FASHION
IN

fb

IN
FASHION

SECOND EDITION

ELAINE STONE

PROFESSOR EMERITA

FASHION INSTITUTE OF TECHNOLOGY

NEW YORK

FAIRCHILD BOOKS, INC. | NEW YORK

Executive Editor: Olga T. Kontzias
Senior Associate Acquisitions Editor: Jaclyn Bergeron
Assistant Acquisitions Editor: Amanda Breccia
Assistant Art Director: Sarah Silberg
Production Director: Ginger Hillman
Senior Production Editor: Elizabeth Marotta
Copyeditor: Jeff Klingman
Ancillaries Editor: Noah Schwartzberg
Executive Director & General Manager: Michael Schluter
Associate Director of Sales: Melanie Sankel
Cover Design: Carolyn Eckert and Michael Miranda
Cover Art: Courtesy of WWD/Giovanni Giannoni: Elie Saab, Fall 2011 RTW
Text Design: Carolyn Eckert and Barbara Barg Medley
Feature Design and Photo Research: Carly Grafstein
Text Layout: Barbara Barg Medley and Carly Grafstein
Production Assistance: Suzette Lam and Lauren Vlassenko
Illustrations: Vanessa Han

Library of Congress Catalog Card Number: 2011930036
ISBN: 978-1-60901-222-9
GST R 133004424
Printed in the United States of America
TP08

CONTENTS

EXTENDED CONTENTS

PREFACE

InFashion, 2nd edition—What a wonderful career choice! Fashion offers a career that is exciting and exhilarating, challenging and changing, fast and furious, and, of course, encourages fun, fame, and fortune. Because fashion is all of this, I have developed *InFashion*, which prepares students to be on the cutting edge of what is happening in the business known as Fashion. This text will help students to learn and understand the facts and figures that are essential for a successful career in the global world of today's fashion business.

InFashion brings new perspectives of the fashion business to students' attention. It covers the broad scope of fashion and adds the newest, most up-to-date facts and figures used by professionals to keep the industry a vital and challenging career path.

InFashion reflects the survey nature of an introductory course and is structured so that the concepts and practices developed are equally applicable to all career paths. To keep the students current in the most recent happenings, each chapter concludes with a discussion of the latest developments and upcoming trends.

ORGANIZATION OF THE TEXT

This edition of *InFashion* uses the same classroom-tested organization that has been so successful in my previous textbooks.

PART ONE
THE CHANGING WORLD OF FASHION

The first part examines how and why fashion evolves and changes. It explains the principles around which fashion revolves and the role that economic, sociological, and psychological elements play in the cyclical nature of fashion. It also covers the business scope of the industry including recent growth and expansion.

Fashion operates in a far different way today than it did years ago. It moves faster and reaches more people. And perhaps most important, it is more businesslike. To understand the changes that have occurred and will occur in the future of the fashion industry, you must first understand the dynamics that underlie the fashion business.

PART TWO
THE PRIMARY LEVEL—THE MATERIALS OF FASHION

The growers and producers of the raw materials of fashion, fibers, fabrics, leather, and fur are covered in this unit, along with the sustainability of products made from recycled materials. New and fast-moving advances in these industries coupled with an increasing variety of fashion goods using these materials are also explained.

PART THREE
THE SECONDARY LEVEL—THE PRODUCERS OF FASHION

The third part begins with a chapter on Product Development explaining how each fashion product is developed and the systems that are used. Then, industry trends in apparel (women's, men's, children's, and teen's) and accessories are highlighted. Each market sector is compared and contrasted with the factors that are common to all: supply chain management, licensing, private label, brand extension, specification buying, offshore production, with examples and concepts for the students to put them in a "real world" context. This unit explains how each industry functions and covers current and future practices and trends.

PART FOUR
THE RETAIL LEVEL—THE MARKETS FOR FASHION

This part focuses on the elements of fashion marketing and reveals how markets operate to help manufacturers sell their products and how retailers satisfy the needs of their target customer. It details both domestic and foreign markets and global sources. Different types of retailers and current trends are detailed. Also discussed are the many fashion services that work with all levels of the fashion industry including magazines, newspapers, broadcast, television, the Internet and social media, fashion reporting services, as well as trade associations.

Text Features

InFashion includes a wide range of examples and illustrations, and has many exciting features that make the people, principles, practices, and techniques of the fashion business come alive in the minds of students. I believe that these features will help students to learn about the fashion business in an enjoyable and lasting manner. All these features are appropriate for class discussion, library research projects, and group projects.

In the Fashion Spotlight

The feature "In the Fashion Spotlight" highlights interesting people, places, and/or products that have an impact on the subject matter. This feature is found in every chapter and makes the chapter material more relevant to the student. Some examples are Michael Kors: Michael's Magic Moment; Jason Wu; Teens, Tweens, and Justin Bieber: Talking Technology; and Jessica Simpson: Billion-Dollar Baby.

Everything Old Is New Again

"Everything Old Is New Again" is a feature that encourages the student to understand the cyclical movement of fashion and its lasting imprint on fashion then and now. Some examples are Roberto Cavalli: Four Decades in Fashion's Jungle; Lilly Pulitzer: Life in Lilly Land; It's a Mad, Mad World!; and Recycled Fashion: From Discarded to Divine.

Timeless Treasures

"Timeless Treasures" is a feature that explains the lasting effects of certain people, products, and policies that have remained successful for long periods of time. Some examples are Betsey: Fashion's Magic Johnson; Pierre Cartier: Good Things Come in Red Packages; Roots: What Inspires Designers?; and Ralph Lauren: New in an Old World.

Tools of the Trade

"Tools of the Trade" is a feature that reinforces the importance of technology in today's fashion business and explains how much impact it has had in the growth of the fashion business. Some examples are RFID: Radio Frequency Identification; eBay: Looming Even Larger in Fashion; and Digital Fitting Experiences.

Top 100 Apparel Designers

A revised compilation of famous designers, both old and new, that includes noteworthy elements of their designs.

Glossary

The glossary contains industry terms called "Trade Talk." A knowledge and understanding of the "language" of fashion gives the students a firm footing upon which they can "step out" into the industry and know they are speaking the right language.

Summary and Review

Each of the twelve chapters in the text concludes with four kinds of student-oriented activities designed to enrich and reinforce the instructional material. They are Summary, Trade Talk, For Review, and For Discussion.

The **Summary** gives a quick review and reminder of key concepts covered in the chapter.

The **Trade Talk** section lists fashion and industry terms introduced for the first time in that chapter. The student will recognize these terms when they appear in subsequent chapters. All the Trade Talk terms are defined in the Glossary.

For Review asks questions about the key concepts of each chapter. These questions provoke thought, encourage classroom discussion, and develop recall of the material presented in the text.

For Discussion asks the student to explain the importance and significance of a major concept and to support the explanation with specific illustrations. This activity gives the student an opportunity to apply theory to actual situations and to draw on his or her own background and experiences.

ACKNOWLEDGMENTS

Thank you to the many educators and businesspeople who have given me encouragement, information, and helpful suggestions. Among these are my teaching colleagues at the Fashion Institute of Technology and the very helpful staff of professionals at the FIT library.

I am also indebted to the industry experts and professionals, both domestic and foreign, who gave their time and expertise to ensure the timeliness and accuracy of the information in this book. Comments from readers selected by the publisher were also very helpful.

My gratitude and sincere appreciation go to the staff at Fairchild Books. I would like to thank Jaclyn Bergeron, Senior Associate Acquisitions Editor, for all of her helpful notes and guidance. I particularly want to mention Elizabeth Marotta, the senior production editor at Fairchild, and the person who really made this edition possible by her complete attention to every detail, and most of all for being a friend in need, who helped me on all phases of producing this book. To Carly Grafstein for her enthusiasm and doing the fantastic photo research and feature layouts, which really make this edition so wonderful. I would also like to thank the creative team for their artistic design and illustrations: Carolyn Eckert, Barbara Barg Medley, Michael Miranda, Vanessa Han, and Sarah Silberg. To Olga Kontzias, I say a heartfelt "thank you" for all the years we have worked together.

I regret that space does not permit me to personally list and thank my friends in all segments of the fashion business who supplied their encouragement as well as significant amounts of current trend and trade information. As always, I welcome instructors' and students' comments. You can send these to me through Fairchild Books or to the following e-mail address: elaine_stone@fitnyc.edu

This book is dedicated to Minnie M. Stone, who served as a mentor, friend, and critic throughout my career. Best of all, she was a terrific mother. And a belated thank you to Professor Helen Watson, who was responsible for me going into the fashion business.

FASHION
IN

PART 1

THE CHANGING WORLD OF FASHION

In this part, you will learn how and why fashion evolves and changes. You will begin to develop a basic vocabulary and a working knowledge of the following:

* The principles around which the fashion world revolves are featured in Chapter 1.

* The environmental forces—the role that economic, demographic, sociological, and psychological elements play in the fashion business—in Chapter 2.

* The cyclical forces—how fashions change and how an understanding of this constant cycle of change can be used to predict and analyze current and future fashion—in Chapter 3.

* The business forces—the scope of the industry, its recent growth and expansion, and various new forms of ownership, along with the design forces, and the roles played by designers, manufacturers, and retailers in creating fashion—in Chapter 4.

The world of fashion operates in a far different way today than it did years ago. It moves faster and reaches more people. And perhaps, most important, it is more businesslike. To understand the changes that have occurred and will occur in the future of the fashion industry, you must first understand the dynamics that underlie the fashion business.

THE NATURE OF FASHION

KEY CONCEPTS

- Marketing and merchandising in the fashion business
- The terminology of the fashion business
- The stages of the fashion cycle
- The intangibles of fashion

Behold the many faces of fashion—fun, fantastic, frivolous, frantic, fabulous, futuristic, flirtatious, fresh, and financial. Fashion is all of this, and much more. Fashion is the most dynamic of American businesses. It thrives on change—and change is the engine that fuels it. Life might be easier if we never had to change. **However, if the fashion business did not change, it would not survive.**

A billowing, floral-inspired gown at the Christian Dior Fall 2010 Couture show in Paris.

THE IMPORTANCE OF FASHION

In recent years, general interest in fashion has increased. Fashion has a great impact on our country's economy. Changes in fashion result in new consumer goods. At the same time, such changes encourage consumers to purchase new products because the thought of being unfashionable is a fate worse than death to many people!

Webster's defines fashion as "prevailing custom, usage, or style,"[1] and in this sense, it covers a wide range of human activity. In this book, however, fashion is used in a narrower sense. Fashion here means the style or styles of clothing and accessories worn at a particular time by a particular group of people. It also includes fashion in cosmetics, fragrances, and home furnishings.

THE FASHION BUSINESS

Fashion is big business and millions of people are employed in fashion-related activities. The **fashion industries** are businesses that are engaged in manufacturing the materials and finished products used in the production of apparel and accessories for men, women, and children. The broader term **fashion business** includes all the industries and services connected with fashion: design, manufacturing, distribution, marketing, retailing, advertising, communications, publishing, and consulting—in other words, any business concerned with fashion goods or services.

Marketing

Today, **marketing** has become a major influence in the fashion business. The process of marketing includes many different activities that identify consumer needs; develop good products; and price, distribute, and promote them effectively so that they will sell easily.

Fashion Marketing and Merchandising

The fashion business has been rather slow in adopting the marketing techniques of consumer goods, such as automobiles and packaged foods. For many years, fashion producers were concerned only with what was economical and easy for them to produce. They would spend considerable time and money trying to convince the consumer that what they had produced was what the consumer wanted. The producer had little or no interest in the wants and needs of the consumer.

Today, the total process of marketing has been adopted by the fashion business and is being applied to the products and services of the fashion industries. The result is called fashion marketing. Marketing must be understood not in the old sense of making a sale—"telling and selling"—but in the new sense of satisfying customer needs. If the marketer understands consumer needs; develops products and services that provide superior customer value; and prices, distributes, and promotes them effectively, these products will sell easily.

We are also concerned with fashion **merchandising**. Webster's defines merchandising as sales promotion as a comprehensive function, including market research, development of new products, coordination of manufacture and marketing, and effective advertising and selling.[2] It refers to the *planning* required to have the right fashion-oriented merchandise at the right time, in the right place, in the right quantities, at the right prices, and with the right sales promotion for a specified target customer. This is better known in the industry as the five Rs of merchandising.

MISCONCEPTIONS ABOUT FASHION

The first and most common misconception is that designers and retailers dictate what the fashion will be and then force it upon helpless consumers. In reality, consumers decide what the fashion will be by influencing new designs and by accepting or rejecting the styles that are offered.

The second misconception is that fashion acts as an influence on women only. Men and children are as influenced by and responsive to fashion as women. Fashion is the force that causes women to raise or lower their skirt lengths from minis to maxis, straighten or frizz their hair, and change from casual sportswear to dressy clothes. Fashion is also the force that influences men to grow or shave off their mustaches and beards, choose wide or "skinny" ties and lapels, and change from casual jeans into three-piece suits. And fashion is the force that makes children demand specific products and styles.

The third misconception is that fashion is a mysterious and unpredictable force. Actually, its direction can be determined and its changes predicted with remarkable accuracy by those who study and understand the fundamentals of fashion. Fashion was once considered an art form controlled by designers who dictated its content, but today fashion can be measured and evaluated.

THE TERMINOLOGY OF FASHION

What is the difference among fashion, style, and design? Just what do high fashion, mass fashion, taste, classic, and fad mean?

Style

The first step in understanding fashion is to distinguish between "fashion" and "style." In general terms, a style is a characteristic or distinctive artistic expression or presentation. Styles exist in architecture, sculpture, painting, politics, and music, as well as in popular heroes, games, hobbies, pets, flirtations, and weddings.

In apparel, **style** is the characteristic or distinctive appearance of a garment—the combination of features that makes it different from other garments. For example, T-shirts are as different from polo shirts as they are from peasant blouses. Riding jackets are as different from safari jackets as they are from blazer jackets.

Although styles come and go in terms of acceptance, a specific style always remains a style, whether it is currently in fashion or not. Some people adopt a style that becomes indelibly associated with them and wear it regardless of whether it is currently fashionable. Carmen Miranda's platform shoes, Katharine Hepburn's pleated trousers, the Duchess of Windsor's jewelry, Marilyn Monroe's white halter dress, Michael Jackson's glove, Mary J. Blige's sunglasses, and Snooki's pouf are all examples of personal style.

Some styles are named for the period of history in which they originated—Grecian, Roman, Renaissance, Empire, Gibson Girl (early 1900s), flapper (1920s). When such styles return to fashion, their basic elements remain the same. Minor details are altered to reflect the taste or needs of the era in which they reappear. For example, the flapper style of the 1920s was short, pleated, and body slimming. That style can be bought today but with changes for current fashion acceptance.

Fashion

Alternatively, a **fashion** is a style that is accepted and used by the majority of a group at any one time, no matter how small that group. A fashion is a result of social emulation and acceptance. Miniskirts, square-toed shoes, mustaches, and theatrical daytime makeup have all been fashions. And no doubt each will again be accepted by a majority of a group of people with similar interests or characteristics—for example, college students, young career men and women, retired men and women.

Fashions appeal to many different groups and can be categorized according to those groups. **High fashion** refers to a new style accepted by a limited number of fashion leaders who want to be the first to adopt changes and innovation in fashion. However, if the style can appeal to a broader audience, it is generally copied, mass-produced, and sold at lower prices. The fashion leaders or innovators who first accepted it then move on to something new.

To contrast with high fashion, **mass fashion** or **volume fashion** consists of styles that are widely accepted. These fashions are usually produced and sold in large quantities at moderate to low prices and appeal to the greatest majority of fashion-conscious consumers. Mass fashion accounts for the majority of sales in the fashion business. Mass fashion is the "bread and butter" of the fashion banquet.

Mannequins dressed in 1920s flapper chic in the Costume Institute's "American Woman: Fashioning a National Identity" exhibit.

Design

There can be many variations of detail within a specific style. A **design** is a particular or individual interpretation, version, or treatment of a style. A style may be expressed in a great many designs—all different, yet all related, because they are in the same style. A sweatshirt, for example, is a distinctive style, but within that style, variations may include different types of necklines, pockets, and sleeves. Another example is a satchel handbag, which may be interpreted with different closures, locks, or handles. These minor variations are the different interpretations that change the design of a style.

In the fashion industries, manufacturers and retailers assign a number to each individual design produced. This is the **style number**. The style number of a product identifies it for manufacturing, ordering, and selling purposes. In this instance, the term style number is used rather than design number, even though a design is being identified.

A steak-clad Lady Gaga accepts her "Video of the Year" award with typically provocative flair at the 2010 MTV Video Music Awards.

Taste

In fashion, **taste** refers to prevailing opinion of what is and what is not appropriate for a given occasion. Good taste in fashion, therefore, means sensitivity not only to what is artistically pleasing but also to what is appropriate for a specific situation. A style, such as an evening gown, may be beautiful. But if it is worn to a wedding breakfast, for example, it may not be considered in good taste.

While the time an individual fashion takes to complete this course may vary, the course is always a cyclical one. A new style is often considered daring and in dubious taste. It is gradually accepted, then widely accepted, and finally gradually discarded.

For many decades, Laver's cycle (see "The Fashion Cycle," p. 15) has been accepted as the movement of most fashions. However, in the past few decades some fashions have deviated from this pattern. The fashion cycles have become shorter and have repeated themselves within a shorter space of time. For the student of fashion this presents an interesting challenge. What factors determine which fashions will follow the accepted cycles and which fashions will not? To understand the movement of fashion, it is important to understand that fashions are always in harmony with the times in which they appear.

Classic

A **classic** is a style or design that satisfies a basic need and remains in general fashion acceptance for an extended period of time. They are exceptions to the usual movement of styles through the fashion life cycle.

Depending upon the intended fashion statement, a person may have only a few classics or a wardrobe of mostly classics. A classic is characterized by a simple design that keeps it from being easily dated. The Chanel suit is an outstanding example of a classic because its simple lines have made it acceptable for many decades. Although it reappears now and then as a fashion, many women always have a Chanel suit in their wardrobes. Other examples of classics are denim jeans, blazer jackets, cardigan or turtleneck sweaters, button-down oxford shirts, and T-shirts. Among accessories, the pump-style shoe, the loafer, the one-button glove, the pearl necklace, and the clutch handbag are also classics. For young children, overalls and one-piece pajamas have become classics.

Fad

A fashion that suddenly sweeps into popularity, affects a limited part of the total population, and then quickly disappears is called a **fad**. It comes into existence by the introduction of some feature or detail, usually exaggerated, that excites the interest of the customer. The fad starts by being quickly accepted and then imitated by others. Fads

often begin in lower price ranges, are relatively easy to copy, and therefore flood the market in a very short time. Because of this kind of market saturation, the public tires of fads quickly, and they end abruptly.

Fads follow the same cycle as do fashions, but their rise in popularity is much faster, their acceptance much shorter, and their decline much more rapid than that of a true fashion. Because most fads come and go in a single season, they have been called "miniature fashions." In recent decades we have had the "punk" multicolored hair favored by certain pop stars, the "King Tut" design fad, the "Urban Cowboy" fad, and the "grunge" fad. Fads, like fashions, invade every field: sports, literature, religion, politics, and education.

Trend

A **trend** is a general direction or movement. For example, you will often read in fashion magazines that "there is a trend toward longer skirts"; it means that several designers, including some leading ones, are showing longer skirts, leading retailers are buying them, and fashion-forward customers are wearing them. It is often difficult to tell a trend from a fad; even the experts get caught. However, marketers always want to know whether a new development is going to be a trend or a fad because they want to cash in on trends but avoid getting burned by fads.

A massive Chanel coat dwarfs models at the brand's Spring 2008 Haute Couture show at the Grand Palais in Paris [left]. A model poses at the hem of the show's iconic set piece [right].

MICHAEL KORS

Michael's Magic Moment

Michael Kors

THE YEAR 2011 IS MICHAEL KORS'S 30TH YEAR IN BUSINESS—HIS MAGIC MOMENT! In 2010 he received the CFDA Lifetime Achievement Award, to add to previous honors—the 1999 CFDA Award for Womenswear Designer of the Year and the 2003 CFDA Award for Menswear Designer of the Year.

Kors began designing clothes at the age of 19 and studied fashion design at the Fashion Institute of Technology in New York. In 1981, he launched the Michael Kors womenswear line at Bloomingdales, Bergdorf Goodman, Lord & Taylor, Neiman Marcus, and Saks Fifth Avenue. Building on his success, Kors was named the first ever women's ready-to-wear designer and creative director for the French fashion house Celine in 1997. He turned the fashion house around with his critically acclaimed ready-to-wear line and blockbuster accessories. Kors left Celine in 2003 to concentrate on his own brand, which now includes menswear.

In addition to the Michael Kors runway collection, the MICHAEL Michael Kors and KORS Michael Kors lines were launched in 2004. KORS is considered the mid-tier line, between the runway and MICHAEL collections. The MICHAEL line includes women's handbags and shoes as well as women's ready-to-wear apparel. The KORS line contains footwear and jeans. Currently, Kors has full-collection boutiques in New York, Beverly Hills, Palm Beach, and Chicago. He has boutiques in London, Milan, and Munich and is looking forward to having more Kors boutiques globally.

Though very successful, Kors says one thing has not changed for the many aspirants: the fashion business remains a hard-knock life. While he applauds American fashion's current, glorious young designer moment, Kors suspects that many of its stars won't celebrate 30 years in the business.

Kors's own ongoing success spans decades, and adding to his success and reputation is his part in the success of *Project Runway*. His turn as a judge on *Project Runway* has transformed him into fashion's Simon Cowell—shrewd, blunt, and in command. He is known for his supreme gift for wit and graciousness, and for his modern take on American fashion. The show has made him the de facto authority on what is and what isn't "fashion" in living rooms all over the world.

The accolades just keep coming for Michael Kors. Barely a week after receiving the CFDA's Geoffrey Beene Lifetime Achievement Award and being inducted into the Fragrance Foundation's hall of fame, the designer was honored on June 16, 2010, by the Cancer Research Institute for his commitment to promoting awareness and raising funds for breast cancer. Friends and associates including Ron Frasch, Marjorie Gubelmann, the Gregorys, and event co-chair John Idol gathered at the Mandarin Oriental for dinner and the ceremony, during which Joan Allen, clad in a black-and-white gown by the designer, presented Kors with the Oliver R. Grace Award for Distinguished Service in Advancing Cancer Research.

Spring 2011   Spring 2011   *Project Runway*   Fall 2010   Fall 2010

COMPONENTS OF FASHION DESIGN

Fashion design does not just happen, nor does the designer wave a magic wand to create a new design. Fashion design involves the combination of four basic elements or components: silhouette, detail, texture, and color. Only through a change in one or more of these basic components does a new fashion evolve.

Silhouette

The **silhouette** of a costume is its overall outline or contour. It is also frequently referred to as "shape" or "form." It may appear to the casual observer that women have worn countless silhouettes throughout the centuries. In the 1930s, Agnes Brooke Young's research showed that there are actually only three basic forms—bell-shaped or bouffant; bustle, or back fullness; straight or tubular—with many variations.[3] Today, most fashion experts include four variations on the tubular silhouette: slim, rectangle, wedge, and A-line.

Details

The individual elements that give a silhouette its form or shape are called **details**. These include trimmings; skirt and pant length and width; and shoulder, waist, and sleeve treatment.

Silhouettes evolve gradually from one to another through changes in detail. When the trend in a detail reaches an extreme, a reversal of the trend takes place. For example, dresses and suits featured wide shoulders with much padding in the 1940s and 1950s. This was reversed in the late 1960s and 1970s, when the look became casual and unstructured. This casualness reached such extremes that by the start of the 1980s, structured clothing was back in fashion and dress and suit shoulders began once again to grow wider as padding was inserted. By the 1990s, the unstructured look was predominant again; and entering the 2000s, structured suits and wide shoulders were back on the runways.

a   b   c   d   e   f   g

Silhouettes are categorized as belonging to one of three basic groups: a) bell-shaped or bouffant, b) bustle or back fullness, and c) straight or tubular. Variations of the straight silhouette are d) slim, e) rectangular, f) wedge, and g) A-line.

Texture

One of the most significant components of fashion is **texture**. Texture is the look and feel of material, woven or nonwoven.

Texture can affect the appearance of a silhouette, giving it a bulky or slender look, depending on the roughness or smoothness of the materials. A woman dressed in a rough tweed dress and a bulky knit sweater is likely to look larger and squarer than she does in the same dress executed in a smooth jersey and topped with a cashmere sweater.

Texture influences the drape of a garment. Chiffon clings and flows, making it a good choice for soft, feminine styles, while corduroy has the firmness and bulk suitable for more casual garments.

Texture affects the color of a fabric by causing the surface to either reflect or absorb light. Rough textures absorb light, causing the colors to appear flat. Smooth textures reflect light, causing colors to appear brighter. Anyone who has tried to match colors soon discovers that a color that appears extremely bright in a shiny vinyl, satin, or high-gloss enamel paint seems subdued in a rough wool, suede, or stucco wall finish.

Color

Color has always been a major consideration in women's clothing. Since World War II, color in men's clothing has been regaining the importance it had in previous centuries. Today, color is a key factor in apparel selection for both genders. Color is important in advertising, packaging, and store decor as well.

Historically, colors have been used to denote rank and profession. Purple, for instance, was associated with royalty, and in some periods, could be worn only by those of noble birth. Black became customary for the apparel of the clergy and for members of the judiciary.

Today, a fashion designer's color palette changes with consumers' preferences. In some seasons, all is brightness and sharp contrast, and no color is too powerful to be worn. In other seasons, only subdued colors appeal. Fashion merchants must develop an eye for color—not only for the specific hues and values popular in a given season but also for indications of possible trends in consumer preference.

From "Honeysuckle" to "Silver Cloud"— the color experts at Pantone select hues for a Spring season.

THE FASHION CYCLE

All fashions move in cycles. The term **fashion cycle** refers to the rise, wide popularity, and subsequent decline in acceptance of a style. The word "cycle" suggests a circle. However, the fashion cycle is represented by a bell-shaped curve.

Some authorities compare the fashion cycle with a wave, which shows first a slow swell, then a crest, and finally a swift fall. As with the movement of a wave, the movement of a fashion is always forward, never backward. As with waves, fashion cycles do not follow one another in regular, measured order. Some take a short time to crest, while others take a long time. The length of the cycle from swell to fall may be long or short. And, again like waves, fashion cycles overlap.

Stages of the Fashion Cycle

Fashion cycles are not haphazard; they don't "just happen." There are definite stages in a style's development that are easily recognized. These stages can be charted and traced, and in the short run, accurately predicted. Being able to recognize and predict the different stages is vital to success in the designer's buying and selling of fashion.

Every fashion cycle passes through five stages: (1) introduction, (2) rise, (3) culmination, (4) decline, and (5) obsolescence.

The fashion cycle serves as an important guide for fashion merchandising. Fashion merchants use the fashion cycle concept to introduce new fashion goods, to chart their rise and culmination, and to recognize their decline and obsolescence.

THE FASHION CYCLE

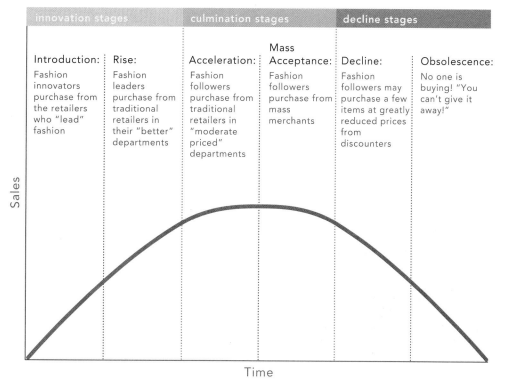

innovation stages		culmination stages		decline stages	
Introduction:	Rise:	Acceleration:	Mass Acceptance:	Decline:	Obsolescence:
Fashion innovators purchase from the retailers who "lead" fashion	Fashion leaders purchase from traditional retailers in their "better" departments	Fashion followers purchase from traditional retailers in "moderate priced" departments	Fashion followers purchase from mass merchants	Fashion followers may purchase a few items at greatly reduced prices from discounters	No one is buying! "You can't give it away!"

Sales

Time

The basic life cycle of fashion can be represented by a bell-shaped curve.

Spring 2011

Spring 2011

Fall 2011

Show-ending cartwheel

Betsey Johnson

BETSEY
Fashion's Magic Johnson

THERE ARE TWO "MAGIC JOHNSONS" IN THE WORLD OF CELEBRITY: IN SPORTS, MAGIC JOHNSON—THE BASKETBALL SENSATION—AND, IN FASHION, BETSEY JOHNSON—FASHION'S ALL-TIME GOOD-TIME GIRL. She celebrated her label's big 30 in 2008, proof to anyone who's dismissed her as a silly eccentric—or kooky and funky, adjectives that inevitably appear alongside her name. But look at her staying power! For more than 30 years Johnson has made a big business—more than 70 stores worldwide, 800 wholesale accounts, and ten licensees—because of staying true to her ultra-specific style of tulle, tutus, poufy petticoats, leopard spots, and hearts. Her most recognizable stuff, prom dresses and sheath dresses, became her business.

But—now is the time for change! Johnson's new goal is getting back to her roots, which weren't in ruffles, but sportswear. Johnson wants a five-pocket jean. "I'm a T-shirt and jeans, sloppy show-skin type," she said of her renewed vision. "And I'm vintage-inspired like crazy." She has since been obsessively collecting her early work, scouring eBay, and buying her original designs, many of which will be remade for the Betsey Johnson Vintage Collection.

Johnson's career has been colorful from day one! Obsessed with dance, the costumes, the-atrics, and performance value all influence her designs and exuberant runway presentations. Betsey didn't make it to Broadway, but while studying art at Syracuse University, she won a contest that landed her in London. There she was introduced to 60s superstars Mary Quant, Biba, and Penelope Tree, as well as a job guest-editing at *Mademoiselle*. By the time British retailer Paul Young trapped Betsey to design for his Paraphernalia boutique in 1965, she was fully immersed in New York's 60s hipster scene.

In 1969 she ventured into retail, opening the Betsey Bunki Nini Boutique. In 1978, Johnson found three things she needed to move ahead in the fashion game: confidence, cash, and her longtime business partner, Chantal Bacon. They launched the Betsey Johnson collection on August 10, Johnson's birthday. She closed that first show with a cartwheel—now her signature final bow! Her work has attracted style-setting celebrity shoppers Joan Jett, Madonna, Cyndi Lauper, and Amy Winehouse.

In 2007 Johnson and Bacon sold a major-ity stake to Cambridge-based equity group Castanea Partners. Bacon left the company after Steve Madden, Ltd, took over control in Oc-tober 2010. Steve Madden already had ties to Betsey Johnson, holding licenses for accessories including handbags, and its expertise with shoes should help the company expand in that area. Of Johnson's future role in the company, Betsey Johnson CEO Jonathan Friedman said, "She will continue to be the namesake of the brand, and do what she does so well—design."

If anything, these recent events have re-charged Johnson's mission, giving her all the more reason to stick to her stylistic guns. "I love the support and exposure I've had. I love girls yelling 'Go, Betsey!' or—'You're the Bomb.' To me, that means I really stand for something."

VARIATIONS IN THE FASHION CYCLE

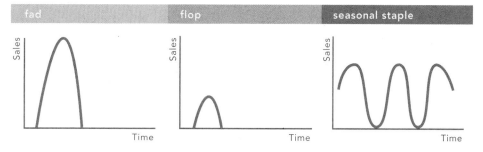

Variations can occur to the height to which a fashion rises at its peak and the length of time it takes to get to that point and then to decline in popularity.

Introduction Stage

The next new fashion may be introduced by a producer in the form of a new style, color, or texture. The new style may be a flared pant leg when slim legs are popular, vibrant colors when earth tones are popular, or slim body-hugging fabrics such as knit jersey when heavy-textured bulky looks are being worn.

New styles are almost always introduced in higher-priced merchandise. They are produced in small quantities because retail fashion buyers purchase a limited number of pieces to test the new styles' appeal to targeted customers. This testing period comes at the beginning of the buying cycle of fashion merchandise, which coincides with the introduction stage of the fashion cycle. The test period ends when the new style either begins its rise or has been rejected by the target customer. Because there can be many risks, new styles must be priced high enough so that those that succeed can cover the losses on those that do not succeed. Promotional activities, such as designer appearances, institutional advertising, and charity fashion shows, all of which appeal to the fashion leaders of the community and also enhance the store's fashion image, take place at this point.

Rise Stage

When the new original design (or its adaptations) is accepted by an increasing number of customers, it is considered to be in its **rise stage**. At this stage, the buyer reorders in quantity for maximum stock coverage.

During the rise stage of a new original design, many retailers will offer line-for-line copies—or **knockoffs**, as they are referred to in the fashion industry. These are versions of the original designer style duplicated by manufacturers. These copies look exactly like the original except that they have been mass produced in less expensive fabrics. Because production of the merchandise is now on a larger scale, knockoff prices are generally lower.

As a new style continues to be accepted by more and more customers, adaptations appear. **Adaptations** are designs that have all the dominant features of the style that inspired them, but do not claim to be exact copies. Modifications have been made, but distinguishing features of the original, such as a special shoulder treatment or the use of textured fabric, may be retained in the adaptation. At this stage, the promotion effort focuses on regular price lines, full assortments, and product type ads to persuade the customer of the store's superiority in meeting his or her fashion needs.

Culmination Stage

The **culmination stage** of the fashion cycle is the period when a fashion is at the height of its popularity and use. At this stage, the fashion is in such demand that it can be mass produced, mass distributed, and sold at prices within the range of most customers. This stage may be long or brief, depending on how extended the peak of popularity is. The culmination stage of a fashion may be extended in the following two ways:

1. If a fashion becomes accepted as a classic, it settles into a fairly steady sales pattern. An example of this is the cardigan sweater, an annual steady seller.
2. If new details of design, color, or texture are continually introduced, interest in the fashion may be kept alive longer. Shoulder-strap handbags are a perfect example. Another example is the continued fashion interest in running shoes, fostered by new colors, designs, and comfort innovations.

Decline Stage

When boredom with a fashion sets in, the result is a decrease in consumer demand for that fashion. This is known as the **decline stage**. It is a principle of fashion that all fashions end in excess.

As a fashion starts to decline, consumers may still be wearing it, but they are no longer willing to buy it at its regular price. The outstanding fashion merchandiser is able to recognize the end of the culmination stage and start markdowns early. At this point, production stops immediately or comes slowly to a halt. The leading fashion stores abandon the style; traditional stores take a moderate markdown and advertise the price reduction. This will probably be followed in a short while by a major price-slash clearance or closeout. At this stage, the style may be found in bargain stores at prices far below what the style commanded in earlier stages.

Obsolescence Stage

When total lack of interest for a style has set in and it can no longer be sold at any price, the fashion is in its **obsolescence stage**. At this stage, the style can be found only in thrift shops, garage sales, or flea markets.

Lengths of Cycles

Predicting the time span of a fashion cycle is impossible because each fashion moves at its own speed. However, one guideline can be counted on. Declines are fast, and a drop to obsolescence is almost always steeper than a rise to culmination. At this point, as they say in merchandising: "You can't give it away."

The speed with which products move through their cycles is becoming faster and faster. Rapid technological developments and "instant" communications have much to do with this speedup, as do fast-changing environmental factors. The result is an intense competition among manufacturers and retailers to provide consumers with what they want and expect—constantly changing assortments from which to choose.

Consumers either give a new style enough acceptance to get it started, or they immediately reject it. Because more new fashions are always ready to push existing ones out of the way, it is no wonder that with each passing year, the time required for a fashion to complete its cycle becomes shorter and shorter.

Studies recognize the importance of assortment rotation, universally called **fast fashion**. This strategy of keeping fashion fresh, as if it were a perishable good, has been successful for many retailers, including Zara, H&M, and Uniqlo. For any retailer with variety-seeking customers, some degree of fast fashion is important, and it allows retailers to develop ways that allow variety to be managed officially.[4]

Breaks in the Cycle

In fashion, as in everything else, there are always ups and downs, stops and starts. The normal flow of a fashion cycle can be broken or abruptly interrupted by outside influences. The influence can be as simple as unpredictable weather or a change in group acceptance. Or it can be much more dramatic and far reaching—war, worldwide economic depression, or a natural disaster, for example.

Although no formal studies have been made of the phenomenon of the broken cycle, manufacturers and merchants have a theory about it. They believe that a broken cycle usually picks up where it has stopped once conditions return to normal or once the season that was cut short reopens. Widespread economic depressions also temporarily interrupt the normal progress of a fashion cycle. When there is widespread unemployment, fashion moves much more slowly, resuming its pace only with economic recovery and growth.

Wars also affect fashion. They cause shortages that force designers, manufacturers, retailers, and consumers to change fashions less freely or to restrict styles. People redirect their interests, and fashion must take a back seat.

CONSUMER BUYING AND THE FASHION CYCLE

Every fashion has both a consumer buying cycle and a consumer use cycle. The curve of the consumer buying cycle rises in direct relation to that of the consumer use cycle. But when the fashion reaches its peak, consumer buying tends to decline more rapidly than consumer use. Different segments of society respond to and tire of a fashion at different times. So different groups of consumers continue to wear fashions for varying lengths of time after they have ceased buying them. While each group is using and enjoying a fashion, the producers and retailers serving that group are already abandoning the style and marketing something newer. Their efforts in this direction are most profitable when they anticipate, rather than follow, the trend of consumer demand. Consumer buying is often halted prematurely. This happens because producers and sellers no longer wish to risk making and stocking an item they believe will soon decline in popularity. Instead, they concentrate their resources on new items with better prospects for longevity. This procedure is familiar to anyone who has tried to buy summer clothes in late August or skiwear in March.

CONSUMER BUYING CYCLE versus CONSUMER USE CYCLE

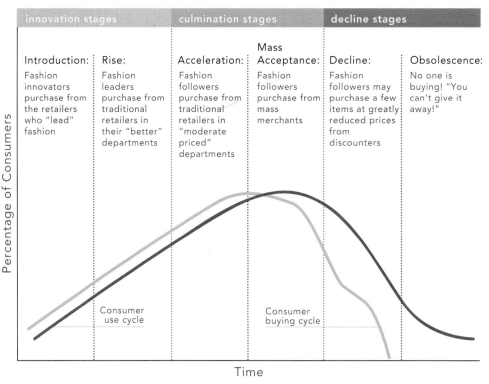

innovation stages		culmination stages		decline stages	
Introduction:	Rise:	Acceleration:	Mass Acceptance:	Decline:	Obsolescence:
Fashion innovators purchase from the retailers who "lead" fashion	Fashion leaders purchase from traditional retailers in their "better" departments	Fashion followers purchase from traditional retailers in "moderate priced" departments	Fashion followers purchase from mass merchants	Fashion followers may purchase a few items at greatly reduced prices from discounters	No one is buying! "You can't give it away!"

Percentage of Consumers

Consumer use cycle

Consumer buying cycle

Time

Consumer use of a fashion product follows a cycle similar to the buying cycle; however, the use cycle begins after the buying cycle and endures beyond the buying cycle's decline and obsolescence stages.

THE INTANGIBLES OF FASHION

Fashion itself is intangible. A style is tangible, made up of a definite silhouette and details of design. But fashion is shaped by such powerful intangibles as group acceptance, change, the social forces important during a certain era, and people's desire to relate to specific lifestyles.

Group Acceptance

The fig leaf, the first fashion creation, was widely accepted, and we have since come a long way. Basically, fashion is acceptance: group acceptance or approval is implied in any definition of fashion. Most people have a great wish to express themselves as individuals, but they also want to be part of a group and belong. However, acceptance need not be universal. A style may be adopted by one group while other segments of the population ignore it.

The way we dress is a personal signature. The dress or suit we wear is not just a confirmation of the old adage that "clothes make the man . . . or the woman," but rather an example of the fact that our need for acceptance is expressed largely in the way we dress. Acceptance also means that a fashion is considered appropriate to the occasion for which it is worn. Clothes considered appropriate for big-business boardrooms would not be considered acceptable for casual weekends.

If any of you should doubt the power of acceptance in fashion, try a simple experiment. Put on clothes that were worn 10 or 20 years ago by family members or friends or that are totally different in style from what is considered the fashion. Then go out casually among your friends, acquaintances, or even strangers, and note their reactions toward you and then your feelings toward yourself. There will be quizzical looks, doubtful stares, and in some cases smirks and laughter. No one can really "belong" to a chosen group and at the same time choose to be completely "out" of present-day fashion. Such is the power of fashion acceptance.

Change

Fashion changes because ideas about politics, religion, leisure, democracy, success, and age change. This is particularly true when the society is no longer able to provide identity and maintain social order through custom or tradition. In the United States and across the globe fashion is one means of providing a social bond.

Fashion is subject to change—both rapid and gradual. Modern communications play a major role in today's accelerated rate of fashion change. The mass media spreads fashion news across the face of the globe in hours, sometimes seconds. Even slight fashion changes are given faster and wider publicity than ever before. Fashion coverage of events around the world enables us to see not only what people are doing but also what they are wearing. Our morning newspapers, television shows, blogs, and websites show us what fashion leaders wore to a party the night before. Today, we even know what they are wearing at the moment with live postings via Twitter, Facebook, and other social media networks.

The cast of *Beverly Hills 90210,* dressed at the height of 1990s fashion.

Another change that is affecting today's fashion world is that a growing number of environmentally conscious consumers are demanding eco-friendly products. The fashion industry is working hard to satisfy this need. With advances in technology, the industry is producing more "green" or sustainable fibers and fabrics. Marketers are also affected by these changes and must rethink how to successfully target these types of consumers. According to a study from *Adweek*, researchers evaluated more than 200 million "green consumers" in the United States and separated these consumers into the following different groups: [5]

- **Alpha Ecos** (43 million adults): Committed to green causes and saving the planet.
- **Eco-Centrics** (34 million adults): Concerned about how environmental products benefit them personally.
- **Eco-Chics** (57 million adults): Understand the cachet of being seen as "green." This younger generation uses social networking to show others just how green they are.
- **Economically Ecos** (53 million adults): Less concerned about saving the planet— more concerned about saving money.
- **Eco-Moms** (33 million moms of children under 18): Interested in cost-effective, socially responsible practices and products with an emphasis on kids.

With any fashion industry change, when consumers like what they see, they demand it from merchants, who in turn demand it from manufacturers.

Styles from 1968

Spring/ Summer 2011

Spring 2011

PIERRE CARDIN

He's Everywhere and Into Everything

PIERRE CARDIN IS THE LAST POST-WAR COUTURIER STILL HEADING HIS OWN LABEL, a source of considerable pride to the son of Italian immigrants, who had left home at 17 and opened his own Paris fashion house by 30.

Cardin started his career at the house of Paquin, where he designed costumes for Jean Cocteau's film *Beauty and the Beast*. After a short time at Schiaparelli, he joined the brand-new house of Christian Dior, where he was instrumental in helping to launch the "New Look" in 1947.

In 2010 he celebrated the 60th anniversary of his label with a series of outstanding events, including a catwalk show during Paris Fashion Week and a book charting creations such as the bubble dress and his signature outfits based on geometric patterns and circles. The book he wrote with his longtime collaborator, Jean-Pascal Hesse, *Pierre Cardin, 60 Years of Innovation*, is now a best-seller, and he holds book-signing parties at his Paris restaurant Maxim's.

At age 87, he says, "I never expected when I started out that I would live to such an advanced age. It's a pleasant surprise…. I have the enthusiasm, I have a reason for existing, a passion—I feel useful. I have a goal in life, which is to continue working until the very last moment." It's a perfect example of the fearlessness that drove Cardin to pioneer Space Age fashion in the 60s and put his name on everything

from cigarette lighters to orthopedic mattresses! He is the king of licenses—licensing more than 900 products in 140 countries. Today, the Cardin empire employs more than 180,000 workers in 70 countries. He has become the world's richest haute couture designer, but despite his success, he shuns advertising. This is the designer who felt that haute couture should be equally available to more people, and he was the first designer to open a boutique and show and sell his new ready-to-wear line, the first of its kind in 1959. It scandalized the fashion powers in France, the Chambre Syndicale, who expelled him for attempting to make designer clothes more accessible. They later reinstated him, but he never showed his collection with them ever again!

To call Cardin hyperactive is an understatement. From his headquarters across the road from the French president's palace, he runs his various empires and plans new buildings, music festivals, art exhibitions, theater performances, and even a golf course.

Pierre Cardin

pierre cardin
60 ANS DE CRÉATION

The Futility of Forcing Change

Fashion expresses the spirit of the times, and in turn influences it. Fashion designers are successful or not, depending on their abilities to sense and anticipate changes—if not to initiate them. Changes can be initiated, but there are as many examples of failures as there are of successful changes. Efforts have been made from time to time to force changes in the course of fashion, but they usually fail. Fashion is a potent force that by definition requires support from the majority.

In the late 1980s, designers and retailers tried to repeat the 1960s with a change to very short skirts. The public disliked the radical change and refused to buy miniskirts when they were first introduced—as they did in the 60s. Today, however, women are seen wearing both miniskirts and long skirts.

Meeting the Demand for Change

After World War II, a new French designer, Christian Dior, caught and expressed the desire for a freer line and a more feminine garment in his first collection, which achieved instant fashion success. Using fabric with a lavishness that had been impossible in Europe or the United States during the war years, he created his "new look," with long, full skirts, fitted waistlines, and feminine curves.

Dior did not change the course of fashion; he quickened it—from a slow evolutionary course to a revolutionary one. He recognized and interpreted the need of women at that time to get out of stiff, short, narrow, unfeminine clothes and into soft, free, longer, feminine ones. Consumers wanted the change, and the lifting of the very limiting wartime restrictions made it possible to meet their demands.

A Mirror of the Times

Fashion is a nonverbal symbol. A study of the past and careful observation of the present make it apparent that fashions are social expressions that document the tastes and values of an era, just as the paintings, sculpture, and architecture of the times do. The extreme modesty of the Victorian era was reflected in bulky and concealing fashions. The sexual emancipation of the flappers in the 1920s was expressed in their flattened figures, short skirts, "sheer" hosiery (the first time the bare leg was exposed), and short hair. The individualistic fashions of the 1990s and 2000s are a true reflection of the current freedom of expression and lifestyle.

Social Class

Fashions mirror the times by reflecting the degree of rigidity in the class structure of an era. Although such ideas are difficult to imagine today, throughout much of history certain fashions were restricted to the members of certain defined social classes. In some early eras, royal declarations regulated both the type of apparel that could be worn by each group of citizens and how ornate it could be. Class distinctions were thus emphasized. Certain fashions have also been used as indications of high social standing and material success. During the 19th century, the constricted waists of Western women and the bound feet of high-caste Chinese women were silent but obvious evidence that the male head of the household was wealthy.

Reality television personalities, like the dramatically poufed *Jersey Shore* star Nicole "Snooki" Polizzi, provide a time-stamped picture of personal fashion in early-21st-century America.

A modern homage celebrates the 40th anniversary of hippie fashions from the late 1960s.

Today, social classes are far more fluid and mobile than ever before. Because there is no universal way of life today, people are free to choose their own values and lifestyles—and their dress reflects that choice. Many fashions exist simultaneously, and we are all free to adopt the fashions of any social group. If we do not wish to join others in their fashion choices, we can create our own modes and standards of dress. The beatniks of the 1950s and the hippies of the 1960s had their typical fashions, as did the bohemians of the 1920s and the liberated groups of the 1970s. In the 1980s, the phenomenon of the punk rockers existed side by side with the yuppies. In the 1990s, hip-hop fashion coexisted with Ralph Lauren's Polo Sport. In the 2000s, vintage has found a home alongside celebrity glamour.

Lifestyle

Fashions also mirror the times by reflecting the activities in which the people of an era participate. The importance of court-centered social activities in 17th- and 18th-century Europe was evident in men's and women's ornately styled apparel. Fashions became less colorful and more functional when a new working class was created by the industrial revolution.

Currently, our clothes vary according to lifestyle. More casual and active sportswear in wardrobes reflects our interest in active sports and leisure pastimes. The difference in the lifestyle of an urban, career-oriented woman and that of a suburban housewife is reflected in their choice of wardrobes.

PRINCIPLES OF FASHION

Diversification of fashion has added new dimensions to the interpretation of the principles of fashion. While the intangibles of fashion can be vague and sometimes difficult to predict and chart, certain fundamental principles of fashion are tangible and precise. For many decades these principles served as the solid foundation for fashion identification and forecasting. They still do, but today's student of fashion must recognize that in the current vibrant and changing atmosphere, the application of these principles becomes a more intricate and challenging task.

The five principles we will discuss are the foundations upon which the study of fashion is based.

1. Consumers establish fashions by accepting or rejecting the styles offered. The popular belief that designers create artistic designs with little regard for the acceptance of these designs by the public is quite false. No designer can be successful without the support and acceptance of the customer.

A customer is a patron or potential purchaser of goods or services. Thus, a retail store's dress buyer is a customer of a dress manufacturer, and the dress manufacturer is a customer of a fabric producer. The consumer is the ultimate user: the person who uses the finished fashion garment.

Designers create hundreds of new styles each season, based on what they think may attract customers. From among those many styles, manufacturers choose what they think will be successful. They reject many more than they select. From the manufacturers' offerings retailers choose styles they believe their customers will want. Consumers then make the vital choice. By accepting some styles and rejecting others, they—and only they—dictate what styles will become fashions.

2. Fashions are not based on price. Just because something is expensive does not mean it will be successful. Although new styles that may eventually become fashions are often introduced at high prices, this is happening less and less. What you pay for an item of apparel is not an indication of whether the item is considered fashionable.

In the fashion diversity offered to consumers today, successful fashions are to be found at every price level. Upper-income consumers will accept fashions at very low prices, and consumers at the opposite end of the income scale will often splurge and buy a very expensive item—if it is in fashion.

3. Fashions are evolutionary in nature; they are rarely revolutionary. In these days of rapid cultural and national revolutions, it is hard to believe that a worldwide phenomenon such as fashion is evolutionary in nature—not revolutionary. To the casual observer it appears as though fashion changes suddenly. Actually, fashion change comes about as a result of gradual movements from one season to the next.

Throughout history there have probably been only two real revolutions in fashion styles. One occurred during the 20th century: the Dior "New Look" of 1947. The other was the abrupt change of styles brought about by the French Revolution when the fashion changed overnight from elaborate full skirts, low-cut daring bodices, and ornate and glamorous fabrics to simple, drab costumes in keeping with the political and moral upheaval.

Consumers buy apparel and accessories to supplement and update the wardrobes they already own, some of which they purchased last year, some the year before, some the year before that, and so on. In most cases, consumers will buy only if the purchase complements their existing wardrobe and does not depart too radically from last year's purchases.

4. No amount of sales promotion can change the direction in which fashions are moving. Promotional efforts on the part of producers or retailers cannot dictate what consumers will buy, nor can they force people to buy what they do not want. The few times that fashion merchants have tried to promote a radical change in fashion, they have not been successful.

Also, promotional efforts cannot renew the life of a fading fashion unless the extent of change gives the fashion an altogether new appeal. This is why stores have markdown or clearance sales. When the sales of a particular style start slumping, store managers know they must clear out as much of that stock as possible, even at much lower prices, to make room for newer styles in which consumers have indicated interest.

5. All fashions end in excess. This saying is sometimes attributed to Paul Poiret, a top 1920s Parisian designer. Eighteenth-century hoop-skirts ballooned out to more than eight feet in width, which made moving from room to room a complicated matter. The French tried to accommodate these skirts by designing doors that could be opened to a width far beyond that of regular doors. They became known as "French doors" and can still be found in architecture today. Similarly, miniskirts of the 1960s became so short that the slightest movement caused a major problem in modesty. This same trend toward excess can be found in men's wear. Just think of the growth of the width of a tie. It will start as a thin string tie and become wider and wider until it becomes as wide as a bib!

Once the extreme in styling has been reached, a fashion is nearing its end. The attraction of the fashion wanes, and people begin to seek a different look—a new fashion.

This Dior Spring 2011 couture dress proves the concept that all fashions end in excess!

SUMMARY AND REVIEW

In its narrow sense, fashion is the prevailing way a group of people at a particular time and place dress themselves. The fashion industries, which manufacture the materials and finished products of clothing, also produce related goods, including cosmetics, fragrances, and home fashions. Fashion designers attempt to determine what styles—characteristic appearances of garments and other fashion items—will appeal to their target group of consumers. The designs that are offered to the public are versions of a style that are distinguished by their silhouettes, details, textures, and colors.

Public acceptance of a fashion follows a course called the fashion cycle, which includes the following stages: introduction, rise, culmination, decline, and obsolescence. A fashion that reaches the culmination stage and then declines over a brief period of time is called a fad. A classic, alternatively, may not necessarily reach its peak of popularity very quickly, but its decline is gradual, and it never reaches the obsolescence stage.

Any fashion evolves according to the demands of its market. Neither pricing nor promotion by the producers can force consumers to embrace a new fashion. Usually changes evolve gradually, building up to an extreme and then reversing and moving toward the other extreme. The success of fashion merchandisers depends on their abilities to predict the changing tastes of their public with scientific accuracy and to use their artistic creativity to satisfy those tastes.

FOR REVIEW

1. What group ultimately decides whether a style will be "fashionable" or not? Explain your answer.

2. Apparel styles are often named for the periods in history in which they were introduced. Name three such styles and the historic period in which they originated.

3. Give two examples of "classics" that are in style today for each of the following groups: (a) men, (b) women, and (c) children.

4. Distinguish among (a) style, fashion, and design, and between (b) classic and fad.

5. Fashions go through a five-stage life cycle. Name and explain each stage.

6. In what respects does the consumer buying cycle differ from the consumer use cycle? How is such information useful to fashion merchants?

7. Can designers, manufacturers, or retailers force unwanted fashion on consumers? Explain your answer.

8. What are the five basic principles relating to fashion? What are the implications for fashion merchants?

FOR DISCUSSION

The following statements are derived from the text. Discuss the significance of each, giving examples of how each applies to merchandising fashion goods.

1. Men today are as influenced by and responsive to fashion as women.

2. Predicting the time span of a fashion cycle is impossible because each fashion moves at its own speed.

3. Because there is no universal way of life, people are free to choose their own values and lifestyles.

TRADE TALK

Define or briefly explain the following terms:

adaptation

classic

culmination stage

decline stage

design

details

fad

fashion

fashion business

fashion cycle

fashion industries

fast fashion

high fashion

knockoff

marketing

mass or volume fashion

merchandising

obsolescence stage

rise stage

silhouette

style

style number

taste

texture

trend

THE ENVIRONMENT OF
FASHION

KEY CONCEPTS

- The four major factors affecting fashion
- How research is used by fashion producers and retailers to help them with market segmentation
- The five basic psychological factors that motivate human behavior—and how each affects fashion

A cardinal rule in any business is "know your customer." This rule is especially true in the fashion business. Accurate facts about customers who are properly interpreted help designers, manufacturers, and retailers make major decisions about what to offer them. Guesswork and misinterpreted facts can lead to major business failures.

To satisfy the greatest number of customers and make them want to buy their products, every designer, manufacturer, and retailer must know the answers to the following questions:

- How many potential customers for your products and services are there in a given community?
- How old are these customers?
- How much are they willing to spend on your product?
- What level of service do they expect?
- Are they married or single, homeowners or renters?
- How many children do they have?
- What kind of work do they do?
- What is their annual income?
- What is more important to the customer—value or style? Prestige or price?
- How much do they have to spend on "extras"?
- Do they like to shop early or late in the day? Weekdays or weekends?
- What motivates them to shop in a particular store?
- How do they spend their leisure time?

In other words: who are your customers?

One major source of information about the consumer market is the U.S. Census Bureau. The Bureau produces more than three billion separate statistics about the American people and the conditions that affect their lives and influence their actions. It helps businesspeople who are interested in translating the data and projections drawn from them into new product and profit opportunities.

Collectively, the conditions under which we live are called our **environment**. Just as the environment of one nation or society differs from that of another nation or society, so the environment of one neighborhood differs from that of another. In fashion merchandising, it is important to be aware of the conditions that affect a particular customer's environment and to know how the environment differs from one group to another.

The following four major environmental factors affect fashion interest and demand:
1. Market segmentation by geographics, demographics, psychographics, and behavior.
2. The degree of economic development and well-being of a country or society.
3. The sociological characteristics of the class structure.
4. The psychological attitudes of consumers.

MARKET SEGMENTATION

Both manufacturers and retailers try to identify and select target markets for their goods. **Target markets** are specific groups of potential customers that a business is attempting to turn into regular customers. Businesses attempt to determine who their customers are, what those customers want, how much the customers are willing to pay for goods, where potential customers are located, and how many targeted customers exist. Today, geographic, demographic, psychographic, and behavioral research studies are a vital part of determining these important factors.

Most manufacturers and designers are concerned with national trends. Retailers, however, must consider the impact of statistics in their local areas as well as statistics from national studies. **Market segmentation** is the separation of the total consumer market into smaller groups. These are known as market segments. By identifying and studying each market segment, producers and retailers can target their goods and services to their special markets. Markets are divided or segmented in four major ways: by geographics, demographics, psychographics, and behavior.

Geographics

Geographics are population studies that focus on where people live. These studies organize data by region of the country, by county or city size, by population density, and by climate.

Demographics

Demographics are population studies that divide broad groups of consumers into smaller, more homogeneous market segments. The variables covered in a demographic study include the following:

- Age
- Gender
- Family size
- Stages in family life cycle
- Income
- Occupation
- Education
- Religion
- Race and ethnicity or nationality

Psychographics

Psychographics are studies that develop more extensive and personal portraits of potential customers and their lifestyles. Psychographic studies more fully predict consumer purchase patterns and distinguish users of a product. The variables covered in a psychographic study include social class, values and lifestyle, and personality. Sometimes researchers request information about the actual product benefits desired by consumers. These studies help greatly in matching the image of a company and its product with the type of consumer using the product.

Many research firms combine geographic and demographic studies for retailers and manufacturers. One such firm, the Nielsen Corporation, produces the PRIZM system, which divides and then clusters the population of the United States into 62 market segments or "clusters" based on postal zip codes, housing, and lifestyle choices.

In order to reach and keep profitable customers you must know what drives their purchasing decisions. PRIZM combines demographics, consumer behavior, and geographic data to help fashion industry marketers identify and understand their customers and prospects.[1]

Fall 2011

Donna Karan

Urban Zen Spring 2011

Nature-inspired designs

Donna Karan & Sonja Nuttall

URBAN ZEN

DONNA KARAN

DONNA KARAN REMADE FASHION IN HER OWN IMAGE, now she's working to change our ideas about death and healing, encompassing new approaches to health and wellness practices and introducing her Urban Zen Collection.

The year 2010 marked the twenty-fifth anniversary of Karan's fashion label, which she originally started "to design modern clothes for modern people." Her goal was to create the kind of clothes that she and her friends needed, and Karan's now-iconic system of "seven easy pieces" offers busy women a wardrobe that could be mixed and matched to go anywhere.

In her new direction the uniting principle is Karan's conviction that nontraditional health and wellness practices can enhance the lives of everyone from schoolchildren to cancer patients, and she is working hard to extend such techniques to a range of disciplines.

Through a hectic private life, Karan kept working. She eventually left Anne Klein to start her own label, Donna Karan New York, which was followed by DKNY, DKNY for Men, DKNY Active, and other DKNY lines. It was while juggling business and family that Karan also got involved with charitable causes. "My first true philanthropic passion was when the AIDS epidemic broke out," she says. "I thought, there is an emergency here; how do you bring a community to-

gether? You get the retailers, the manufacturers and designers, and the consumers—and now you have a movement."

Karan went to work with Elizabeth Glaser's Pediatric AIDS Foundation and cofounded the fashion industry's Seventh on Sale events and the annual Super Saturday ovarian cancer research fund-raiser in the Hamptons, both of which she continues to support. Donna Karan's goals for her foundations are ambitious. "My three major passions are preserving culture, improving health and well-being, and empowering children," she says, "and I see Urban Zen [Foundation] as being about past, present, and future: the wisdom of cultures of the past; the health care of today; and education and children, which is the future. Urban Zen is a center where we create, collaborate, and communicate change of the minds who want to be catalysts for change."

As far as Karan is concerned, this is only the beginning. "Right now we're located in New York City, but I think this is a model that can be duplicated," she says. "The vision for the future is that we have Urban Zen centers around the world."

PRIZM tells you what people buy, but not why. To get closer to that information, many people turn to another widely used research system that uses demographics and psychographics: the VALS 2 system, offered by Strategic Business Insights. The VALS 2 (Values and Life Styles) system sorts customers into eight major categories based on psychological attributes. The categories are arranged into a framework that puts consumers with the most resources on the top and those with the fewest on the bottom. It also arranges consumers into three groups horizontally: principle-oriented, status-oriented, and action-oriented. The main dimensions of the segmentation framework are the primary motivation (the horizontal dimension) and resources (the vertical dimensions).

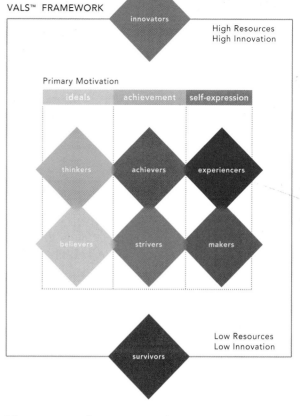

VALS™ FRAMEWORK

innovators

High Resources
High Innovation

Primary Motivation

ideals | achievement | self-expression

thinkers | achievers | experiencers

believers | strivers | makers

Low Resources
Low Innovation

survivors

In the VALS 2 system, each diamond-shaped box represents one of the eight consumer markets.

Behavior

In an attempt to gather even more insight into customer preferences, some retailers and manufacturers use behavioral research. These studies group consumers according to their opinions of specific products or services or their actual rate of use of these products or services. Behavioral studies help companies understand and predict the behavior of present and potential customers. If you segment your market by behavior, you might be able to identify the reasons for one group's refusal to buy your product. Once you have identified the reason, you may be able to change the product enough to satisfy their objections. A more recent extension of VALS, GeoVALS, uses psychographics to identify where customers live and further explain their behavioral trends.

THE ECONOMIC ENVIRONMENT

The growth of fashion demand depends on a high level of economic development, which is reflected in consumer income and population characteristics, including technological advances.

Consumer Income

Consumer income can be measured in terms of personal income, disposable personal income, and discretionary income. Many people use the amount of personal income as an indicator of "arriving" in their particular social set. The more personal income they have, the more socially acceptable they consider themselves to be. We will also discuss how the purchasing power of the dollar affects consumer income later in this chapter.

Personal Income

The total or gross income received by the population as a whole is called **personal income**. It consists of wages, salaries, interest, dividends, and all other income for everyone in the country. Divide personal income by the number of people in the population and the result is **per capita personal income**.

Disposable Personal Income

The amount a person has left to spend or save after paying taxes is called **disposable personal income**. It is roughly equivalent to take-home pay and provides an approximation of the purchasing power of each consumer during any given year.

Disposable income per household and per capita varies according to age groups and gender. While household after-tax income starts to drop after age 49, individual after-tax income does not peak until ages 60 to 64, showing that consumers in the 50- to 64-year-old age bracket have the highest disposable income of any group.

Discretionary Income

The money that an individual or family can spend or save after buying necessities—food, clothing, shelter, and basic transportation—is called **discretionary income**. Of course, the distinction between "necessities" and "luxuries" or between "needs" and "wants" is a subjective one.

In the 2010 Annual Report of the White House Task Force on the Middle Class, various definitions, middle-class values, and aspirations were examined. The principle findings of the report are as follows:

- Middle-class families are defined by their aspirations more than their income. The report assumes that middle-class families aspire to home ownership, a car, a college education for their children, health and retirement security, and occasional family vacations.
- Families at a variety of income levels aspire to be middle class, and under certain circumstances can put together budgets that allow them to obtain all the items that are assumed to be part of a middle-class lifestyle.
- Estimates of a middle-class family budget for married-couple families with two school-age children range from about $51,000 to about $123,000.[2]

The lucky few are like consumer royalty, able to buy a wide variety of goods and services. Although marketers like to target these consumers, it may not be a wise long-term strategy. The superrich have greater purchasing power, but they are declining in number. While middle-class households have less money, they still have overwhelming strength in numbers.

Purchasing Power of the Dollar

Even if the average income increases, it does not mean that people have an equivalent increase in purchasing power. The reason for this is that the value of the dollar—its **purchasing power** or what it will buy—has steadily declined since 1950.

A decline in the purchasing power of money is caused by **inflation**. Webster's defines inflation as a continuing rise in the general price level usually attributed to an increase in the volume of money and credit relative to available goods and services.[3] Inflation, therefore, is an economic situation in which demand exceeds supply. Scarcity of goods and services, in relation to demand, results in ever-increasing prices.

When income taxes increase, the purchasing power of the family income drops; a decrease in income taxes has the reverse effect. With an inflationary economy, the

PURCHASING POWER OF THE DOLLAR: 1950–2008

year	average*
1950	4.15
1960	3.37
1970	2.57
1980	1.22
1990	0.77
2000	0.58
2005	0.51
2008	0.46

*as measured by consumer prices

The value of the dollar has steadily declined since 1950.

working time required to acquire the necessities of life—basic food, clothing, transportation, and shelter—increases. The increase is not, however, uniform among all items.

A **recession** is one of several discrete phases in the overall business cycle. The beginning of a recession is known as a business cycle "peak," and the end of a recession is referred to as a business cycle "trough." The National Bureau of Economic Research (NBER) has a more precise definition:

> A recession is a significant decline in economic activity spread across the economy lasting more than a few months, normally visible in real GDP, real income, employment, industrial production, and wholesale retail sales. A recession begins just after the economy reaches a peak of activity and ends as the economy reaches its trough. Between trough and peak, the economy is in an expansion.[4]

Both inflation and recession affect consumers' buying patterns. Fashion merchants in particular must thoroughly understand the effects of inflation and recession when planning their inventory assortments and promotional activities. Manufacturers must also understand how consumers are affected by economic factors.

Population

The majority of the population of the United States has some discretionary income and thus can influence the course of fashion. Two factors relating to population, however, have an important bearing on the extent of fashion demand.

1. The size of the total population and the rate of its growth
2. The age mix of the population and its projection into the future

Executive Vice President Catherine Moellering

Executive Vice President Catherine Moellering & CEO Abbey Doneger

TOBÉ REPORTS
The Original Trend Spotter Just Got Trendier

TOBÉ (PRONOUNCED TOE-BEE) WAS ESTABLISHED IN 1927 IN THE EARLY DAYS OF FASHION FORECASTING. Tobé's founder was syndicated newspaper columnist Taube Coller Davis—who changed her name to Tobé, with an accent, in a fit of French fabulousness.

To peruse the trends in Tobé's archives is to travel to a time when styles were designed in Europe, and women waited to buy a version of the line at their local department and specialty stores. Back then, Tobé performed the job of a modern-day "fashion director," helping big-store buyers understand and interpret trends from Europe before placing their orders.

Tobé once counted among its clients all the big department-store chains—Kaufman's, Bullock's, Marshall Field's—most of which have vanished during the past 20 years of industry consolidation. In 2005, Federated Department Stores, Inc. formed the behemoth now known as Macy's, Inc. by acquiring its rival May Department Stores Co. May had been Tobé's biggest client, so it was no coincidence that 2005 was the year that Tobé's then president, Kathy Deane—daughter of one of five executives who would continue to run the Tobé report after the Tobé founder's death in 1962—decided to sell the company.

Enter Abbey Doneger—CEO of the Doneger Group, the world's largest fashion and retail advisory firm. Mr. Doneger had heard about the Tobé Report from his own retail clients back in the 1970s and was impressed with their record. He bought Tobé Reports in 2005 and realized that their business needed to embrace change!

When Kathy Deane retired in 2009, Mr. Doneger hired Catherine Moellering, a merchant trained in the executive program at Bloomingdale's, to put Tobé ahead of the trends again. New to forecasting, Ms. Moellering spent her career in apparel retailing at Bloomingdale's and Liz Claiborne. She was aware of the impact of the Web and was quick to get the Tobé Report up to speed on the use of the Web for clients.

But the competitors grasped how significant the Web would be for trend spotting and grabbing market share. Worth Global Style Network, known as WGSN, was founded in 1998 and now has 36,000 unique users. It sped up fashion forecasting with "up-to-the-minute information with no time delay" from a network of 200 trendspotters around the world. Another rival Stylesight, founded in 2004, has image banks and customizable trend analyses available in English, Spanish, Chinese, Japanese, and Turkish.

Tobé's dozen or so trendspotters go to fashion shows, work retailer's selling floors, visit showrooms, and shoot photos on the street. Rather than carving the market up into categories like "junior knits" and "career separates," Tobé editors now scope and classify trends by consumers.

The website WGSN.com, accessible mostly to clients, has tools like "taking last year's best-seller forward," which tells retailers how to move sales volume from this year's hot item (cargo pants) to next season's version (slouchy "boyfriend" khakis). It also features on-the-street trend observations and other content that can be filtered according to an individual retailer's specifications.

Size of Population

The size of the population relates to the extent of current fashion demand. The rate of population growth suggests what tomorrow's market may become. In 1920, the United States had a population of about 106 million. By 1950, that figure had reached 151 million, and by 1980 it was 227.6 million. In 2008, the population reached 304.1 million. By 2025, the U.S. population is estimated to reach 357.5 million[5] and by 2050, it is expected to reach 439 million.[6]

Age Mix

The age mix and its projection into the future affect the characteristics of current fashion demand and suggest what they may be in the future. While the overall population continues to grow, the growth rate is not the same for all age groups or for both genders. Since each group has its own special fashion interests, needs, and reactions, changes in the age mix serve as vital clues to future fashion demand.

Because both men and women are living longer, the over-age-65 group is steadily growing. People who are 50 years old and older account for more than one half of all discretionary spending power. This mature group becomes increasingly important in the fashion world as their earlier retirement—and in many cases, increased retirement incomes—allows them to spend many active years wherever and however they choose. They are healthier, better educated, more active, and will live longer. Their interests and discretionary purchases vary radically from those of their younger counterparts, offering a real challenge to businesses to meet the demands of the "new old." The demand of older consumers for items such as package travel tours, cosmetic aids, and apparel that suits their ages and retirement lifestyles will offer growth opportunities for marketers, especially in fashion.

The aging of the population has several causes: healthier lifestyles and improved medical treatment have increased life expectancies, and with birthrates on the rise, there is a slow increase of the population in younger age groups.

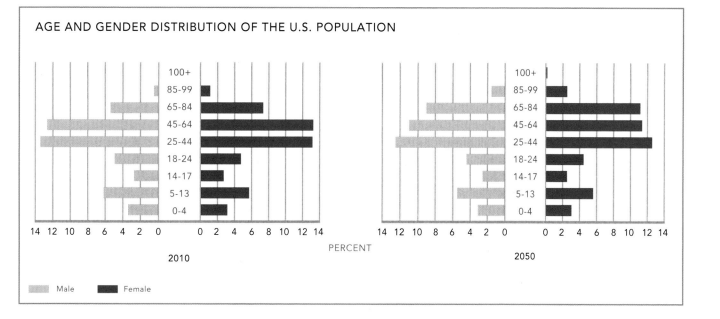

AGE AND GENDER DISTRIBUTION OF THE U.S. POPULATION

2010

2050

PERCENT

Male   Female

The modest dress
exhibited by female
tennis players of the
1930s [left] is a far cry
from the sportswear
of today's athletes,
as seen in Maria
Sharapova's Nike
ensemble [right].

THE SOCIOLOGICAL ENVIRONMENT

To understand fashion, one needs to understand the sociological environment in which fashion trends begin, grow, and fade away. Simply stated, changes in fashion are caused by changes in the attitudes of consumers, which in turn are influenced by changes in the social patterns of the times. The key sociological factors influencing fashion today are: leisure time; ethnic influences; status of women; social and physical mobility; instant communications; and wars, disasters, and crises.

Leisure Time

One of the most precious possessions of the average U.S. citizen today is leisure time, partly because it is also one of the most scarce. The demands of the workplace compete with the demands of family and home for much of people's waking hours, leaving less and less time for the pursuit of other activities, whether those activities be a fitness regimen, community work, entertainment, relaxation—or even shopping.

The ways in which people use their leisure time are as varied as people themselves. Some turn to active or spectator sports; others prefer to travel. Many seek self-improvement, while growing numbers improve their standard of living with a second job. The increased importance of leisure time has brought changes to people's lives in many ways—in values, standards of living, and scope of activities. As a result, whole new markets have sprung up. Demand for larger and more versatile wardrobes for the many activities consumers can now explore and enjoy has mushroomed.

Casual Living

A look into the closets of the U.S. population would probably reveal one feature that is much the same from coast to coast, in large cities and in small towns: Most would contain an unusually large selection of casual clothes and sportswear. The market for casual apparel developed with the growth of the suburbs in the 1950s and led to "dress-down Fridays" at work in the 1990s. The choice as to what is suitable for an activity is still largely left to the individual, and into the 2000s a shift in the direction of casual dress has begun a reverse trend as an interest in "dressing up" starts to grow again.

Active Sportswear

There is no doubt about it, the superstar of the fashion market in the 1970s, the 1980s, and the 1990s was sportswear. Its growth was phenomenal! While sports clothes have been around since the turn of the century, when they first appeared they were not particularly distinctive. Women's sport dresses for playing tennis or golf were not much different from their regular streetwear, and men's outfits similarly varied little from business suits. By the 1920s, consumers began demanding apparel that was appropriate for active sports or simply for relaxing in the sunshine. But it is the emphasis on health and self in the past three decades that has caused the fantastic growth of the active sportswear market.

From 2000 through today, sports-minded people play tennis in specially designed tennis fashions. Golfers want special golfwear. Joggers want only jogging outfits. And cyclists seem able to bike only in spandex biker shorts and high-tech helmets. Rollerbladers also want helmets, wrist and knee guards, and appropriate fashions. The same goes for ice-skaters, skiers, runners, hang gliders, sky divers, and climbers. Health clubs, exercise classes, and workout gyms exploded in popularity in the 1980s and a whole new and vast world of leotards, exercise suits, warm-up suits, and other self-improvement fashions and accessories were born. Whatever the activity, the specialized fashions—from jogging suits to biker shorts—quickly followed and became *de rigueur*. Today, even those who do not participate in a particular sport beyond watching the pros on television feel the need to look the part!

Ethnic Influences

In recent years, minority groups in the United States, representing more than 30 percent of the nation's total population, have experienced vast population increases and sociological changes. The future holds even more change. In 2005, African Americans slipped from the largest minority group in the United States to the second largest. Hispanics outnumber

Projections show the proportion of the non-Hispanic white majority shrinking, the Hispanic population replacing African Americans as the largest minority, and the percentage of Asian Americans increasing at a fast rate.

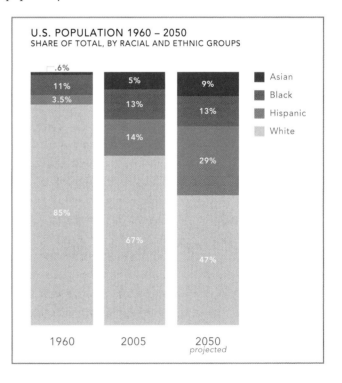

U.S. POPULATION 1960 – 2050
SHARE OF TOTAL, BY RACIAL AND ETHNIC GROUPS

Legend:
- Asian
- Black
- Hispanic
- White

1960: .6%, 11%, 3.5%, 85%
2005: 5%, 13%, 14%, 67%
2050 projected: 9%, 13%, 29%, 47%

Alexander McQueen's 2011 Spring collection shows a heavy influence toward South American styles and colors.

African Americans, and Asians continue to exhibit a rapid growth rate. This historic shift in the racial and ethnic composition of the U.S. population will have many long-range implications. For example, the growth of the Hispanic and Asian populations has brought about an increased demand for clothing in smaller sizes because both men and women in these groups are typically smaller in stature than people whose ethnic heritage is Northern European.

Hispanics

The United States added nearly 1.2 million people of Hispanic origin to the population between 2007 and 2008, and new Hispanic immigrants are expected to continue to come in large numbers for the foreseeable future. Projections show the Hispanic population will reach 20 percent of the population by 2020 and over 30 percent by 2050. Hispanic customers will be a large part of the shopping experience and in fashion this has been evidenced with the success of fiery new colors and prints reminiscent of lush South American rain forests.[7]

African Americans

At 13.3 percent of the population in 2008, African Americans were the second largest minority in the United States.[8] They are better educated and hold higher-level jobs than they did in the past. With better education comes a stronger sense of oneself and one's heritage. Many black people show the pride they feel in their African heritage by wearing African styles, fabrics, and patterns. Other ethnic groups have adopted these styles as well. Fashion companies have acknowledged the changes that have occurred among the African American population and have reflected these changes in the products they market and the models they use. Cosmetics are available that emphasize the beauty of dark skin. African American men and women have become world famous modeling clothing and advertising various items in magazines and on television.

Asians

According to the 2008 Census statistics, the Asian American population was estimated at 15.5 million. Between 2000 and 2008, Asians alone accounted for 13.1 percent of the change in the U.S. population. They are considered the second-fastest growing minority group, following the Hispanic population.[9] But they are not one homogenous group. They come from more than a dozen countries and speak at least 41 different languages!

In 2009 Asians in the United States were more geographically concentrated than African Americans or Latinos. The states that account for roughly half of the Asian population are California (35 percent), New York (10 percent), and Texas (6 percent). In Hawaii, our nation's only majority-Asian state, Asians made up the highest proportion of the total population (53 percent). This includes both Asian alone or Asian in combination with one or more other races.[10]

The end of the Vietnam War and the influx of thousands of refugees from Cambodia and Vietnam brought additional traditions and costumes to be shared. This stimulated interest in some of the more exotic fashions of the East and in the everyday comfort of the Chinese sandal and quilted jacket.

Immigration from many Asian countries continues to rise. As of 2009, Chinese Americans were the largest Asian group, followed by Filipinos, Asian Indians, Vietnamese, Koreans, and Japanese.[11]

Status of Women

In the early 1900s, the U.S. woman was, in many ways, a nonperson. She could not vote, serve on a jury, earn a living at any but a few occupations, own property, or enter public places unescorted. She passed directly from her father's control to her husband's control, without rights or monies. In both households, she dressed to please the man and reflect his status.

Profound changes began to occur during World War I and have accelerated ever since. The most dramatic advances have happened since the mid-1960s and the advent of the women's movement. Women's demands for equal opportunity, equal pay, and equal rights in every facet of life continue to bring about even more change. These changes have affected not only fashion but also the entire field of marketing.

Jobs and Money

The number of women ages 20 and over who work has increased dramatically since 1975. This represents a staggering increase of more than 15 million women who have entered the workforce since 1975. This figure has doubled, despite the fact that women's salaries are still, on average only about 80 percent of men's salaries.[12] In the age groupings of those 35 years and older, women had earnings that were roughly three-fourths as much as their male counterparts. Among younger workers, the earning differences between women and men were not as great. Women earned 89 percent as much as men among workers 25 to 34 years old and 93 percent as much among 16- to 24-year-olds.

Japanese designer Issey Miyake, whose Spring 2011 collection is pictured here, is representative of the ever-growing influence of Asian fashion.

LILLY PULITZER
Life in Lilly Land

Fall 2008

Lilly Pulitzer sleepwear

Lilly Pulitzer

Fall 2008

Inside a Lilly Pulitzer store

LONG BEFORE "LIFESTYLE DRESSING" WAS THE FASHIONABLE WAY TO GO, BEFORE RALPH AND TORY, THERE WAS A LADY NAMED LILLY PULITZER ROUSSEAU. Whether Lilly can believe it or not, over 50 years have passed since she launched the preppy girls' warm-weather wardrobe—simple shifts, capri pants, and tennis skirts in flashy, pastel print patterns.

Her story has been told often over the years: Born Lilly McKim, she attended all the right schools with all the right people, such as Jacqueline Bouvier (Kennedy). She eloped in 1952 with newspaper scion Peter Pulitzer and moved to Palm Beach, Florida. Bored with the society life, she looked to keep busy and discovered she had a talent for designing simple clothes, and an eye for colorful prints. Together with a textile business called Key West Fabrics, they dreamed up lime green palm trees, bursting sunflowers, and sky blue shells, all whimsical motifs based on Lilly's sun-drenched life.

Within a year, she was shipping orders to retailers from Lord & Taylor and Saks Fifth Avenue to specialty stores. In 1961, a Lilly Pulitzer shop opened off Worth Avenue in Palm Beach. Her fame was cemented a year later when Lilly's school pal first lady Jackie Kennedy appeared in *Life* magazine wearing the Lilly Pulitzer Classic Shift.

Told by one retailer that she had to start making fall clothes, Lilly replied, "Oh, but you don't understand, it's always summer somewhere." Thus, she introduced what may have been one of the first resort collections, a year-round summery lineup that grew to include men's, children's, and swimwear. Soon after, Lilly Pulitzer boutiques opened across the country.

By the early 80s, however, the working-girl wardrobe and a neutral palette had taken over fashion; sales were on a downward trend, and Lilly shut the business down in 1984. In 1993, the Lilly Pulitzer brand was for sale and Lilly wanted someone to resurrect it. Enter Scott Beaumont and James Bradbeer Jr., two Pennsylvania businessmen looking for a business to buy. They bought Lilly's brand and it became a tremendous success. Today the Lilly Pulitzer brand brings in over $100 million in wholesale volume annually.

It's often said that there's very little that's truly original in fashion these days. But when Lilly Pulitzer first offered her sunny prints, there wasn't much like them anywhere, and they turned into a fashion and lifestyle brand. Here, in honor of its jubilee, the company collected thoughts from some designers and fashion-world observers about the Lilly phenomenon.

"Lilly Pulitzer created a very distinct look—her personal style of bright colors and prints has an important place in fashion." —*Ralph Lauren*

"Lilly Pulitzer is one of the few designers worthy of copying. You can't be an American designer without a little nod to Lilly." —*Isaac Mizrahi*

"With her bold prints and sunny colors, Lilly taught the world about Palm Beach style. Like a Levi's 501, a Lilly shift can work on everyone from age seven to 70. A true American classic." —*Michael Kors*

"When you think of classic American resortwear, you cannot help but think of Lilly Pulitzer." —*Trina Turk*

"Lilly Pulitzer makes everyone look happier, richer, and more fun-loving than they probably are. Lilly equals sunshine." —*Jonathan Adler*

Spring 2004

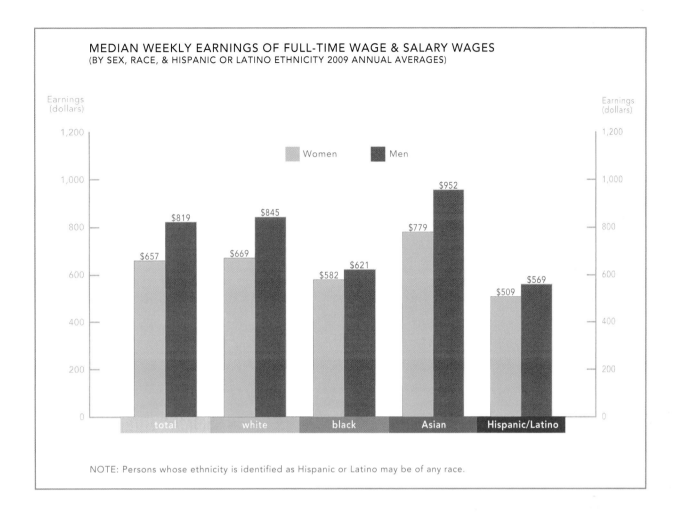

MEDIAN WEEKLY EARNINGS OF FULL-TIME WAGE & SALARY WAGES
(BY SEX, RACE, & HISPANIC OR LATINO ETHNICITY 2009 ANNUAL AVERAGES)

Earnings (dollars)

Women   Men

	total	white	black	Asian	Hispanic/Latino
Women	$657	$669	$582	$779	$509
Men	$819	$845	$621	$952	$569

NOTE: Persons whose ethnicity is identified as Hispanic or Latino may be of any race.

Both financial pressures and career satisfaction should keep the number of working women growing.[13]

The dramatic increase in working women has led to a surge in fashion interest because a woman who works is continuously exposed to fashion. It is everywhere around her as she meets people, shops during her lunch hour, or goes to and from home. As a member of the workforce, she now has the incentive, the opportunity, and the means to respond to fashion's appeal.

Finally, women in general today have more money of their own to spend as they see fit. Approximately four women in every six have incomes, earned and unearned, of their own. These women and their acceptance or rejection of offered styles have new importance in the fashion marketplace.

Education

Often the better educated a woman becomes, the more willing she is to learn new things. She is also more willing to try new fashions, which of course serves to accelerate fashion change. And with more women today receiving more education than ever before, the repercussions on fashion are unmistakable. According to the U.S. Bureau of

According to the U.S. Census Bureau, Asian women and men earned more than their white, black, and Hispanic counterparts.

Labor Statistics, young women are outnumbering men in education attainment, with nearly 1 in 4 women earning bachelor's degrees by the age of 23, in comparison to 1 in 7 men.[14] Today's educated women have had wider exposure than their mothers or grandmothers to other cultures and to people of different backgrounds. Consequently, they are more worldly, more discerning, more demanding, and more confident in their tastes and feels for fashion.

Social Freedom

Perhaps the most marked change in the status of women since the early 1900s is the degree of social freedom they now enjoy. Young women today are free to apply for a job and to earn, spend, and save their own money. They are free to go unescorted to a restaurant, theater, or other public place. Women travel more frequently than they did in the past. They travel to more distant locations at younger ages and often alone. Many own their own cars. If they can afford it, they may maintain an apartment or share one with others. It is difficult to imagine that the social freedoms and responsibilities that today's young women accept as normal were considered unfeminine or outrageous as recently as 40 years ago.

Short skirts, popular in the 1920s, the early 1940s, the 1960s, and the 2000s are commonly interpreted as a reflection of women's freedom. So, too, is the simplicity of the styles that prevailed in those periods: chemises, sacks, tents, shifts, other variations of loose-hanging dresses, and pants.

Different theories exist about why these changes came about. Some people believe that stiff, unyielding corsets went out with a stiff, unyielding moral code. Others believe that the changes had no particular social significance. They believe that women rejected inflexible corsets not because of a change in the moral code, but because the new materials were simply more comfortable. Similarly, pants may be viewed as an expression of women's freedom or merely as suitable garments for hopping in and out of the indispensable car.

Whatever the reasons, the lifestyles of U.S. women, and their opinions and attitudes about fashion, have changed radically in the past four decades. U.S. women have gained hard-won freedoms in their social and business lives. They are just as definite about their freedom of choice in fashion. The thought of today's independent women accepting uncomfortable and constricting clothing or shoes just to follow the dictates of some fashion arbiter, as they did years ago, is ludicrous. Today's busy, active women, whether at home or at the office, have very carefully defined preferences for fashions that suit their own individual needs and comfort. Successful designers recognize these preferences and make sure their drawing boards reflect them.

Social Mobility

Almost all societies have classes, and individuals choose either to stand out from or to conform to their actual or aspired-to class. Sociologists have related fashion change to changes in **social mobility**, when an individual or group moves within a social hierarchy. There is also an effort to associate with a higher class by imitation.

The United States is sometimes called a classless society, but this is valid only in that there are no hereditary ranks, royalty, or untouchables. Classes do exist, but they are based largely upon occupation, income, residential location, education, or avocation, and their boundaries have become increasingly fluid. They range from the immensely wealthy (self-made millionaires or their descendants—the Vanderbilts, Whitneys, and Rockefellers, for example) at the top through the very wealthy (mostly nouveau riche) through the many middle-income levels and finally to the low-income and poverty levels. At the very bottom are the unemployed and the homeless.

Middle-Class Influence

Most fashion authorities agree that there is a direct relationship between the growth and strength of the middle class and the growth and strength of fashion demand. As discussed earlier, the middle class has the highest physical, social, and financial mobility. Because it is the largest class, it has the majority vote in the adoption of fashions. Members of the middle class tend to be followers, not leaders, of fashion, but the strength of their following pumps money into the fashion industry. And the persistence of their following often spurs fashion leaders to seek newer and different fashions of their own. They have both fashion interest and the money to indulge it. Despite fluctuations in the economy, this growth generally means a widespread increase in consumer buying power, which in turn generates increased fashion demand.

Physical Mobility

Physical mobility, like social mobility, encourages the demand for and response to fashion. One effect of travel is "cross-pollination" of cultures. After seeing how other people live, travelers bring home a desire to adopt or adapt some of what they observed and make it part of their environment.

Thus, Marco Polo brought gunpowder, silks, and spices from the Orient, introducing new products to medieval Europe. In the 19th century, travelers brought touches of Asian and African fashions to Western dress and home furnishings. In the 20th century, Latin American and pre-Columbian influences were introduced into North America, dramatically changing the direction and emphasis of fashion in this country.

In the United States, people enjoy several kinds of physical mobility. For example, the daily routine for many people involves driving to work or to a shopping center, often in a different city. Among the broad range of influences they are exposed to during their daily trips are the fashions of others and the fashion offerings of retail distributors.

A second form of physical mobility popular among Americans is vacation travel. Whether travelers are going to a nearby lake or around the world, each trip exposes them to many different fashion influences and each trip itself demands special fashions. Living out of a suitcase for a few days or a few months requires clothes that are easy to pack, wrinkle-resistant, suitable for a variety of occasions, and easy to keep in order.

A third form of physical mobility is change of residence, which, like travel, exposes an individual to new contacts, new environments, and new fashion influences.

Fashion bloggers like Bryanboy and Tavi Gevinson are exerting style influence from their bedrooms, evidence of social media's evolving role in fashion.

Faster Communications

Related to physical mobility is faster communications. Not many years ago, news of every sort traveled more slowly. This meant that life not only moved more slowly but also fashions changed more slowly. It could take weeks or months for people in one section of the country to learn what was being worn in another part of the country. Fashion trends moved at a pace that was as leisurely as the news.

Our electronic age has changed all that. We now enjoy rapid communication in ever-increasing quantities and infinite varieties. By means of satellites, round-the-clock broadcasting, radio, Twitter, Facebook, iPhone applications, and blogs, we have the world at our fingertips. Thus, these have become important mediums for transmitting fashion information.

A significant shift began in 2009 when fashion bloggers, for the first time, were seated in the front row of fashion shows with the press. They have become the new celebrities. For example, Marc Jacobs named his ostrich bag, the BB, after blogger Bryanboy, and 13-year-old blogger Tavi Gevinson inspired Rodarte's collection for Target.[15] Fast communication is becoming even faster and is essential for the ever-changing world of fashion.

War, Disaster, and Crises

War, widespread disaster, and crises shake people's lives and focus attention on ideas, events, and places that may be completely new. People develop a need for fashions that are compatible with the changes in their attitudes and environments.

Such changes took place in women's activities and in fashions as a result of the two world wars. World War I brought women into the business world in significant numbers and encouraged their desire for independence and suffrage. It gave them a reason to demand styles that allowed freer physical movement. World War II drew women into such traditionally masculine jobs as riveting, for which they previously had not been considered strong enough. It put them in war plants on night shifts.

THE PSYCHOLOGICAL ENVIRONMENT

The five basic psychological factors that influence fashion demand are boredom, curiosity, reaction to convention, need for self-assurance, and desire for companionship.[16] These factors motivate a large share of people's actions and reactions.

1. **Boredom.** People tend to become bored with fashions too long in use. Boredom leads to restlessness and a desire for change. In fashion, the desire for change expresses itself in a demand for something new and satisfyingly different from what one already has.

2. **Curiosity.** Curiosity causes interest in change for its own sake. Highly curious people like to experiment; they want to know what is around the next corner. There is curiosity in everyone, though some may respond to it less dramatically than others. Curiosity and the need to experiment keep fashion demand alive.

3. **Reaction to convention.** One of the most important psychological factors influencing fashion demand is the reaction to convention. People's reactions take one of two forms: rebellion against convention or adherence to it. Rebellion against convention is characteristic of young people. This involves more than boredom or curiosity: It is a positive rejection of what exists and a search for something new. However, acceptance by the majority is an important part of the definition of fashion. The majority tends to adhere to convention, either within its own group or class or in general.

4. **Need for self-assurance.** The need for self-assurance or confidence is a human characteristic that gives impetus to fashion demand. Often the need to overcome feelings of inferiority or of disappointment can be satisfied through apparel. People who consider themselves to be fashionably dressed have an armor that gives them self-assurance. Those who know that their clothes are dated are at a psychological disadvantage.

5. **Desire for companionship.** The desire for companionship is fundamental in human beings. The instinct for survival of the species drives individuals to seek mates. Humans' innate gregariousness also encourages them to seek companions. Fashion plays its part in the search for all kinds of companionship. In its broader sense, companionship implies the formation of groups, which require conformity in dress as well as in other respects. Flamboyant or subdued, a person's mode of dress can be a bid for companionship as well as the symbol of acceptance within a particular group.

SUMMARY AND REVIEW

Fashion marketers determine their customers' wants and needs by examining various market segments, identified by geographics, demographics, psychographics, and behavior. Each marketer identifies the group or groups within the general population that are its target customer. Determining the average customer's personal income helps marketers make pricing decisions and estimate sales, especially when population trends are matched with income figures. For example, businesses that target middle-age and retirement-age consumers know that their customers are increasing in number and that the average income for consumers in these age groups is also increasing. The teenage and young adult markets are a smaller portion of the population than they were earlier in the century, but they are an influential market segment, often spending their discretionary income on fashion merchandise. The growing value placed on leisure time and leisure-time activities has increased the market for casual clothing and active sportswear.

Marketers also track trends in the population of targeted ethnic groups. Changing patterns of immigration bring with them new influences from different parts of the world. The Hispanic market has become the largest ethnic minority in the United States in the 21st century, superseding the African American market in size. The Asian American market is the second-fastest growing minority, following Hispanics. The non-Hispanic Caucasian population is expected to remain the majority, but by a reduced percentage.

The role of women in society changed dramatically in the 20th century, and their increased freedom, better education, and growing presence in the labor force increased their average income and changed their buying habits.

Other social forces that affect business include greater mobility and more rapid communication, which bring individuals wider choices in their purchases. Political, economic, and natural upheavals also affect fashion marketing, often leading to trends that last beyond the crisis. As consumers become more knowledgeable about their growing choices in their buying behavior, marketers are paying more attention to psychographic factors as they attempt to identify and meet the demands of their target customers.

FOR REVIEW

1. Name the four major environmental influences on fashion interest and demand in any era.

2. Market segmentation is vitally important to producers and retailers of fashion merchandise. Explain why, giving at least two examples of how such information could be used by the fashion industry.

3. How does the size and age mix of a population affect current fashion demand? What does information about size and age mix today tell us about the future of fashion demand?

4. In what ways has increased availability of leisure time affected the fashion market?

5. How has the changing status of ethnic groups affected fashion interest and demand? Cite at least two examples.

6. How does a higher level of education affect fashion interest and demand?

7. What is social mobility? How does the degree of social mobility affect fashion interest and demand? Illustrate your answer with examples.

8. Upon what factors are classes in the United States usually based? Why is it more difficult to identify an individual's social class in this country than it is in other countries?

9. Describe three kinds of physical mobility that people in the United States enjoy today, explaining how each influences fashion demand.

10. Five basic psychological factors motivate much of human behavior. List them, explaining how each affects fashion interest and demand.

FOR DISCUSSION

1. Is discretionary income or disposable personal income the more significant figure to fashion producers and marketers? Why?

2. Discuss the similarities and differences between the GeoVALS and PRIZM 2 systems.

3. How has the status of women changed during the 20th century? How have these changes affected fashion interest and demand?

4. How are the changes in technology and social media affecting fashion today?

TRADE TALK

Define or briefly explain the following terms:

demographics

discretionary income

disposable personal income

environment

geographics

inflation

market segmentation

per capita personal income

personal income

psychographics

purchasing power

recession

social mobility

target market

THE MOVEMENT OF FASHION

KEY CONCEPTS

- The factors influencing the movement of fashion
- How to predict the movement of fashion
- The theories of fashion adoption
- How to identify fashion leaders and fashion followers

Fashion is, in many ways, like a river. A river is always in motion, continuously flowing—sometimes it is slow and gentle; other times it is rushed and turbulent. It is exciting and never the same. It affects those who ride its currents and those who rest on its shores. Its movements depend on the environment.

All of this is true of fashion, too. The constant movements of fashion depend on an environment made up of social, political, and economic factors. These movements, no matter how obvious or how slight, have both meaning and definite direction. There is a special excitement to interpreting these movements and estimating their speed and direction. Everyone involved in fashion, from the designer to the consumer, is caught up in the movement of fashion.

The excitement starts with the textile producers. Fully 12 to 18 months before they offer their lines to manufacturers, the textile people must choose their designs, textures, and colors. From three to nine months before showing a line to buyers, apparel manufacturers begin deciding which styles they will produce and in which fabrics. Then, two to six months before the fashions will appear on the selling floor, the retail buyers make their selections from the manufacturers' lines. Finally, the excitement passes on to the consumers, as they select the garments that will be versatile, appropriate, and suitably priced for their individual needs and wants.

How can all these people be sure their choices are based on reliable predictions? Successful designers, manufacturers, buyers, and consumers have a good understanding of basic cycles, principles, and patterns that operate in the world of fashion. Their predictions are based on this understanding.

FACTORS INFLUENCING FASHION MOVEMENT

The movement of fashion can be accelerated or retarded by a variety of factors. We will also discuss later in this chapter how recurring fashions affect this movement.

Accelerating Factors

There are general factors that speed up fashion cycles. These influences are, themselves, ever growing and accelerating in the 21st century as the pace of life becomes more and geographically all encompassing. The accelerating factors are as follows:

- Widespread buying power
- Leisure time
- Increased education
- Improved status of women
- Technological advances
- Sales promotion
- Seasonal change

Widespread Buying Power

Widespread income means there are more people with the financial means to respond to a fashion change. The more consumers flock to a new fashion, the sooner it will reach its culmination. The more widespread the financial ability of consumers to turn to yet a newer fashion, the sooner the current fashion will plunge into obsolescence.

Leisure Time

In the past, the majority of the population worked long hours and had little leisure time, so they paid scant attention to fashion. More leisure time usually means people have more time to buy and enjoy fashion of many kinds. Since 1900, decreases in working hours and increases in paid vacations have encouraged more use of at-home wear, casual clothes, sports apparel, travel clothes, and different types of ordinary business dress. Increased purchases of these types of apparel give impetus to their fashion cycles.

One result of today's frantic pace has been the return to catalog buying and the emergence of other forms of nonstore retailing. Catalog buying originally evolved because people in farming societies lived far from stores and had little leisure time for shopping. Today's leisure time has allowed people to add new physical and mental activities to their lives, such as sports and hobbies, leaving little time for shopping once again. Realizing that their customers are using leisure time for other pursuits, retailers are bringing shopping into the consumers' homes with catalogs, cable TV shopping channels, and websites. Consumers can browse at any time of day and, with customer service telephone lines and computer connections available all day, every day, customers can place their orders whenever they wish.

Increased Education

The increasingly higher level of education in the United States helps to speed up fashion cycles in two ways. First, more people have broadened their horizons and have new interests and new wants. Second, more people are better educated and earn more money to satisfy those wants. These two factors provide significant impetus to the adoption of new fashions.

Improved Status of Women

In a society with few artificial social barriers, women with discretionary income can spend it as they choose. No law or custom in the United States prevents any woman from buying the newest and most prestigious styles in dresses, hats, or shoes if she can afford to do so. Sex discrimination in the job market has steadily decreased, and social acceptance of women who manage both homes and jobs has steadily increased. As a result, today's women have more discretionary income and are influencing the speed of fashion cycles by the way they spend it.

Technological Advances

Today we live in an "instant" world. The stunning advances in technology in almost every area have put us in immediate possession of facts, fantasies, and fashions. We see news as it happens around the world. Goods are sped to retail stores by land, air, and sea more rapidly than would have been dreamed of just a few decades ago.

You did not have to be at the 2010 catwalk shows at Lincoln Center in order to see New York fashion. Audiences in Tokyo, Paris, and Dubai watched the designer shows that were streamed live to their computers and mobile devices. More and more designers are live-streaming their shows on the Web. You can now enjoy the feeling of being at the show—and in the front row![1] Technological advances combine to make goods available almost at the instant that the consumer is psychologically and financially ready to buy. Thus, the cycle of fashion becomes more accelerated.

Fall 2011

Spring 2011

Jason Wu &
First Lady
Michelle Obama

Jason Wu
branded
eyewear

JASON WU

UNTIL ONE COLD NIGHT IN JANUARY 2008, MOST PEOPLE OUT-SIDE THE FASHION WORLD WOULD HAVE ASKED, JASON WHO?
But that was before Michelle Obama picked Wu's one-strap ivory gown to wear to the inaugural ball. Instant fame! But the publicity blitzkrieg came at a perfect time for Jason Wu. He was riding high from a 2009 spring show, which was only his sixth collection but was a huge success. He has been busy ever since. After a jump of $1.2 million in sales, Wu said, "We were ready for that next area of expansion."

And expand he has. In the past year, the Taiwanese designer launched a pre-fall collection, which had sales of 45 percent over initial projections. He has also designed sunglasses, with Modo Eyewear; his own G.E. digital camera, licensed by General Imaging; and a capsule collection with Tse Cashmere. He also created two collections of Madame Alexander dolls, in addition to his ongoing role as creative director of Integrity Toys, where he started at age sixteen.

Born in Taiwan, Wu moved to British Columbia at age 9. He learned how to sew by designing and sewing dolls, and then went to study sculpture in Tokyo. He decided to become a fashion designer in his senior year of high school and went on to The Loomis Chaffee School in 2001, and then studied at Parsons School of Design.

A former Narcisco Rodriguez intern, Wu launched his line in 2006 with the earnings from his years of doll designs. He won the Fashion Group International's Rising Star Award in 2008 and was also nominated for the *Vogue* Fashion Fund Award.

His early clients included Ivanka Trump, January Jones, and Amber Valletta and he was introduced to Michelle Obama by André Leon Talley, *Vogue* magazine's editor-at-large in 2007. Since then she has worn many of his dress designs, leading the media to consider Michelle Obama his "career-launcher."

Fall 2011

Sales Promotion

The impact of sales promotion is felt everywhere in the fashion world. Magazines, television, newspapers, billboards, direct mail, the Internet, and mobile ads all expose the public to a never-ending procession of new fashions. While there is no way to force consumers to accept new fashions, nor any way to save a fashion if consumers reject it, sales promotion can greatly influence a fashion's success by telling people it exists.

Seasonal Change

Nothing is so consistent in bringing about change in fashions as the calendar. As the seasons change, so do consumer demands. After months of winter, people want to shed their heavy clothing for light-weight spring and summer fashions, which is natural in climates where there are radical seasonal changes, even though our homes, schools, cars, and places of business are kept at desired temperatures through central heating and air-conditioning. However, even in areas such as Florida and Hawaii, where the weather is constant year-round, people change their wardrobes with the seasons. Even if the 21st century brings complete climate control, people will never accept the boredom of a year-round wardrobe.

Because people are so accustomed to travel at all times of the year to all types of climates, the seasonal changes are accelerated and a kind of preseason testing occurs. Resort wear appears in retail stores in time for selection by the public for winter vacations in tropical areas. The late June appearance of the first fall fashions in leading stores makes it possible for the style conscious to make their selections well in advance of the first cold wind. Consumer responses to these early offerings allow manufacturers and retailers alike to know what appeals.

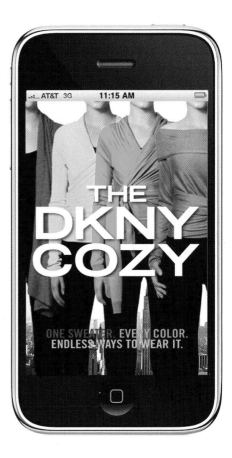

Brands now keep in touch with their customers via updates delivered straight to personal smart phones.

Retarding Factors

Factors that retard the development of fashion cycles either discourage people from adopting incoming styles or encourage them to continue using styles that may be considered on the decline. Retarding factors include the opposites of the accelerating factors, for example, decreased buying power during recessionary periods. Major retarding factors are habit and custom, religion, sumptuary laws, and reductions in consumers' buying power.

Habit and Custom

By slowing down the acceptance of new styles and prolonging the life spans of those that are already accepted, habit and custom exert a braking effect on fashion movement. Habit slows the adoption of new skirt lengths, silhouettes, necklines, or colors whenever shoppers unconsciously select styles that do not differ perceptibly from those they already own. It is easy for an individual to let habit take over, and some consumers are more susceptible to this tendency than others. Their loyalty to an established style is less a matter of fashion judgment than a natural attraction to the more familiar.

Custom slows progress in the fashion cycle by permitting vestiges of past fashions, status symbols, taboos, or special needs to continue to appear in modern dress. Custom is responsible for such details as buttons on the sleeves of men's suits, vents in men's jackets, and the sharp creases down the fronts of men's trousers.

Religion

Historically, religious leaders have championed custom, and their ceremonial apparel has demonstrated their respect for the old ways. In the past, religious leaders tended to associate fashion with temptation and urged their followers to turn their backs on both. Religion today, however, exerts much less of a restraining influence on fashion. Examples of the new relaxation may be found in the modernization of women's dress in most religious orders and in the fact that most women no longer consider a hat obligatory when in a house of worship.

Sumptuary Laws

Sumptuary laws regulate what we can and cannot purchase. For example, sumptuary laws require that children's sleepwear be flame retardant. In the past, sumptuary laws regulated extravagance and luxury in dress on religious or moral grounds. Height of headdress, length of train, width of sleeve, value and weight of material, and color of dress have all at times been restricted by law to specific classes. Such laws were aimed at keeping each class in its place in a rigidly stratified society.[2]

School uniforms in public schools were common before the 1960s, but they were largely abandoned in the free spiritedness of that decade. However, in the 1990s, when school violence and classroom disruption increased across the country, uniforms became popular once again. People in favor of uniforms argued that they would promote a sense of discipline and belonging and serve as a concrete and visual means of restoring order to the classroom.

Reductions in Consumers' Buying Power

Consumers' buying power has a powerful effect on the movement of fashion cycles. When buying power increases, fashion cycles often speed up. Decreased buying power, conversely, can retard the movement of fashion cycles. During economic recessions, with their resultant high unemployment, consumers' buying power is sharply reduced. Many people make do with clothes they have and buy only necessities. A similar caution is shown by consumers affected by strikes, inflation, high taxes, or changes in interest rates. All these factors have a slowing influence on fashion cycles. The poorer people are, the less impact they have on fashion's movements. They become bystanders in matters of fashion and, as a result, do not keep cycles moving. James Laver emphasized the importance of buying power when he said that nothing except poverty can make a style permanent.[3]

Recurring Fashions

In the study of fashion history, we see that styles reoccur, with adaptations that suit the times in which they reappear. Occasionally, an entire look is reborn. The elegant, simple look of the late 1940s and early 1950s, for example, was born again for the generation of the 1980s, and for Spring 2011 the look of the 1970s was on every runway, recalling the colorful and glamorous days of "hot pants" and dancing at Studio 54.[4]

Sometimes a single costume component or a minor detail that had exhausted its welcome stages a comeback, like the chandelier earring. At other times, a single article of clothing, like the sandals of the ancient Greeks, returns to popularity.

Research indicates that in the past, similar silhouettes and details of design in women's apparel have recurred with remarkable regularity. Despite widely held opinions to the contrary, the three basic silhouettes (bell-shaped, backfullness, and straight) always follow one another in a 100-year sequence. Each silhouette with all its variations dominates the fashion scene for a period of approximately 35 years. Having reached an excess in styling, it then declines in popularity and yields to the next silhouette in regular sequence.

PLAYING THE APPAREL FASHION GAME

According to Madge Garland, a well-known English fashion authority: "Every woman is born with a built-in hobby: the adornment of her person. The tricks she can play with it, the shapes she can make of it, the different portions she displays at various times, the coverings she uses or discards" all add up to fashion.[5]

Models in oversized hats during the Marc Jacobs Spring 2011 runway show display an example of a recurring fashion trend.

Many clothing authorities read a clear message into the alternate exposure and covering of various parts of the body—sex. J.C. Flügel cited sexual attraction as the dominant motive for wearing clothes.[6]

Another expert, James Laver, explained fashion emphasis in terms of the sexuality of the body. "Fashion really began," he said, "with the discovery in the fifteenth century that clothes could be used as a compromise between exhibitionism and modesty."[7] He also suggested that those portions of the body no longer fashionable to expose are "sterilized" and are no longer regarded as sexually attractive. Those that are newly exposed are **erogenous**, or sexually stimulating. He viewed fashion as pursuing the emphasis of ever-shifting erogenous zones, but never quite catching up with them. "If you really catch up," he warned, "you are immediately arrested for indecent exposure. If you almost catch up, you are celebrated as a leader of fashion."[8]

With ever-shifting erogenous zones, only certain parts of the body can be exposed at a given time, as seen in Giambattista Valli's miniskirt from Spring 2011 [left] and Louis Vuitton's designs from Spring 2011 [right].

Pieces of the Game

The pieces with which the women's fashion game is played are the various parts of the female body: waist, shoulders, bosom, neckline, hips, derrière, legs, and feet, as well as the figure as a whole. Historically, as attention to a part of the anatomy reaches a saturation point, the fashion spotlight shifts to some other portion.

Rules of the Game

In the game of emphasizing different parts of the female body at different times, as in any game, there are rules.

The first and strongest rule is that fashion emphasis does not flit from one area to another! Rather, a particular area of the body is emphasized until every bit of excitement has been exhausted. At this point, fashion attention turns to another area. For example, when miniskirts of the 1960s could go no higher and still be legal, the fashion emphasis moved on.

The second rule of the fashion game is that only certain parts of the body can be exposed at any given time. There are dozens of examples throughout fashion history that back up this theory: floor-length evening gowns with plunging necklines, high necklines with miniskirts, turtlenecks on sleeveless fashions.

A third rule of the fashion game is that, like fashion itself, fashion attention must always go forward.

PREDICTING THE MOVEMENT OF FASHION

Designing and selling fashion merchandise to consumers at a profit is what fashion merchandising is all about. To bring excitement and flair to their segment of merchandising, producers, designers, and retailers must have a well-defined plan and follow the movement of general fashion preferences.

The success of fashion merchandising depends on correctly predicting which new styles will be accepted by the majority of consumers. Suggested steps in developing a fashion forecast:

1. Identify facts about past trends and forecasts.
2. Determine the causes of change in the past.
3. Investigate the difference between past forecasts and actual behavior.
4. Analyze the factors likely to affect trends in the future.
5. Apply forecasting tools and techniques, using accuracy and reliability.
6. Study the forecast continually to determine reasons for significant deviations from expected plans.
7. Revise the forecast when necessary.

With information on these points, projections—a prime requisite in successful fashion merchandising—become possible.

ROOTS
What Inspires Designers?

The secret behind the success of some of the world's greatest designers is their past.

BETSEY JOHNSON
"All my dancing costumes forever and ever from the years I took ballet, tap, Hindu, and jazz classes. [They] were a super-big-time influence. My dancing teacher let me design my two solo recital costumes each year—yes, I was the sta-a-r-r."

OSCAR DE LA RENTA
"From my Dominican Island side comes my love for the exotic color and light. From my Spanish side comes my love of gypsies and bullfighters."

MICHAEL KORS
"The early 70s of my childhood and the great mini-maxi debate."

DONATELLA VERSACE
"When I was a teenager, I wore black, fitted shirts with tight black pants and a leather jacket. Over the years this was my signature look and became the basis of many of my designs."

STELLA MCCARTNEY
"Some of my earliest memories are of horses. I grew up with horses. They were my mother's favorite animals. She was passionate about them, and was a keen horse rider."

KARL LAGERFELD
"When I was a child, I wanted to be a grown-up. I liked the way my father was dressed, I hated everything about children. I loved Austrian clothes—and still do. The famous Chanel jacket is inspired by Austrian men's clothes, so all that is perfect with me."

GIORGIO ARMANI
"My mother had her own style that was extremely personal. She was a woman who had succeeded in matching her style to her temperament, rejecting artificiality, ostentation, and caricatures. This had a definite effect on me. To this day, she is a constant inspiration."

TOMMY HILFIGER
"My mom was a classic dresser. She didn't have a lot of clothes, but she wore what she had really well—she was always pulled together. At holiday time she wore tartan pants, [and] in the summer she wore tartan Bermuda shorts. We come from a Scottish heritage, so it is something of our past, our personal family history."

Identifying Trends

A fashion trend, as discussed in Chapter 1, is a direction in which fashion is moving. Designers, manufacturers, and merchants try to recognize each fashion trend to determine how widespread it is and whether it is moving toward or away from maximum fashion acceptance. They can then decide whether to actively promote the fashion to their target customers, wait, or abandon it.

For example, assume that wide-leg pants have developed as a fashion trend. At the introduction and rise stages, retailers will stock and promote more wide-leg pants. When customer response begins to level off, retailers will realize that a saturation point is being reached with this style and will begin introducing narrower pants into their stocks in larger and larger numbers. If the retailers have correctly predicted the downturn in customer demand for wide-leg pants, they will have fewer on hand when the downturn occurs. And while some customers may continue to wear the wide-leg style, they will not be buying new wide-leg pants and certainly not at regular prices. One of the outstanding Trend and Forecasting companies is Tobé Reports, which is covered in Chapter 2.

Sources of Data

Modern fashion forecasters bear little resemblance to the mystical prognosticators of old. Their ability to predict the strength and direction of fashion trends among their customers has almost nothing to do with what is often called a "fashion sense." Nor does it depend on glances into the future through a cloudy crystal ball. Successful fashion forecasters depend on a most valuable commodity: information. Good, solid facts about the willingness of customers to accept certain goods are the basis of successful merchandising decisions.

Merchants can keep "instant" records on sales, inventories, new fashion testing, and a myriad of other contributing factors that aid the fashion merchandising process. In addition, wise merchants keep their eyes open to see what is being worn by their own customers as well as by the public as a whole. They are so familiar with their customers' lifestyles, economic status, educational levels, and social milieu that they can determine at just what point in a fashion's life cycle their customers will be ready to accept or reject it. Merchants turn to every available source for information that will help ensure success. They use their hard-earned sales experience but do not rely just on their own judgment; they rely on the judgment of others, too. From the producers of fashion—resident buying, merchandising, and developing offices—to special fashion groups, they learn about the buying habits of customers other than their own. Successful merchants look at the larger fashion picture to predict more ably just where their local scene fits in.

Interpreting Influential Factors

In fashion forecasting, all the data in the world can be collected by merchants, producers, or designers, but this is of little importance without interpretation. That is where the forecasters' knowledge of fashion and fashion principles comes into the picture.

From collected data, they are able to identify certain patterns. Then they consider the factors that can accelerate or retard a fashion cycle among their target group of customers. Among these factors are current events, the appearance of prophetic styles, sales promotion efforts, and the standards of taste currently in vogue. Analysts estimate that crowd-sourced and customized products could eventually make up as much as 10 percent of the total market for apparel, accessories, and footwear. Sometimes, trends remake design in the following ways:

• Crowd-sourcing: while definitions are controversial, generally it means using the many social possibilities of the Web to either create something or solve a problem. Examples could include open-source software and news aggregation sites such as Digg and Wikipedia.
• Mass-customization: Levi's, Selve, Timberland, Kenneth Cole, and Lori Coulter Swimwear are some of the companies that have used technology and factory production rather than traditional craftsmanship to produce a custom product at a popular price.
• Desktop manufacturing: digital printers can create three-dimensional objects, such as eyeglasses, jewelry, and electronics, by fusing layers of plastic or metal. [9]

Current Events

The news of what is going on in the country or the world can have a long-term or short-term influence on consumers and affect their responses to a fashion. For example, in the mid-1980s, many newspapers, magazines, and TV shows were discussing opportunities for women at mid- and upper-management levels. Success in responsible positions in the business world demanded "dressing for success," and career-minded women responded by adopting the severely tailored business suit look. By their very appearance, these women indicated their determination to succeed in the still male-dominated world of business. A reaction to this strictly tailored look occurred in the early 1990s, when women turned to a softer, less tailored look and many men abandoned the business suit "uniform" that had been the standard for generations. Today, men and women choose what "fashion" is right for them.

Prophetic Styles

Good fashion forecasters keep a sharp watch for what they call **prophetic styles**. These are particularly interesting new styles that are still in the introduction phase of their fashion cycle. Taken up enthusiastically by the socially prominent or by the flamboyantly young, these styles may gather momentum very rapidly or may prove to be nonstarters. Whatever their future course, the degree of acceptance of these very new styles gives forecasters a sense of in which directions fashion may go.

Importance of Timing

Successful merchants must determine what their particular target group of customers is wearing now and what this group is most likely to be wearing one month or three months from now. The data these merchants collect enable them to identify each current fashion, who is wearing it, and what point it has reached in its fashion cycle.

Since merchants know at what point in a fashion's cycle their customers are most likely to be attracted, they can determine whether to stock a current fashion now, one month from now, or three months from now.

THEORIES OF FASHION ADOPTION

Fashions are accepted by a few before they are accepted by the majority. An important step in fashion forecasting is isolating and identifying those fashion leaders and keeping track of their preferences. Once these are known, the fashion forecaster is better able to forecast which styles are most likely to succeed as fashions, and how widely and by whom each will be accepted.

Three theories have been advanced to explain the "social contagion" or spread of fashion adoption: the **downward-flow theory** or *trickle-down* theory, the **horizontal-flow theory** or *mass-market* theory, and the **upward-flow theory**. Each theory attempts to explain the course a fashion travels or is likely to travel, and each has its own claim to validity in reference to particular fashions or social environments.

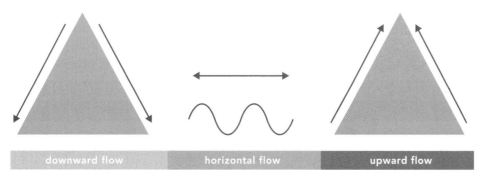

downward flow | horizontal flow | upward flow

THEORIES OF FASHION FLOW

The three theories of fashion flow.

Downward-Flow Theory

The oldest theory of fashion adoption is the downward-flow theory (or the trickle-down theory). It maintains that to be identified as a true fashion, a style must first be adopted by people at the top of the social pyramid. The style then gradually wins acceptance at progressively lower social levels.

This theory assumes the existence of a social hierarchy in which lower-income people seek identification with more affluent people. At the same time, those at the top seek disassociation from those they consider socially inferior. The theory suggests that fashions are accepted by lower classes only if, and after, they are accepted by upper classes, and upper classes will reject a fashion once it has flowed to a lower social level.

Implications for Merchandising

To some extent, the downward-flow theory has validity. Some fashions may appear first among the socially prominent. Eager manufacturers then quickly mass-produce lower-priced copies that many consumers can afford, and the wealthier consumers seek newer styles.

ESPRIT
Looking Back and Forward

1968: Esprit is founded as Susie and Doug Tompkins sell clothes bearing the new brand out of the back of their station wagon in San Francisco.

1971: Esprit Far East Group begins when Doug and Susie Tompkins meet Michael Ying, who would become the group's chairman and a shareholder of Esprit.

1978: Sales top $100 million and international partnerships in Hong Kong and Germany are formed.

1979: John Casado designs the famous Esprit stencil-effect logo. Despite worries that the triple-bar "E" would not be legible to customers, the new logo becomes one of the most recognized in international fashion.

1986: The first Esprit store opens in Germany. Cologne is chosen for the first Esprit site in that nation and it is designed by Ettore Sottsass.

1987: Susie and Doug Tompkins urge the public to confront the growing AIDS epidemic. In the same year the company expands into Taiwan, the Netherlands, Belgium, and Denmark.

1992: The "What would you do to change the world?" campaign becomes famous worldwide.

1994: The operating divisions of Esprit Apparel, Footwear, and Accessories are combined to create the Esprit Wholesale division, with Andrew Cohen as president of the new unit.

1995: The Esprit design philosophy is applied to new product categories: eyewear, timepieces, bed and bath, and hosiery.

1996: Esprit is represented in 44 countries, and ranked 28th out of the 100 most recognized brands in the U.S. Jay Margolis, a former executive with Tommy Hilfiger and Liz Claiborne, becomes chairman and chief executive at Esprit de Corp., based in San Francisco.

1997: The Labor Department adds Esprit de Corp. to its Trendsetter List, the good-guy roster of companies deemed to be taking exemplary steps to guard against buying apparel made under sweatshop conditions. Esprit de Corp. licenses Beach Patrol Inc. to produce its first full swimwear collection, which will also include selected beach-related sportswear styles.

1998: Esprit de Corp. launches an online store at esprit.com, replacing its original website.

1999: Joseph E. Heid, former president of Revlon International, is named chairman, CEO, and president of Esprit de Corp., San Francisco, succeeding Jay Margolis.

2000: Esprit Holdings Ltd. becomes a constituent stock of Morgan Stanley's MSCI Hong Kong Index. New product lines such as sportswear, clothes for newborns, and toys are introduced.

2001: Worldwide brand awareness grows, especially in Germany, by 84 percent, a record for the company. Esprit Holdings Ltd. opens its first flagship on Regent Street in London.

2004: In the Global Business Headquarters, Esprit commemorates Ettore Sottsass with an exhibition. This partnership with the designer has existed since 1982. His design and architecture formed the Esprit stores and showrooms worldwide. Ettore Sottsass was substantially involved in building up the brand.

2006: The Esprit brand is sold on five continents and in more than 40 countries, with 640 freestanding stores and over 12,000 wholesale customers. More than 20,000 products are designed each year for 12 product lines for women, men, and kids—and a wide variety of licensed products.

2007: Esprit launches de.corp. Trendier and more progressive than its "big sister," Esprit women casual, the new Esprit division addresses 18- to 25-year-olds who are in search of a clean, urban, and young style. The first set of garments presented by de.corp, Esprit Urban Casual, features a cool eighties-inspired look. MTV Networks and edc by Esprit announce an extensive partnership with the first solo performance of the edc by Esprit brand as a sponsor of Europe's biggest music event—the MTV Europe Music Awards.

2008: Esprit celebrates its 40th anniversary with a number of activities across all divisions and license partners.

2010: Esprit opened a new 18,000-square-foot store on 34th street in New York City, one of the city's busiest shopping corridors. The three-level flagship features a new interior design and carries the casual and collection lines for men and women, the trendy and playful Esprit de Corp, and de.corp, a modern, urban label.

Inside an Esprit store

An Esprit taxi in New York City

Doug, Susie, & Quincy Tompkins

Because our social structure has radically changed, this theory has few adherents today. The downward-flow theory of fashion dissemination can apply only when a society resembles a pyramid, with people of wealth and position at the apex and followers at successively lower levels. Our social structure, however, is more like a group of rolling hills than a pyramid. There are many social groups and many directions in which fashion can and does travel.

This altered pattern of fashion acceptance is also a result of the speed with which fashion news now travels. All social groups know about fashion innovation at practically the same time. Moreover, accelerated mass production and mass distribution of fashion goods have broadened acceptance of styles. They are available at lower prices and more quickly than ever before.

Industry Practice

For the reasons given above, those who mass-produce fashion goods today are less likely to wait cautiously for approval of newly introduced styles by affluent consumers. As soon as significant signs of an interesting new style appear, the producers are ready to offer adaptations or even copies to the public.

Horizontal-Flow Theory

A newer theory is the horizontal-flow theory (or mass-market theory) of fashion adoption. This theory claims that fashions move horizontally among groups on similar social levels rather than vertically from one level to another.

Implications for Merchandising

The theory of horizontal fashion movement has great significance for merchandising. It points out the fallacy of assuming that there is a single, homogeneous fashion public in this country. In reality, a number of distinctly different groups make up the fashion public. Each group has its own characteristics and its own fashion ideas and needs. The horizontal-flow theory recognizes that what wealthy society people are wearing today is not necessarily what middle-class suburbanites, college students, or office workers will either wear tomorrow or wait until tomorrow to accept. This theory acknowledges that there are separate markets in fashion goods as in any other type of merchandise.

Retailers who apply the horizontal-flow theory will watch their own customers closely rather than being guided solely by what more exclusive stores are selling. They will seek to identify the groups into which customers can be divided in terms of income, age, education, and lifestyle. Among their customers, they will look for the innovators and their style choices as well as the influentials and their selections. Charles King defined a **fashion innovator** as a person who is quicker than his or her associates to try out a new style. A **fashion influential** is a person whose advice is sought by associates. A fashion influential's adoption of a new style gives it prestige among a group. The two roles may or may not be played by the same individual within a specific group.

Industry Practice

A distinction can be drawn between the spread of fashion within the industry itself and its adoption by consumers. A vertical flow definitely operates within the industry. Furthermore, as any reader of *Women's Wear Daily* knows, the hottest news in the industry concerns what the top designers and the top producers are showing.

Moreover, the innovation process in the industry represents a great filtering system. From an almost infinite number of possibilities, manufacturers select a finite number of styles. From these, trade buyers select a small sampling. Finally, consumers choose from among retailers' selections, thereby endorsing certain ones as accepted fashions.

This process is quite different from the consumer reaction in the downward-flow theory. The difference lies in the fact that today the mass market does not await the approval of the "class" market before it adopts a fashion.

Upward-Flow Theory

The third theory that attempts to explain the process of fashion adoption is relatively new. It reflects the enormous social changes that have occurred in the past five decades. Because the process of fashion dissemination that evolved in the decades of the 1950s through the 2000s was the exact opposite of that which prevailed throughout much of recorded history, this theory has important implications for producers and retailers alike.

This theory of fashion adoption is called the upward-flow theory. It holds that the young—particularly those of low-income families and those in higher-income groups who adopt low-income lifestyles—are quicker than any social group to create or adopt new and different fashions. As its name implies, this theory is exactly the opposite of the downward-flow theory. The upward-flow theory holds that fashion adoption begins among the young members of lower-income groups and then moves upward into higher-income groups.

The decades of the 1950s through today have outstanding examples of the upward-flow theory. In the 1950s, young people discovered Army/Navy surplus stores and were soon wearing khaki pants, caps, battle jackets, fatigues, and even ammunition belts. In the 1960s, led by the Hell's Angels, the motorcycle clubs introduced the fashion world to black leather—in jackets, vests, and studded armbands. Soon the jet set was dressed in black leather long coats, skirts, and pants. Meanwhile, other young people were discovering bib overalls, railroad worker's caps, and all-purpose laborer's coveralls that were soon translated into jumpsuits. Peasant apparel, prairie looks, and styles and designs from various minority groups followed the same pattern. They began as part of a young and lower-income lifestyle and were then quickly adopted among older people with different lifestyles and incomes.

One of the more dramatic illustrations of this has been the T-shirt. In its short-sleeved version, it has long been worn by truckers, laborers, and farmworkers. In its long-sleeved version, it was the uniform of local bowling and softball teams. In the 1970s, the T-shirt became a message board and sprouted a brand-new fashion cottage industry. The ultimate T-shirt was the Chanel No. 5; first the perfume, then the T-shirt.

The T-shirt, once a fashion only for the streets, has transitioned to couture. Here, celebrity Sarah Jessica Parker sports a design by Dior.

Actually, the Chanel T-shirt was a logical application of a tenet long held by the late Coco Chanel, who believed that fashion came from the streets and was then adapted by the couture.

In the 1980s, sources of inspiration for fashion styles representing the upward-flow theory were everywhere, especially in the world of rock music. By following the fashion statements of rock-and-roll idols, America's youth were dressed in worn-out denim, metal, leather, lace, bangles, spandex, and glitter.

In the 1990s and the early 2000s, rap artists not only composed lyrics that spoke of "ghetto" life in street language but also introduced and popularized hip-hop clothing styles.

Implications for Merchandising

For producers and retailers, this new direction of fashion flow implies radical changes in traditional methods of charting and forecasting fashion trends. No longer can producers and retailers look solely to name designers and socially prominent fashion leaders for ideas that will become tomorrow's best-selling fashions. They also must pay considerable attention to what young people favor, for the young have now become a large and an independent group that can exert considerable influence on fashion styling.

As a result, today fewer retailers and manufacturers attend European couture showings, once considered fashion's most important source of design inspiration. Now producers and retailers alike are more interested in ready-to-wear (prêt-à-porter) showings. Here they look for styles and design details that reflect trends with more fashion relevance for American youth.

Blake Lively, walking the red carpet in Jimmy Choo heels, is an example of the young actress as fashion leader.

Industry Practice

Apparently, fashion will never again flow in only one direction. Of course, customers will always exist for high fashion and for conservative fashion. But producers and retailers must now accept that they will be doing a considerable proportion of their business in fashions created or adopted first by the lower-income young and by those who choose to be allied with them.

FASHION LEADERS

As different as they may be, the three theories of fashion flow share one common perspective: They recognize that there are both fashion leaders and fashion followers. People of social, political, and economic importance here and abroad are seen as leaders in the downward-flow theory. The horizontal-flow theory recognizes individuals whose personal prestige makes them leaders within their own circles, whether they are known elsewhere. Finally, the important fashion role played by young, lower-income groups is recognized in the upward-flow theory.

The theories of fashion adoption stress that the fashion leader is not the creator of the fashion; nor does merely wearing the fashion make a person a fashion leader. If a fashion parade is forming, fashion leaders may head it and even quicken its pace. They cannot, however, bring about a procession; nor can they reverse a procession.

Innovators and Influentials

Famous people are not necessarily fashion leaders, even if they do influence an individual style. Their influence usually is limited to only one striking style, one physical attribute, or one time. The true fashion leader is a person constantly seeking distinction and therefore likely to launch a succession of fashions rather than just one. People like Beau Brummel, who made a career of dressing fashionably, or the Duchess of Windsor, whose wardrobe was front-page fashion news for decades, influence fashion on a much broader scale.

What makes a person a fashion leader? Charles King made it clear that more than just daring to be different is required. In his analysis, a person eager for the new is merely an innovator or early buyer. To be a leader, one must be influential and sought after for advice within one's coterie.[10]

Royalty

In the past, fashion leadership was exclusively the province of royalty. New fashions were introduced in royal courts by such leaders as Empress Eugenie and Marie Antoinette. In the 20th century, the Duchess of Windsor, although an American and a commoner by birth, was a fashion innovator and influential from the 1930s through the 1960s. When the King of England gave up his throne to marry "the woman he loved," style and fashion professionals throughout the world copied her elegance. The Sotheby auction in the late 1980s of the Duchess of Windsor's jewelry sparked new interest in her style, and designers are still showing copies of her jewelry.

Until Princess Diana and Sarah Ferguson married into the British royal family, few royal personages had qualified as fashion leaders. In 2011, Kate Middleton is continually seen on best-dressed lists and has become a fashion icon for the younger generation. Despite the belief held by some people that kings and queens wear crowns and ermine, the truth is that modern royalty has become a hardworking group whose daily lives are packed with so many activities that sensible and conservative dress is necessary for most occasions.

The Rich

As monarchies were replaced with democracies, members of the wealthy and international sets came into the fashion spotlight. Whether the members of "society" derive their positions from vast fortunes and old family names or from recent wealth, they bring to the scene a glamour and excitement that draws attention to everything they do. Through the constant eye of television, magazines, newspapers, and blogs the average person is able to find fashion leadership in a whole new stratum of society—the jet set.

What these socialites are doing and what they are wearing are instantly served up to the general public by the media. As far as fashion is concerned, these people are not just in the news; they *are* the news. Any move they make is important enough to be immediately publicized. What they wear is of vital interest to the general public. The media tell us what the social leaders wear to dine in a chic restaurant, to attend a charity ball, or to go shopping. Because they are trendsetters, their choices are of prime interest to designers and to the world at large.

Of course, this inundation of news about what social leaders wear influences the public. The average person is affected because so many manufacturers and retailers of fashion take their cues from these social leaders. Right or wrong, fashion merchants count on the fashion sense of these leaders. They know that the overwhelming exposure of these leaders in the media encourages people of ordinary means to imitate them—consciously or unconsciously.

Kourtney and Kim Kardashian have used their wealth and fame to influence fashion, even launching their own K-Dash by Kardashian line through the QVC network.

FASHION STYLES NAMED FOR THE FAMOUS

trendsetters	styles
Amelia Bloomer	Bloomers
Earl of Chesterfield	Chesterfield jacket
Dwight D. Eisenhower	Eisenhower jacket
Geraldine Ferraro	"Gerry cut" (hairstyle)
Mao Tse Tung	Mao jacket
Jawaharlal Nehru	Nehru jacket
Madame de Pompadour	Pompadour (hairstyle)
Nancy Reagan	"Reagan plastics" (costume jewelry), red
Duke of Wellington	Wellington boots
Earl of Cardigan	Cardigan sweater
Duke of Windsor	Windsor knot (tie)
Duke of Norfolk	Norfolk jacket
Nelson Mandela	Madiba smart (shirt)
The Beatles	Hairstyle

table 3.1

The Famous

Fashion today takes its impetus and influence from people in every possible walk of life. These people have one thing in common, however: they are famous. Because of some special talent, charisma, notoriety, or popularity, they are constantly mentioned and shown in the media. They may or may not appear in the society pages.

In this group can be found presidents and princesses, movie stars and religious leaders, sports figures and recording stars, and politicians and TV personalities. Because they are seen so frequently, the public has a good sense of their fashions and lifestyles and can imitate them to the extent of the public's means and desires.

Athletes

Today, there is strong emphasis on sports. And what prominent sports figures wear is of great importance to the people who seek to imitate them. Television has increased the public acceptance of several sports. For example, people have enjoyed going to baseball, football, or basketball games for years. But sports of a more individual nature, such as tennis and golf, were of minor interest. Now these sports are brought into the living rooms of an increasing number of viewers. As a result, fashions for participating in these sports have grown remarkably in importance. Tennis is now a very popular participation sport and has given rise to an entire specialized fashion industry. Today, every aspiring tennis player has endless fashion styles, colors, and fabrics to choose from. A wide selection of fashion is also available for golf, jogging, running, swimming, skating, cycling, snorkeling, snowboarding, and other sports. The names of Michael Jordan, Tiger Woods, Venus and Serena Williams, Lance Armstrong, and Sean White are known to most Americans.

FASHION FOLLOWERS

Filling out forms for his daughter's college entrance application, a father wrote of his daughter's leadership qualities: "To tell the truth, my daughter is really not a leader, but rather a loyal and devoted follower." The dean of the college admissions responded: "We are welcoming a freshman class of 100 students this year and are delighted to accept your daughter. You can't imagine how happy we are to have one follower among the 99 leaders!"

Established movie stars, like Scarlett Johansson, are often used in ads to reinforce a brand's desired identity.

Most people want to be thought of as leaders, not followers. But there are many people who are followers, and good ones. In fact, followers are in the majority within any group. Without followers the fashion industry would certainly collapse. Mass production and mass distribution can be possible and profitable only when large numbers of consumers accept the merchandise. Though they may say otherwise, luckily, more people prefer to follow than to lead. The styles fashion leaders adopt may help manufacturers and retailers in determining what will be demanded by the majority of consumers in the near future. Only accurate predictions can ensure the continued success of the giant ready-to-wear business in this country, which depends for its success on mass production and distribution. While fashion leaders may stimulate and excite the fashion industry, fashion followers are the industry's lifeblood.

Reasons for Following Fashion

Theories about why people follow rather than lead in fashion are plentiful. Among the explanations are feelings of insecurity, admiration of others, lack of interest, and ambivalence about the new.

Feelings of Insecurity

A person about to face a difficult interview or attend the first meeting with a new group carefully selects new clothes. Often a person can hide feelings of inadequacy by wearing a style that others have already deemed appropriate.

Admiration

Flügel also maintained that it is a fundamental human impulse to imitate those who are admired or envied. A natural and symbolic means of doing this is to copy their clothes, makeup, and hairstyles. Outstanding illustrations of this theory have been provided by movie stars and models—Mary Pickford, "America's Sweetheart" of the 1910s; Clara Bow, the "It" girl of the 1920s; Ginger Rogers, Katharine Hepburn, and Rosalind Russell of the 1930s; Veronica Lake and Ann Sheridan, the "Oomph Girls" of the 1940s; Doris Day and Marilyn Monroe in the 1950s; Twiggy in the 1960s; Farrah Fawcett in the 1970s; Christie Brinkley in the 1980s; Elle McPherson and Cindy Crawford in the 1990s; Jennifer Lopez, Cameron Diaz, and Britney Spears at the beginning of the 21st century; and today the Kardashians, Snooki, Lady Gaga, and Justin Bieber. Their clothes and hairstyles were copied instantly among many different groups throughout this country and in many other parts of the world. On a different level, the young girl who copies the hairstyle of her best friend, older sister, or favorite aunt demonstrates the same principle, as do college students who model their appearance after that of a campus leader.

Lack of Interest

Edward Sapir suggested that many people are insensitive to fashion and follow it only because "they realize that not to fall in with it would be to declare themselves members of a past generation, or dull people who cannot keep up with their neighbors."[11] Their response to fashion, he said, is a sullen surrender to but by no means an eager following of the Pied Piper.

Ambivalence

Another theory holds that many people are ambivalent in their attitudes toward the new; they both want it and fear it. For most, it is easier to choose what is already familiar. Such individuals need time and exposure to new styles before they can accept them.

Varying Rates of Response

Individuals vary in the speed with which they respond to a new idea, especially when fashion change is radical and dramatic. Some fashion followers apparently need time to adjust to new ideas. Merchants exploit this point when they buy a few "window pieces" of styles too advanced for their own clientele and expose them in windows and fashion shows to allow customers time to get used to them. Only after a period of exposure to the new styles do the fashion followers accept them.

FASHION AND INDIVIDUALITY

In the early part of the 21st century, a strange but understandable trend became apparent across the nation. People were striving, through their mode of dress, to declare individuality in the face of computer-age conformity.

People had watched strings of impersonal numbers become more a part of their lives—zip codes, bank and credit card account numbers, employee identification numbers, department store accounts, automobile registrations, Social Security numbers, and so on. An aversion to joining the masses—to becoming "just another number"—became prevalent. So while most people continued to go along with general fashion trends, some asserted their individuality. This was accomplished by distinctive touches each wearer added to an outfit. A freedom in dress, color and texture combinations, use of accessories, and hairstyles allowed people to assert their individuality without being out of step with the times.

We have all known people who at some point in their lives found a fashion that particularly pleased them. It might have been a certain style of dress, a certain shoe, or a hairstyle. Even in the face of continuing changes in fashion, the person continued to wear that style in which she or he felt right and attractive. Instead of slavishly adopting any one look, today's young person seeks to create an individual effect through the way he or she combines various fashion components. For instance, if a young woman thinks a denim skirt, an ankle-length woolen coat, and a heavy turtlenecked sweater represent her personality, they will likely be considered acceptable by others in her group. Having experienced such fashion freedom, young people may never conform again. Yet, despite individual differences in dress, young experimenters have in common a deep-rooted desire to dress differently from older generations. This is an assertion of individuality in the face of conformity.

Most social scientists, however, see this as a paradox—an endless conflict between the desire to conform and the desire to remain apart.

Designers and Self-Expression

Forward-looking designers recognize a consumer's desire for self-expression. Designers say that basic wardrobe components should be made available, but that consumers should be encouraged to combine them as they see fit. For instance, they advise women to wear pants or skirts, long or short, according to how they feel, not according to what past tradition has considered proper for an occasion. They suggest that men make the same choice among tailored suits, leisure wear, and slacks, to find the styles that express their personalities.

Designer Kenneth Cole said, "Clothing is maybe the single greatest form of self-expression. Whether you're fashion-impaired or fashion-inspired, I urge everyone to take a few extra minutes every day to contemplate the message you're sending to the world."[12]

The Paradox of Conformity and Individuality

For decades, experts have tried to explain why people seek both conformity and individuality in fashion. One suggestion is that two opposing social tendencies are at war: the need for union and the need for isolation. The individual derives satisfaction from knowing that the way in which he or she expresses a fashion represents something special. At the same time, people gain support from seeing others favor the same style.

Retailers know that although some people like to lead and some like to follow in fashion, most people buy fashion to express their personality or to identify with a particular group. To belong, they follow fashion; to express their personalities, they find ways to individualize fashion.

SUMMARY AND REVIEW

It is the nature of fashion to change, but the speed and direction of its changes are difficult to predict. Some factors that accelerate the pace of change are widespread buying power, increased leisure time, increased education, the improved status of women, technological advances that bring new and improved products to the market, sales promotion, and seasonal changes. However, the pace of change can be slowed by habit and custom, religious restrictions, sumptuary laws (laws placing limits or requirements on the construction of apparel), and reductions in consumers' buying power.

Some types of fashion merchandise change more slowly than other types. For example, men's fashions change more slowly than women's. Some fashion historians have tracked the basic shapes of apparel, particularly women's wear, and concluded that three basic silhouettes dominate fashion in turn, each for about 35 years, creating a cycle that lasts about 100 years. Other details of line, such as sleeve shape and skirt length have similar cycles.

Fashion also focuses on different parts of the body at different times, accentuating the seductive appeal of each part in turn. For fashion merchandisers, success depends on the accuracy of predictions of trends and judging when and to what degree a fashion will be adopted by the producer's or retailer's target market. Inventory and sales records and a careful following of current events, the reception of new styles at the introductory stage of the fashion cycle, sales promotion, and current canons of taste help forecasters make accurate predictions.

Three theories attempt to explain the movement of fashion; they are the downward-flow, horizontal-flow, and upward-flow theories. The acceptance of a fashion depends on innovators, who are the first to wear it, and influentials, whose personal style is copied by others. On a broad scale, public figures are often innovators and influentials. The buying public watches the fashions of royalty, high society, athletes, entertainers, and other celebrities. On a smaller scale, individual communities have their own fashion innovators and influentials, but a fashion's acceptance ultimately depends on fashion followers. They are the people who spread a fashion and account for the number of sales. Each person adjusts his or her wardrobe to balance a sense of belonging to a group and being an individual.

FOR REVIEW

1. Describe the theory of fashion cycles and explain why it accelerated in the 20th century.

2. According to leading fashion authorities, what are the three basic rules that govern the fashion game?

3. What basic resources are available to the fashion merchant to predict fashion?

4. Explain the term *prophetic style*.

5. Is the downward-flow theory of fashion adoption as valid today as it was in years past? Explain your answer.

6. How does the horizontal-flow theory of fashion adoption affect fashion merchants today? How are merchants today affected by the upward-flow theory?

7. Explain why rich people, famous people, and athletes are prime candidates for positions of fashion leadership.

8. Give four reasons why most people follow, rather than lead, in regard to fashion. Explain each.

9. How can fashion be used as a means of expressing individuality?

FOR DISCUSSION

1. Give at least one current example of each of several factors that are accelerating the forward movement of fashions today.

2. Certain factors tend to retard the development of fashion cycles by discouraging the adoption of newly introduced styles. List these factors and give at least one example of how each factor exerts a braking influence on fashion development.

3. Why do people today seek both conformity and individuality in fashion? How does this affect the fashion designer or manufacturer? The fashion retailer?

TRADE TALK

Define or briefly explain the following terms:

downward-flow theory

erogenous

fashion influential

fashion innovator

horizontal-flow theory

prophetic style

upward-flow theory

4

THE BUSINESS OF FASHION

- The four levels of the fashion business
- The three common forms of business ownership
- The roles of franchising and licensing
- The roles of the designer, the manufacturer, and the retailer in the fashion business

Fashion is a business, affected by the same technological advances, investment patterns, and economic forces that affect other major businesses in the world. Fashion is not just limited to apparel, and it impacts our complete lifestyle as well as the products that we buy. Fashion influences the automobile, housing, and entertainment industries, and like these industries, it is shaped by the basic principles of business and economics.

What is business? Business is the activity of creating, producing, and marketing products or services. The primary objective of business is to make a profit. **Profit**, or net income, is the amount of money a business earns in excess of its expenses. Consequently, in the United States, business can be defined as the activity of creating, producing, and marketing products or services for a profit.

ECONOMIC IMPORTANCE OF THE FASHION BUSINESS

The business of fashion contributes significantly to the economy of the United States, and the world, through the materials and services it purchases, the wages and taxes it pays, and the goods and services it produces. The fashion business is one of the largest employers in the country, despite the decline in employment since the industry boom in the early 1970s. As of 2008, roughly 497,000 people in the United States were employed either in factories that produce apparel for men, women, and children or in textile plants that produce the materials from which garments are made.[1]

The growth and development of mass markets, mass-production methods, and mass distribution have contributed to the creation of new job opportunities in the fashion industry—not only in the production area, but in design and marketing as well. Young people are entering the fashion business in greater numbers each year and are having a marked effect on the business. Innovation and change have become increasingly important factors in the economic growth of the fashion business.

SCOPE OF THE FASHION BUSINESS

The fashion business is composed of numerous industries all working to keep consumers of fashion satisfied. A special relationship exists among these industries that makes the fashion business different from other businesses. The four different levels of the fashion business—known as the primary level, secondary level, retail level, and auxiliary level—are composed of separate entities, but they also work interdependently to provide the market with the fashion merchandise that will satisfy consumers. Because of this unique relationship among the different industries, the fashion business is unusually exciting.

The Primary Level

The **primary level** is composed of the growers and producers of the raw materials of fashion—the fiber, fabric, leather, and fur producers who function in the raw materials market. The earliest part of the planning function in color and texture takes place on the primary level. It is also the level of the fashion business that works the furthest in advance of the ultimate selling period of the goods. Up to two years' lead time is needed by primary-level companies before the goods will be available to the consumer. Primary-level goods may often be imports from Third World emerging nations, where textiles are usually the earliest form of industrialization.

The Secondary Level

The **secondary level** is composed of industries—manufacturers and contractors—that produce the semifinished or finished fashion goods from the materials produced on the primary level. On the secondary level are the designers and manufacturers of

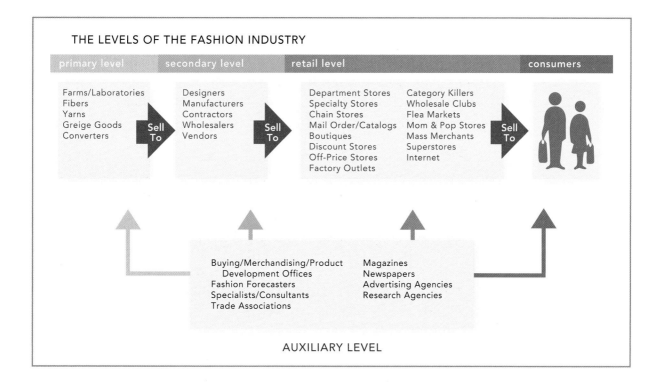

women's, men's, and children's apparel and also legwear, bodywear, and underwear; accessories; cosmetics and fragrances; and home furnishings.

Manufacturers who function on the secondary level may be based in the United States or overseas. Fashion goods are produced in the Far East, the Caribbean, South America, and Europe. Secondary-level companies work from six months to one and a half years ahead of the time that goods are available to the consumer.

The Retail Level

The **retail level** is the ultimate distribution level. On this level are the different types of retailers who buy their goods from the secondary level and then supply them directly to the consumer. In many cases, the retail level works with both the primary and secondary levels to ensure a coordinated approach to consumer wants. The relationship among the primary, secondary, and retail levels is vertical. The further removed a level is from the consumer, the further in advance it must be planned. Retailers make initial purchases for resale to customers from three to six months before the customer buying season.

The Auxiliary Level

The **auxiliary level** is the only level that functions with all the other levels simultaneously. This level is composed of all the support services that are working constantly with primary producers, secondary manufacturers, and retailers to keep consumers aware of the fashion merchandise produced for ultimate consumption. On this level are all the advertising media—print, audio, and visual—and fashion consultants and researchers.

The fashion industry operates collaboratively on four levels to serve the customer.

Tom Ford
sunglasses

Tom Ford

Tom Ford
ad campaign
Spring/Summer
2009

TOM FORD

Tom Ford
directing
A Single Man

TOM FORD

"You Ought to Be in Pictures": From Fashion to Film

FORD'S ROLE AT GUCCI RAPIDLY EXPANDED WHEN THE DESIGN DIRECTOR RESIGNED IN 1992. Ford took over the job and was in charge of the brand's ready-to-wear, fragrances, image, advertising, and store design. In 1994, Ford was promoted to creative director and has been credited with putting the glamour back into fashion. Sales at Gucci increased by 90 percent from 1995 to 1996. By 1999, Gucci, which had been almost bankrupt when Ford joined, was worth $4.3 billion. When Ford left in 2004, the Gucci Group was valued at $10 billion! When Gucci acquired the house of Yves Saint Laurent (YSL), Ford was named creative director of that label as well and went on to win numerous awards from the Council of Fashion Designers of America. But in 2004, Tom Ford and Domenico de Sole, CEO of the Gucci Group, left because of disagreements with the management.

In 2005, Ford announced the creation of the TOM FORD brand, where he specialized in menswear and signed licensing deals for frames and sunglasses. With Estée Lauder he created the TOM FORD Beauty Brand. In April 2007, his first directly owned flagship store opened in N.Y.C. Presently there are 21 free-standing stores and shop-in-shop locations such as Milan, Tokyo, Las Vegas, Dubai, Zurich, and Russia.

Since the launch of his menswear collection, Ford has dressed many of Hollywood's leading men: Brad Pitt, John Hamm, Colin Firth, Tom Hanks, Bradley Cooper, Pierce Brosnan, and Johnny Depp. In March 2005, he announced the opening of his film production company, FADE TO BLACK. In 2009 he made his directorial debut with *A Single Man*. The film was greeted with fantastic reviews from both critics and the moviegoing public. It also garnered many important awards both in Europe and America, making Tom Ford one of the most successful moviemakers.

Ford made his return to women's fashion in 2010 with a fantastic runway show. Ford proved what a movie star personality is when he narrated the show in his newly grown beard and impeccable tuxedo. The clothes were very Ford, glamorous but real. They all sent the message that Ford has never changed: "Looking good, looking chic, looking right is worth a little effort."

Does Tom Ford have it all now? Other people may think so, but we look forward to many more "firsts" in both men's and women's fashion—and many more films. He really should be in pictures.

Bradley Cooper
wearing Tom Ford

DIVERSITY AND COMPETITION

The enormous variety and diversity that exist in the kinds and sizes of firms that operate on each level of the fashion industry make it a fascinating and competitive business. There are giant firms, both national and international, and small companies with regional or local distribution, doing business side by side as privately or publicly owned corporations, partnerships, or sole proprietorships. Fashion-producing companies may also be part of conglomerates, which also own, for example, entertainment companies, oil wells, professional sports teams, or consumer foods and products divisions.

Whether large or small, the different types of producers have one need in common—the need to understand what their ultimate customer will buy. Only through complete understanding and cooperation can the four levels of the fashion business be aware of new developments in fashion and apply them to satisfy the wants of their customers. This cooperation allows them to have the right merchandise at the right price, in the right place, at the right time, in the right quantities, and with the right sales promotion for their customers.

However, when you begin to try to sell a product or service in our economic system, chances are that someone else will be trying to sell something similar. No matter what the size of the firm involved, potential customers are free to buy where and what they please. Each company must compete with the others for those customers' business. A company can choose to compete in one of three ways: price, quality, or innovation.

Competition and Price

Selling blue jeans for less than your competition may bring you more business. However, you are taking in less money than your rival does on each pair sold, and you still have to cover the same cost and expenses. The hope is that your lower price will attract more customers, sell more jeans than your competition, and so come out with a good overall profit. Head-to-head competition like this tends to keep prices down, which is good for the buying public. At the same time, it allows a company to look forward to a promise of profits if it can sell more of its product or service than competitors do. In 2011, amid the recession, makers of luxury apparel, home furnishings, and other high-end goods are selling their unsold merchandise on members-only shopping sites, such as Gilt Groupe. Gilt Groupe and other private shopping sites like Rue La La and Ideeli help fuel pent-up demand by limiting membership, forcing potential clients to be on either a waiting list or referred to the site by existing members.[2] Through the use of these private-sale shopping sites, businesses are increasing their competitiveness.

Competition and Quality

Rather than sell your jeans for less than your competition, you may choose to compete for customers by offering higher-quality goods. Although you may charge more for your jeans, you offer a better fit, more durable fabric, or better styling. This possibility provides a practical incentive for businesses to maintain high standards and increases the choices available to consumers.

KEY FEDERAL LAWS AFFECTING THE FASHION INDUSTRY

laws affecting competition	purpose and provisions
Sherman Antitrust Act—1890	Outlawed monopolies. Outlawed restraint of competition.
Clayton Act—1914	Same purpose as Sherman Act but reinforced Sherman Act by defining some specific restraint—(e.g., price fixing).
Federal Trade Commission (FTC) Act—1914 (Wheeler–Lee Act of 1938 amended the FTC Act)	Established the FTC as a "policing" agency. Developed the mechanics for policing unfair methods of competition (e.g., false claims, price discrimination, price fixing).
Robinson–Patman Act—1936	Designed to equalize competition between large and small retailers (i.e., to reduce the advantages that big retailers have over small retailers—outgrowth of 1930 depression and growth of big chain retailers in 1920s.) Examples of provision of law: 1. Outlawed price discrimination if both small and large retailers buy the same amount of goods. 2. Outlawed inequitable and unjustified quantity discounts (e.g., discounts allowable if (a) available to all types of retailers and (b) related to actual savings that vendors could make from quantity cuttings or shipments.) 3. Outlawed "phony" advertising allowance monies (i.e., advertising money must be used for advertising). 4. Outlawed discrimination in promotional allowances (monies for advertising, promotional display, etc.)—equal allowances must be given under same conditions to small and large retailers alike.
Wool Products Labeling Act—1939; amended in 2006	Protects consumers from unrevealed presence of substitutes or mixtures. FTC responsible for enforcing law.
Cellar–Kefauver—1950	This law made it illegal to eliminate competition by creating a monopoly through the merger of two or more companies.
Fur Products Labeling Act—1951; amended in 2000	Protects consumers and retailers against misbranding, false advertising, and false invoicing.
Flammable Fabrics Act—1954; amended in 1972	Prohibits manufacture or sale of flammable fabrics, interior furnishings, and apparel. Transferred responsibility to the Consumer Product Safety Commission.
Textile Fiber Identification Act—1960; amended in 2000	Protects producers and consumers against false identification of fiber content.
Fair Packaging and Labeling Act—1966	Regulates interstate and foreign commerce by prohibiting deceptive methods of packaging or labeling.
Care Labeling of Textile Wearing Apparel Ruling—1972; amended in 1984, 1997	Requires that all apparel have labels attached that clearly inform consumers about care and maintenance of the article.

table 4.1

Competition and Innovation

Our economic system not only encourages variations in quality and price but also encourages immense variety in the types of merchandise and services offered to the public. Changes in taste and new technology bring about innovation, so that your jeans could be trimmed or untrimmed, designer made, or French cut. The economy and the competitive environment are constantly creating new business opportunities. The result is an astonishing diversity of businesses.

GOVERNMENT REGULATION OF BUSINESS

The right of government to regulate business is granted by the U.S. Constitution and by state constitutions. There are two basic categories of federal legislation that affect the fashion industry: laws that regulate competition, and labeling laws designed to protect consumers. Key federal laws that affect and (or both) regulate the fashion industry are shown in Table 4.1.

FORMS OF BUSINESS OWNERSHIP

Ownership of a fashion business—or of any business—may take many different legal forms, each carrying certain privileges and responsibilities. The three most common forms of business ownership are the sole proprietorship, the partnership, and the corporation. Corporations tend to be large-scale operations that account for the greatest share of the profits earned by U.S. business. However, sole proprietorships are more numerous, accounting for almost 70 percent of all business.

Each form of ownership has a characteristic structure, legal status, size, and field to which it is best suited. Each has its own advantages and disadvantages and offers a distinctive working environment with its own risks and rewards (Table 4.2).

ADVANTAGES AND DISADVANTAGES OF EACH FORM OF BUSINESS OWNERSHIP

form of ownership	advantages	disadvantages
Sole proprietorship (single owner)	• Ability to keep all profits • Simple to form and easiest to dissolve • Ownership flexibility	• Unlimited financial liability • Limited capital • Management deficiencies • Lack of continuity
Partnership (a few owners)	• Ease of formation • Greater financial capacity than sole proprietorship • Less red tape than corporation	• Unlimited financial liability • Interpersonal conflicts • Lack of continuity if partner dies • Harder to dissolve than sole proprietorship
Corporation (Inc.) (many owners)	• Limited financial liability • Specialized management skills • Greater financial capacity than other forms of ownership • Economies of larger-scale operation • Easy to transfer ownership	• Difficult and costly ownership form to establish and dissolve • Tax disadvantage • Legal restrictions • Depersonalization

table 4.2

BUSINESS GROWTH AND EXPANSION

The news media is filled with reports of businesses buying and selling other businesses and seeking new methods to make themselves more efficient and competitive.

One of the most distinct changes in the fashion business has been the rise of corporate giants, which grew through mergers, acquisitions, and internal expansion. The growth of these giants has changed the methods of doing business and has led to the demise of old-time famous-name sole proprietorships, partnerships, and small companies that could no longer compete.

Growth and expansion are fundamental to today's business world. Corporate growth has become a major economic, political, and social issue. Growth and expansion can occur in a variety of ways—internal growth, mergers, and acquisitions. Many large corporations grow by more than one of these methods. For example, cosmetics giant Estée Lauder developed the Prescriptives brand to expand to a more upscale consumer market. The company also acquired several smaller companies that cater to a younger market, including Bobbi Brown and MAC.

Internal Growth

A company's ability to grow internally determines its ability to offer more services and broader assortments of merchandise and to increase profits. This is true because internal growth is real growth, in terms of creating new products and new jobs. Internal growth can be accomplished through horizontal means, vertical means, or both. When a company has **horizontal growth**, it expands its capabilities on the level at which it has been performing successfully. An apparel company could add new lines to diversify its product offerings; a retail store could open new branches. When a company has **vertical growth**, it expands its capabilities on levels other than its primary function. An apparel company could begin to produce its own fabric or could retail its manufactured goods in stores that the apparel company owns.

Mergers and Acquisitions

In a **merger** (or acquisition), one company is sold to another company, with the purchasing company usually remaining dominant. Companies merge to form a larger corporate organization for many reasons. They may wish to take advantage of a large corporation's greater purchasing power, or they may want to sell stock to obtain the financial resources needed for expansion. The desire to constantly increase sales is often able to be fulfilled only by a merger. At the retail level, for example, the acquisition of The May Department Stores Company by Federated Department Stores extended the conglomerate's market. In 2007, Federated Department Stores then changed its name to Macy's, Inc.

Operating economies can often be achieved by combining companies. Many times duplicate facilities can be eliminated, and marketing, purchasing, and other operations can be consolidated. **Diversification**, the addition of various lines, products, or services to serve different markets, can also be a motive for a merger. For example, the acquisition of Banana Republic by Gap broadened Gap's market to reach customers for clothing at higher price points. Then Gap started Old Navy to reach even lower price points. Now the company covers three price points.

The Franchise

A growing business arrangement is the franchise. The **franchise** arrangement is a contract that gives an individual (or group of people) the right to own a business while benefiting from the expertise and reputation of an established firm. In return, the individual, known as the franchisee, pays the parent company, known as the franchisor, a set sum to purchase the franchise and royalties on goods or services sold. Franchises may be organized as sole proprietorships, partnerships, or corporations, although the

Lululemon Athletica is a fast-growing franchise.

form of business organization that the franchise must use may be designated in the franchise contract.

Franchises have generated one-third of all retail sales in the United States. Between 2001 and 2008 franchises grew by more than 40 percent. While there was a decline by 0.1 percent between 2008 and 2009, franchises are steadily growing again.[3] The franchise arrangement is most widespread among fast-food restaurants, convenience stores, and automobile dealers, but franchises are found at many levels of the fashion business, especially in retailing.

The growth in the number of manufacturer-franchised shops is phenomenal. One of the outstanding examples of this is the very popular Athlete's Foot stores. Although we will learn much more about designer-name franchising when we cover the apparel industries, it is important to note that Ralph Lauren, Donna Karan, and Oscar de la Renta are all involved in designer-franchised boutiques and shops in major cities throughout the United States, Europe, and Asia.

Advantages

Franchising offers advantages to both the franchisee and the franchisor. The franchisee can get into business quickly, use proven operating methods, and benefit from training programs and mass purchasing offered by the franchisor. The franchisee is provided with a ready market that identifies with the store or brand name, thus assuring customer traffic. The franchisor has a great deal of control over its distribution network, limited liability, and less need for capital for expansion. Expansion is therefore more rapid than would be possible without the franchising arrangement. Royalty and franchise fees add to the profits of the parent company, and the personal interest and efforts of the franchisees as owner-managers help to assure the success of each venture.

Disadvantages

Franchising also has drawbacks for both parties. The franchisee may find profits small in relation to the time and work involved and often has limited flexibility at the local level. In addition, there is the risk of franchise arrangements organized merely to sell franchises, rather than for their long-range profitability to all parties involved. The franchisor may find profits so slim that it may want to own stores outright rather than franchise them. Attempts to buy back franchises often lead to troubled relations with the remaining franchises.

Licensing

Licensing is an increasingly popular method of expanding an already existing business. **Licensing** is a legal arrangement whereby firms are given permission to produce and market merchandise in the name of the licensor for a specific period of time. The licensor is then paid a percentage of the sales (usually at the wholesale price) called a **royalty fee**. The royalty fee usually ranges from 2 to 15 percent.

Licensing grew tremendously in the late 1970s through the 1990s. The United States and Canada have accounted for about two thirds of worldwide retail sales to licensed merchandise, though the percentage has dropped somewhat since the 1990s. Retail sales of licensed merchandise worldwide totaled $149.77 billion in 2009. Today, the U.S. is the largest single market for licensed merchandise worldwide, valued at $83.15 billion.[4]

The first designer to license his name to a manufacturer was Christian Dior, who lent his name to a line of ties in 1950. Many of the best-known women's and men's apparel designers are licensing either the use of their original designs or just their names without a design for a wide variety of goods, from apparel to luggage. Many fashion labels—Ralph Lauren and Laura Ashley, for example—also extend into home furnishings through licensing. Among the many American designers involved in licensing are Michael (Michael Kors), Bill Blass, Calvin Klein, Ralph Lauren, and Oscar de la Renta. Most customers are not aware that some of the fashion merchandise they buy is licensed. For example, to customers every Kenneth Cole product is made by Kenneth Cole. In fact, this licensor manufactures *no* merchandise in house.

The licensing phenomenon is not limited to name designers. Manufacturers of athletic shoes expand their business enormously by licensing their logos and names to producers of active sportswear. Nike, Reebok, and Adidas have been particularly successful. Popular movies and TV shows, such as *Alice in Wonderland* and *Glee,* have spawned apparel and other products based on their themes or characters. Disney, for example, released an exclusive line of *Toy Story 3* T-shirts retailing for $70 to $108 at Revolveclothing.[5] Cartoon characters, like Mickey Mouse, Dora the Explorer, Spider-Man, and Strawberry Shortcake, are also frequently licensed, as are most professional sports teams and many players or athletes.

The advantage of a licensing arrangement to a manufacturer is that the merchandise is identified with a highly recognizable name, which also generally connotes high quality. Of course, the manufacturer also runs the risk of the designer's popularity fading. However, many manufacturers produce licensed goods for several designers.

The recognition factor can be valuable to retailers in presenting their own fashion images. And to consumers, the designer name not only indicates a certain quality of merchandise but symbolizes status or achievement as well. Because of that built-in appeal, stores have stocked up on designer goods from socks to fragrances and jewelry.

THE DESIGNER'S ROLE

There are unlimited opportunities in the field of design for those who have the special talents, both artistic and practical, that are needed to shape the consumer's world. Designers are everywhere and they design everything—fashions, furnishings, housewares, and office equipment. Their tools range from pencil and sketchpad to computer programs.

In creating designs that will not only reflect consumer attitudes and needs but also give expression to artistic ideas, fashion designers are continually influenced and limited by many factors. Of particular importance are practical business considerations.

VERA WANG

Skating Her Way to Fashion Success

A TALENTED FIGURE SKATER, VERA WANG COMPETED PROFESSIONALLY THROUGHOUT HER TEENS. In the 1968 and 1969 U.S. National Championships she and her partner, James Stuart, placed fifth in the junior pairs' competition. However, in 1971 after graduating from college, she left her skating career and began to work for *Vogue*. Within a year, at age 23, Vera Wang was promoted to senior fashion editor. She held that title for 15 years and in 1987 she left *Vogue* to take a job as design director for accessories at Ralph Lauren.

Vera Wang figure skating as a young girl

In 1989, Vera wed her longtime boyfriend Arthur Becker. Frustrated with the slim selection of existing bridal wear, she sketched her own design and commissioned a dressmaker to tailor the elaborate gown at a cost of $10,000. The next year, with financial backing from her new family, Wang opened her own bridal boutique in the upscale Carlyle Hotel in New York City. Catering mostly to celebrities and socialites, the Vera Wang Bridal House initially sold couture gowns by the famous designers like Guy Laroche, Arnold Scaasi, Carolina Herrera, and Christian Dior. Over the next few years, Wang honed her skills as a fashion designer and eventually launched a signature collection of streamlined and sophisticated bridal wear.

Wang first received international fashion attention during the 1994 Olympics when she designed a hand-beaded ensemble for figure skater Nancy Kerrigan. Since then, Wang has introduced an equally popular line of eloquent evening wear, as well as Vera Wang Made to Order—a collection of couture designs that are available exclusively at the Manhattan boutique. Both her bridal and evening apparel are sold in more than 55 upscale retailers, including Saks Fifth Avenue and Neiman Marcus.

Vera Wang, the firm, has grown into an important licensing-based operation, and Vera Wang, the designer, into a major fashion force. Today, Wang's licenses form the backbone of her business and surpass what is done in volume for ready-to-wear and bridal.

Here is a quick look at Wang's world in licensing:

F.T.D.: Wang formed a partnership with F.T.D. in 2007 and is now reinventing bouquets.

Waterford, Wedgwood, Royal Doulton: In 2002 she entered into china and crystal. Since then, the collection has grown steadily to include silverware, tabletop, and gifts.

Kohl's Department Stores: Simply Vera Wang launched in 2007 and has been growing ever since. She is also working with Kohl's to expand this line into cosmetics.

Kenmark Group: Launched eyewear in 2003 and has complete control over design and distribution.

William Arthur: The Vera Wang stationery collection, which launched in 2005, goes beyond the expected wedding announcements and invitations.

Brown Shoe Co.: Boots, heels, and ballet flats reflect Wang's designs.

David's Bridal: After two decades of designing for the Tony wedding market—and getting major celebrity clients—Wang is going for the proletarian wedding gowns. In 2010 she signed a long-term agreement with David's Bridal.

Bridal Fall 2011

Glam Princess perfume

Pre-fall 2011

Vera Wang for Waterford Wedgwood Royal Doulton dishes

Bridal Spring 2010

All designs must be produced at a profit and within the firm's predetermined whole-sale price range. Consequently, designers must consider the availability and cost of materials, the particular image that the firm wants to maintain, available production techniques, and labor costs. Great designers use their creativity to overcome all these limitations and to produce salable, exciting designs.

Types of Designers

Most designers can be classified in one of the following three categories:

1. High-fashion or "name" designers: They are responsible for the full range of decisions of a fashion house, as well as for establishing the image and creating designs for the company. They design ready-to-wear lines as well as custom designs, and many license the use of their prestigious names to manufacturers of accessories, fragrances and cosmetics, and home fashions.

2. Stylist-designers: They work for manufacturers and adapt the designs of others, typically of name designers. Usually they create variations in less-expensive fabrics to appeal to a market for lower-priced merchandise at the late rise or early culmination stage of the fashion cycle.

3. Freelance designers: They sell sketches of their original designs or adaptations to manufacturers. Freelancers typically work out of design studios. They are not involved in the selection of fabrics and colors or in the business decisions that are required to manufacture the products based on their designs.

Sources of Design Inspiration

Where does the designer get ideas and inspiration for new fashion? The answer, of course, is everywhere! Through TV, the designer experiences all the wonders of the entertainment world. In films, the designer is exposed to the influences of all the arts and lifestyles throughout the world. Because consumers are exposed to movies through international distribution, films prime their audiences to accept new fashions inspired by the costumes. Museum exhibits, art shows, world happenings, expositions, theater, music, dance, and world travel are all sources of design inspiration to fashion designers. The fashions of the past are also a rich source of design inspiration.

While always alert to the new and exciting, fashion designers never lose sight of the recent past. They know that consumers need to anticipate something new each season. But they also recognize that whatever new style is introduced will have to take its place with what consumers already have in their wardrobes. No one starts with all new clothes each season. Rarely does a revolutionary new style succeed. Instead, it is the evolutionary new style that so often becomes the best-selling fashion.

THE MANUFACTURER'S ROLE

Manufacturers would agree with Dwight E. Robinson that "every market into which the consumer's fashion sense has insinuated itself is, by that very token, subject to [the] common, compelling need for unceasing change in the styling of its goods."[6]

Even in such mundane items as writing paper, the need for change has produced rainbows of pastels, brilliant deep shades, and the traditional white with dainty or bold prints. Similarly, in basics such as bedsheets or men's dress shirts, the once traditional white has yielded to a variety of colors, stripes, and prints. There is scarcely an industry serving consumers today in which the manufacturer's success does not depend, in part, on an ability to attune styling to fashion interest and demand. A current trend is to hire merchandisers who do market research for the manufacturer, specializing in identifying the correct customer and his or her needs and wants.

Types of Manufacturers

In general, manufacturers of fashion goods can be divided into five groups, differentiated by styling and price. One group is made up of designers or firms that produce innovative, high-fashion apparel that is very expensive. Another group bridges the price range between custom designs and high-quality but less-expensive merchandise, hence the name bridge market. Some high-fashion designers also produce bridge lines. The next group is usually identified as the better market. Its price range is just below that of the bridge lines. A fourth group of firms sometimes produces originals. But it usually turns out adaptations of styles that have survived the introduction stage and are in the rise stage of their fashion life cycle. This group of firms is usually identified as the moderate-priced market. A fifth group of manufacturers makes no attempt to offer new or unusual styling. Rather, these firms mass-produce close copies or adaptations of styles that have proved their acceptance in higher-priced markets. This group is usually identified as the budget market.

Fashion Influence

In the field of women's apparel, manufacturers are committed to producing several new lines a year. A **line** is an assortment of new designs with a designated period for delivery to the retailer. Some of these may be new in every sense of the word and others merely adaptations of currently popular styles. Producers hope that a few of the designs in a given line will prove to be "hot"—so precisely in step with demand that their sales will be profitably large.

For the most part, the fashion industries are made up of manufacturers whose abilities to anticipate the public's response to styles is excellent. Those who do badly in this respect, even for a single season, usually reap small sales and large losses. Unless they are unusually well financed, they quickly find themselves out of business. In the fashion industry, the survival of the fittest means the survival of those who give the most able assistance in the birth and growth of fashions that consumers will buy.

THE RETAILER'S ROLE

Although retailers do not usually create fashion, they can encourage or retard its progress by the degree of accuracy with which they anticipate the demands of their customers. They seek out from manufacturers styles that they believe are most likely to win acceptance from these target groups.

Some large retailers work directly with manufacturers and firms at the primary level to develop styles for exclusive sale at their stores. Thus, retailers such as Gap and The Limited can stock only their own labels. Others, such as Macy's, Inc., sell private label merchandise along with national brands. (We will examine the practice of product development by retailers in more detail in Chapter 7.)

Types of Retailers

There are many ways to classify retail firms. However, when firms are evaluated on the basis of their leadership positions, they tend to fall into three main categories.

First, there are firms that are considered "fashion leaders." They feature newly introduced styles that have only limited production and distribution. These styles, called "Designer Collections," are usually very expensive. Examples of these firms include Bergdorf Goodman, Neiman Marcus, and Nordstrom.

A second group, called "traditional retailers"—by far the largest in number—features fashions that have captured consumer interest in their introduction stage and are in the late rise or early culmination stages of their life cycles. These styles are from designer "bridge collections" or from "better" or "moderate" manufacturers. Since these styles

Brands that are limited in distribution or exclusive to certain stores, such as Tommy Hilfiger's sportswear to Macy's, are a growing trend in the industry.

Fall
2011

Roberto Cavalli

Fall
201

ROBERTO CAVALLI
Four Decades in Fashion's Jungle

"DON'T ASK ME TO SKETCH OR FIT A MANNEQUIN, THAT'S NEVER BEEN MY STYLE," SAID ROBERTO CAVALLI AT THE COMPANY'S 40TH ANNIVERSARY GALA IN SEPTEMBER 2010. "The strength of my fashion has been to distinguish right from wrong, ugly from attractive, good from bad—that's how I became a great designer." And those "great designer" qualities have generated a $250 million business with 60 signature stores and fantastic international stature.

Flowers, ribbons, and a first taste of animal prints were his favorite motifs. Eventually a Dalmatian-spotted print grabbed the attention of Krizia's Mariuccia Mandelli and soon more famous design houses such as Hermès wrote orders for Cavalli's prints.

It was in 1970 that the idea of opening his own business became his dream. "I believe it was July 1970, and I was flying back from Paris when I thought that if I did my own collection, I would be part of the fashion world," Cavalli said.

In 1972, he opened a small shop called Tembo in Saint-Tropez, which was so successful that the following year he was invited to show his leather wares in the Sala Bianca in Florence, Italy, alongside the most important designers including Armani, Missoni, Krizia, Fendi, and Basile.

During his 40-year run, Cavalli noted how his fashion "inventions"—namely printed knitwear, leather, and a trail-blazing approach to denim via special treatment, embroideries, and a stretch connotation—"revolutionized."

He launched men's wear in 1999, with hopes to change classic dress for men. "I always thought men should have more fun in dressing and use more fantasy, especially at night," he said. "Otherwise, they all look the same with all those boring jackets and shirts."

Over the years, Cavalli has grown his success. "It is well known that we are strong in women's ready-to-wear dress, but there are still many opportunities in leather accessories, shoes, and perfumes," he said.

In the U.S., the brand is available at prominent specialty stores like Bergdorf-Goodman, Saks Fifth Avenue, and 30 smaller specialty retailers. There are 60 Roberto Cavalli stores globally and the company's goal is to reach 100 over the next five years.

As he says, "Roberto Cavalli is me, the signature collection is me. I have built it all my life."

Cavalli runway show, Shangha

are usually widely produced by this time, they are most often offered at more moderate prices. Examples of these firms include Macy's, Dillard's, and Bloomingdale's. The distinction between the traditional retailers and fashion leaders is somewhat blurred in that the fashion leaders may also carry "traditional" merchandise, and the traditional retailers may have designer departments.

A third group of retailers, often called "mass merchants," features widely accepted fashions that are well into the culmination phase of their life cycles. Since fashions at this stage of development are usually mass produced, mass merchants can and do offer fashions at moderate to low prices. Examples of these firms include JCPenney and Sears. At the low end of the mass market are the discounters, like the off-price Dress Barn, for example, which sells merchandise at discounted prices. Other examples include Wal-Mart and Kmart.

Fashion Influence

Sometimes, because of their constant and intimate contact with their customers, retailers are so intuitive or creative that they lead their suppliers in anticipating the styles their customers will accept. Such retailers accelerate the introduction and progress of new fashions by persuading manufacturers to produce styles that answer an upcoming need or demand. Because of this ability, retailers are doing more and more product development for their own customers.

CONSUMER BUYING CYCLE versus RETAILER BUYING CYCLE

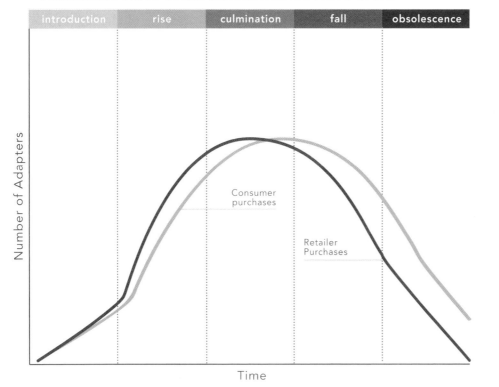

Retailers have to stay just a step ahead of their target customers. Retailers need to have sufficient stock available when customers are ready to buy a new fashion, but need to avoid being overstocked when customers' interests shift to a new fashion.

SUMMARY AND REVIEW

The fashion industry is a major business sector in the United States and around the world. It employs people at four levels: producers of materials, such as natural and manufactured textiles, leather, fur, and materials used in decorative trimmings; manufacturers of apparel, accessories, cosmetics and fragrances, and home fashions; fashion retailers; and auxiliary services to the other three levels, including market research and forecasting and promotional services. Businesses at all four levels collaborate to capture their share of the market.

Companies compete with others at their level by offering advantages of price, quality, and innovation. The federal government regulates the production and sale of fashion goods to ensure safe, functional products for consumers and fair marketing practices among competitors.

Like other businesses, fashion businesses at all levels may be sole proprietorships, partnerships, or corporations. Fashion companies grow horizontally by getting into new markets or vertically by expanding into levels beyond the level of their original business. They may expand internally, acquire or merge with other companies, or franchise or license a part of their businesses. Continuing into the 21st century, licensing is an important part of virtually every major designer's business strategy, and businesses outside the fashion industry license their names and logos to apparel producers.

At all levels, fashion business executives must be able to predict the tastes of the consumers who wear and use their merchandise. Depending on level, a company must anticipate consumer demand from six months to one year and a half in advance of the day a new fashion becomes available at retail.

FOR REVIEW

1. What is the primary objective of all businesses? Explain your answer.

2. Describe the four levels of the fashion business. Give examples.

3. How does the auxiliary level differ from the other levels?

4. Compare the advantages and disadvantages of a sole proprietorship and a partnership as a form of business for a fashion retailer.

5. Why do companies seek growth through mergers and acquisitions?

6. What are the practical obstacles that limit fashion designers? What additional factors must be considered in developing each fashion design?

7. List the three types of designers commonly serving the U.S. fashion industry today. List the responsibilities of each.

8. If you were the president of a national chain of shoe stores, what are five laws and regulations that would affect how you do business? Which of these laws would not affect a small, privately owned bridal shop?

9. What is the difference between a license agreement and a franchise?

10. How is a licensed designer name an advantage to the manufacturer? To the consumer? To the retailer?

FOR DISCUSSION

1. What initial decisions need to be made by an individual or group of individuals who plan to form a company with regard to the form of ownership that will be most beneficial to all?

2. What does the statement "You're only as good as your last collection" mean in regard to fashion designers?

TRADE TALK

Define or briefly explain the following terms:

auxiliary level

diversification

franchise

horizontal growth

licensing

line

merger

primary level

profit

retail level

royalty fee

secondary level

vertical growth

PART 2

THE PRIMARY LEVEL— THE MATERIALS OF FASHION

In this part, you will examine the primary market suppliers—the growers and producers of the raw materials of fashion. You will begin to develop a basic vocabulary and a working knowledge of the following:

- The history, manufacture, and uses of natural and manufactured fibers and fabrics—in Chapter 5.

- The history, processing, and politics of manufacturing leathers and fur—in Chapter 6.

The earliest part of the planning function—in both color and texture—takes place on the primary level. It is also the level of the fashion business that works the furthest in advance of the ultimate selling period for the finished goods. Primary-level companies need up to two years' lead time before the goods will be available to the consumer. Goods at the primary level may often be imports from Third World emerging nations, where textiles are usually the earliest form of industrialization. The primary level is the foundation upon which the merchandisers and marketers of fashion products build their ideas and designs that will answer the needs and wants of the customer.

TEXTILES
FIBERS AND
FABRIC

- The difference between a natural fiber and a manufactured fiber
- The major steps in the production of most fabrics
- The effect of imports on the U.S. fiber and fabric industries
- The effects of new technology on textiles

Fashion and the materials from which they are made are inseparable.

Have you ever bought a fashion product simply because you loved the

feel of it? Perhaps it was rough and coarse or silky and smooth. Maybe it

was incredibly soft to the touch. If so, then you, like almost everyone else,

have responded to a fabric rather than to the style or color of a fashion

product.

The designer creating a style at the drawing board must consider the material best suited for the particular silhouette and details of design. The manufacturer must then consider the various weights of material currently desired as well as the cost factors. Finally, the retailer must select fashions made of those materials considered appropriate and desirable by their target customers.

The material or fabric a garment is made of is so important that Christian Dior, the world-famous designer, once said of it: "Fabric not only expresses a designer's dream, but also stimulates his own ideas. It can be the beginning of an inspiration. Many a dress of mine is born of the fabric alone."[1]

The enormous appeal of fabric—and the fibers of which it is composed—lies in its many varied textures, finishes, uses, and colors. These are created, as we shall learn, by the fiber and fabric industries that work closely together to produce an end product, which is called fashion textiles.

The production of fiber and fabrics is the first step in the manufacture of clothing, accessories, and home fashions. As a result, textile fiber and textile fabric manufacturers are considered **primary suppliers**. The makers of **trimmings** are also at the primary level of the fashion business.

THE FIBER INDUSTRY

A **fiber**—an extremely fine, hairlike strand almost invisible to the eye—is the smallest element of a fabric. It is also the starting point of a fabric. Fibers can be spun or twisted into continuous threads called **yarn**, and yarns can be knitted, woven, or bonded into **fabrics**. Although tiny, fibers have enormous influence on fashion. They are what give a fabric its color, weight, texture, and durability.

Fibers are either natural or manufactured. Natural fibers are found in nature, that is, they come from plant or animal sources. In contrast, **manufactured fibers** are made in a chemist's laboratory. Natural fibers may be made from substances that occur in nature, such as wood pulp, air, petroleum, or natural gas, but these natural substances must be converted into fibers before they can be made into fabric. Manufactured fibers are sometimes called "man-made" or "synthetic fibers." Because manufactured fibers are invented in the laboratory, they are more plentiful than natural fibers. Currently, 25 manufactured fibers are available. Some of the manufactured fibers whose names you may recognize are rayon, nylon, acetate, acrylic, spandex, and polyester.

HISTORY AND DEVELOPMENT

The use of natural fibers is ancient, whereas most of the manufactured fibers have been invented in the past 50 years. Despite their relatively short life span, however, rapid advances have been made in the use of manufactured fibers. In contrast, the natural fiber industry has developed much more slowly. In fact, many of the developments in natural fibers are actually advances made in the manufactured fiber industry that were transferred to the natural fiber industry.

Designer Jean Paul Gaultier makes dramatic use of silk in his Fall 2010 couture show in Paris.

The Development of Natural Fibers

The use of natural fibers predates written history. Prehistoric humans are known to have gathered flax, the fiber in linen, to make yarns for fabrics. There are four major natural fibers: cotton, silk, flax (linen), and wool. Two other minor natural fibers are ramie and hemp. In addition, there are many other natural fibers that are in short supply, and so limited to luxury items. (See Table 5.1.)

Cotton, the most widely used of all the natural fibers, is the substance attached to the seed of a cotton plant. Cotton fibers are composed primarily of cellulose, a carbohydrate that especially lends itself to the manufacture of fibrous and paper products. Cotton fibers absorb moisture quickly, dry quickly, and have a cooling effect that makes cotton a good fiber for hot or warm weather. Usually the fluffy cotton boll is white, but other growing methods have brought about naturally colored cotton. This type of cotton can be grown in many colors, thus eliminating the need for dyes. Long and extra-long cotton fibers (or staple) produce the finest fabrics. The United States leads the world in the production of long staple Pima cotton, while Egypt is a close second.[2]

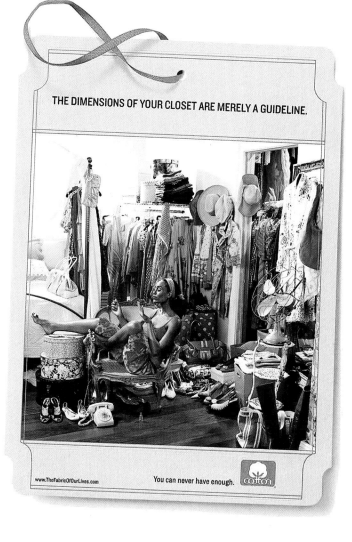

This ad for Cotton Inc. highlights the ubiquity of cotton in everyday life.

Wool is the fiber that forms the coat of sheep. Sheep produce one of the few replenishable natural commodities. Shear a sheep's coat time after time, and it quickly grows a new one. An animal fiber, wool is composed mostly of protein. Wool fiber is a natural insulator and is used to make warm clothes. Wool fiber, in fact, has a natural crimp that is ideal for the production of bulky yarns that trap air to form insulating barriers against the cold. Wool absorbs moisture more slowly and dries more slowly than cotton. A lightweight summer wool has been developed to be machine washable.

Silk comes from a cocoon formed by a silkworm. The silkworm forces two fine streams of a thick liquid out of tiny openings in its head. These streams harden into filaments, or fibers, upon contact with the air. Silk, best known for its luxurious feel, is a breathable fabric that can be worn year-round. For many years, silk required dry cleaning, but much of today's silk is washable.

COTTON INCORPORATED
Keeping Cotton Growing and Going

Cotton plant

DROUGHTS, INSECTS, CONSUMER DEMAND, ATTACKS FROM OTHER FIBERS, ENVIRONMENTAL GROUPS, AND LET'S NOT FORGET GLOBAL RECESSIONS—the foes have been formidable—but Cotton Inc. has weathered the storms over the past 40 years, becoming the leading voice and advocate for the cotton industry worldwide.

Best known to the general public as the company behind the famous "The Fabric of Our Lives" advertising campaign, Cotton Inc. works on behalf of cotton producers and importers of cotton products with the sole objective of increasing the demand and profitability of U.S. cotton through promotion and research activities.

The company was created by an act of Congress to help farmers recapture cotton's plummeting market share. Based in the United States, Cotton Inc. conducts agricultural, fiber, and textile research and testing, utilizing state-of-the-art equipment. It disseminates market information and provides technical services; creates ad campaigns for print, TV, radio, and the Internet; and provides market intelligence, fashion forecasts, and retail promotions.

The cotton industry faced a crisis as the 60s gave way to the 70s. By 1975, cotton's share of the textile marketplace had fallen to an all-time low of 34 percent, from 78 percent in 1960, as synthetic and man-made fibers made high inroads in the fashion industry. The new synthetic fibers even threatened the historically all-cotton jeans category. Fibers such as nylon, rayon, and polyester had become household names. Terms like "wash and wear" and "wrinkle free" associated with synthetic fibers helped erode cotton's market share.

Fast forward to 2010: cotton apparel and home fabrics now account for more than 60 percent of textile products sold at retail. A large part of the resurgence owes its success to Cotton Inc., which has seen its logo and advertising reach iconic status. In the four decades since it was founded, Cotton Inc. has used marketing and innovative technological advancements to position cotton as a brand—not just an agricultural commodity.

As Wally Darneille, president and CEO of the Plains Cotton Cooperative Association in Lubbock, Texas, said, "If it hadn't been for what Cotton Inc. did for cotton farmers all over the world, we'd all be wearing polyester leisure suits."

Key milestones for Cotton Inc.:

1966: Cotton Research and Promotion Act passes Congress, establishing funding from producer assessments aimed at conducting a campaign to recapture cotton's market share.

1970: Cotton Incorporated is created.

1973: The iconic "Seal of Cotton" is introduced.

1976: Cotton Inc. sponsors the Winter Olympic Games

1980: Cotton Inc. hosts the first Textile Designer Awards in New York. The awards recognize designers' abilities to add creativity and functionality to cotton apparel and home textiles.

1982: Engineered Fiber System launches, which allows for greater precision in processing cotton and selecting for the highest-quality fibers.

1987: Cotton Inc. introduces wrinkle-resistant technology. Farah is the first company to market it.

1989: "The Fabric of Our Lives" advertising campaign launches, with the jingle sung by popular musician Richie Havens.

1993: Cotton Inc. forges a marketing partnership with Procter & Gamble Co. to display the Seal of Cotton trademark on laundry detergents.

1994: Cotton Inc. launches The Lifestyle Monitor Survey and moves into the field of consumer research.

1997: Cotton Inc. opens its Shanghai office to service mills, manufacturers, and retailers in China that use U.S. cotton, illustrating how global the cotton market has become.

2000: Cotton Inc. moves into a new state-of-the-art facility in Cary, N.C.

2002: Cotton Inc. develops a marketing campaign for India called the Cotton Gold Alliance, further expanding its global research.

2010: Cotton Inc. celebrates its 40th anniversary and reintroduces "The Fabric of Our Lives" ad campaign with singers Leona Lewis and Colbie Caillat giving new twists to the famous jingle.

NATURAL LUXURY ANIMAL FIBERS

name	source	characteristics and uses
Alpaca	Member of the llama family found in the Andes Mountains in South America	Fine, hollow-core fleece; annual shearing yields 6–12 pounds of fibers; 22 natural shades; strongest, most resilient wool; scarce
Angora	Rabbit hair	Soft fibers, dyes well; sheds easily
Camel hair	Camel	Usually left in natural tones; used in coats, jackets, artists' brushes
Cashmere	Kashmir goat (60% found in China but also bred in United States)	Rare (1/100 of wool crop); sheared annually; one goat produces enough for one-quarter of a sweater
Goose down (often mixed with goose feathers to cut cost)	Goose	Most compressible insulation; lightweight warmth for jackets, vests, comforters, pillows, sleeping bags, feather beds
Llama	Llama found in Andes Mountains of South America, United States, Canada, Australia, and New Zealand	Coarser, stronger than alpaca; used in utilitarian items such as sacks
Marabou	African marabou stork or turkey	Soft, fluffy material from feathers
Mohair	Angora goat, originally from Turkey, now from South Africa, Texas, and New Zealand	Twice-yearly shearing; 2.5 times as strong as wool; less allergenic than sheep's wool
Ostrich feathers	Ostrich	Used in high-fashion apparel, feather dusters
Pashmina	Mountain goats from Himalayas	Softer than cashmere-fiber
Qiviut	Musk ox down from Canada, Alaska	Natural taupe color; soft, light, 8 times warmer than sheep's wool; rare ($20–$25/oz)
Vicuna	Rare llama-like animal from Peru	World's finest natural fiber

table 5.1

Flax, used to make linen, comes from the stem of a flax plant. Only after the flax fiber is spun into yarn and woven or knit into fabric is the product called linen. Flax is the strongest of the vegetable fibers (it is twice as strong as cotton), and like cotton, it absorbs moisture and dries quickly. These features make linen an excellent fabric for warm-weather apparel. However, even with new technology that makes linen less apt to wrinkle, it still has a tendency to wrinkle and is harder to iron than cotton. Most flax is imported from Europe, especially Belgium, Ireland, France, and the UK.

Ramie comes from a woody-leafed Asian plant grown mostly in China. It has been available in the United States only since 1979, when the United States and China reopened trade with each other. A linen-like fabric suitable for warm-weather apparel, ramie is also inexpensive.

Hemp is a fibrous plant, which was an agricultural staple in America for hundreds of years. A number of other natural fibers are used in apparel and home furnishings. They are relatively rare and thus expensive.

THE DEVELOPMENT OF MANUFACTURED FIBERS

Manufactured or synthetic fibers have been improving the quality of our lives since rayon, the first synthetic fiber, went into production in 1910. Since then, many other manufactured fibers have been introduced in literally thousands of new apparel, upholstery, and industrial applications.

Manufactured fibers offer a variety of characteristics that are mostly unavailable in natural fibers. Each year, manufactured fibers find new uses in our wardrobes, homes, hospitals, and workplaces. Designers like Georgio Armani, Calvin Klein, and Joseph Abboud all use high-tech, stretch, and classic fabrics to illustrate the constant innovation of their product lines.[3]

All manufactured fibers start life as thick liquids. Fibers of continuous, indefinite lengths are produced by forcing the liquid through the tiny holes of a mechanical device called a **spinnerette**. This is similar to the way pasta dough is pushed through a pasta machine to make spaghetti.

Fibers are then cut into short lengths and spun into yarn, as is the case with natural fibers, or they are chemically processed into yarn directly. In the latter case, the production of fiber and yarn occurs simultaneously.

There are two basic types of manufactured fibers: cellulosic and noncellulosic. Cellulosic fibers include rayon, acetate, triacetate, and lyocell. Noncellulosic fibers are made of petroleum, coal, natural gas, air, and water.

Generic Names for Manufactured Fibers

The Federal Trade Commission (FTC) has assigned **generic names**, or nontrademarked names, to 25 manufactured fibers. Within any of these broad generic categories, fiber producers can modify the composition to produce a new fiber, called a *variant*. The variant is then given a brand name by the producer. There are hundreds of **brand names**, or trademarks, which are registered with the U.S. Patent Office; only the manufacturer of a variant is allowed to use the registered name. For example, polyester is the generic name, and Dacron is the DuPont trademark for polyester.

The properties of these fibers greatly influence the behavior of the finished fabric made from them. Polyester, for example, is strong and wrinkle resistant, which contributes to its durability and washability. Once scorned as the dull material of inexpensive leisure suits, today's polyester has the subtle sheen of fine silk.

Manufactured fibers of varying lengths are produced by forcing thick liquids through the tiny holes of a device known as a spinnerette.

MANUFACTURED FIBERS

date	fiber	first commercial production	end use
1910	Rayon	The first manufactured fiber. The first commercial production of rayon fiber in the United States was in 1910 by the American Viscose Company. By using two different chemicals and manufacturing techniques, two basic types of rayon were developed. They were viscose rayon and cuprammonium rayon. Today, only viscose rayon is being produced in the United States.	Blouses, coats, dresses, jackets, lingerie, linings, millinery, rainwear, and nonwoven fabrics. Non-apparel includes draperies and medical products.
1924	Acetate	The first commercial production of acetate fiber in the United States was in 1924 by the Celanese Corporation.	Lining fabric, lingerie, ribbons, and foundation garments.
1938	Nylon	The first commercial production of nylon in the United States was in 1939 by the E. I. DuPont de Nemours & Company, Inc. It is the second-most-used manufactured fiber in this country, after polyester.	Wide range of products in apparel (blouses, hosiery, lingerie, underwear, raincoats, windbreakers); interior furnishings (bedspreads, curtains, upholstery); and industrial areas (sleeping bags, tents, luggage).
1950	Acrylic	The first commercial production of acrylic fiber in the United States was in 1950 by E. I. DuPont de Nemours & Company, Inc.	Sweaters, blankets, carpeting, children's garments, socks. Also includes outdoor products like awnings.
1953	Polyester	The first commercial production of polyester fiber in the United States was in 1953 by E. I. DuPont de Nemours & Company, Inc. Polyester is the most-used manufactured fiber in the United States.	Suits, skirts, career apparel, performance fabrics, curtains, and sheets. Also includes fiberfill for pillows, sails, and tire cord.
1954	Triacetate	The first commercial production of triacetate fiber in the United States was in 1954 by the Celanese Corporation. Domestic triacetate production was discontinued in 1985.	Good for apparel that requires pleats or creases, such as dresses or skirts. Also used in knitted sleepwear and robes.
1959	Spandex	The first commercial production of spandex fiber in the United States was in 1959 by E. I. DuPont de Nemours & Company, Inc. It is an elastomeric manufactured fiber (able to stretch at least 100 percent and snap back like natural rubber). Spandex is used in filament form.	Denim, undergarments, support products, ski pants, athletic apparel in which stretch is needed, and swimwear.
1961	Olefin/ Polyolefin	The first commercial production of an olefin fiber manufactured in the United States was by Hercules Incorporated in 1991. A polypropylene-type olefin fiber followed and both are commercially produced.	Athletic clothing, specifically for running, cycling, diving, and surfing. Also used in upholstery, industrial fabrics, and geotextiles.
1993	Lyocell	The first commercial production of lyocell in the United States was in 1992 by Courtaulds Fibers. The fabric was given the generic name Lyocell in 1996. Environmentally friendly, lyocell is produced from the wood pulp of trees grown specifically for this purpose. It is specially processed, using a solvent spinning technique in which the dissolving agent is recycled, reducing environmental effluents.	Blouses, dresses, pajamas, shirts, and coats.
2002	Polylactide (PLA)	The first commercial production of PLA in the United States was in 2002 by Cargill Dow Polymers. PLA is a plastic derived from natural plant sugars, bridging the gap between natural fibers and conventional synthetic fibers.	Primary uses include pillows, comforters, and mattress pads. Also suitable for activewear and apparel.

table 5.2

Source: Adapted from Fabric Link/Fabric University, http://www.fabriclink.com/Fabric University/Man-made Fibers, http://www.Fibersource.com, and http://www.fta.gov.

Lacroix home furnishings

DVF Collection bedding

Blumarine chair

Designer Angel Sanchez's living room

HOME TEXTILES
"You Can't Live Without Them!"

THE NOTION THAT FASHION IS JUST ABOUT CLOTHES IS AS OLD-FASHIONED AS THE LOW-RISE JEAN. Today, designers are rethinking our living spaces. Home furnishings, or soft furnishings, are the happening thing in the textile and fashion business today. In Fall 2010, the Council of Fashion Designers of America (CFDA) moved from the runways into designer home fashions featuring textiles.

"Home Textiles" refer to the textiles used in manufacturing home furnishings. It has an extensive range of functional as well as decorative products with both natural and man-made fabrics used. The textile fabrics most commonly used for home furnishings are silk, cotton, jute, rayon, wool, nylon, polyester, and satin.

Just as clothing designers always credit the fabrics they use to make their designs perfect for their customers, the same is true for home furnishings. Fabric is the prime contributor in home furnishing products, and, therefore, it must provide the texture, color, character, scale, and anything that is missing in the architecture. It brings style, reflects one's taste, and controls the mood. It also is the most flexible, as it can be easily changed, added to, or replaced. Fabrics increase livability and workability, reduce noises, and make music—and even speech—richer and more resonant.

Home textiles are used in upholstery, window textiles, bed linens, bathroom textiles, kitchen linens and accessories, table linens, tablecloths, and rugs and carpets, as follows:

- Upholstery fabrics are used to cushion and cover furniture.
- Window textiles include curtains, drapes, and blinds. This is one of the biggest areas of fabric development in home textiles.
- Bed linens and other bed textiles include bedsheets, pillowcases, spreads, quilt covers, duvet covers, cushions, blankets, mattresses, and throws.
- Bathroom textiles include shower curtains, bath mats and rugs, and towels.
- Kitchen linens and accessories include aprons, mittens, dish cloths, and kitchen towels. Flame-retardant kitchen wears are also in great demand.
- Table linens include table mats, napkins, placemats, chair covers, table runners, and coasters.
- Rugs and carpets are a very important part of floor coverings, which have gained worldwide popularity.

GENERIC NAMES AND TRADE NAMES
OF MANUFACTURED FIBERS USED IN THE UNITED STATES

generic name	trade names
Acetate	Celanese, Chromspun, Estron, Microsafe
Acrylic	Acrilan, Bio Fresh, Bounce-Back, Creslan, Cystar, Cystar AF, Duraspun, Fi-lana, Pil-Trol, Sayelle, So-Lara, Smart Yarns, Wear-Dated, Wintuk
Aramid	Kevlar, Nomex
Lyocell	Lenzing Lyocell, Tencel
Modacrylic	SEF Plus
Nylon	A.C.E., Anso, Antron, Assurance, Avantige, Cantrece, Capima, Caplana, Caprolan, Captiva, Cordura, Creme de Captiva, Crepeset, DuraSoft, DyeNAMIX, Eclipse, Hardline, Hydrofil, Hytel, Matinesse, Microsupplex, No Shock, Power-Silk, Resistat, Shimmereen, Silkey Touch, Solution, Sportouch, Stainmaster, Stay Guard, Supplex, Tactel, Tru-Ballistic, Ultra Image, Ultra Touch, Ultron, Wear-Dated, Wellon, Wellstrand, WorryFree, Zefsprot, Zeftron
Olefin	Alpha, Essera, Impressa, Inova, Marvess, Patlon III, Polystrand, Spectra, Synera, Trace
Polyester	A.C.E., Ceylon, Comfort Fiber, Compet, Coolmax, Corebond, Dacronfi, ES.P, Fortrel, Hollofi, Kodaire, Kodel, KodOfill, KodOsoff, Pentron, Premafill Plump, Premafill Soft, Trevira, Trevira Finesse, Trevira Microness, Universe
PBI	PBI Logo
Rayon	Beau-Grip, Fibro, Galaxy
Spandex	Lycra
Sulfar	Ryton

table 5.3

Adapted from: www.fibersource.com/f-tutor/q-guide.htm and American Fiber Manufacturers Association, www.afma.org/afma/afma.html

Microfibers

A major technological breakthrough occurred in 1989 with the first commercial production of microfiber in the United States by DuPont. A **microfiber** is a fiber that is two or three times smaller than a human hair—smaller than wool, cotton, or silk fibers. Microfiber is the thinnest and finest of all manufactured fibers. It has a touch and texture similar to silk or cashmere, but is wrinkle resistant and can usually be machine washed and dried. Today, microfiber is produced in a number of manufactured fibers—for example, nylon, acrylic, and polyester. Designers have used it widely in womenswear, menswear, activewear, outerwear, and home furnishings.

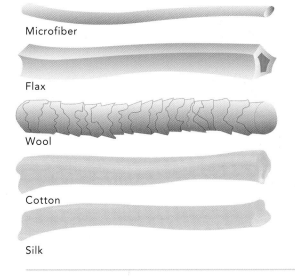

A microfiber compared with silk, cotton, wool, and flax.

ORGANIZATION AND OPERATION

Because of the differences in the origin and characteristics of fibers, each industry—the natural fiber industry and the manufactured fiber industry—is organized along different lines.

The Natural Fiber Industry

Cotton is produced in four major areas of the United States: the Southeast; the Mississippi Delta; the Texas-Oklahoma panhandle; and New Mexico, Arizona, and California. Nearly all cotton growers sell their product in local markets, either to mill representatives or, more typically, to wholesalers. The cotton wholesalers bargain at central markets in Memphis, New Orleans, Dallas, Houston, New York City, and Chicago.

The wool produced in the United States comes from relatively small sheep ranches in the Western states. Boston is the central marketplace for both domestic and imported wool.

Linen, silk, and ramie are not produced in any great quantities in the United States. As with hemp, these fibers are imported from foreign sources.

The natural fiber industry in the United States has been greatly affected by the advent of manufactured fibers. The ability to tailor the manufactured fibers to the demands of the ever-changing marketplace has forced the natural fiber industries to become more attuned to the needs of their customers. To compete, the natural fiber industries have become more aggressive about developing new uses for their products and promoting themselves. Cotton, usually a warm-weather fiber, is now promoted as a year-round fiber, largely through the use of heavier cotton fibers used to make cotton sweaters. And wool, usually designed for cold-weather wear, is now being treated to make new light-weight fibers suitable for year-round wear. Through advanced technology and innovative chemical processing, many natural fibers are treated with special finishes to give them care-and-wear properties equal to those of manufactured fibers.

The Manufactured Fiber Industry

Obviously, climate and terrain have nothing to do with the production of a manufactured fiber. Chemical companies are extremely adaptable, requiring only supplies of raw chemicals, power, and labor. Chemical companies have built their factories in every part of the United States—up and down the East Coast, in the South, the Midwest, and increasingly on the West Coast. Operations are located wherever companies have found raw materials or railroads and waterways for convenient shipment of those materials. Most of these factories are huge.

With manufactured fibers, the producing company can also serve as its own market. It purchases fibers from chemical companies, spins them into yarn, and knits or weaves the yarn into fabric. Burlington Industries and Swift Galey LLC are two of the giants that consolidate all operations, from spun yarn manufacture to finished fabric.

Fiber Development

The fierce competition among various producers of manufactured fibers is tied to the fact that in one season, a need may arise for fiber that is stretchable, offers warmth without weight, and is also wrinkle resistant. Armed with a list of customer preferences, competing laboratories go to work to develop new products to meet these preferences. It is no wonder that several of them come up with the same answer at the same time.

Under the Textile Fibers Products Identification Act of 1960, consumer products that use textile fibers are required to carry labels indicating the country where the fiber was processed or manufactured and the generic names and percentages of each fiber that is used, assuming that it is more than 5 percent, in order, by weight. Brand names or trademarks may also be used on the label, but they are not required by law.

Fiber Distribution

Producers of manufactured fibers sell their fibers to fabric manufacturers in one of three ways:

1. As unbranded products, with no restrictions placed on their end use and no implied or required standards of performance claimed
2. As branded or trademarked fibers, with assurance to consumers that the quality of the fiber has been controlled by its producer, but not necessarily with assurance as to either implied or required standards of performance in the end product
3. Under a licensing agreement, whereby the use of the fiber trademark is permitted only to those manufacturers whose fabrics or other end products pass tests set up by the fiber producer for their specific end uses or applications

MERCHANDISING AND MARKETING

No matter how familiar producers and consumers may be with the qualities of each fiber, there is always the need to articulate/publicize information about the newest modifications and their application to fashion merchandise. To do this, producers of both natural and manufactured fibers make extensive use of advertising, publicity, and market research. They also extend various customer services to manufacturers, retailers, and consumers.

Usually a producer of manufactured fibers, such as DuPont or Monsanto, undertakes these activities on behalf of its own individual brands and companies. The American Fiber Manufacturers Association (AFMA), a domestic trade association whose members produce more than 90 percent of the total U.S. output of manufactured fibers, filaments, and yarns, also carries on a very active program of consumer education about manufactured fibers.[4]

NATURAL FIBER TRADE ASSOCIATIONS

fiber	organization
Cotton	Cotton Incorporated National Cotton Council, Supima
Linen	Masters of Linen (European)
Mohair	The Mohair Council of America
Silk	International Silk Association
Wool	America Wool Council, The Woolmark Company (Australian)

table 5.4

Source: Hemp Industries Association. Available at http://www.thehia.org/

DuPont uses advertising to promote their swimwear products that have Lycra.

So that they can better promote their new products (and themselves), the natural fiber industries also have organized trade associations that carry their message to the textile industry as well as to the customer.

Advertising and Publicity

As you might suspect, given their greater potential for competition, the manufactured fiber industries spend considerably more money on advertising than the natural fiber industries. They maintain a steady flow of advertising and publicity directed at both the trade and consumer markets. Sometimes an advertising campaign will promote an entire range of textile fibers; at other times, it will concentrate on only a single fiber. Fiber companies give most of their advertising dollars to support the manufacturers who use their fibers.

Some natural fiber groups are putting more effort and money into campaigns to combat the growing domination of manufactured fibers. Because these campaigns are mainly handled by trade associations, they promote the fiber itself, not the products of an individual natural fiber producer. One of the most eye-catching campaigns is that of Cotton Incorporated. The ads and posters not only emphasize cotton's advantages as a fiber but also point to the cotton industry's importance in the economy and to cotton's ecological appeal (see page 101).

Fiber sources also provide garment producers and retailers with various aids that facilitate mention of their fibers in consumer advertising, adding to the recognition already achieved by the fiber producer's name, trademark, slogan, or logo. For example, Woolmark encourages the use of its ball-of-yarn logo in producer and retailer advertising of all wool merchandise, as well as in displays.

Advertising undertaken by fiber producers in cooperation with fabric and garment manufacturers and retailers benefits the fiber industry in two ways. First, consumers begin to associate the fiber name with other names that are already familiar, such as the name of the fiber source or the name of the retail store selling the garment. This is particularly important in introducing a new manufactured fiber. Second, fabric and garment producers, as well as retailers, are encouraged to use and promote the fiber because the fiber producer's share of advertising costs subsidizes its local or national advertising.

Research and Development

Both natural fiber producers and manufactured fiber producers are constantly seeking ways to improve their products. Individual large manufactured fiber producers conduct research and development. The natural fiber producers, which tend to be small in size, often work through the trade group for a particular fiber.

Customer Services

All major producers of manufactured fibers and many smaller firms offer a number of services to direct and secondary users of their products. Producers of natural fibers, working through their associations, also offer many such services. These include the following:

- Technical advice as well as know-how on weaving and knitting techniques
- Assistance to textile and garment producers and retailers in locating supplies
- Fabric libraries that include information about sources, prices, and delivery schedules (research in a fabric library saves precious time spent shopping the market for trend information)
- Fashion presentations and exhibits for the textile industry, retailers, garment manufacturers, the fashion press, and—occasionally—the public
- Extensive literature for manufacturers, retailers, educators, and consumers about fiber properties, use, and care
- Fashion experts who address groups of manufacturers, retailers, or consumers, staging fashion shows and demonstrations
- Educational films and audiovisual aids for use by the trade, schools, and consumer groups

Trends in the Fiber Industry

The most dramatic trend in the fiber industry is the increasing use of blends of natural and manufactured fibers. This trend will be discussed in more detail in the next section of this chapter, as will the second most widespread trend, the use of microfibers.

The fiber industry is fighting hard to overcome a major problem: the onslaught/ rapid increase of imports into its domestic markets. Since manufactured fibers account for more than 85 percent of fiber usage annually in the United States, it is obvious that this will be a continuing and ongoing problem. The U.S. fiber industry will have to fight harder than ever for its share of the international—and even the domestic—market. Added to this challenge is consumers' interest in sustainable products.

Improvement in technology is also playing an important role in the fiber industries' abilities to service their customers more quickly and efficiently. In addition to facilitating communications, computers offer important linkages between the various industries and enable them to do such things as coordinate delivery schedules and provide bar coding.

To many observers, the manufactured fiber story is just beginning, and the upcoming years promise to be even more exciting than the previous ones. Despite the economic challenges the United States has faced in recent years, textile productivity has continued to improve as of 2010, and it appears as though there is a stronger industry on the horizon. According to *Textile World*, U.S. mills have shown few signs of cutting back on purchases of new plants and equipment, and there were less plant closings in recent years than there had been in the early part of the 21st century.[5]

THE TEXTILE FABRIC INDUSTRY

Midway between the fiber and the finished apparel, accessory, or home furnishing product is the fabric. **Textile fabric** is any material that is made by weaving, knitting, braiding, knotting, laminating, felting, or chemical bonding. It is the basic material from which most articles of apparel, accessories, and home fashions are made.

Americans use a lot of textile fabric. Each person consumes nearly eighty-six pounds of textile fabric annually. We use all types of fabrics for different purposes, including clothing, home furnishings, transportation, defense, recreation, healthcare, and space exploration.

The production of most fabrics begins with the creation of yarn from fibers. With the exception of felted fabric and a few other nonwoven fabrics, fibers cannot be made into fabrics without first spinning or twisting them into yarn. Yarns are then woven or knit into **greige** (pronounced "gray") **goods**, or unfinished fabrics. Greige goods are converted into finished fabrics for consumer or industrial use.

ORGANIZATION AND OPERATION

For decades, there was no pattern of organization in the textile fabric industry. Some textile fabric companies were large corporations employing thousands of people, but many remained small operations with only a few dozen employees.

Imports overpowered the U.S. textile industry in the late 1970s and 1980s. Currently, industry experts predict that the merger mania will continue and result in fewer but stronger companies. The pace of mergers and acquisitions continues to accelerate at a dizzying rate.

Because of the tremendous rise of textile imports, the U.S. textile industry was forced to close 40 mills in 2009. There were also more than 159,000 jobs lost between 2004 and 2009 in the textile industry alone.[6] However, as of 2010, U.S. textile mills started adding jobs and reopening plants.[7]

Because commitments to specific weaves, colors, and finishes must be made 6 to 18 months in advance, the textile fabric industry is extremely well informed about fashion and alert to new trends. Information about these trends comes from fashion designers, predictive services, fashion directors for fiber or yarn companies, and advance textile shows throughout the world. But because they are geared to mass-production methods, most mills were reluctant to produce short experimental runs for individual designers. This is changing as new technology is developed.

The market centers for textile fabrics are not at the mills but in the fashion capital of the country: New York City. There, on the doorstep of the garment industry, every mill of importance has a salesroom. A fabric buyer or designer for a garment maker, or a retail store apparel buyer or fashion coordinator, has only to walk a block or two to obtain firsthand information on what the fabric market offers.

MERCHANDISING AND MARKETING

Many designers let the fabric act as the creative impetus for their designs. Good designers respond to new fabrics and search for that special fabric that will drape in the way they want or has just the color or texture they need. It is the job of the fabric industry to introduce designers to the particular fabric needed.

The textile industry works several seasons ahead. Fiber producers usually work two years ahead of a season. They must present their products this early to textile mills and converters so they will have enough lead time to plan their color and fabric lines. The fabric market presents its products a year ahead of a season. Their first presentation is to the manufacturers of apparel and accessories, after which they present their finished products to retail stores and the press—all ahead of season—so they can publicize upcoming trends.

Since the textile industry must work several seasons ahead of consumer demand, it must also take the lead in recognizing new fashion directions.

The Industry's Fashion Experts

To guide them in future planning, textile firms employ staffs of fashion experts. These experts work with textile designers to create fabrics in the weights, textures, colors, and patterns they anticipate consumers will want. Because most of the early decisions in both the fiber and the fabric market are based on color, the industry's fashion experts also work closely with specialized associations within the fashion industry that provide advanced research and trend information.

Most prominent among these groups are the ones that work exclusively with color, such as the Color Association of the United States, the International Color Authority (ICA), the Color Box, and Pantone. One of Pantone's partnerships includes Clariant International, one of the largest colorant and chemical companies in the world.

Australian wool on display at the Pitti Filati textile show in Florence, Italy.

The Pantone Fashion and Home Color System uses SMART colors, which are more environmentally friendly and help to shorten the color development timeline.

Color forecasting services provide their clients with reports and newsletters, color swatches, palette predictions, and color-matching services—all geared to each of the apparel markets (men's, women's, and children's).

In addition to making decisions about color, the fabric industry must also consider fabrication and texture. If the trend is toward structured clothing, firm fabrication will be necessary, but when a soft, layered look is in, fabrication can be lightweight and soft. Since trends must be spotted so far in the future, the fashion experts play an important role as they work with fiber and fabric mills as well as designers and buyers.

Textile Trade Shows and Fairs

New trends are also introduced at trade shows and fairs held throughout the world. Usually semiannual events, these shows are attended by designers, manufacturers, and retailers. Here are some of the important textile shows:

- China (Guangzhou) International Trade Fair for Home Textiles
- China International Trade Fair for Apparel Fabrics and Accessories
- Ideacomo (Ideas from Como), Como, Italy
- Interstoff Textile Fair, Asia
- Los Angeles International Textile Show
- Pitti Filati (Pitti Yarns), Florence, Italy
- Premiere Vision (First Look), Paris, France

- SpinExpo, New York City
- Techtextil India

The failure to identify and act on a trend seen at a major textile show, for example, would mean that retailers and apparel manufacturers would be unable to supply the fashions that consumers want.

Tables strewn with samples at the Los Angeles International Textile Show.

Advertising and Publicity

Unlike fiber producers, fabric manufacturers rarely advertise these days. But when they do, their advertising usually features the brand names of their products and frequently the names of specific apparel manufacturers that use their goods. Either with the cooperation of fiber sources or on their own, these fabric houses run advertisements in a wide variety of mass-circulation magazines and newspapers and share the cost of brand advertising run by retail stores. Their advertising generally makes consumers aware of new apparel styles, the fabrics of which they are made, and often the names of retail stores where they may be purchased.

Research and Development

Fabric producers, like fiber producers, now devote attention to exploring the market potential of their products and anticipating the needs of their customers. Success in the fashion industry depends on supplying customers with what they want. Swift changes are the rule in fashion. Anticipation of such changes requires close attention to the market and a scientific study of trends. Market research is used to identify changing lifestyles as well as geographic demands.

Many of the large fabric producers maintain product- and market-research divisions. Their experts work closely with both the trade and consumer markets in studying fabric performance characteristics. Many fabric producers provide garment manufacturers with sample runs of new fabrics for experimental purposes. The market researchers conduct consumer studies relating to the demand for or acceptance of finishes, blends, and other desired characteristics. Such studies also help fabric and garment producers to determine what consumers will want in the future, where and when they will want it, and in what quantities.

The Green Scene

The public is being asked to recycle waste, fly less frequently, and drive smaller cars. Being eco-friendly in the production of fibers and fabrics is at the forefront of customers' concerns, and textile manufacturers are responding to this need. They are collecting plastic bottles, used clothing, and cotton and wool scraps, then turning them into first-quality fleece fabrics. For example, the company Hagger Clothing Co., one of the most recognized brands in men's apparel, has partnered with Unifi, Inc., a global leader in sustainable textiles solutions, to create a line of sustainable men's pants featuring Repreve recycled fiber. Unifi's Repreve is a family of recycled fibers made from 100 percent recycled materials. According to Unifi, Inc., "on average a pair of Haggar pants that contains Repreve saves ten 16 oz. plastic bottles from becoming landfill."[8]

There are a variety of companies that are taking on a greater interest in sustainability with recycling programs and policies. One example is Patagonia, which launched its Common Threads Garment Recycling program in 2005. Five years later in 2010, they were able to take back and recycle 62 percent of their entire Fall 2010 line.[9]

Other well-known companies that offer recycling programs include DuPont; Foss Manufacturing Company, Inc.; Polartec; Toray Industries, Inc.; and the Carpet America Recovery Effort (CARE).

There is also a crop of textiles with exceptional properties. Working hand-in-hand with Mother Nature, mills are developing some of the most comfortable, sanitary performance products, using hemp, soy, and bamboo, which are good for moisture absorption and have antibacterial properties. While the original materials are considered more eco-friendly, it is important to note that some manufacturing processes may not be. The overall process and chemicals that are used must be evaluated to determine if the finished product really is "green."

Customer Services

Today's well-integrated and diversified fabric companies speak with great fashion authority. They also employ merchandising and marketing staffs whose expertise in fashion trends is available to apparel manufacturers, retailers, the fashion press, and frequently to consumers. Fashion staffs attend fashion forecasts. They conduct in-store sales training programs, address consumer groups, and stage fashion shows for the trade and press. They help retail stores arrange fashion shows and storewide promotions featuring their products, and they assist buyers in locating merchandise made from their fabrics.

TRENDS IN THE TEXTILE FABRIC INDUSTRY

A dramatic change in the mind-set of the textile producers and marketing managers has broadened the product mix, quickened the response time required to meet customer demand, and made possible shorter runs of more innovative and fashionable fabrics. Currently, retailers, apparel manufacturers, and the fiber and fabric industries are working together to explore new and innovative ways to move textile products through the pipeline to the ultimate consumer more quickly and efficiently.

Fortunately, the consumption rate of textiles increases every year. Economists forecast that this trend will continue. The role of the textile fiber and fabric industries in the global economy has been an important one. Some of the major trends that affect both the fiber and fabric industries are the following:

- Innovations in high-tech fabrics
- Growing global competition
- Increased exports
- Greater diversification of products
- Increased government regulations
- New technology and equipment

Recycled polyester and Lycra spandex make up this beautiful white parka by Lundström.

Production of High-Tech Fabrics

We live in a high-tech age, when almost every new product is a result of combined effort and sophistication in research and development. Fabric is no exception, as evidenced by the frequent introduction of new textiles endowed with some novel and valuable property, characteristic, or performance.

A fabric that has been constructed, finished, or processed in a way that gives it certain innovative, unusual, or hard-to-achieve qualities not normally available can be described as **high-tech fabric**.

Protective Uses of High-Tech Fabrics

Many common fabrics have been transformed into high-tech fabrics by coating or laminating them or by making them with innovative yarns such as Kevlar, Nomex, Spectra, and so on. These fabrics are engineered to be capable of **wicking** or transporting moisture; have resistance to radiation, corrosive chemicals, and other stresses; and adjust to extreme weather changes.

A bright future is ahead for these specialized fabrics in a variety of situations, as follows:

- Activewear—Apparel for jogging, golfing, cycling, skating, sailing
- Rainwear—Raincoats, capes, hats

From left to right: The Mac
was created using 18 trench
this garment was created us
copies of the *Financial Time*
Green Shows were sponsore
natural beauty company We
and its Skin Food lotion was
honored in this creation.

RECYCLED FASHION

From Discarded to Divine

FASHION DESIGNERS ARE VERY IMAGINATIVE PEOPLE, MERGING THE WORLDS OF FANTASY AND REALITY. More designers are utilizing unusual materials for their creations, and the famous are wearing them. Some materials include paper products like newspaper, toilet tissue, currency, human hair, cans, and plastic bags—and let's not forget Lady Gaga's meat outfit that she wore to the MTV Music Awards in 2010.

However, the most exciting part of the sustainable and eco-friendly movement in fashion is people's perception of secondhand clothing. Starting in 2008 fashion designers began recasting used apparel and fabric into chic cocktail dresses, evening gowns, and tuxedos.

At the 2010 NY Fashion Week the Green Shows showcased models strutting down the runway wearing the best in sustainable, recycled, and awesome attire. Gary Harvey, who was previously creative director of Levi Strauss and Docker Europe, opened the show with his recycled couture. There were newspapers, laundry bags, old sweatshirts, and baseball jackets repurposed into eighteen dresses. Harvey believes, "Too many garments end up in landfill sites. They are deemed aesthetically redundant and get discarded at the end of the season when there are often years of wear left."

Coat made from vintage
duffel bags and army
tents by Greg Lauren

- All-weather wear—Apparel for hunting, fishing, skiing, mountaineering, and so forth
- Swimwear—Bathing suits, bodysuits for diving, life vests
- Protective clothing—Garments to protect the wearer from hazardous waste; medical contamination; bullets or shrapnel; radiation; cutting or abrasion; electronic, computer, and pharmaceutical manufacture
- Heat and fire protection clothing—Occupational clothing for firefighters, blast furnace workers, car racers, tank crews
- Chemical protection clothing—Occupational clothing for chemical workers, workers at toxic waste sites and spills

An outstanding example is a knit fabric blending Hydrofil, polyester, and Lycra spandex that moves moisture away from the body. It is used in cross-country ski tights, sports tops, cycling jerseys, jackets, face masks, and gloves. High-tech fabrics can help to keep an athlete's or worker's mind and body more comfortable, thus allowing the person to improve his or her performance or make that extra effort.

Other high-tech fabrics are seen in home furnishings. For example, KromaLon, an olefin fiber, is used to make carpets that are antimicrobial as well as stain and bleach resistant.

A see-through raincoat protects much, but conceals little on the runway for designer Sonia Rykiel.

Use of High-Tech Fabrics and Materials in Apparel

Designers at all price points are incorporating a range of materials besides natural fibers—metallic threads, plastic, vinyl, rubber, and reflective material. In one of his early collections, Alexander McQueen attracted a lot of attention when he cut out pieces of lace, backed them with latex, and splattered them on nude chiffon. The late Gianni Versace used clear vinyl extensively, as well as a chain-mail fabric that drapes easily. Helmut Lang adopted the reflecting strips commonly found on backpacks, running shoes, and firefighters' uniforms for reflective jeans. Fredric Molenac, designing for the Madame Gres collection, used Lycra with neoprene, a rubberlike fabric. And the list goes on. As the expanding field of textiles grows, more designers are finding inspiration and aesthetic value in high-tech fabrics and all kinds of materials.

Growing Global Competition

The major concern of the U.S. textile industry is the competition of global markets. Although the domestic fiber and fabric industries produce a large amount of goods, the United States still imports vast quantities of fiber, yarn, and fabric from around the world. Industry experts estimate that Central America's apparel and textile industry could attract significant apparel investment by 2015, and European brands may shift activities to offset the "deepening sourcing woes in Asia." While Asia, and particularly China, has received large orders from U.S. and European brands for years, some of those contracts are now expected to go to Central America as China's domestic clothing

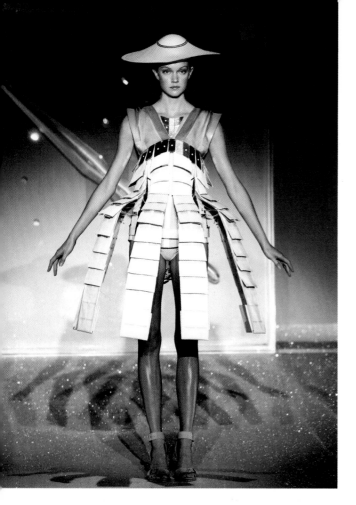

Hussein Chalayan is a designer at the forefront of the high-tech fabric movement, using microchip technology.

demand soars and labor costs are on the rise.[10] Another increase is expected to be seen in the Indian textile and apparel industry. It is estimated that this market will grow as much as three times by the year 2020, from $70 billion to $220 billion, according to a report by consultants KSA Technopak.[11]

Increased Exports

Apparel import trade to the United States from regions including Guatemala, El Salvador, Honduras, Nicaragua, Costa Rica, and the Dominican Republic has not only become a vibrant sourcing platform but it also serves as a major export market for U.S.-made fabrics and yarns. Textile exports rose 21 percent in 2010 to $2.49 billion, according to the National Council of Textile Organizations.[12] India's exports reported a 20 percent growth in export orders in 2010, and its share of world trade has the potential to almost double, from 4.5 percent to 8 percent by 2020.[13]

With these shifts in the global market, the textile industry continues to focus on a number of corporate strategies, as follows:

- Increasing the focus on foreign markets and operations for apparel fabrics, since most studies indicate that the major growth in apparel markets will be outside the United States
- Developing overseas manufacturing operations, or exploring licensing in conjunction with foreign mills, to attain a stronger foothold on the international scene
- Devoting increased resources to market research
- Continuing technological advances

The United States is the third-largest exporter of textile products in the world. Nearly two-thirds of U.S. textile exports during 2009 went to developing countries.[14] The industry is focusing more of its manufacturing and marketing activities abroad on fabrics for home furnishings, offices, hotels, military, and industrial end uses.

Greater Diversification of Products

The textile industry produces a more diversified range of fibers and fabrics than ever before. The specialization that once divided the industry into separate segments, each producing fabrics from a single type of fiber, has all but faded. To meet the needs of consumers, it is often necessary to blend two or more fibers into a yarn or to combine yarns of two fibers. Mills are learning to adjust their operations to any new fiber or combination of fibers.

Another bright spot for the domestic textile market is **geotextiles**, or manufactured permeable textiles that are currently used in reinforcing or stabilizing civil engineering projects. Two examples of industrial fabrics are Kevlar and Tyvek, which are used for diverse applications such as book covers and wrapping houses to prevent moisture penetration.

An example of an industrial protective coating is Teflon—yes, the coating used on nonstick frying pans—which is now being used to protect delicate fabrics. With fashion designers searching for new fabrics every day, can apparel applications for industrial and geotextiles be far behind?

Increased Government Regulation

One of the biggest impacts on the textile industry over the years has been the intervention of the federal government in every aspect of the industry: health and safety, noise levels and chemical pollution, consumer product liability, environmental impact, and hiring practices.

Until recently, federal regulation of the textile industry was mainly concerned with the fiber content labeling of fabrics and products made of those fabrics. The law requires that most textile and wool products have a label listing the fiber content, the country of origin, and the identity of the manufacturer or business responsible for marketing or handling the item. In 1953, the Flammable Fabrics Act was passed, but it served to ban from the market only a few very ignitable fabrics and apparel made from them. The increasing strength and direction of the consumerism movement, however, resulted in more government regulation of the textile industry on both the federal and state levels.

In July 1972, two important changes in federal textile regulations took effect: the Federal Trade Commission's (FTC) rule on Care Labeling of Textile Wearing Apparel and the revision of the Flammable Fabrics Act. The FTC's care-labeling rule requires that all fabrics—piece goods as well as apparel and accessories made of fabric—be labeled to show the type of care they require. They indicate whether the fabric can be hand washed or machine washed or should be dry-cleaned. The symbols also indicate whether ironing is required, and if so, at what temperature. The manufacturer must sew a permanent label with these care symbols into each garment.

According to the Bureau of Consumer Protection, "recyclable" claims on labels and advertisements mean that the products can be collected, separated, or recovered—or reused in the manufacture or assembly of another product through an established recycling program.[15]

New Technology in Equipment

"New technology is totally revolutionizing the textile industry," says Jack Lenor Larsen, an eminent textiles designer in the home furnishings industry. The trend toward increased mechanization and automation is clearly apparent throughout the industry as it has changed from one that is labor intensive to one that is equipment intensive.

Over the years the textile industry has experienced a number of technological developments; for example, the shuttleless loom and computer design of fabrics. In the mills, new machines combine higher production speeds with lower energy consumption. Automated weaving and knitting machines produce more with fewer operators.

The industry is also experimenting with new printing techniques. Digital printing on fabrics has yet to outstrip screen printing, but it is catching up fast with a push of innovative applications.[16] Rotary-screen printing is truly the technology of the 21st century and will replace flat-screen and roller printing techniques. Powerful computers will enable the industry to set the cost and price of fabrics before they are knitted or woven. Industry leaders need to be competitive in the global textile market.

Computer technology is playing a key role in Quick Response programs that improve communications among fiber, fabric, apparel, and retail businesses. Quick response shortens the time between the placement of orders by retailers and the delivery of goods. Bar codes have been established by the Fabric and Supplier Linkage Council so that vendors can label shipments with standard bar codes that purchasers can enter immediately into inventory records. This reduces inventory costs, warehouse time, forced markdowns, and stock outs.

Although new technology has potential for creating job losses, it will ultimately help the industry by attracting bright, ambitious young workers and leaders who want to work in a progressive environment.

U.S. textile plants are characterized by computer-run looms that feed a mile of yarn per minute, as well as completely automated yarn spinning plants that can run 24 hours a day, 7 days a week. Technological advances have long been introduced at the Bobbin Show, a three-day event held annually in the United States. Other major shows that focus on these areas are the International Machinery Show in Germany and the Japanese International Apparel Machinery Show.

SUMMARY AND REVIEW

Textiles begin with fibers, which may be natural (cotton, wool, flax, and silk) or manufactured. Manufactured fibers are either cellulosic (made of cellulose, which is also the substance of natural plant fibers) or noncellulosic (combining chemicals in a laboratory). Variants of generic manufactured fibers bear the trade name of the manufacturer. For example, Dacron is DuPont's brand of polyester.

The main market for fibers is the textile fabric industry, which weaves, knits, or otherwise turns fibers into greige goods. These goods are then finished by either the textile mill or converters who add treatments such as dye, waterproofing, and fire-retarding and permanent-press finishes. Finishes added to natural fibers allow them to compete more effectively with manufactured fibers by taking on some of the properties that consumers demand in apparel and other textile products.

Textiles are sold primarily to manufacturers of apparel and home fashions, but marketing of fibers and textiles is directed at retailers and consumers, too, to build demand. U.S. textile manufacturers compete with foreign imports through technological advances that speed production, minimize pollution, and improve the performance of fabrics in terms of colorfastness, insulation, and other desirable features. Computerized systems expedite order fulfillment.

FOR REVIEW

1. What is the difference between a natural and a manufactured fiber? Give five examples of each and indicate the source of each natural fiber you name.

2. What has the natural fiber industry done to counteract the effects of manufactured fibers in the marketplace?

3. Trace the steps through which a new or newly modified manufactured fiber passes as it goes from conception to general availability.

4. Name and explain the three ways in which producers of manufactured fibers usually sell their products to fabric manufacturers.

5. Describe the three major merchandising and marketing activities of natural and manufactured fiber producers.

6. Describe the major steps in the production of most fabrics.

7. What is the function of the textile converter? What are the advantages of dealing with a converter for a fabric mill and an apparel producer?

8. How do textile fabric producers keep informed about new fashion trends?

9. How have increased fiber, yarn, and fabric imports affected the U.S. textile industry?

10. What are the provisions of the Flammable Fabrics Act of 1953 and the FTC's rule on Care Labeling of Textile Wearing Apparel of 1972?

FOR DISCUSSION

1. What is the role of trade associations in the marketing of fibers and textile fabrics?

2. When a major designer designed his collection for a mass merchandiser, he went directly to the textile mills with specifications for his fabrics in regard to width, pattern repeats, and so on. Can most designers do this? Why or why not?

3. Discuss the relationship of the designer and the manufacturer of fashion merchandise to the textile industry.

TRADE TALK

Define or briefly explain the following terms:

brand names

fabrics

fiber

generic names

geotextiles

greige goods

high-tech fabric

manufactured fibers

microfiber

primary supplier

spinnerette

textile fabric

trimmings

wicking

yarn

LEATHER AND FUR

- The three major types of companies in the leather industry and their functions
- The nine different categories of leather and the special finishes used on leather
- The history and development of the fur industry in the United States
- The functions of the three major groups in the fur industry
- The steps in transforming fur pelts into finished garments

The most glamorous and sought-after textiles—leather and fur—are also the two oldest. Prehistoric people discovered that the animals they killed for food could serve another purpose, that of providing them with warmth and protection from the elements. Today, leather and fur are vital to the apparel, home furnishings, and automotive industries, contributing the raw materials for coats and jackets, handbags, shoes, gloves, and an ever-widening range of fashion products.

The leather jacket, de- and re-constructed by Roberto Cavalli.

The leather industry is currently expanding its markets in ways that no one even dreamed of ten years ago. New processing methods have created leathers so thin and supple that designers can use them for everything from bikinis to shirts to evening wear—all available in an incredible array of colors.

After several years of decline because of environmental concerns over the use of scarce or rare animal skins, furs are making a comeback, especially with the young, first-time customer. The demand for furs has never been greater, at the very time when the fur industry is experimenting with new colors and styles.

THE LEATHER INDUSTRY

Leather-making is a highly specialized and time-consuming operation. Because of the time involved, the leather industry must anticipate and predict trends far in advance of other textile suppliers. Leather producers typically decide what production method, textures, finishes, and colors they will use 8 to 16 months before a leather will reach apparel and accessory manufacturers. As a result, those in other fashion industries often look to the leather industry for leadership, particularly in terms of color and texture.

Because leather is a by-product of the meatpacking industry, it is not as much of a target of animal rights activists as is the fur industry. Few animals are raised specifically for their hides. Most animals are raised to feed people, and their skins and hides, which have no food value, are then sold to the leather trade.

Categories of Leather

Almost all leather comes from cattle. But the hides and skins of many other animals from all parts of the world are also used in fashion apparel and accessories. There are nine major categories of leather, and they are listed in Table 6.1 on page 127.

The Equine Group

Horses provide a rugged leather. Some horsehide is tanned into cordovan leather, which makes extremely durable and sturdy shoe uppers. The hide is also used for leather jackets. But it is important to know that most of what is called "pony skin" is really stenciled calfskin, which is used because it is more pliable than real pony skin. Real top-quality pony skin comes from wild horses in Poland and Russia.[1]

NINE MAJOR CATEGORIES OF LEATHER

cattle group	sheep and lamb group
Steer, cow, and bull hides, producing leather for: • Shoe and slipper outsoles, insoles, uppers, linings, counters, welts, heels, etc. • Traveling bags, suitcases, briefcases, luggage straps, etc. • Gloves and garments • Upholstery for automobiles, furniture, airplanes, buses, decoration • Handbags, purses, wallets, waist belts, other personal leather goods • Harnesses, saddles, bridles, skirting (for saddles), etc. • Machinery belting, packings, washers, aprons, carders, combers, pickers, etc. • Footballs, basketballs, volleyballs, and other sporting goods • Laces, scabbards, holsters, etc.	Wooled skins, hair skins (cabrettas), shearlings, producing leather for: • Shoe and slipper uppers and linings • Gloves and garments • Chamois • Handbags and other personal leather goods • Moutons and shearlings (skins with wool on) • Parchment • Textile rollers • Hats, hat sweat bands, millinery, and caps • Bookbindings • Piano actions • Sporting goods (balls, gloves, etc.)

	pig and hog group
Kips or kipskins (from large calves or undersized cattle), producing leather for: • Shoe and slipper uppers and linings • Handbags and other personal leather goods • Gloves and garments • Sweat bands for hats • Rawhide and parchment • Athletic helmets • Bookbindings • Handicrafts, etc.	Pig, hog, boar, peccary, carpincho (a Brazilian rodent) skins, producing leather for: • Gloves • Innersoles, contours, etc. • Fancy leather goods, luggage • Saddlery and harnesses • Shoe uppers • Upholstery

equine group	buffalo group
Horse, colt, ass, mule, and zebra hides, producing leather for: • Shoe soles and uppers • Luggage • Gloves and garments • Belts • Aviator's clothing • Sporting goods (baseball covers and mitts, etc.)	Domesticated land and water buffalo (not American bison, whose hide is not tanned for leather), producing leather for: • Shoe soles and uppers • Handbags • Fancy leather goods, luggage • Buffing wheels

deer group	goat and kid group
Fallow deer, reindeer, elk, and caribou skins, producing leather for: • Shoe uppers • Gloves • Clothing • Piano actions • Moccasins • Mukluks • Fancy leather goods	Skins producing leather for: • Shoe and fancy uppers, linings • Gloves and garments • Fancy leather goods, handbags • Bookbindings

kangaroo and wallaby group	exotic leathers
Skins producing very strong leather for: • Shoe uppers, including track and basketball shoes	Hides from: • Aquatic group—frog, seal, shark, walrus, and turtle • Land group—camel, elephant, ostrich, and pangolin • Reptile group—alligator, crocodile, lizard, and snake

table 6.1

Source: Leather Industries of America, *Dictionary of Leather Terminology*, 8th ed. (Washington, D.C.: Leather Industries of America).

Ralph Lauren
Fall 2011

Prada
Fall 2011

Valentino
Fall 2011

Gucci
Fall 2010

Luxurious
LEATHER

**LONG BEFORE WE LEARNED TO WEAVE FABRICS, MANKIND WAS PROB-
ABLY WEARING AND USING ANIMAL SKINS FOR UNTOLD GENERATIONS.**
Over this time, leather evolved from a practicality to a luxury material. But
that cycle may be starting over.

According to well-known and respected specialists, leather is known as "one of the most fascinating natural products." Most everyone likes the luxurious look, feel, and smell of leather—it appeals to multiple senses: sight, touch, and smell!

Leather's performance qualities are unparalleled. It is good to wear next to skin—it is breathable and transmits humidity. A leather garment can absorb perspiration off skin, which then evaporates off the surface of the leather. This is why leather is such a desirable material for shoes.

There are obviously pros and cons to genuine leather as a fabric, but the alternatives are equally controversial. Leather alternatives are often made from vinyl and polyurethane, easy to work with but not eco-friendly. However, leather and suede alternatives also provide "animal-friendly" options for vegetarians,

vegans, and others who may object to leather on philosophical or ethical grounds.

The future of leather and leather alternatives is bright as far as consumer demand is concerned. However, because of growing population in the coming decades, there will be less farmland available to feed people, much less animals. The proportion of cattle to people will decrease as we run out of land to graze them. Since the leather industry is a by-product of the meat industry, the proportion of available leather will shift away from cowhide to smaller animals like sheep, pigs, and goats.

Whether natural or synthetic, it's unlikely that future consumers will end their timeless love affair with luxurious leather. But shorter supplies may mean that for many people, this ancient and well-loved material will become a true luxury once more.

The Exotic Leathers

Supplies of the so-called "exotic leathers" are diminishing worldwide, driving prices up sharply. There is some good news, however. From 1967 to 1987, the American alligator was listed as an endangered species. The alligator is now out of danger because of a policy called **sustainable use**. This refers to an environmental program that encourages landowners to preserve alligator eggs and habitats in return for the right to use a percentage of the grown animals. Louisiana leads the United States in the production of alligator skins. After rebuilding the population through research, management, and law enforcement, the wild harvest from 1972 through 2008 has produced over 800,000 wild skins with an estimated value of $212 million. The farm/ranch harvest from 1972 through 2007 produced 3.5 million skins with an estimated value of $299 million.[2] The United States is the only source of raw alligator hides, and half of all alligator tanneries are owned by major fashion houses in the United States or Europe. The main competitor of alligator hides are crocodile hides. To unfamiliar consumers, these two are almost identical. In more high-end stores, customers mistakenly identify alligator products as crocodile products.[3]

Leather Processing

Animal pelts are divided into three classes, each based on weight. Those that weigh 15 pounds or less when shipped to the tannery are called **skins**. This class consists mostly of calves, goats, pigs, sheep, and deer. Those weighing from 15 to 25 pounds, mostly from young horses and cattle, are referred to as **kips**. Those weighing more than 25 pounds, primarily cattle, oxen, buffalo, and horse skins, are called **hides**.

The process of transforming animal pelts into leather is known as **tanning**. The word is derived from a Latin word for oak bark, which was used in early treatments of animal skins. Tanning is the oldest known craft.

Three to six months are needed to tan hides for sole leather and saddlery. Less time is required for tanning kips and skins, but the processes are more numerous and require more expensive equipment and highly trained labor. The tanning process involves minerals, vegetable materials, oils, and chemicals, used alone or in combination. The choice of a tanning agent depends on the end use for which the leather is being prepared.

Tanning Methods

Mineral tanning uses chrome salts. Chrome tanning is now used to process nearly two-thirds of all leather produced in the United States. This is a fast method that takes hours rather than weeks. It produces leather for shoe uppers, garments, gloves, handbags, and other products. Chrome-tanned leather can be identified by the pale, blue-gray color in the center of the cut edge. Vegetable tanning uses the tannic acids that naturally occur in the bark, wood, or nuts of various trees and shrubs and in tea leaves. Vegetable tanning is used on cow, steer, horse, and buffalo hides. Vegetable-tanned leather can be identified by a dark center streak in the cut edge. Because it is so labor intensive, relatively little vegetable tanning is done in the United States.

Processing with oil is one of the oldest methods of turning raw animal skins into leather. A fish oil—usually that of codfish—is used. Oil tanning is used to produce chamois, doeskin, and buckskin—relatively soft and pliable leathers used in making gloves and jackets. The most widely used and quickest method of tanning relies primarily on the chemical formaldehyde. Because the processing turns the leather white, it can be easily dyed. Formaldehyde-tanned leather is washable. It is often used for gloves and children's shoe uppers. It is possible to combine tanning agents. A vegetable and mineral combination is used to "retan" work shoes and boots. Combinations of alum and formaldehyde or oil and chrome are common.

Finishing

The finishing process gives leather the desired thickness, moisture, color, and aesthetic appeal. Leather can now be dyed in nearly 500 different colors. Dyed leather is also sometimes finished with oils and fats to ensure softness, strength, or waterproofing. Special color effects include sponging, stenciling, spraying, or tie-dyeing. Other finishes include matte, luster or pearl, suede, patent, or metallic. It is important to note that suede is a finish, not a kind of leather.

MERCHANDISING AND MARKETING

Because of the lead-time needed to produce leather, the leather industry must stay abreast of fashion, and be several steps ahead of it. Months before other fashion industries commit themselves to colors and textures, leather producers have already made their decisions. They have started the search for the right dyes and treatments to meet expected future demand. As a result, the leather industry's forecasters are considered the best and most experienced in the fashion industry.

Fashion Information Services

Because they make their assessments of fashion trends so far in advance, others in the industry look to the leather industry for information. Like other fashion industries, the leather industry retains experts to disseminate information about trends and new products. They often produce booklets that forecast trends, describe new colors and textures, and generally promote the leather industry. Samples of important textures and looks are included.

Fashion experts also work directly with retailers, manufacturers, and the press to help crystallize their thinking about leather products. One-on-one meetings, seminars, and fashion presentations are used to educate the fashion industry and consumers about leather.

Despite all this activity, individual tanners are not known by name to the public. Nor is a fashion editor, in describing a leather garment, likely to mention its manufacturer. Leather producers are not named in retail stores or in leather manufacturers' advertising. Consumers who can name several fabric and fiber producers would have a difficult time naming any leather tanners.

Trade Associations and Trade Shows

For more than 80 years, Leather Industries of America (LIA) has served its members by providing environmental, technical, educational, statistical, and marketing services—all at the direction of its membership and to the benefit of the leather industry. Leather membership is available to any U.S. business involved in the tanning, finishing, manufacturing, or selling of leather. General membership is available to foreign companies and those with an interest in the industry, including hide brokers, consultants, chemical suppliers, and equipment and leather product manufacturers. The Leather Industries of America provides the following:

- Government Representation: Leather Industries of America's legal team works for congressional and regulatory action, which promotes the acceleration of leather exports and the elimination of protectionist trade restrictions.
- Environmental Regulation: For more than two decades, it has been involved in the development and communication of fair and sensible environmental regulations affecting the tanning industry.
- Leather Research Laboratory: It provides valuable technical and consulting services through the state-of-the-art Leather Research Laboratory at the University of Cincinnati.[4]

Trade shows are another important source of information within the leather industry. Two years before the ultimate consumer sees finished leather products in retail stores, the leathers are introduced in several industry trade shows.

The Asia Pacific Leather Fair (APLF) (formerly known as the Hong Kong Leather Fair) began 26 years ago. Over the years APLF has expanded its scope and currently organizes six premium events in Hong Kong, China, and India, covering a wide range of industry sectors.[5] There is also the Shoes and Leather Guangzhou, which is held in China in June, and the India International Leather Fair (IILF) held in February.

LINEAPPELLE, started in 1981, is the most important international exhibition dedicated to leather, accessories, components, synthetics, and models for footwear, leather goods, garments, and furniture. The exhibition is reserved exclusively for the operators of the leather sector and is held in April for Spring/Summer and in October for Fall/Winter.[6]

Research and Development

The leather industry retains and expands its markets by adapting its products to fashion's changing requirements. Before World War II, relatively few colors and types of leather were available in any one season, and each usually had a fashion life of several years. A major tannery today may turn out hundreds of leather colors and types each season, meanwhile preparing to produce more new colors and textures for the next season.

TRENDS IN THE LEATHER INDUSTRY

Until just a few decades ago, the leather industry concerned itself primarily with meeting consumer needs in relatively few fashion areas—mainly shoes, gloves, belts,

handbags, luggage, and small leather goods. The use of leather for apparel was restricted largely to a few items of outerwear, such as jackets and coats. These were stiff, bulky, and primarily functional in appeal. Now designers offer colorful, supple leather vests, jeans, pants, blazers, anoraks, skirts, and suits of every description, in addition to jackets and coats.

But the leather industry has changed. These changes are the result of three trends: enlarging market opportunities, increased competition from synthetics, and increased foreign trade.

Enlarging Markets

Improved methods of tanning are turning out better, more versatile leathers with improved fashion characteristics. In general, these improvements fall into three categories.

1. The new leathers are softer and more pliable. Tanners' abilities to split full-grain leather thinner and thinner create this new suppleness.
2. The new leathers can be dyed more successfully in a greater number of fashion colors.
3. Washable leather finishes and improved cleaning techniques have made it easier for consumers to care for leather garments.

Prada and Gucci are two upscale fashion companies built on leather. They continue to expand their offerings season after season. Other designers working with leather include Vakko, Donna Karan, Ralph Lauren, Escada, Michael Kors, and Calvin Klein.

Increased Competition from Synthetics

In the past few decades, the leather market has been eroded by synthetics. Leather heel lifts, which used to be commonplace, are now more often than not replaced with plastic. Synthetics that look and feel like leather but are less susceptible to scratches and easier to maintain are used to make handbags and other small leather goods.

Because most synthetic leather products were not as attractive as leather, synthetics did not offer leather any real competition for a long time. However, imitation leathers and suedes that were true substitutes began to be marketed. The most important one, Ultrasuede, quickly became a fashion classic. Although a washable synthetic, Ultrasuede does not look fake or cheap, and it is used by high-fashion designers. Another artificial suede called Facile has improved suppleness. It is also widely used by high-fashion designers. Vinyl is widely used for shoes, handbags, and other accessories, and its appearance has improved over the years.

Industry Growth Factors

Several factors point to overall industry growth. Foremost among these is the trend toward a classic and elegant fashion look with an emphasis on quality. When quality is desired, consumers want real leather with all its mystique and will not settle for substitutes. Another hopeful sign is the fact that the supply of raw hides is large enough to allow for growth in production. Actively supported by a federal export program, the industry's aggressive efforts to develop foreign markets ensures future growth for the industry, as does the industry's expanded research programs.

THE FUR INDUSTRY

Long before prehistoric people learned how to plant crops, weave cloth, or build shelters, they figured out how to use fur. They spread it on the floor and used it as rugs. They used it to cover and create walls, thus bringing some warmth into otherwise cold and drafty caves.

By the Middle Ages, the wearing of fur announced one's wealth and status. Sable, marten, ermine, and fox were the favored furs of nobility. Italian cardinals wore ermine as a symbol of purity; English nobles wore it as a sign of power. Fur was also a valued commodity, something that was used in trading. For centuries in Northern Europe, furs were valued more than gold and silver. Fur was still as good as gold in 1900, when Chile banked chinchilla skins as security for a loan.

Fur accents enhance the drama at John Galliano's Fall/Winter 2010 show for Dior.

FUR
Makes a Comeback

THERE MAY BE NO ITEM OF CLOTHING QUITE AS CONTROVERSIAL AS FUR, AND, YET, FUR IS EVERYWHERE—in ways that designers hope will take some of the edge away from its usual critics.

The comeback of fur has less to do with newly humane treatment than with the return of luxury to the fashion industry. "There is a comeback of fur as there is an acceptance of luxury again," says Gilles Mendel of J. Mendel. "After the difficult years in retail, in the economy, and in the world of fashion, now people want to think about luxury that is precious and offers longevity."

Today, fashion is aiming for a balance, positioning fur as a versatile item that will outlast a fancy handbag or sequined top while playing up softness and warmth.

"The beauty about fur—fake or real—is that it can glam up everything. If you have a little cardigan that's sitting in your closet, a little fur trim can make it special," says *Marie Claire* fashion director, Nina Garcia.

The use of faux fur could fuel the market for real fur, even inadvertently. If people see it, they want it and that increases demand; then more people will want it and it becomes a trend. Any time fur is available, no matter what the source, demand will increase.

This go-around of fur started in street fashion, not in couture boutiques, says famous footwear designer Stuart Weitzman, whose fur-inspired boots have been his best sellers.

Animal fur has a very practical side, its warmth, and this is what makes it popular. However, today instead of a thick cozy fur coat—a status symbol for generations—the fashion trend is toward knit or tightly sheared furs or just fur on accessories. It's a marriage of sportswear and sophistication that caters to modern day-to-night wear, workwear, and weekend wardrobes.

Wearing fur is a personal choice, but whether you prefer faux or real fur, it's a fashionable way to stay warm.

Each winter, when it gets very cold, you see people wrapped in fur taking care of themselves and being warm—even for a few minutes. For a huge part of the world, winter is something people have to live with for a long time—and fur makes it better!

Humane consciousness notwithstanding, the truth is that more designers than ever are working with fur, including many in the ready-to-wear market, such as Donna Karan, Calvin Klein, Dennis Basso, and J. Mendel.

Alber Elbaz for Lanvin
Pre-Fall 2011

J. Mendel
Fall 2011

Gucci
Fall 2011

Rene Caovilla
Fall/Winter 2011

Emanuel
Ungaro
Fall 2011

Fur is still big business in America, and men and women of all ages are buying it. Fur is found in designer boutiques, specialty retailers, sporting goods stores, accessories shops, as well as the more traditional fur salons and department stores.

History and Development

The search for a northwest passage that would shorten the route between Europe and the Orient led to the establishment of the fur trade in North America. The first posts were situated along the St. Lawrence and Hudson Rivers, but they soon dotted the continent. Early fur-trading posts played a role in establishing cities such as St. Louis, Chicago, Detroit, St. Paul, and Spokane.

The plentiful supply of furs helped the colonists in other ways. They were able to export furs and use the money to bring European necessities—and even some luxuries—to the New World. Furs were an important source of clothing and furnishings. For a while in the mid-18th century, furs were virtually the currency of North America.

It is the beaver, however, that truly deserves a special place in North American history. The discovery of this fur led to a "fur rush" that rivaled the Gold Rush. Settlers pushed west in search of beaver fur, leaving behind communities with names like Beaver Creek, Beaver Falls, and Beaver Lake. Fortunes were made. John Jacob Astor was among the first to become a millionaire in the beaver trade. He dreamed of a beaver-fur empire stretching from New York to the Northwest Territory.

Fashions in furs do change, although they change less quickly than do other apparel styles because furs are expensive. While mink coats account for half of all furs sold today, 50 years ago a woman who wanted to look glamorous chose an ermine cape. Today, an ermine cape would be valuable only as a theatrical prop—and it could be picked up fairly cheaply in a secondhand store.

More than at any other time in the history of fur fashion, the current list of furs is long and varied. Mink is the overwhelming favorite among consumers. Sable is a distant second, followed by fox and beaver. A new category, called "sport" or "contemporary," includes such furs as raccoon, fox, beaver, coyote, muskrat, tanuki (Japanese raccoon), and nutria (a South American beaverlike animal).

Sometimes an interest in a fur comes about because fur manufacturers invent a finishing technique that makes a fur seem new. A renewed interest in raccoon can be traced to a technique that eliminated much of its bulkiness. In the 1940s, beaver was invariably sheared to look like a short fur; today it is sometimes left unplucked, giving it a totally new look.

Animal Rights Groups

For more than 30 years, animal rights groups have protested the wearing of animal fur as cruel and inhumane. Some groups are opposed to trapping fur-bearing animals in the wild. Others also protest fur farming. Some groups, like **PETA** (People for the Ethical Treatment of Animals) and the Friends of Animals, have staged confrontations and demonstrations to get media attention. Still other groups, like the Animal Liberation Front, have raided mink and fox farms and let the animals loose. They also destroyed pedigree cards containing irreplaceable genetic data.[7]

SELECTED POPULAR FURS AND THEIR CHARACTERISTICS

fur	characteristics	what you should look for
Beaver	Sheared: Soft, plushy texture.	Silky texture. Well-matched pelts, evenly sheared.
	Natural: Long, lustrous guard hairs over thick underfur.	Lustrous sheen of guard hairs and thickness of underfur.
Calf	Short, sleek, flat hairs. Comes in many natural colors and patterns and may be dyed.	Lustrous, supple pelt with bright luster. Marking should be attractive.
Chinchilla	A short, dense, very silky fur. Originally from South America, but now wholly ranch-raised.	Lustrous slate-blue top hair and dark underfur, although mutation colors are now available.
Coyote	A long-haired fur, often pale gray or tan in color. Durable and warm.	Long guard hair and thick, soft underfur.
Ermine	A fur with very silky white guard hairs and dense underfur.	Clear white color.
Fox	The widest range of natural mutation colors of any fur except mink; silver, blue, white, red, cross, beige, gray, and brown. Can also be dyed in a wide variety of colors.	Long, glossy guard hairs and thick soft underfur. Also clarity of color.
Lamb	American Processed: Pelts of fine wool sheep sheared to show the pattern near the skin. Naturally white but may be dyed.	Silky, lustrous moire pattern, not too curly.
	Broadtail: A natural (unsheared) flat moire pattern. Color may be natural browns, gray, black, or dyed in more exotic colors.	Silky texture and uniformity of pattern.
	Mongolian: Long, wavy, silky guard hair. May be natural off-white, bleached, or dyed in more exotic colors.	Silky texture, with wavy—not frizzy—hair.
	Mouton: Pelts are sheared, hairs are straightened for soft, water-repellent fur, generally dyed brown.	Uniformity of shearing.
	Shearling: Natural sheepskin (lamb pelt), with the leather side sueded and worn outside. The fur side (or inside) is often sheared.	Softness of leather side and even shearing.
	Persian lamb: From karkul sheep raised in Southwest Africa, or central Asia. Traditionally black, brown, and gray, new mutation colors available; also dyed.	Silky curls or ripples of fur and soft, light, pliable leather.
Lynx	Russian lynx is the softest and whitest of these long-haired furs, with the most subtle beige markings. Canadian lynx is next, while Montana lynx has stronger markings. Lynx cat or bobcat is reddish black fading to spotted white on longer belly hairs.	Creamy white tones and subtle markings.
Marten	See also sable.	Texture and clarity of color.
	American: Long silky guard hairs and dense underfur. Color ranges from blue-brown to dark brown.	
	Baum: Softer, silkier, and shinier than American marten.	
	Stone: The finest marten has soft, thick guard hairs and a bluish-brown cast with pale underfur.	
Mink	Soft and lightweight, with lustrous guard hairs and dense underfur.	Natural luster and clarity of color. Fur should be full and dense.
	Mutation: Most colors of any natural ranched fur, from white to grays, blues, and beiges.	
	Ranch: Color ranges from a true, rich brown to a deep brownish black.	
	Wild Pieced*: Generally brown in color. Color and pattern depend on pieces used. This is the least expensive mink.	Pattern and well-made seams.

table 6.2

(continued)

fur	characteristics	what you should look for
Nutria	Similar to beaver, often sheared for a sporty, more lightweight feel. Popular for linings and trims. Often dyed in a variety of colors.	Clarity of color.
Rabbit	Generally long hair in a variety of natural colors, including 14 natural mutation colors in ranch rabbit. May be sheared and grooved. Not very durable, shed easily.	Silky texture and uniformity.
Raccoon	Long silver, black-tipped guard hairs over woolly underfur. May also be plucked and sheared and dyed.	Silvery cast. Plenty of guard hair with heavy underfur.
Sable	Member of marten family. Russian sable has a silver cast; the most expensive. Crown sable is brown with a blue coat. Canadian golden sable, an amber tone, is less expensive.	Soft, deep fur in dark lustrous brown, with silky guard hairs.
Tanuki	Also called Japanese raccoon. Color is light amber brown with distinctive cross markings.	Clarity of color and dense, full texture.

*The same piecing technique can be used for almost any fur. The most common pieced furs are mink, sable, marten, fox, Persian lamb, raccoon, and beaver.

Adapted from a number of sources, including the booklet *Choosing Fur* published jointly by The Fur Council of Canada and the Fur Information Council of America, Herndon, Virginia, pp. 4–5.

The industry response has been strong on a number of fronts. It is working with the U.S. and Canadian governments and the International Standards Organization to develop global humane trapping standards. Fur farmers are proposing legislation to make the crime of releasing fur-bearing animals a felony. Associations of American and Canadian fur farmers have also offered rewards for information leading to the arrest of fur raiders. Fur auction houses are offering farmers vandalism insurance. The industry has done a great deal of consumer education to stress that today's farmed furs come from only nonendangered species.

Manufactured Furs

Manufactured, synthetic, or "fake" furs were long regarded as beneath the notice of serious designers and were limited to inexpensive garments. Technological developments in the 1980s and animal rights activism changed that. The new manufactured furs looked so good that fashion writers dropped the word "fake" and began calling them "faux" furs. (*Faux* is the French word for "false".)

ORGANIZATION AND OPERATION

The fur industry in the United States is divided into three groups, which also represent the three stages of fur production: the trappers, farmers, and ranchers who produce the pelts and sell them at auction; the fur-processing companies; and the manufacturers of fur products.

RACHEL ZOE
Stylist, Designer, and Mother of Invention

FIRST THERE WERE "DESIGN CELEBRITIES," THEN "CELEBRITY DESIGNERS," and the latest phenomenon: "Stylists-turned-celebrities-turned designers."

Rachel Zoe is the most famous of the "stylists" who moved from helping dress stars and celebrities for photo shoots and "red carpet talks" to working with fashion houses, beauty firms, advertising agencies, and magazine editors.

As a stylist, she worked with Nicole Richie, Keira Knightley, and Mischa Barton. Today her client list includes Cameron Diaz, Jennifer Garner, Liv Tyler, Eva Mendes, and Anne Hathaway.

In 2008, Zoe's television reality series, *The Rachel Zoe Project*, debuted on Bravo. It was an immediate success and the audience grows with each new season, now including well over one million viewers with double-digit growth among viewers 18 to 49 years old.

Zoe officially announced her move into designing her own clothing line in 2011. It contains accessories, shoes, and apparel featuring leather and her passion for fur vests.

The Rachel Zoe Collection is a lifestyle brand that had its launch in better department stores, specialty stores, and on e-commerce sites worldwide. It was done with LF USA, and it made a major strategic move for both companies.

The collection is priced at the contemporary level and sits alongside Diane von Furstenberg, Marc by Marc Jacobs, and Alexander Wang. The look is predominantly tailored with suits and jackets with matching wool trousers. There's even outerwear—"Zoe's obsession"—with an emphasis on capes with leather trim as well as fur and leather coats. "It was this dream that I never thought would be reality because I was petrified—I was," Zoe recalled.

It is now time to stop calling Rachel Zoe a celebrity stylist. Absolutely, she is a fashion designer who understands her customers' needs and wants—and fulfills them!

Rachel Zoe and Cameron Diaz

Fall 2011

Rachel Zoe

Pelt Production

The first step in the production of fur is to obtain the necessary pelts. A **pelt** is the skin of a fur-bearing animal.

Trappers are the primary source of wild-animal pelts, which must be taken only during the coldest season of the year to be of prime quality. In 2009 there were 278 mink farms compared to 771 in 1990. The number of mink pelts produced in 2009 were 2,855,700 compared to 3,365,700 in 1990. In 2009 the average price for a pelt rose to $65.10 from $25.50 in 1990, and the value of mink pelts was $185,906,070, far surpassing the $82,825,350 of 1990.[8]

The majority of furs come from farms or ranches, where fur-bearing animals are bred and raised strictly for their fur. Almost all mink, rabbit, fox, and—more recently—chinchilla, Persian lamb, and broadtail are ranched. **Fur farming** offers two important advantages. First, animals can be raised under controlled conditions. Second, they can be bred selectively. When wild mink roamed North America, they came in one color, a dark brown with reddish highlights. Today, many beautiful colors, some of which are trademarked and denote a manufacturer's private label, are available. Among the better-known names are Azurene, Lunaraine, Rovalia, Lutetia, Jasmin, Tourmaline, Cerulean, and the most recognizable name of all, Blackgama.[9]

Fur Auctions

Fur pelts are sold at auctions today, much as they were in the 13th century. Fur buyers and manufacturers bid on the pelts, which are sold in bundles. Buyers look for bundles that are matched in quality and color. This enables a manufacturer to make up a garment of uniform beauty.

Competition has increased among buyers to purchase a "top bundle"—that is, an unusually beautiful bundle that goes for an unusually high price. This, in turn, results in a much-touted coat—often costing $100,000 or more—that is made from the top bundle.

The auction trail is an international one, although except for England, Tokyo, and Beijing, each market sells indigenous furs. Fur buyers from the United States travel to Canada, Scandinavia, China, and Russia. To buy North American furs, fur buyers travel to auction houses in New York, Seattle, Toronto, and North Bay, Canada.

Fur Processing

After manufacturers of fur goods buy the pelts, they contract with fur-dressing and fur-dyeing firms to process them.

The job of fur dressers is to make the pelts suitable for use in consumer products. The pelts are first softened by soaking and mechanical means. Then a flesher removes any unwanted substances from the inner surface of the skin. For less expensive furs, this is done by roller-type machines. At this point, the pelts are treated with solutions that tan the skin side into pliable leather. The fur side may be processed at the same time. This involves either plucking unwanted guard hairs or shearing the underfur to make the fur more lightweight. Although fur dressing has traditionally been a handcraft industry, modern technology is turning it into a more mechanical process.

After dressing, the pelts may go to a dyer. Fur dyes were once made from vegetable matter but are now mostly derived from chemical compounds. New dyes are constantly being developed, making it possible to dye fur more successfully and in more shades than ever before.

Fur Manufacturing

Most fur manufacturers are small, independently owned and operated shops, although a few large companies have emerged largely as a result of the explosion in the number of fur products. New York City's fur district on Seventh Avenue between 23rd and 30th Streets is the main center for fur manufacturing. The production of fur garments lends itself neither to mass production nor to large-scale operations. Skill and judgment are required at every stage of manufacturing. Doing each step by hand lets a worker deal with each pelt's color, quality, and peculiarities. The following steps transform pelts into finished garments:

1. A design of the garment is sketched.
2. A paper pattern is made of the garment.
3. A canvas pattern is made.
4. The skins are cut in such a way as to conform to the designer's sketch, exhibit the fur to its best advantage, and minimize waste.
5. The cut skins are sewn together.
6. The skins are wetted and then stapled to a board to dry, a process that sets them permanently.
7. The garment sections are sewn together.
8. The garment is lined and finished.
9. The garment is inspected.

For some luxurious furs, the cutting operation becomes extremely complex. Short skins must be **let out** to a suitable length for garments. Letting out mink, for example, involves cutting each skin down the center of a dark vertical line of fur (the grotzen stripe). Each half skin must then be cut at an angle into diagonal strips one-eighth to three-sixteenths of an inch wide. Then each tiny strip is re-sewn at an angle to the strips above and below it to make a long, narrow skin. The other half-skin is sewn in a similar manner.

The two halves are then joined, resulting in a longer, slimmer pelt that is more beautiful than the original. Considerable hand labor is required to do all of these operations. Ten miles of thread and more than 1,200 staples may be used in a single coat.

In an industry that for generations has produced furs in much the same way as in ancient times, a revolutionary process was developed through technology in 1989. The famous Fendi sisters of Italy showed an entire collection of furs based on a process that made them all, from sables to squirrels, reversible. Interfacing, lining, and construction are all eliminated, and the result is fur coats of incredible lightness and minimal bulk. These coats are so light, in fact, that a full-length fur coat can be folded up and put into a knapsack. Changing from the fur side to the leather side can be done in a minute and there is no bulky look—no matter which side is outside. The fact that all inner construction was eliminated changed the look of the coats themselves. Eliminating the shoulder pads makes everything fit naturally, and the lightness of the fur makes the coat swing and swirl as if it were made of chiffon.

RETAIL DISTRIBUTION OF FURS

There are approximately 1,100 retailers and 100 fur manufacturers in the United States. About 85 percent are small, family-run businesses that have been passed from generation to generation. In the global fur market, the United States ranks among the top countries for retail fur sales.[10] That said, the line between manufacturing and retailing is less clear in the fur industry than in most other industries. Retail fur merchants, for example, typically make up an assortment of garments to sell off the rack to customers, but they also maintain a supply of skins in their workrooms for custom work.

In retail stores, fur departments are either leased or consignment departments. Both operations permit a retail store to offer its customers a large selection without tying up a lot of capital in inventory.

A leased department is situated in the store but run by an independent company such as BC International (it sells luxurious fur fashion in Bloomingdale's, Saks Fifth Avenue, and Macy's). It also pays a percentage of sales to the store as rent. The operator either owns or leases the stock. Lessees often run several similar departments in many stores and can, if necessary, move garments and skins from one location to another. Lessees, who are a unique kind of retailer, are usually well capitalized and have expert knowledge in both furs and retailing.

In consignment selling, a fur manufacturer supplies merchandise to a retail store, which has the option of returning unsold items. In effect, the manufacturer lends stock to a store. Consignment selling is influenced by the state of the economy. When interest rates are high, stores tend to buy less stock. Ritz is an example of a consignment seller.

MERCHANDISING AND MARKETING

Fur traders, dressers, producers, and their labor unions all work through their various trade associations to encourage the demand for fur.

Trade Associations

Trade associations mount their own campaigns to promote furs, and they also work with retailers. The leading trade association is the Fur Information Council of America (FICA), which represents fur retailers and manufacturers. It has placed ads in various fashion magazines to counter some of the animal-rights arguments.

The ranch mink association, American Legend Cooperative, is a not-for-profit formed through the combination of two major mink-producing groups: Emba Mink Breeders Association (EMBA) and Great Lakes Mink Association (GLMA). It serves as a marketing cooperative made up of more than 220 mink farmers within the United States and Canada.[11] American Legend has a program to protect its trademarks from infringement. The association supplies labels and other point-of-purchase materials only to retailers and manufacturers who can prove they purchased the group's pelts at an American Legend auction.

Trade associations not only monitor the industry but also help to educate consumers. Fur is a product that is most successfully purchased when the consumer has some specialized knowledge about what he or she is buying. Consumers need to know, for example, that the rarer the breed, the more expensive the fur. Another important factor in the quality of fur is whether the pelts are female or male. Most female skins are softer and lighter. Although there are exceptions, such as fitch, for which the male skins are preferred, a coat of female mink costs more than one of male mink.

International Fur Fairs

As the demand for fur increases, and the world supply of fur pelts decreases, people are traveling farther than ever before to get the best buys. Designers, manufacturers, retailers, importers/exporters, wholesalers, and the media all attend one or more of the leading international fur fairs.

Labeling

The Fur Products Labeling Act of 1952 requires that all furs be labeled according to the following:
1. The English name of the animal
2. Its country of origin
3. The type of processing, including dyeing, to which the pelts have been subjected
4. Whether or not parts have been cut from a used garment or from the less desirable paw or tail sections

Years ago, such labeling would have been helpful, for example, to prevent a customer from buying a less expensive, dyed muskrat that was touted as the much rarer and more expensive Hudson seal. Such labeling is helpful in distinguishing one fur from another in an industry that, without intending to defraud, has learned to capitalize on fashion trends by treating less expensive furs to look like more expensive ones.

TRENDS IN THE FUR INDUSTRY

As a general rule, the demand for furs is related to the economy. During the Depression, fur sales dropped off dramatically. After World War II, when the economy was expanding, fur sales boomed. In the early 1970s, conservationists' concerns about the diminishing wildlife species put a temporary damper on fur sales, but the industry rebounded in the 1980s. Mid-1987 saw the highest point, the $2 billion mark. But in the early 1990s, a combination of anti-fur activism and mild winters brought a rapid downturn in fur sales. Synthetic fur sales rose rapidly. But then the record-breaking bad weather in the mid-1990s saw a renewed interest in real fur. From 2002 to 2006 the number of U.S. mink farms fell by 16 percent, while average pelt production per farm rose 31 percent. The continued decline in 2007 came in spite of favorable weather conditions through the winter of 2007–2008. The decline instead has been attributed to growing concerns about the state of the economy and a decrease in discretionary spending.[12] According to FICA, there was an overall sales increase of 3.1 percent for 2010 versus 2009. This

brings total U.S. retail fur sales to $1.3 billion. "The combination of a cold winter and fur's presence as a major fashion trend worked together to support sales increases," noted FICA's Executive Director, Keith Kaplan.[13]

Fur can be both elegant [left] and rock and roll [right].

Growth will be affected by the following four major trends:
1. Renewed fashion interest in furs
2. Increased foreign trade
3. Restrictive legislation that actually helps the industry
4. New channels of retail distribution

Renewed Fashion Interest

Once worn only by the rich or for formal occasions, furs are now bought and worn by many kinds of consumers for many occasions. The average customer no longer buys one conservatively cut coat, either. Furs are now sporty and casual, elegant and classic, or faddish and trendy—and with such choices, many customers have been persuaded to buy more than one. As designer Michael Kors has said: "At this point, people who think of fur as a separate category make it very old-fashioned. It's getting rid of that idea of my one great mink coat of my lifetime, and instead treating fur like another fabric, another texture."[14]

Today, there are more than 400 renowned designers using fur in their collections.[15] Some American designers, like Oscar de la Renta and Jerry Sorbara, have produced fur collections for years. Marc Jacobs, Byron Lars, and Dennis Basso have also developed signature looks, establishing a following of fashion insiders.

Increased Foreign Trade

According to the International Fur Trade Federation, global retail for fur increased about 5.4 percent in 2010 from 2009, with sales rising from $13.334 billion to $14.053 billion. China has historically been one of the world's greatest markets for furs, and there is still increased interest for fur garments in the Far East. The United States also continues to produce innovative, high-style furs that are in great demand around the world.[16]

Restrictive Legislation

The Federal Trade Commission and the fur industry are constantly engaged in talks about fur labeling. Ironically, the most important recent legislation, which was intended to restrict the fur industry, has actually been a boom to sales. The Endangered Species Act of 1973 forbade the sale of furs made from endangered species such as leopard, tiger, ocelot, cheetah, jaguar, vicuna, and a few types of wolf. Since women no longer have to worry about wearing an endangered species, many have returned to the fur market.

New Channels of Retail Distribution

Hotel, armory, and arena fur sales are held almost every fall and winter weekend in New York City and other large cities. Fur manufacturers can conduct these sales for a fraction of the cost in wages and rent that would be required if they were to maintain comparable facilities year-round. Even better, the average hotel ballroom, armory, or arena showroom is suitable for displaying thousands of coats, far more than the average fur salon can attractively exhibit. The sales appeal to customers, who like the hands-on approach and lower prices. The same customers who frequent weekend sales also can shop in manufacturer-leased discount and off-price stores such as Filene's Basement and Syms and Loehmanns.

SUMMARY AND REVIEW

In the United States, the tanning of leather for clothing and footwear dates back to the pre-colonial Indian populations. The industry consists of three major types of businesses: regular tanneries, contract tanneries, and converters.

Most leather comes from cattle as an offshoot of the meatpacking industry, but leather is also produced from the pelts of eight other animal groups. Tanneries tend to specialize according to the end use of the leather. Tanning may involve one or more processes using minerals, vegetable materials, oils, and chemicals, alone or in combination, to achieve the desired color and textural finish.

Leather Industries of America (LIA), the industry's trade association, advises its members on fashion and technical issues and promotes the industry to its markets.

Fur has been used for warmth in clothing and shelter since prehistoric times. Fur trading, especially in beaver skins, was a major industry in the European colonization of America, and it remained so well into the 19th century. For much of the 20th century, fur was considered a luxury fashion item for women, but in recent years, fur has been used as a trim for various types of apparel. The efforts of animal rights activists, periods of economic downturn, and competition from imports and from faux furs have challenged the industry, but, most recently, economic prosperity and industry campaigns to educate the public about humane industry practices have had a positive effect on sales.

The fur industry is made up of three groups: trappers, farmers, and ranchers; fur-processing companies, who buy furs at auctions; and manufacturers of fur products. Processing pelts and turning them into fashion products require skilled labor although some mechanization has been introduced into the process. The distinction between levels in the fur industry is less precise than in other segments of the fashion industry. Because of the specialized knowledge and the financial investment required, furs are often sold to consumers by consignment or leased departments in retail stores, by mail order, or in manufacturers' shows in hotels or other large spaces.

FOR REVIEW

1. In what ways have technological advances in machinery and chemistry benefited the leather industry?

2. Name and describe the three major types of companies in the leather industry.

3. What are the nine major groups of fur-bearing animals?

4. What has Leather Industries of America done to broaden the leather market and soften the impact of competition from synthetics?

5. What factors point to growth for the leather industry?

6. Describe the history and development of the fur industry in the United States.

7. Into what three groups is the fur industry divided? Briefly describe the function of each.

8. What are the advantages of fur farming over trapping?

9. Outline the steps in transforming processed fur pelts into finished garments.

10. Differentiate between leased departments and consignment selling as these terms apply to retail distribution of fur garments. What major advantages does each have for retail merchants?

TRADE TALK

Define or briefly explain the following terms:

fur farming

hide

kip

let out

pelt

PETA

skins

sustainable use

tanning

FOR DISCUSSION

1. Discuss the following statement from the text and its implications for leather merchandising: "The leather industry not only must stay abreast of fashion but also must be several steps ahead of it."

2. Discuss current trends in the leather industry that relate to enlarging markets, competition from synthetics, and increased foreign trade.

3. Discuss the pros and cons of trapping and raising animals for their fur. Explain your support or rejection of the arguments advanced by animal rights activists and by the fur industry.

4. Discuss current trends in the fur industry as they relate to fashion interest, increased foreign trade, new channels of retail distribution, low-cost imports, rising overhead, and lack of skilled workers and managers.

PART 3

THE SECONDARY LEVEL—THE PRODUCERS OF FASHION

In this part, you will learn how the fashion apparel manufacturing business has changed from an industry of many small companies into an industry dominated by a growing group of giants. You will begin to develop a basic vocabulary and a working knowledge of the following:

- The six-stage process of developing and producing a line and the major industry practices of licensing, private label, specification buying, offshore production, factors, and chargebacks in Chapter 7.

- The history of the women's, men's, children's, and teen's apparel industries and the categories, size ranges, and price zones, as well as the roles of brand names and designer names, in the marketing process in Chapter 8.

- The history, merchandising, and marketing of accessories in Chapter 9.

- The increased size of companies has influenced the way apparel is designed, manufactured, and merchandised. To understand these developments, you need to explore the aspects of apparel production, as well as the history and current activities of the producers of accessories.

147

PRODUCT
DEVELOPMENT

KEY CONCEPTS

- The major advantages and disadvantages of the contractor system
- The six-stage process of developing and producing a line of apparel
- The major industry practices of licensing, brand extension, private label and specification buying, offshore production, CAD/CAM, PLM, use of factors, chargebacks, and SIC/NAICS codes
- The supply chain management movement and the mass customization theory and their effects on the product development chain
- How bar codes, scanners, and RFID are integral parts of supply chain management

Apparel manufacturers seeking to serve today's world-class brands and retailers will need a continued uptick in their product development and design skills, **an ability to innovate in both product and process**, savvy risk management, and operational transparency.[1]

If new apparel and fashion-related products are not developed, sales and profits decline, technology and markets change, or innovation by other firms makes the original product obsolete. All of this points to the importance of product development for the continued success of a company.

Product development is the teaming of market and trend research, with the merchandising, design, and technical processes that develop a final product. Product development is used by both wholesale manufacturers, who develop products for signature brands, and retailers who use it for private label development at their own stores.

Whether making plain T-shirts or elaborate evening gowns, the men's, women's, and children's apparel industries in the United States have managed to settle into a basic cycle of design and production that repeats itself more or less unchanged from season to season. However, before an article of clothing reaches the retail store racks, a great deal of work and planning are involved. (There are similar cycles for accessories, cosmetics and fragrances, and home fashions; they will be discussed in Part Four.) This chapter will focus on the design and production of apparel for men, women, and children; Chapter 8 examines each area in detail.

WHAT IS A PRODUCT LINE AND WHO DEVELOPS IT?

Product lines of apparel are created and styled for wholesale presentation several times, or seasons, per year. In the fashion industries, a product line is referred to simply as a **line**. A line not only encompasses the individual item of apparel or accessories but also the entire season's production from that manufacturer as well. The term "line" is used for moderate- and popular-priced apparel. The term **collection** is used to describe an expensive line in the United States or in Europe. Lines are divided into **groups** of garments, linked by a common theme like color, fabric, or style. Each garment is known as a style number or number, such as 401 or 57.

It is important to note here that in the United States, designs cannot be copyrighted, as they are in France. Copying from creative designers is common throughout the fashion industry; it is not considered piracy. At some firms, few if any designs are original, rather they are copied **line-for-line** in a similar fabric, adapted from another designer in a cheaper fabric (knockoffs), or reworked from a previous season in a different color or fabric (**anchors**).

Designers typically work on three seasonal lines at a time. They monitor the sales of the current season's line, put the finishing touches on next season's line, while they begin to develop the new line for the following season. Clearly, this is a challenging undertaking.

We will now examine the roles played by the merchandiser, designer, and producer in the product development process.

Role of the Merchandiser

The merchandiser channels the creativity of the designer and design staff so that the six "rights" of merchandising can be successfully accomplished. These rights are the right merchandise, at the right price, at the right time, in the right place, in the right quantity, with the right promotion. To these rights must be added another—the right customer! Because this customer is so important, the merchandiser is given the responsibility to research who the "right" customer is.

Some people in the industry have described the merchandiser as the "glue" that holds the whole product development concept together. In fact, the merchandiser is the link among the design staff, production facilities, and sales staff. The merchandiser has to view the line from the design point of view and also has to be knowledgeable about production and sales efforts.

Role of the Designer

Designers can create by sketching or by drawing on a computer (computer-aided design [CAD]) or by draping cloth on a model. Although artistic excellence is the goal, designers must keep practical business considerations in mind. All designs must be produced at a profit and within the firm's wholesale price range. Consequently, designers must consider the availability and cost of materials, the cost of cutting and sewing the garment, and labor costs.

Role of the Producer

The fashion apparel industry consists of three types of producers: manufacturers, jobbers, and contractors. An **apparel manufacturer** performs all the operations required to produce apparel, from buying the fabric to selling and shipping the finished garments. An **apparel jobber** handles the designing, the planning, the purchasing, usually the cutting, the selling, and the shipping, but not the actual sewing operation. An **apparel contractor** is a producer whose sole function is to supply sewing services to the industry, where it is sometimes called an **outside shop**. Contractors that specialize in the production of one product are sometimes referred to as **item houses**. Increasingly, the term "manufacturer" is being used more loosely to describe any firm that handles any part of the cutting or sewing process, and the terms "jobber" and "contractor" are used less often.

Manufacturers

A manufacturer is a producer who handles all phases of a garment's production. Each line is planned by the company executives. After the staff produces the original design or buys an acceptable design from a freelance designer, the company purchases the fabric and trimmings needed. The cutting and sewing are usually done in the company's factories. On certain occasions, however, a manufacturer may use the services of a contractor if sales of an item exceed the capacity of the firm's sewing facilities and if shipping deadlines cannot otherwise be met. Finally, the company's sales force and traffic department handle the selling and shipping of the finished goods. One great advantage of this type of operation is that close quality control can be maintained. When producers contract out some part of their work, they cannot as effectively monitor its quality.

PHILLIPS-VAN HEUSEN

Big-Bigger-Biggest in the World

Phillips-Van Heusen shirt

PHILLIPS-VAN HEUSEN CORP. (PVH) WANTS TO BE NUMBER ONE IN THE FASHION BUSINESS. Presently number three after Polo Ralph Lauren Corp. and VF Corp., this is clearly long-range thinking. Or is it?

Emanuel Chirico, PVH's Chairman and CEO, made this declaration at the company's annual meeting in July 2010. With the acquisition of the Tommy Hilfiger business in May 2010, PVH is a $4.8 billion business behind the #1 VF Corp. at $7.22 billion and #2 Polo Ralph Lauren at $4.98 billion.

The power of the PVH company is the power of their brands. They own, design, source, and market a selection of world-renowned brands in the dress shirts, sportswear, neckwear, footwear, and accessories categories. These brands are Calvin Klein, Arrow, Izod, and Van Heusen. PVH also holds licenses in the dress shirt, neckwear, and sportswear categories. They include Chaps, DKNY, Donald J. Trump, Geoffrey Beene, Kenneth Cole, Reaction, Michael Kors, Nautica, Sean John, Timberland, Jones New York, and Tommy Hilfiger.

Historically, Phillips-Van Heusen has not had a strong advertising of its own, preferring to let its department store customers market their products within its stores. However, in October 2007, PVH took over naming rights to the Meadowlands Sports Complex arena in East Rutherford, New Jersey. The arena's name was changed to the Izod Center. This was a major marketing move because the Izod Center is the home to many famous sports teams and that kind of audience is a major consumer of the PVH Brands.

No time frame has been set for the goal of being the "Biggest in Business." However, there is a possibility of future acquisitions because of the proven success of the 2003 acquisition of Calvin Klein, Inc. as a "transformational transaction," and the Tommy Hilfiger acquisition in 2010.

Like the Calvin Klein purchase, Tommy Hilfiger should also provide a solid platform for international growth for PVH provides products to many popular department stores, such as Macy's, Kohl's, JCPenney, and Dillard's, both through its own labels and private label agreements.

Shirt and tie by Van Heusen

TOMMY ■ HILFIGER

Emanuel Chirico, Tommy Hilfiger, and Fred Gehring

Van Heusen button-down collars

Apparel Jobbers

Apparel jobbers handle all phases of the production of a garment except for the actual sewing and sometimes the cutting. A jobber firm may employ a design staff to create various seasonal lines or may buy sketches from freelance designers. The jobber's staff buys the fabric and trimmings necessary to produce the styles in each line, makes up samples, and grades the patterns. In most cases, the staff also cuts the fabric for the various parts of each garment. Jobbers arrange with outside factories run by contractors to perform these manufacturing operations. The sales staff takes orders for garments in each line, and the shipping department fills store orders from the finished garments returned by the contractor.

Contractors

Contractors usually specialize in just one phase of the production of a garment: sewing. In some cases contractors also perform the cutting operation from patterns submitted by a jobber or a manufacturer.

If a contractor is used, cut pieces of the garment are provided by the manufacturer. For an agreed price per garment, the article is sewn, finished, inspected, pressed, hung or packaged, and returned to the manufacturer for shipment to retail stores.

In the mass production of ready-to-wear, a single sewing-machine operator rarely makes a complete garment. Each operator sews only a certain section of the garment, such as a sleeve or a hem. This division of labor, called **section work** or **piece work**, makes it unnecessary for an operator to switch from one highly specialized machine to another or to make adjustments. Any change or adjustment in equipment takes time and increases labor costs. In the fashion trade, time lost in making such changes also causes delays in getting a style to consumers. Delays in production could mean the loss of timeliness and sales appeal before an article reaches market.

A contractor may arrange to work exclusively with one or more jobbers or manufacturers, reserving the right to work for others whenever the contractor's facilities are not fully employed. Such agreements are necessarily reciprocal. If a contractor agrees to give preference to a particular jobber's or manufacturer's work, the jobber or manufacturer gives preference to that contractor when placing sewing orders.

The advantages and disadvantages of the contractor system for the manufacturer are as follows:

Advantages

- Large amounts of capital are not required for investment in sewing equipment that may soon become obsolete.
- Difficulties in the hiring and training of suitable workers are minimized.
- The amount of capital necessary to meet regular payrolls is greatly reduced.
- By providing additional manufacturing facilities in periods of peak demand, contractors help speed up delivery of orders.
- It is unnecessary to keep one factory busy all year.

Disadvantages
- No individual has full responsibility for the finished product.
- Other manufacturers (jobbers) may use the same facilities and get preferential treatment because they place larger orders, offer repeat business, or even guarantee future business.
- The quality of the work and inspection tends to be uneven.

THE PRODUCT DEVELOPMENT PROCESS

In a study published in the *Journal of Textile and Apparel Technology and Management,* the authors listed the following functions for an effective integrated system of product development: [2]
- Marketing
- Forecasting
- Merchandising
- Product Line Development
- Product Design and Specifications
- Material Requisition Planning
- Inventory Control
- Costing
- Production Planning and Scheduling
- Sourcing and Manufacturing
- Quality Control
- Human Resources
- Purchasing
- Logistics
- Warehouse Inventory Movement Systems
- Finance
- Sales
- Field Sales Support
- Performance Measurement
- External Communication

Currently, many variations exist in the product development process, but we will discuss a simple six-stage process that covers the functions performed at every firm, regardless of size. The major differences are the number of people involved and how they communicate and interact. The six-stage product development process is outlined as follows:
- Stage 1: Planning a line
- Stage 2: Creating the design concept
- Stage 3: Developing the designs
- Stage 4: Planning production
- Stage 5: Production
- Stage 6: Distributing the line

Stage 1: Planning a Line

The first step of the product development process involves the work of a designer or a product development team, working under the direction of a merchandiser. It is these people who are charged with creating a line. Their first task is research. They review information on trends, colors, fabrics, and other materials. Because they must keep in mind previous fashion successes or failures, past sales records are reviewed, as well as markdown reports. Some firms develop "trend boards" that contain visual or graphic representations of developments that are affecting their target customer. All of this research helps designers or product development teams to formulate some idea of what the new line will contain.

Using all their merchandising and marketing skills, merchandisers or designers help to form and maintain a positive image in the marketplace for the manufacturer. It is this image that influences a specific consumer group to buy a particular line at the retail level.

In most cases, design has to be disciplined and directed so that the particular image of the manufacturer and the merchandise that is produced will continue to fit the needs and wants of a specific consumer group.

Stage 2: Creating the Design Concept

Next come designs for individual garments. Each one is sketched or developed in muslin. At this stage, the designer or design staff considers his or her work and weighs it on two points: first, on its own individual merit and, second, for its suitability in the line as a whole. Many designs are discarded at this point.

Tropical birds and other flights of fancy grouped in clusters on the inspiration board for Jonathan Saunders' Fall 2009 collection.

Price is also a critical factor in determining whether a design is deleted from a line. A cost analysis is often done at this stage, and designs that are too expensive to produce profitably at the desired price point are rejected.

Stage 3: Developing the Designs

Those designs that seem most likely to succeed are made up as finished sample garments. A patternmaker creates a production pattern in the garment size the company uses to produce its samples. From this pattern, one or more samples are cut. Finally, the garment is sewn by a designer's assistant who is also a seamstress. This person is called a **sample hand**. Another option that is common in the industry is producing products offshore by hired vendors.

Now the design is presented to various executives and managers of the company—people in sales, purchasing, production, and cost accounting. Both the cost of the fabric and the cost of producing the garment are carefully analyzed. Many designs are again discarded at this point, while others are sent back to the design department for modification. A few are accepted. The accepted design is assigned a style number. At this point, it is officially part of a manufacturer's line.

Key stages of the product development process: Planning a line [top left], creating the design concept [top right], developing the line [bottom left], and production [bottom right].

Computer-Aided Design

Although the day has not yet arrived when designers will throw away their sketch pads and pencils, the advancements of **computer-aided design (CAD)** are giving designers the freedom to explore and manipulate their designs in relatively easy, quick, and inexpensive ways. A designer does not have to take a chance that he or she is having a sample made up in the best color. CAD is used to test various colors and color combinations, fabrics, and styles. CAD allows three-dimensional (3-D) contouring of objects on screen. Folds, creases, and textures are simulated so that CAD-generated garments drape and hang accurately. Once the design is set on the computer, the computer image is used to create a pattern that is complete with darts, seams, and tailor's markings. Because the computer can create the design in 3-D, the computer image can be rotated to see all sides of the garment. Many companies are thus reducing the number of costly sample garments that they produce. Instead of a physical sample, they use the computer image in merchandising and sales presentations.

Linked CAD/CAM/CIM

CAD systems are continuing to expand with new technology and developments in the industry. In addition, CAD could be linked to **computer-aided manufacturing (CAM)** and **computer-integrated manufacturing (CIM)** systems to provide information internally, to suppliers, and even to retailers across the country and across the world. Linked CAD/CAM/CIM technology and **product lifecycle management (PLM)** software will be discussed in more detail later in this chapter.

Stage 4: Planning Production

This stage of the product development process begins with sourcing, or determining where the components of a garment (fabric, thread, linings, facings, buttons, trim, etc.) will be purchased and, in some cases, where the garments will be cut and sewn. It is now that the vital question of domestic or foreign manufacture must be decided. (The role of supply chain management in this decision is discussed later in this chapter.) Reservations for production must be made, so that the garments will be available when needed. The fabric must be ordered, along with orders for the other components of the garment. Finally, each garment must be costed out, so that the selling price can be set. The samples are used to determine the cost of producing the garment. The money needed to finance production must be obtained. Only when all of these steps have been completed can actual production begin.

The samples, each with its style number, are then presented to retail buyers at the manufacturers' seasonal shows. Most manufacturers have set minimum orders for the quantity, number of styles, and/or dollar amount required to accept the retail buyer's order.

Because the manufacturer usually has not yet begun production when a line is shown to the buyers, it may be possible to fine-tune production to the buyers' orders. When a particular style receives a lot of attention from buyers, it is then scheduled for production. Items that generate little or no enthusiasm are dropped from the line.

BIRTH OF A NOTION

Designers say there is no rhyme or reason to when and how inspiration will strike—and that's half the fun! Here are some sketches by famous designers for their designs and what each felt inspired them.

1. "Polished elegance." —*Oscar de la Renta*
2. "Evening pajamas." —*Isaac Mizrahi*
3. "It's a reimagining of what defines sexy; a collision of chaos-chic." —*Jill Stuart*
4. "Spring is a modern dream state of euphoria." —*Monique Lhuillier*
5. "Always pushing the boundaries, a pioneer in her own right.... She is the American legend."
   —*Diane von Furstenberg and Yvan Mispelaere*
6. "Luxurious textures and masculine shapes." —*Max Azria*

1 Oscar de la Renta
Fall 2010

3 Jill Stuart
Fall 2010

5 Diane von Furstenb
Fall/Winter 2011

2 Isaac Mizrahi
Spring 2011

4 Monique Lhuiller
Spring 2011

6 Max Azria
Fall/Winter 201

Stage 5: Production
Cutting

One of the most important steps in the mass production of apparel is the cutting of the garment pieces. Once a garment is slated for production, it is **graded**, or sloped, to each of the various sizes in which it will be made. After a pattern has been graded to the various sizes, the pieces are laid out on a long piece of paper called a **marker**. The success of cutting depends on the accuracy with which each of the many layers of material are placed on top of one another. A **spreader**, or laying-up machine, carries the material along a guide on either side of the cutting table, spreading the material evenly from end to end. The marker is laid on top of these layers.

For many years, material was cut by hand, but the cutting process is now either computer-assisted or totally computerized. Computers are programmed to feed instructions to laser, blade, or high-speed water jet machines that do the actual cutting.

Once the cutting is completed, the pieces of each pattern—the sleeves, collars, fronts, and backs—are tied into bundles according to their sizes. This process is called **bundling**, and it must be done by hand. The bundles are then moved to the manufacturers' sewing operators, who may be on the premises or in contractors' shops.

Sewing

Technology has dramatically changed the sewing stage of production. The industrial sewing machine sews much faster than a home sewing machine. Further, home sewing machines perform many functions, while industrial machines perform specialized

A worker at an embroidery plant in Bangladesh manually rethreads one of many industrial machines.

functions. Some sew only seams, while others sew blind hems. Button machines sew on buttons. Computerized sewing machines that do embroidery can be set up to stitch whole patterns without a machine operator. Robotic sewing equipment is being developed.

Meanwhile, single-hand operations, in which one operator sews the entire garment, still exist. They are used for very high-priced garments that are produced in very small quantities. Today, most manufacturers use a combination of mass production systems, including the popular modular manufacturing system, in which teams of seven to nine workers produce entire garments, passing them on to each other stage by stage, until the garment is complete. This system requires extensive cross-training, so each team member can learn all the tasks involved and perform them as the flow of work demands.

Finishing the Product

The sewn garment is still far from ready for the retail floor. Pants, for example, are sewn with the legs inside out. They must be turned right side out. A label must be sewn in. Buttons and buttonholes may be added at this stage.

Some fabrics are washed at this stage to prevent shrinkage. Others have a wrinkle-resistant finish applied. Still others are dyed at this point, called garment-dyeing, which gives the manufacturer last-minute control of color.

The garment is then pressed and folded or hung on a hanger with a plastic bag over it. Some manufacturers also offer services that make their apparel **floor ready**, that is, with bar-coded price tickets attached, cartons labeled, and shipping documents attached. Of course, this adds to the cost, but many retailers find that this portion of the supply chain management strategy makes up in speed for the cost. See "Stage 6: Distributing the Line."

Inspecting the Product

Garments are inspected many times during the production process. First the fabric and the dye quality are checked. Cutting is checked for pattern matching and size specs, among other things. Sewing is also checked repeatedly along the way, for stitch length, seam type, buttonhole stitching, and hem stitching. **Quality assurance**, or **QA**, which refers to the product meeting the standards established for it, includes the inspection of each ingredient of the garment: fabric, thread, buttons, snaps or zippers, hem tape, linings, shoulder pads, and so forth.

Stage 6: Distributing the Line

Once the line is completed, it still requires more work before the retailer can sell it. Sales tickets and bar codes must be added. These time-consuming tasks are frequently done by the manufacturer, except for the smallest stores. Then shipments must be consolidated and, finally, sent to retailers by truck, rail, air, or sea.

As the season progresses, manufacturers remain sensitive to retail sales. For example, when reorders come in, they recut only the garments that are most in demand—and therefore, the most profitable. Manufacturers may also recut "hot sellers" in different fabrics and colors to maximize the sales generated by high customer demand.

SPECIALIZING BY PRODUCT

Apparel producers have typically been specialists, producing apparel for a particular gender and age, a particular size range, and a specific price range. A women's blouse manufacturer, for example, seldom makes dresses, and a dress manufacturer usually does not turn out dresses in both women's and junior sizes. A coat and suit manufacturer does not usually produce both expensive and popular-priced lines.

Historically, the U.S. apparel industry has been divided into three major categories: women's, men's, and children's. These three categories are discussed in detail in Chapter 8. Despite a move toward greater diversification, producers and retailers still have to think and work like specialists. For instance, a producer must out of necessity choose an inexpensive fabric for a popular-priced line and a more expensive fabric for a better-priced line. Retail buyers still shop one group of producers for sportswear, another for coats, and still another for bridal wear—and this is not likely to change in the near future.

Jean Paul Gaultier adjusts his upcoming looks on a live model in his atelier ahead of their runway debut [left], and designer Giles Mendel inspects a J. Mendel resort pleated dress on a mannequin [right].

Brands and Labels

A special Infotracs supplement to *Women's Wear Daily* listed the following five distinct kinds of brands or labels used by apparel industry insiders:[3]

1. National/designer brand
2. Private label
3. Retail store brand
4. Other brands
5. Nonbrands

Customers, of course, realize few of these distinctions. They think of them all as "brands" or "nonbrands." But to retailers and manufacturers, these distinctions are vital, impacting heavily on their profits and offering differentiation in an era when customers complain of the "sameness" of many stores and the goods they offer.

National/Designer Brands

National brands are those that are owned by a manufacturer that advertises them nationally. Examples include Fruit of the Loom, Levi's, Reebok, Hanes, and Revlon. Some of the first apparel brands to gain national recognition were the Arrow Shirt Company and the B.V.D. Company, a maker of men's underwear, in the 1930s. National brands continued to grow in number over the next five decades, and the 1980s and 1990s saw a tremendous leap in sales for national brands. In part, this resulted from a huge increase in the number of national advertising campaigns directed at consumers. As a result of the recession in the early 2000s, there was a decrease in spending overall, but by 2011, the apparel industry saw increased growth. Specifically, there was a surge in men's wear categories, including basics—like underwear and socks, fleece, outerwear—and tailored clothing.[4]

Designer labels carry the name of a designer; they have grown enormously in number and importance since the 1940s. As mentioned previously, the four U.S. megadesigners are Ralph Lauren, Calvin Klein, Donna Karan, and Tommy Hilfiger. Hundreds more are working in the United States today. Many other designer names continue to be featured, although the original designer has retired or died. Examples include Anne Klein, Halston, Bill Blass, and Calvin Klein.

Designer labels are no longer limited to apparel. They are frequently found on accessories of every kind, on fragrances and cosmetics, and on home furnishings.

Private Labels

A **private label** is one that is owned by a retailer and found only in its stores. Examples of private label apparel are Mossimo at Target, the Jaclyn Smith line sold by Kmart, the Charter Club line sold by Macy's, Inc., and the Nicole by Nicole Miller line sold by JCPenney. These labels are sold alongside national/designer brands. The proportion of private labels to national and designer brands varies from retailer to retailer.

Retail Store Brand

A retail store brand is the name of a chain that is used as the exclusive label on most of the items in the store or catalog. Examples of retail store brands for apparel and accessories include Gap, The Limited, Ann Taylor, Victoria's Secret, Talbots, L.L. Bean, and Lands' End. Examples of store brands for home furnishings include Pier 1, Crate & Barrel, and Williams-Sonoma. Few, if any, national or designer brands are carried by these stores or catalogs.

Other Brands

This catchall category includes labels not in the preceding three categories, such as cartoon characters, like Disney's Mickey & Co. and Warner Brothers' Looney Tunes; sports teams, like the Chicago Bulls; colleges, like the University of California at Berkeley; and museums, like The Museum of Fine Arts—Chicago. These brands are often licensed.

Nonbrands

This is a label to which customers attach little or no importance. These labels are usually used by firms that manufacture low-priced goods and do little or no advertising to consumers. These labels are found in discount and off-price stores.

INDUSTRY PRACTICES

Every industry has its own particular way of conducting business, and the apparel industry is no exception. Some of the practices discussed in this section developed as responses to specific industry problems. These practices were once considered "trends," but they are so well-established now that they represent business as usual. The six major industry practices that we will discuss are manufacturers acting as retailers, licensing, brand extension, private label and specification buying, offshore production, and the use of factors, chargebacks, and SIC/NAICS codes.

Manufacturers Acting as Retailers

An increasing number of clothing manufacturers are opening their own stores. Disappointed by the sales, service, and space allotted to them in retail stores and wanting to create the "right" atmosphere for their clothing, they are choosing to enter the retail business themselves. Of course, larger profits are also part of the attraction. The manufacturer can sell the product to consumers at full retail price, rather than at the wholesale price required by retail customers.

Designer Ralph Lauren was the first to take this step. Frustrated by the way department and specialty stores were selling his clothes, he opened the first Polo/Ralph Lauren shop on Rodeo Drive in Beverly Hills in 1971. Since then, he has built an empire of Polo/Ralph Lauren shops that stretches coast-to-coast in the United States and across the oceans to Europe and Asia. Calvin Klein, Donna Karan, Adrienne Vittadini, Marc Jacobs, and Vivienne Tam have also opened their own retail outlets.

But whether all manufacturers and designers will be successful retailers remains to be seen. A producer first has to compete for good retail talent, which can be expensive, as well as retail space in a prime location. The risks escalate if the manufacturer franchises, which many must do when they cannot personally oversee their retail empire.

Manufacturer's outlet stores, called "factory outlets," have also grown at a rapid rate. They allow manufacturers to dispose of poor sellers, overstocks, and "seconds" and still make more money on them than they could by selling them to discount retailers as "closeouts."

The opposite of manufacturers acting as retailers is retailers acting as manufacturers through the private label programs of department stores and discounters and through the retail store brands of specialty chains like Gap and Talbots.

Licensing

Licensing, which was described in Chapter 4, experienced a boom in the United States in the 1980s and 1990s. This was largely the result of the emergence of an important new market segment—working women. As a group, they are not quite in the income bracket to buy designer clothes, but designers have learned that they can capitalize on the market these women represent through licensing ventures.

The great appeal of licensing is that merchandise is identified with a highly recognizable name. The advantages for designers include the royalties they receive on the sale of each product (usually from 2 percent to 15 percent), greater exposure of their names, and little investment in product development and manufacturing.

The disadvantages in licensing are few. When designers turn over control to a manufacturer as they do when they license a product, they may lose some quality control. A bigger problem is that a designer will move too far afield for his or her more exclusive customers, but considering the potential profits in licensing, this is unlikely to worry many designers.

A final note on the importance of a company's brand name: **Corporate licensing**, or the use of a company's name on related merchandise, is the fastest-growing segment of licensing today. The Nike "swoosh" is seen worldwide. Harley-Davidson and Disney characters have been licensed for T-shirts and children's wear, Dr. Scholl's has also licensed its name, expanding from foot care to pillows, and Jeep has a line of sunglasses.

Brand Extensions

A common technique in consumer goods marketing is brand extension, which is a strategy in which a company uses a successful brand name to launch new or modified products. Brand extension saves the company the high cost of promoting a new name and creates instant brand recognition of the new product line. It is one way in which a company can diversify its product line.

In the apparel industries, a move into a related category of apparel is the easiest and cheapest way to diversify. A company that makes T-shirts may add a line of cotton sweatshirts, which are also sized small, medium, large, and extra large. A designer of men's suits may add coats. A childrenswear manufacturer may add an infants' line. A woman's shoe manufacturer may add matching handbags.

The move to an unrelated line has traditionally been more difficult—and more costly. One of the first brand extensions by designers was expanding into fragrances and cosmetics.

Private Label and Specification Buying

The terms "private label" and "specification buying" may be used to describe the same items of merchandise, but the meanings are slightly different. If the retailer agrees, the manufacturer may design private label merchandise for the retailer. The private labels of Macy's, Inc. include Alfani, Charter Club, and Tasso Elba. Alternatively, specification buying is a type of purchasing that is done to the store's rather than the manufacturer's standards. JCPenney and Gap are two examples of stores that make extensive use of **specification buying**. These retailers provide the standards and guidelines for the manufacture of clothes they order. Standards cover everything from the quality of materials and workmanship to styling and cost.

Specification buying has become so specialized that many stores now employ a **specification manager** or **product manager** who is trained in specification buying. While keeping an eye on industry and government standards, specification managers

work closely with manufacturers to ensure that their products will be economically successful for both the retailer and the manufacturer.

As they grow more successful with specification buying, stores have begun to use it for their private label lines. Initially intended as a way to keep production at home, a growing amount of private label is now purchased offshore. (See the following section and Chapter 10.)

Offshore Production

U.S. manufacturers are increasingly turning to **offshore production**, that is, the manufacture of U.S. goods in foreign countries with inexpensive labor. Offshore production is seen as a way to generally lower costs and, therefore, compete more effectively with low-cost imports. Some industry insiders view this practice as a threat to the health of American labor; others regard it as a necessity if U.S. manufacturers are to remain competitive.

The American Apparel and Footwear Association (AAFA), the major trade association for apparel and footwear, commented that despite 40 years of quotas and import tariffs, the industry has lost more than one million jobs in the United States—today, more than 97 percent of the apparel sold in the United States is imported. The "protections" appear to have done little to protect this industry. We now have to face the challenges of a quota-free world. We need to take a proactive approach by developing and promoting strong trading relationships with customers worldwide.

Although most companies no longer manufacture in the United States, they still employ hundreds of thousands of U.S. workers in research and development,

Offshore production in a factory in China.

marketing, distribution and warehousing, sourcing, and at the retail level. The U.S. market could soon be saturated and foreign markets could hold the key for continued growth for the U.S. apparel and footwear firms in the future. AAFA's Vice President for International Trade, Nate Herman, stated, "Knocking down barriers to trade at home and around the world improves America's competitiveness in the global marketplace."[5]

Use of Factors

Apparel manufacturers and contractors need cash or credit to produce garments the season before they are sold. Some banks have been reluctant to lend money to apparel companies because of the high risks involved. So an alternate system of financing has developed for the apparel industry. Called **factors**, these companies either purchase a manufacturer's accounts receivable or advance cash on the basis of the accounts receivable. Their interest rates are generally higher than those of a bank.

Another development is the use of credit insurance by firms that do not use factors. Credit insurance, used for decades in Europe, protects the insured company from losses as a result of a customer's bankruptcy or very late payment. Credit insurance is also useful for a U.S. manufacturer with international business because it is cheaper than international letters of credit. In today's economy all financial decisions are being more closely examined. As debt analyst Margaret Taylor noted, "It seems like [credit markets] are being more rational than they had been through the credit boom or the credit crisis."[6]

Chargebacks

As retail chains have grown in size, their power over their suppliers has also increased. Apparel manufacturers are increasingly hit with demands for **chargebacks**, which are financial penalties imposed on manufacturers by retailers. The reasons for chargebacks include mistakes in purchase orders or ticketing. Sometimes retailers request chargebacks for partial or late shipments or even for poor-selling products. Chargebacks are also used for cooperative advertising. Naturally, chargebacks can cause financial problems for designers and manufacturers, especially small ones.

SIC/NAICS Codes

The change from the Standard Industrial Classification (SIC) codes to North American Industry Classification System (NAICS) is a reflection of globalization in the industry. SIC was originally developed in the 1930s to classify U.S. establishments by "the type of activity in which they primarily engage and to create a database of comparable information that would describe the parts of the U.S. economy." Over the years, the SIC was revised periodically to reflect the changes in the businesses that make up the U.S. economy. The NAICS codes allow for a high level of comparability in business statistics among the North American countries, and they are also much simpler. Here are some examples of codes that are used in the industry today:
- NAICS 313: Textile Mills
- NAICS 314: Textile Product Mills (non-apparel)

- NAICS 315: Apparel Manufacturing
- NAICS 316: Leather and Allied Apparel Manufacturing

This data is extremely useful among businesses in the fashion industry and is a good aide for decision making.

ADVANCED TECHNOLOGIES AND STRATEGIES

A number of advanced technologies and the strategies used to harness them have been implemented by the U.S. apparel industry. These technologies have already had a profound impact on the profitability of the business and are poised to increase it further in the 21st century. They include the use of computer-integrated manufacturing, PLM, supply chain management, bar codes, scanners, radio-frequency identification (RFID), electronic data interchange (EDI), mass customization, and body scanning.

Computer-Integrated Manufacturing and Product-Lifecycle Management

Stand-alone computerized equipment is now common in most manufacturers' plants. As discussed earlier in this chapter, this is known as CAM. It includes things such as programmable sewing machines, patternmaking machines, and cutting machines.

But the enormous power of the computer lies in its ability to be linked to other computers, so that the computers can direct the entire production process from design to finished garment. In CIM, computer-integrated manufacturing, and PLM, product-lifecycle management, data from many computers within a manufacturing company are linked during all stages. Design, sourcing, sample-making, and shipping departments, as well as overseas factories, can view the same electronic files and see the status of any garment and its components at a moment's notice. For example, design, patternmaking, and grading are linked to cutting equipment as well as to computers that prepare costing reports and specification sheets. In some plants, these computers are even linked to stitching machines. The potential for cost savings is tremendous because repeated data entry is eliminated, along with entry errors.

Large apparel companies, including Liz Claiborne, Marc Jacobs, Tommy Hilfiger, Diane von Furstenberg, and well over a hundred more use these tools to streamline their operations and make better business decisions.[7]

Supply Chain Management

A well-known business strategy that was used in the late 1990s was **Quick Response (QR)**. QR shortened time frames from raw materials to design to production to finished product to the consumer. It was developed to give U.S. manufacturers a powerful weapon against imports and foreign competitors, linking all parts of the supply pipeline directly to the nation's retailers. What it really means is a far closer association among manufacturer, supplier, retailer, and customer. It requires the development of trust and communication, and that goes all the way from the cash register to the apparel people and the textile suppliers. Simply put, it aims at delivering the right product at the right time.

DIGITAL FITTING EXPERIENCES

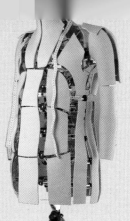

Robotic fitting torso

Levi's Brand Interactive Destination

In 2010, Levi's announced the global launch of the Levi's Digital Fitting Experience, an interactive destination for women to explore and buy their perfect fitting jeans online. It provides women with tools to demystify the process of finding perfect fitting jeans based on their shape, not their size.

The research showed that 80 percent of women around the world fall into three distinct body shapes, so one size can never fit all. The goal is to engage women online with the interactive, custom fit experience that will match them with their perfect Levi's CURVE ID fit, whether they are a Slight Curve, Demi Curve, or Bold Curve.

The Levi's Digital Fitting Experience gives women the opportunity to connect with the Levi's brand across multiple digital channels, allowing them to share content with friends through social media and various mobile platforms. The technology can also be integrated across major e-commerce partner platforms.

Levi's CURVE ID webs

Macy's Magic Fitting Rooms

No need to take clothes off in Macy's Magic Fitting Rooms. At Macy's Herald Square in New York, there is a miracle on 34th Street: the Magic Fitting Room, a temporary space that allows shoppers to "virtually" try on clothes. Equipped with a large, 72-inch digital mirror, boasting 1,024 touch points and connected to an iPad, the Macy's Magic Fitting Room encourages customers to scroll through the store's latest looks and "flick" the pieces they would like to try on. Magic! The virtual clothes are transposed over the shopper's reflection in the mirror. Need a different size? Just "flick" again and the image will be resized to suit your shape.

Need a second, third, or fourth opinion? Shoppers can bring as many "virtual" friends as they would like into the Magic Fitting Room. The mirror is connected to a camera and the Internet, which, after securing a password, allows the shopper to transmit the image to Facebook friends for some advice.

Macy's Magic Mi

A similar, and more recent, strategy is called **supply chain management (SCM)**. Supply chain management has the same benefits of QR, but takes it one step further. It allows companies to share forecasting, point-of-sale data, inventory information, and the supply and demand for materials or products.

Bar Codes, Scanners, and Radio Frequency Identification (RFID)

Bar coding, scanning, and RFID have become integral parts of SCM. Bar coding makes tracking merchandise—from fabric rolls to designer dresses—easier, faster, and more accurate. The **universal product code (UPC)** is one of a number of bar codes used for automatic identification of items scanned at retail cash registers. UPC is the symbol that has been most widely accepted by retailers and manufacturers. Bar codes are made up of a pattern of dark bars and white spaces of varying widths. A group of bars and spaces represents one character.

Scanners "read" the bar code. The UPC symbol does not contain the price of the merchandise; the price is added by the retailer to the store's computerized cash registers and can easily be changed.

Radio Frequency Identification uses electronic tags for storing data. It uses a unique serial number that allows the tracking of products, cartons, containers, and individual items as they move through the supply chain. They hold more data than bar codes and can be read many times faster. With this technology, companies have the ability to increase efficiency and accuracy of counting inventory.[8]

Electronic Data Interchange (EDI)

Electronic Data Interchange is the electronic exchange of machine-readable data in standard formats, linking computers from one company to another. It replaces a large number of paper forms that were the primary link between manufacturers and their retailer customers. These included forms like purchase orders, invoices, packing slips, shipping documents, and inventory forms.

Mass Customization

For the past 80 years, we have lived in a world where mass production was the model for products and services because standardized products meant lower costs. Every time a customer takes home a product with an attribute that he or she really does not want, it is a form of waste. In **mass customization**, the idea is to tailor the product to fit one particular customer—not one size fits all—and to supply thousands of individuals, at mass prices, not custom-made prices.

Body Scanning

As more apparel companies become aware of 3-D body-scanning technology, the fitting room could become a thing of the past. Within seconds, body scanners take a snapshot of the human form and produce a 3-D replica, with complete measurement data.[9] As technology continues to improve and become less costly, scanning of the entire body may become more common, resulting in a better fit for all customers.

GLOBALIZATION

Globalization of the marketplace—finding both foreign competitors and foreign customers—has happened to a wide range of U.S. manufacturing products, such as cars, televisions, electronics, steel, and computers. Starting in the 1970s, globalization occurred in the apparel industries and is still flourishing today. See Chapter 10 for further discussion on Global Sourcing and Merchandising.

SUMMARY AND REVIEW

The men's, women's, and children's apparel industries develop and produce lines of apparel following a standard cycle. The six-stage process of developing and producing a line involves: planning a line, creating the design concept, developing the designs, planning production, production, and distributing the line.

Types of producers include manufacturers, apparel jobbers, and contractors. Producers specialize by gender, age, and size categories, as well as by classification. While consumers generally do not know the differences, industry insiders distinguish among five major types of brands and labels: (1) national/designer brands, (2) private labels, (3) retail store brands, (4) other types of brands, and (5) nonbrands.

Major industry practices that directly affect profitability include licensing, brand extension, private label and specification buying, offshore production, the use of factors, chargebacks, and SIC/NAICS codes.

Advanced technologies affecting product development of apparel include computer-integrated manufacturing, supply chain management, and the use of bar codes, scanners, radio-frequency identification, electronic data interchange, mass customization, and body-scanning computers.

Product development is also affected by globalization and the ongoing changes in our world.

FOR REVIEW

1. How does EDI differ from CIM?

2. How does a jobber differ from a manufacturer?

3. What are the major advantages of the contractor system? What is the key disadvantage?

4. What are the six stages of the product development process?

5. What is a chargeback?

6. What is the goal of supply chain management?

7. Why do most fashion producers sell directly to retail stores rather than through wholesalers?

8. What is the difference between a national brand and a private label?

9. What role do factors play in the fashion industry?

10. Discuss the major problems facing a manufacturer who is also a retailer.

FOR DISCUSSION

1. Compare and contrast the roles of the designer, the merchandiser, and the product manager in developing a line.

2. Give current examples of brand extensions in apparel, accessories, fragrances and cosmetics, and home furnishings.

TRADE TALK

Define or briefly explain the following terms:

anchor

apparel contractor

apparel jobber

apparel manufacturer

bundling

chargeback

collection

computer-aided design (CAD)

computer-aided manufacturing (CAM)

computer-integrated manufacturing (CIM)

corporate licensing

electronic data interchange (EDI)

factor

floor ready

graded

group

item house

line

line-for-line

marker

mass customization

offshore production

outside shop

piece work

private label

product development

product lifecycle management (PLM)

product manager

quality assurance (QA)

quick response (QR)

radio frequency identification (RFID)

sample hand

section work

specification buying

specification manager

spreader

supply chain management (SCM)

universal product code (UPC)

FASHION APPAREL
WOMEN'S, MEN'S, CHILDREN'S, AND TEEN'S

KEY CONCEPTS

- Categories, size ranges, and price zones of women's, men's, children's, and teen's fashion apparel
- Roles of brand and designer names in the marketing of women's, men's, children's, and teen's fashion apparel
- Advertising and promotional activities in the marketing of women's, men's, children's, and teen's fashion apparel

Of necessity, the women's, men's, children's, and teen's fashion industry exists in a constant state of change, reacting on an ongoing basis to the consumer's tastes and styles, to an increasingly global economy, and to new technology. It is an industry that truly thrives on change and novelty.

Taken as a total entity, the women's, men's, children's, and teen's apparel industry is the largest and most recognized part of the fashion business. Although the history, development, and trends in the various apparel are similar in many ways, this chapter addresses each sector separately.

WOMEN'S APPAREL
Organization and Operation

For many decades, the typical women's apparel company was a small, independently owned, and often family-run business. Unlike the automobile industry, no Ford or General Motors dominated the women's apparel industry. In the early 1970s, approximately 5,000 firms made women's dresses. The industry's power came from its collective size. Its 5,000 firms did $3 billion in business every year.

All this changed in the 1970s. An expanding economy led to increased demand for everything, including clothing. Many of the textile companies had grown into huge businesses, as had several major retailers. Pushed from both directions, the clothing manufacturers responded by merging to create large publicly owned corporations.

Within a few years, it became obvious that many of the large corporations and conglomerates were not as successful as the smaller companies had been. The major problem was that the giants lacked the ability to respond quickly, a necessity in the fashion industry. Those that have survived and prospered have combined the advantages of large and small by creating divisions and subsidiaries that function independently within the larger structure.

Regardless of whether a company is part of a conglomerate or a family-owned shop, the way in which clothes are produced does not vary. The operation of the fashion apparel industry remains remarkably similar from business to business. The organization of the industry is currently undergoing changes, however. After years of specialization, the emergence of giant apparel producers has brought diversification. A number of the giants have divisions manufacturing womenswear, menswear, childrenswear, home fashions, and accessories.

Specialization by Product

Apparel producers have typically been specialists, producing apparel for a particular lifestyle, for a particular size range, and for a specific price range. Nowhere in the industry is this truer than in womenswear, the segment with the largest, most varied, and fastest-changing market. A woman's coat manufacturer, for example, seldom makes dresses, and a dress manufacturer does not make bathing suits. This is completely hidden from the customer by the growing practice of putting national brands and licensed designer names on a wide variety of merchandise—from evening gowns to bathing suits to shoes to perfume to sheets.

The Role of Designers

Designers, too, must balance diversification with specialization. From superstars to the new generation struggling to be recognized, all designers specialize to the extent that

Designs from Giorgio Armani's Spring 2011 haute couture show [left] and Oscar de la Renta's Fall 2011 show [right].

they are marketing their own artistic identity to a segment of the population that shares their vision.

As designers from the United States show in Paris and Milan, and European and Japanese designers show in New York, fashion-conscious consumers have a virtually limitless choice of looks they can adopt. There is the street-smart hip-hop style of Rocawear; the casual, gentrified elegance of Ralph Lauren; the spare, clean look of Marc Jacobs; the meeting of Asian and Western sensibilities in the designs of Issey Miyake; and the luxury and sumptuousness of Giorgio Armani and Oscar de la Renta. The established designers of upscale lines not only cater to the people who can afford their clothing but also lead the way for producers of more moderately priced fashion in interpreting trends in fashion and popular culture.

Categories in Women's Apparel

The following are the basic categories in women's apparel and the types of garments generally included in each. The categories of outerwear, suits, dresses, and blouses have been fixtures in the women's ready-to-wear industry from the beginning, and the category of sportswear and separates has been important since the 1940s. Jeans are considered a separate category by many manufacturers and retailers because of their unique position in Americans' wardrobes. The uniforms and aprons category fills a consumer need but does not set fashion trends. The same is true of the special needs category.

The Gibson Girl, 1890-1910s

The Flapper, 1920s

The Bohemian, 1900–1910s

The Screen Siren, 1930s

Various dresses from the 1930s

THE AMERICAN WOMAN
Fashioning a National Identity

AS THE COSTUME INSTITUTE OF THE METROPOLITAN MUSEUM OF ART UNVEILED "THE AMERICAN WOMAN: FASHIONING A NATIONAL IDENTITY" EXHIBIT, the female face and body became a key topic of conversation, particularly among fashion professionals looking to pinpoint just what American style is and how it has evolved since the 1890s Gibson Girl—who serves as the starting point for the exhibit.

In a series of oval and circular rooms, the exhibit brought to life the different stages of the American female identity, from "The Heiress" in a room inspired by Mrs. Astor's Newport mansion and garments by Charles Frederick Worth to "The Gibson Girl" exploring sports in all seasons—and "The Bohemian," who seems right at home in a room decorated in the Tiffany era.

The exhibit struck a particular note in a gallery devoted to "Suffragists" and "Patriots" with actual footage of the movement marches and banners from the era, followed by "The Flapper," which represents the sexual and economic emancipation of women in the Art Deco era.

But the most quintessential symbol of America to the world is the "Screen Siren." It features mannequins in glamorous gowns set against movie screens showing scenes from famous thirties movies, including Hollywood icons such as Marlene Dietrich, Greta Garbo, Jean Harlow, Joan Crawford, and Rita Hayworth.

In the fifties, Hollywood also played a key role in exporting the American lifestyle, and women around the world took their fashions from the movies.

"The American style has absolutely cultivated itself," said Donna Karan. "You see this effortlessness of individuality and comfort."

Ralph Lauren said American style is "really about living, though there is elegance and sophistication to American style, its signature is in its casual and varied attitude. It's less studied, more natural, more about life and less about fashion."

The current "American Idols" were in full view with Oprah Winfrey, Diane von Furstenberg, Taylor Swift, Brooke Shields, and Jessica Alba among others attending opening night in clothes from our favorite American designers.

From now on it is up to American designers and the American woman to work together to fashion the national identity for this century and beyond!

BASIC CATEGORIES IN WOMEN'S APPAREL
AND THE TYPES OF GARMENTS INCLUDED IN EACH CATEGORY

category	types of garments
Outerwear	Coats, rainwear, jackets
Dresses	One- or two-piece designs and ensembles (a dress with a jacket or coat)
Blouses	Dress and tailored
Suits	Jacket/skirt and jacket/pants combinations
After-5 and evening clothes	Formal and prom gowns, and other dressy apparel; this is often called "special occasion"
Bridal wear	Gowns and dresses for brides, attendants, and mothers of the bride and groom
Sportswear and separates	Town-and-country and spectator sportswear, such as pants, shorts, tops, sweaters, skirts, shirts, jackets, casual dresses, and jumpsuits
Activewear	Clothing for participatory sports and athletic activities such as swimwear, tennis dresses, running suits, cycling shorts, exercise apparel, and skiwear
Uniforms and aprons	Aprons, smocks, housedresses, and a variety of uniforms
Maternity	Dresses, sportswear, evening clothes, suits, and blouses designed to accommodate the special needs of pregnant women
Innerwear	Brassieres, panties, shapewear, bodywear, sleepwear, and other intimate apparel
Special needs	Dresses, slops, nightgowns, hosiery, and other intimate apparel designed with snaps or Velcro for ease of use by elderly or physically challenged women

.... table 8.1 ....

Activewear

The "fitness craze" that emerged in the 1980s with workout programs on television and videotape intensified in the 1990s and is still very popular today. People flock to gyms to work out before and after work, and travelers maintain their exercise routines in health clubs that have become an essential hotel service. Running gained favor, and the New York and Boston marathons became national news. Women's sports received a boost in public attention with the formation of the Women's National Basketball Association and the Supreme Court ruling that universities accepting federal funding must offer equal athletic opportunities for male and female students.

All of these developments contributed to the growth of the market for comfortable and fashionable apparel for specific sports and exercise activities. This type of apparel is known in the industry as **activewear**. Leading producers of activewear are the athletic shoe companies Nike, Reebok, and Adidas, all of which have developed lines of clothing. By the 21st century, their women's apparel divisions were given equal attention with the men's.

Nike continues to be a major player in the activewear business.

Kate Middleton's wedding dress, desgined by Sarah Burton for Alexander McQueen, is sure to be an influence on bridal wear for years to come.

Formal Wear

Despite the growing casualness of everyday apparel, people all over the world still like to mark special occasions by wearing formal clothing. Elegant fabrics, trim, and silhouettes—worn with more elaborate jewelry, watches, and other accessories—mark most formal wear. This category is often called "after-5" or "special occasion." It is interesting to note that evening wear gets more media coverage than any other category, especially at the Academy Awards, the Tony Awards, the Grammy Awards, and similar events.

Designers like Bob Mackie and Roberto Cavalli specialize in dressing Hollywood stars for opening nights and award ceremonies. As a result, thousands of women across the country want similar looks for weddings, dances, and formal dinners.

Bridal Wear

Bridal wear has always been a category for which both brides and designers can make personal fashion statements. Designer runway shows in Paris traditionally conclude with the modeling of a bridal gown, and some designers, such as Vera Wang, are known primarily for their work in this category. Weddings of movie stars, royalty, and other celebrities often inspire trends in bridal fashions, but the range of available styles runs from modern interpretations of Victorian designs to unadorned slip dresses.

Maternity

Now that two out of three pregnant women stay on the job almost the entire nine months of their pregnancies, pregnant career women have become an important and growing submarket, and the whole maternity category is receiving new emphasis. The large number of women of child-bearing age has also contributed to renewed interest in maternity fashion.

Destination Maternity Corporation is the world's leading maternity apparel retailer. In the United States and Canada, as of May 31, 2011, Destination Maternity operates 2,361 retail locations, including 663 stores predominantly under the tradenames Motherhood Maternity®, A Pea in the Pod®, and Destination Maternity®, and sells on the web through its brand specific websites.[1]

Size Ranges

Womenswear is produced in the following size ranges:

- **Misses**—Includes regular even-numbered sizes 4 to 20, tall sizes 12 to 20, and sometimes sizes as small as 0–2.
- **Juniors**—Includes regular sizes 5 to 17 and petite sizes 1 to 15.

An upscale maternity dress from A Pea in the Pod® Collection [left] and a more casual chic maternity look from Motherhood Maternity® [right].

- **Petites**—Includes misses' even-numbered sizes 2P to 16P and junior sizes 1P to 15P.
- **Women's** and **Women's Petites**—Includes even-numbered sizes 12WP to 26WP, straight sizes 26 to 52, and XL to 5X.

Major Price Zones

Within the wide range of prices there are certain traditional **price zones**, or series of somewhat contiguous price lines, that appeal to specific target groups of customers. The women's **ready-to-wear** market has six major price zones. Listed from the most to least expensive, they are as follows:

1. **Designer Signature**: The highest price zone includes lines by designers such as Ralph Lauren, Oscar de la Renta, Calvin Klein, Donna Karan, and Jean Paul Gaultier.
2. **Bridge**: This zone is so named because it bridges the price ranges between designer and better prices. Bridge merchandise usually costs one-third to one-half of designer prices. Some designers who produce lines at the designer signature zone or at lower zones also have bridge lines. Examples include Tommy by Tommy Hilfiger, Donna Karan's DKNY, and Calvin Klein's CK.
3. **Contemporary**: This new zone is favored by young designers who want to enter the market with innovative, designer-quality lines but, at the same time, seek a broader market than that of the designer signature zone. By using less-expensive fabrics and locating in lower-rent spaces, they can offer their lines at lower prices. Labels in this zone include Vivienne Tam, Cynthia Rowley, and Laundry by Shelli Segal.
4. **Better**: Apparel in this zone is usually medium to high in price. Familiar labels include Liz Claiborne, Chaus, Nautica, Evan-Picone, and Jones New York. They appeal to a middle-class market, offering fashionable clothes at affordable prices.

5. **Moderate**: As the name suggests, this zone includes lines of nationally advertised makers, such as Guess, Esprit, Levi Strauss, and Jantzen, which have less prestige than lines with designer names but still appeal to middle-class consumers.

6. **Budget**: The lowest price zone is sometimes referred to as the "promotional" or "mass" market. It is primarily a mass market retailer private label such as JCPenney's Arizona line of jeans or Sears' Canyon River Blues line of jeans, or Kmart's Jaclyn Smith line.

There is also a seventh price zone, the new high end, for the superrich. Some designers are trading up, offering special pieces in very limited quantities at astronomical prices. This range is aimed at people who crave exclusivity and have the means to afford it. Ralph Lauren calls his line of hand-tailored women's classic suits and sportswear in luxury fabrics the Purple Label Custom Collection. Donna Karan offers a Limited Edition label with her signature on dresses costing $5,000 to $6,000. Carolina Herrera, Bill Blass, and Oscar de la Renta are also known for developing exclusive designs for special customers.

More recently the industry has seen growth in what is called the **masstige** movement. This is when marquee designers apply their creativity to lower-priced apparel. It started in 2004 when designers like Karl Lagerfeld teamed up with fast-fashion giant H&M. Today there is the popularity of Target's tie-ups with designers such as Isaac Mizrahi, Zac Posen, Alexander McQueen, and Rodarte. Vera Wang is another example with her Simply Vera Wang line sold at Kohl's.[2]

Multiple Price Zones

Some producers offer merchandise in several price zones to capture a share of the business in each of several market segments. Manufacturer/retailer firms such as Gap cater to different price zone markets in each of their member store chains. Gap's stores have a somewhat overlapping price zone structure with Banana Republic merchandise at its highest zones, Gap at the middle of its market, and Old Navy at its low end.

Designers also produce lines segmented by price zone. For example, DKNY is the label of Donna Karan's bridge collection, Donna Karan is the label of her lines in the designer price zone, and the Limited Edition label is her **custom-made** collection. Ralph Lauren is another designer with lines in several different price zones. In order from most to least expensive, a partial list of his lines are Ralph Lauren Purple Label Collection, Ralph Lauren, RL, Polo Sport, Black Label, and Polo.

Private Labels

Traditional department and specialty stores can also compete in pricing by developing their own private labels. Much of this merchandise is priced in the better price zone, but the quality is comparable with that of designer signature or bridge apparel. Some of the same manufacturers who produce the name-brand merchandise that a store is selling at higher prices also make the store's private label goods. Private label merchandise is vigorously promoted to develop brand recognition, and some customers do not distinguish between private and national brands when they shop. (See Chapter 4.)

Merchandising and Marketing

Most fashion producers sell directly to retail stores rather than through intermediaries. The pace of fashion in all but a few staple items is much too fast to allow for the selling, reselling, or warehousing activities of wholesale distributors or jobbers.

As a result, women's apparel producers aim their sales promotion efforts at both retailers and consumers. Such efforts take the form of advertising, publicity, and sales promotion.

An aura of grandiosity pervades Stella McCartney's Fall 2010 show with anxious buyers waiting in the audience.

Fashion Shows, Press Weeks, and Trade Shows

The major public relations effort in womenswear goes into the presentations and fashion shows at which designers show their new collections for retailers, fashion reporters for the press, and the broadcast and Internet media. The shows provide the country's newspapers, magazines, radio, television, and Internet fashion editors and reporters an opportunity to examine the newest American designer collections, as well as those of leading European manufacturers.

Customers gather for Derek Lam's trunk show.

To coordinate shows of their new lines during market weeks, the manufacturers who lease permanent or temporary showroom space at the major regional markets in Los Angeles, Dallas, Miami, Atlanta, and Seattle depend on the services of the management of their market buildings. New York designers (including foreign designers with New York showrooms) are not housed at a single site. Together with IMG Fashion, nearly 250 designers showcase their designs at the biannual Mercedes-Benz Fashion Week. As of 2010, the events in New York moved from the Bryant Park tents to Lincoln Center.[3] IMG also sponsors an annual award show that attracts international press and broadcast coverage. The giant MAGIC show for womenswear is held semiannually in Las Vegas. Also in Las Vegas is the WomensWear in Nevada (WWIN) (formerly The Big and Tall Woman's Show or B.A.T.WOMAN) for plus and tall sizes, which has become an international hit. It specializes in the missy and plus-size markets with apparel and accessories. Other major international women's wear shows include those held semi-annually in Paris, London, Milan, Tokyo, and Hong Kong. These shows are discussed in more detail in Chapter 10.

Trunk Shows

Trunk shows are another excellent form of publicity for the women's apparel industry. **Trunk shows** present a manufacturer's line to a retail store's sales staff and its customers. A representative of the company, sometimes a designer, typically mounts a fashion show of sample garments. After the show, he or she meets with customers to discuss the styles and their fashion relevance. The retail store's customers may review items they have seen and order them.

Everyone benefits from trunk shows. Customers see clothes as the designer planned them and coordinated them, and they experience some of the glamour of the fashion industry. The retailer enjoys the dramatic influx of customers who come to such personal appearances and shows and any profits that result as clothes are ordered. The manufacturer tests the line on real customers to understand real consumers' needs *firsthand*! If customer response is enthusiastic, the designer achieves new status—and larger orders—from the retailer than otherwise expected.

Industry Trends

Throughout the coming decades, the U.S. women's apparel industry and the U.S. apparel industry overall will face dramatic changes. U.S. designers have finally succeeded in rivaling designers from Paris and Milan as definers of high fashion. However, the U.S. manufacturing industry faces what may be its toughest competitive challenge ever—the growth of a global clothing market out of which U.S. manufacturers must carve their market share because a rise in imports has threatened the market they had enjoyed within the United States.

After decades of domination at home, the U.S. wholesale market has been inundated with imports from countries with cheap labor. An increasing number of U.S. manufacturers are using foreign labor, a process called global sourcing, in factories they own or lease in low-wage countries around the world. The U.S. apparel industry is taking steps, however, to enable it to compete more effectively in an increasingly global marketplace. Some of its tactics include the following:

- Emergence of manufacturers as retailers
- Greater emphasis on licensing
- Increased offshore production
- Increased emphasis on supply chain management
- Use of computers and the Internet

MEN'S APPAREL
Organization and Operation

The menswear industry traditionally has been divided into firms that make the following different kinds of clothing:

1. Tailored clothing—suits, overcoats, topcoats, sports coats, formal wear, and separate trousers
2. Furnishings—dress shirts, neckwear, sweaters, headwear, underwear, socks, suspenders, robes, and pajamas
3. Outerwear—raincoats, coats, jackets, and active sportswear
4. Work clothing—work shirts, work pants, overalls, and related items
5. Other—uniforms and miscellaneous items

The federal government uses these five classifications. Although it is not an official classification, sportswear (including active sportswear) has become a vital portion of the business and should be considered a menswear category.

Size and Location of Manufacturers

Menswear is on the rise, representing $52,819,289 in the U.S. apparel market in 2010, a 3.3 percent increase from 2009.[4] Unlike women's apparel, the business has been dominated by large firms at the manufacturing level.

In recent years Levi Strauss, Phillips-Van Heusen Corp., and VF Corporation have been the largest manufacturers of menswear and boys' wear. Because of diversification, mergers, and acquisitions by top menswear producers in the past few years, it has become more difficult to ascertain company size and production figures.

IT'S A MAD, MAD WORLD!

THE SARTORIAL INFLUENCE OF THE EMMY-WINNING TV SHOW *MAD MEN* HAS INSPIRED EVERYTHING FROM RUNWAY COLLECTIONS TO IN-STORE PROMOTIONS—PROVING THE TRUTH OF THE SAYING "WHAT GOES AROUND COMES AROUND." With the show's sleek, cropped suits and skinny ties—staples of sixties office dress worn to dashing perfection by Don Draper, the show's lead character played by John Hamm—have become a marketable touchstone for contemporary tailored clothing vendors and retailers, which, for the past few years, have promoted similarly slim suits. However, *Mad Men* is not the first TV show to influence the suit. Here are some iconic moments on the small and silver screens that redefined men's tailoring.

1. *Dr. No* (1962):

In James Bond, Ian Fleming created an enduring symbol of masculine power—one that was made flesh by a tuxedo-clad Sean Connery in the first Bond film. "Suits project masculinity and stability—all values associated with James Bond," said Andrew Bolton, curator at the Costume Institute. "007 reflects this masculine ideal of being in control; he renders suits cool."

3. *Miami Vice* (1984):

Don Johnson's signature look—T-shirt, jacket, loose pants, and shoes with no socks—became widely popular when the police drama first aired. "It subverted this idea that tailored clothing was formal," Bolton said.

2. *The Great Gatsby* (1974):

Ralph Lauren dressed Robert Redford in the classic American style his brand would come to define. But the suits in the film also advanced the decade's penchant for dandyism, said Bolton. "It really shows the seventies interest in 1920s America. You see it in the width of the lapels."

4. *The King's Speech* (2010):

Pinstripes and tweeds—costume designer Jenny Beavan explains, "I think pinstripes [are] more smart and business-like…. In those days, men had good suits, and they would last for years. Today we are seeing a return to this smart and tailored look."

Designer Names

Currently, an entirely new world of menswear has emerged in which designer labels are promoted as heavily as well-established brand names used to be. A designer who licenses his or her name in suits may also license men's jeans, shirts, jackets, sportswear, activewear, or ties. The manufacturer pays for the design or name of the designer in royalties based on gross sales. Royalties average from 5 to 7 percent on men's suits and 5 percent on men's sportswear, according to industry sources.

Manufacturing companies that license name designers usually establish separate divisions and in many cases allocate separate manufacturing facilities for them. In licensing agreements, the extent of designer involvement varies; designers are not necessarily responsible for all the designs that bear their names. Some licensing agreements simply pay for the use of the designer's name, and the name designer has no design input at all.

The "name game" is big business in all segments of the menswear industry. While there are no hard figures on the amount of designer business alone at the wholesale level, the best market estimates for retail sales are more than $1 billion for all categories combined. One reason for the continuing popularity of designer names is that they are so easily promoted. Consumers associate them with prestige and fashion and recognize them when they see them. Designers have helped by becoming highly visible. Their names are household words, and their faces frequently appear in newspapers and magazines. They lend themselves to the fantasy of the customer who longs for wealth and excitement.

Designer names also get more exposure than brand names in stores because they often appear on many different kinds of goods displayed in several different departments. Designers often have their own boutiques within stores.

Kenneth Cole is a prominent designer in men's fashion.

Market Segments

Most market segments are based on style differences, but some exist because they involve different production methods. The five main market segments in menswear are: tailored clothing, sportswear, activewear, contemporary apparel, and bridge apparel.

Tailored Clothing

A **tailored suit** is structured, or three-dimensional, which gives it a shape even when it is not worn. Until very recently, **tailored clothing** was graded according to the number of hand-tailoring operations required to make it. The grades were 1, 2, 4, 6, 41, and 61, with a grade 1 suit representing the lowest quality.

Men's tailored clothing is produced in the following proportioned sizes, with the number ranges representing chest measurements:

- Short (36–44)
- Regular (35–46)
- Long (37–48)
- Extra long (38–50)
- Portly short (39–48)
- Large (46, 48, 50)

A tailored men's suit from Ermenegildo Zegna; its retro look no doubt is inspired by the popular 60s drama *Mad Men*.

Suit Separates

The steady decline in structured and semistructured tailored menswear has been offset by an increased demand for **suit separates**—sports jackets and trousers that are worn much as the tailored suit used to be. Tailored suits are now the business uniform only in large, sophisticated cities, and even there, only in some firms and industries and for some levels of management. Elsewhere, men often wear suit separates to work—or for almost any occasion except where formal wear is required.

Although an attempt was made in the 1960s to sell menswear consumers on the idea of coordinated sportswear—that is, jackets, vests, and pants that could be mixed and matched with one another—the idea never took hold. Suit separates today refer to sports jackets and trousers.

Suit separates are usually machine-made and, as a result, can be significantly lower-priced than tailored garments. When they are made for better-priced lines, they can also be expensive. Because each item is bought separately, the expensive alterations that manufacturers and retailers must often make on tailored clothes are avoided. One industry expert believes that men who buy separates are more fashion aware than those who need the reassurance of a preassembled look.

Sportswear

Sportswear, or casual wear, runs the gamut from unconstructed jackets, knit and woven sports shirts, slacks, and leisure shorts, to coordinated tops and bottoms.

Sportswear is unstructured or, at minimum, less structured than tailored clothing. Few if any hand-tailoring operations, for example, are required to make a sports jacket. Sportswear lacks padding, binding, and lining, and it takes its shape (if indeed it has any shape these days) from the person who is wearing it.

Activewear

As discussed, clothing worn during active sports participation as well as during leisure time is classified as activewear. The larger segment of this market is men who want to look as if they are doing something athletic, even when they are ambling to the store for the Sunday paper or flopping down in front of the television set to watch a ball game.

Contemporary Apparel

Contemporary menswear refers to a special type of styling that provides high quality and fashion. Contemporary menswear, which produces clothing in all categories, can often be distinguished by its use of bright colors.

Bridge Apparel

Bridge apparel defines clothing that spans the style gap between young men's and men's collections and the price gap between contemporary and designer apparel. In broad terms, the bridge customer is one who has grown out of young men's clothing but cannot yet afford designer clothes. Bridge customers are usually between 25 and 40 years of age and have sophistication and style.

Cargo pants and sweaters dominate this contemporary menswear by Cucinelli.

Fashion-forward rap star Kanye West looks casual mixing whites and bright colors from Phillip Lim.

Merchandising and Marketing

Like the womenswear producers, menswear producers back their lines with advertising and publicity. Menswear fiber and textile producers sometimes promote their products. The largest percentage of promotion is done, however, by the menswear producers, who rely on agencies, freelancers, and less often, on an in-house department for advertising and publicity.

Industry Trends

The dynamics of population growth as well as lifestyle changes and developments in the economy are bringing about changes in all segments of the menswear industry. Some of the most noteworthy trends include a diversification of products on the part of producers, the automation of production processes, an increase in foreign production and sales, and a proliferation of specialty stores. Consumers are showing greater interest in style and are demanding quality in fabric and construction. All of these trends relate to the growing informality of U.S. culture.

CHILDREN'S, TWEEN'S, AND TEEN'S APPAREL
Organization and Operation

There are close to 1,000 companies that make children's apparel, and children's apparel represents nearly 20 percent of the U.S. retail apparel industry. Despite the prominence of giant companies such as Carter's, OshKosh B'Gosh, Gerber Children's Wear, and Health-Tex, most children's clothes are still made by small, family-owned businesses. Many adult apparel producers, including Levi Strauss, Patagonia, Old Navy, Gap, and Reebok, also operate children's apparel divisions. Many adult apparel designers have also begun children's divisions.

Like adult clothing, childrenswear is divided into categories based on price, size, and type of merchandise. Children's clothes are produced in budget, moderate, better-priced, and designer price ranges. Most children's clothes bought by parents are in the budget and moderate price ranges, although better-priced and designer merchandise is a common gift purchase by grandparents and other adults.

Size Categories

A super-sophisticated marketplace makes sizing little customers more challenging than ever before. The industry debates whether the traditional size categories really reflect a child's age and maturity level. Across the country retailers and manufacturers are questioning and reimagining the size standards, each with their own ideas of what would constitute the ideal size categories.[5]

Name-brand designers like Ralph Lauren offer distinct lines of high-quality childrenswear.

SIZE RANGES OF CHILDRENSWEAR

size category	age range	sizes
Infant's	Newborn–1 year	0–24 months (0–3 months, 6-, 9-, 12-, 18-, and 24-months) Newborn, small, medium, large, extra-large
Toddler's	2–3 years	2T–4T
Children's	3–6 years	3–6X for girls 3–7 for boys
Girl's	7–14 years	7–16
Preteen	7–14 years	6–16 for girls
Boy's	6 or 7–14 or 15 years	8–20 (available in husky, regular, and slim)
Young men	8–20 years, concentrating on 14–20 years	8–20

table 8.2

Results from the 2007–2008 National Health and Nutrition Examination Survey indicated that an estimated 16.9 percent of children and adolescents aged 2–19 years are obese.[6]

Some retailers and vendors do offer plus-size clothing, but the availability of attractive, flattering plus sizes is scarce. JCPenney has carried extended sizes for children for more than 10 years.

Although the actual size range is the same, the preteen sizes for girls offer more sophisticated styling than the girls' sizes. Similarly, the young men's size category (also called prep, student, or teen) stresses sophisticated styling more than boys' sized apparel does.

Product Specialization

Childrenswear manufacturers typically specialize by product. One producer will make only girls' knits, while another makes only girls' dresses, and another makes only preteen sportswear. But unlike the producers of adult wear, childrenswear producers often make a single type of clothing in several size ranges. For example, a producer may make boys' sportswear in sizes 8 through 20, while a producer of girls' dresses may make a product in toddlers' through girls' sizes.

The same design and production methods that are used in the manufacturing of adult apparel are used in childrenswear, although they are often simplified. While children's garments require less fabric, they are usually more expensive to make because they require more labor.

The Role of Fashion in Children's, Tween's, and Teen's Wear

Even the most basic lines of children's clothing reflect attempts to make the clothes fashionable, and the demand for style, once primarily an urban phenomenon, is now

Teens, Tweens, and JUSTIN BIEBER
Talking Technology

THERE HAS ALWAYS BEEN A TEEN-HEARTTHROB ICON—FROM FRANK SINATRA TO ELVIS PRESLEY TO THE BEATLES TO THE JACKSON FIVE TO LEIF GARRETT TO 'NSYNC TO THE JONAS BROTHERS. They were then. Now it's Bieber Fever! Biebermania! Justin Bieber has become one of the most-Googled people on the planet with more than one billion YouTube views, 6.3 million Twitter followers, and 16.5 million friends on Facebook.

In just two years since his first auditions, he has the Justin doll, his own fragrance, and a nail-polish line (with colors inspired by his music and a portion of the proceeds going to charity). What is it that binds and bonds Justin Bieber and tweens, teens, and Gen-Y's? Technology—that's what!

Fashion companies catering to these age groups, which range from 7 to 30 years old, are exploring technology multiplatform boundaries. They are trying to build their brands by enticing consumers who are the most savvy and demanding about the Internet, the latest apps, videos, and social media. Statistics predict the 84 million members of Gen-Y will have more spending power than Baby Boomers by 2017. So as the Internet Generation grows larger, teen brands must go high-tech. And as this generation becomes more entranced with celebrities like Justin Bieber, their use of technology will also grow, and the world of digital will become even bigger.

Justin Bieber on tour

Justin Bieber

Bieber fans

Justin B
film pre

felt in every area. The demand for stylish children's clothes, which has risen every year, has most recently culminated in designer clothing for children. Childrenswear, however, must still be viewed as a business that is a *fashionable* rather than a *fashion* business. The difference is that while the childrenswear industry produces fashionable clothing, the styles adapt men's and women's styles. They are not in themselves innovative, nor does new fashion start in childrenswear lines. The backpack is one recent exception.

Producers of children's clothing have typically operated on a one-line-per-season production schedule, and four lines—spring, summer, winter, and fall—are typical. Lines are not updated during a season. Once a line has been shown and accepted, that is all the manufacturer produces.

Increasingly, children look to their own peers and to the group just ahead of them, young adults, for pace-setting styles and trends. Successful childrenswear producers have learned that they, too, must look to the young adult fashion world for inspiration. This means watching fads as well as trends. Popular young adult fads and styles are increasingly being translated into childrenswear lines. The industry has also begun to use fashion forecasting specialists to enable manufacturers to incorporate new styles into their lines as soon as a trend is spotted.

Merchandising and Marketing

Many of the features and activities of the childrenswear industry are similar, if not identical, to those of the women's and men's apparel industries. Sales promotion and advertising activities for childrenswear, however, are considerably more limited.

The few giants in the industry—Carter's, Health-Tex, and OshKosh B'Gosh—advertise aggressively to consumers. Smaller firms—the majority of firms producing budget and moderately priced childrenswear—leave most consumer advertising to retailers. Firms producing higher-priced, name-designer merchandise do a limited amount of consumer advertising. The high cost of this advertising is often shared with textile firms.

In general the industry limits its advertising to the trade press. Specialized publications that are concerned with childrenswear include *Earnshaw's Infants'* and *Girls' and Boys' Wear Review*. Trade publications that report on adult fashions, such as *Women's Wear Daily*, also carry childrenswear advertising and news reports of interest to retailers on a regular basis. More and more companies are going on the Internet, often combining information about the company with a catalog.

Trade Shows

The Los Angeles Kids Show features KIDS ON 6 at the California Market Center in Los Angeles. It is the largest kids and maternity fashion and accessories showcase in the United States, with more than 600 brands from around the globe. The huge MAGIC International shows for men's, women's, and children's apparel and accessories are held in Las Vegas twice a year. Other popular childrenswear trade shows include the New York–based Children's Club trade show, produced by ENK International, and the annual Women & Children's Apparel Market event in Chicago.

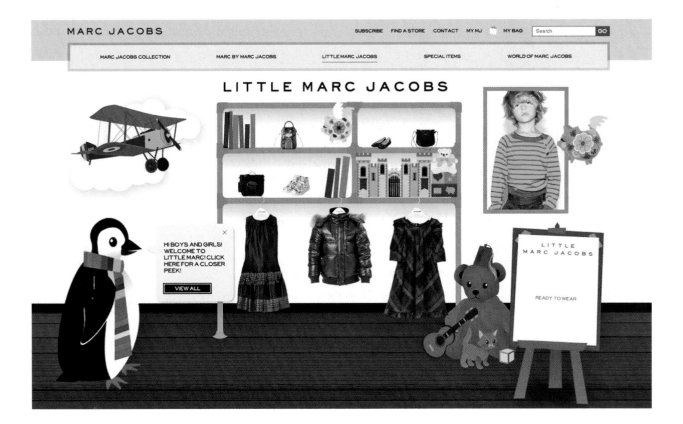

The Marc Jacobs website has prominent page space devoted to the brand's apparel for children.

Designer Labels

Children's designer-label clothing and accessories are highly visible in stores across the country. The appeal of these items seems to rise above income levels. Designer labels are available in stores geared to middle-income as well as high-income customers. Although designer wear for children has been around for a while—Izod introduced a boys' line in the late 1960s—the explosion in designer-label childrenswear took off in the late 1970s with the designer jean craze.

Well-known brand names in childrenswear include Flapdoodles, Gymboree, Little Me, Absorba, Joe Boxer, Cotton Caboodle, and, of course, Guess and Gap. Because they have designer-name status, some childrenswear designers, following in the pioneering footsteps of Florence Eiseman and Ruth Scharf, have acquired celebrity status, such as Hanna Anderson.

Several companies, including Esprit, Guess, Patagonia, and Ralph Lauren, have launched separate divisions of childrenswear. Other designers who offer children's lines include Gucci and Donna Karan's DKNY.

Licensing

Like designer labels, other kinds of licensed names provide a sense of fashion rightness, in addition to giving a garment or line instant identification in consumers' minds. As a result, as the childrenswear industry became more fashion conscious, manufacturers were quick to produce licensed goods. Today, in addition to designer names, the ever-popular cartoon and toy character licenses share the spotlight with a growing number of sports and corporate licenses.

Character Licensing

The first licensed cartoon character was Buster Brown in 1904. Licensed cartoon and toy characters, long a staple with children, are still thriving today. Younger children especially enjoy wearing representations of their favorite characters and television shows. Widespread examples are *Yo Gabba Gabba!*, SpongeBob SquarePants, and Dora the Explorer. Character licenses dominate in children's T-shirts, sweatshirts, and sleepwear, and are also strong in accessories and sportswear.

Disney, a major studio that produces cartoons, has its own retail outlets, where the mix of apparel, accessories, and toys may help to extend the lives of the movie characters. Warner Brothers owns both Superman and Batman, perennial favorites with boys on sleepwear, underwear, and T-shirts. It made a licensing agreement with Spalding Sports Worldwide to put its Looney Tunes characters (Bugs Bunny, Daffy Duck, Road Runner, and Wile E. Coyote) on its leisure products line, including backpacks. Warner Brothers also oversees licensing arrangements for the Hanna-Barbera studio (the Flintstones, Scooby-Doo, and Tom & Jerry). Kmart's exclusive Disney Kids and Sesame Street clothing licenses have been very successful over the years.

Sports Licensing

Sports licensing is another prospering area of licensing. Sports figures and teams both have high visibility in the media and thus enjoy instant recognition among children and young adults. Areas with professional or school teams, college stores, airport shops, and stadium concessions increase the availability of licensed apparel at retail. Sports figures who have successfully put their names on sports equipment for years are now adding them to jogging and running suits, tennis clothes and accessories, as well as less-active casual and sportswear lines. And producers of athletic shoes, sweatshirts, and sports equipment feature their names and logos on active sportswear.

Industry Trends

Like women's apparel manufacturers, childrenswear producers are constantly on the lookout for ways to increase productivity and reduce—or at least minimize—costs while still maintaining quality. Computerized operations have become the norm for manufacturers. Even portions of the design process are now computerized in childrenswear, mostly because this helps producers respond more quickly to fashion trends in the industry.

E-commerce continues to thrive for suppliers, manufacturers, and retailers of childrenswear. Carter's launched two new e-commerce sites, www.carters.com and www.oshkoshbgosh.com, in 2010. Each site features a shopping cart that collects items from both sites, enabling consumers to check out at once.[7] However, the e-commerce sites that attract the most traffic are already attached to a major retail brand, like the Disney Store (www.disneystore.com) and Warner Brothers (www.wbshop.com) for younger children and Abercrombie and Fitch (www.abercrombie. com) and Hot Topic (www. hottopic.com) for teens.

crewcuts
for ages 2–12
crewcutkids.com
A sweet treat for summer... free shipping on all crewcuts orders placed at crewcutkids.com from now through May 31.

J.Crew's "crewcuts" catalog for kids.

Specialty Retail Outlets

Increasing attention is being given to childrenswear by apparel retailers whose main lines are men's and women's clothing. A related trend is the prominence of clothing in the merchandise mix of retail outlets carrying a broader array of children's goods. Even among clothing stores that have not opened freestanding children's outlets, distinctive stores-within-stores are now selling childrenswear exclusively. Carrying the trend to its logical conclusion, the infants' and toddlers' departments of the children's stores and stores-within-stores are being set up as separate outlets.

Separate Stores

Typical of this trend are Gap's GapKids and BabyGap. Begun in 1969 as a retailer of jeans for adults, Gap expanded into a private-label specialty store featuring casual wear for men and women. In 1986, the first GapKids store opened, offering Gap customers basic but fashionable childrenswear that catered to the same tastes as the adult lines. The BabyGap line began in 1990 and became a separate department within GapKids stores and departments, and in 1996, the first flagship freestanding BabyGap store opened in New York. Benetton is another producer/retailer that has developed a successful chain of childrenswear stores. Benetton 0–12 is packed with miniversions of the same stylish merchandise sold to adults.

Catalogs

Major catalog retailers such as Lands' End, J.Crew, and L.L. Bean have also increased their offerings for children in recent years. They offer specialized catalogs, such as J.Crew's Crewcuts. JCPenney has long had a separate catalog geared to kids. It also includes JCPenney for Baby, with furniture and accessories, and JCPenney School Uniforms. Delia's, a catalog for girls and women aged 10 to 24, is another success story.

Resale of Childrenswear

Another important trend in the retailing of childrenswear is the growth of secondhand resale or consignment stores. For parents who are concerned about the price of their children's wardrobe basics, secondhand clothes received as hand-me-downs, or purchased at garage sales or nursery school bazaars have always been a good source of clothing. Because children—especially infants and toddlers—so quickly outgrow their clothes, more budget-minded parents are using this kind of outlet.

Resale shops have emerged as a popular source of "lightly used" childrenswear. Franchise chains like The Children's Orchard, Kid to Kid, and Once Upon a Child have become prominent resale outlets and continue to grow.

SUMMARY AND REVIEW

Womenswear is the largest segment of the fashion industry, and it sets the trends for other segments. In the 20th and 21st centuries, merchandising of ready-to-wear apparel in the United States has been centered in the fashion district of New York City, with other major markets in Los Angeles, Dallas, and Atlanta. Mass production has depended on a unionized labor force.

The production of womenswear is segmented in several ways, and companies may specialize according to categories, such as activewear or bridal wear; sizes, including misses, junior, petite, women's, and half sizes; price zones, ranging from designer signature to bridge to better and contemporary to moderate and budget. Manufacturers and designers change their goods each selling season.

Merchandising and marketing activities include advertising; publicity; fashion shows, press weeks, and trade shows; trunk shows; and other promotion aids.

Five major industry trends include manufacturers acting as retailers, licensing, increased offshore production and imports, increased emphasis on the supply chain management strategy in the United States, and the widespread use of computers and the Internet.

Designer and brand names are part of the push to provide men with up-to-date fashion. And while there will always be a market for classic or traditional men's clothes, industry forecasters predict that menswear will continue to be even more fashion oriented. The Europeanization of the American tailored clothing market has brought an appreciation of quality and fit. Comfort and convenience remain important to the average man, especially in casual wear and active wear.

While menswear changes more slowly than womenswear, the industry saw dramatic change and growth in the 1990s, as dress-down Fridays were adopted by most businesses in the United States. The activewear category also saw dramatic growth as firm, toned bodies became the goal of tens of thousands of men. As the baby boomers aged, more men turned to plastic surgery and cosmetics to hide the signs of aging.

The industry was quick to capitalize on the new interest in menswear, offering increasingly diverse products by using increased automation. Meanwhile, foreign production and imports continued to climb. Retailers jumped on the bandwagon, offering improved visual merchandising, and increased advertising in newspapers, magazines, and on the Internet.

The childrenswear market is segmented by gender and by size categories. The special features of infants' and toddlers' apparel must be taken into consideration by designers and manufacturers.

Designer labels, which are often licensed to manufacturers that specialize in children's products, are becoming increasingly important in this industry, as are character and sports licensing.

Established trends that bear watching are manufacturers offering multiple price lines, and steady offshore production. Retail trends include establishing separate stores, the widespread use of catalogs, and establishing Internet sites.

Most experts are optimistic that the two prevalent trends—a move toward greater fashion in children's and teen's wear and another move toward buying better children's and teen's wear—are unlikely to reverse themselves in the coming years. This situation should serve to make this industry one of the more stable divisions in the fashion industry. The segment that has simply been called childrenswear can now rightly be called children's and teen's fashion.

TRADE TALK

Define or briefly explain the following terms:

activewear

custom-made

price zones

ready-to-wear

masstige

suit separates

tailored clothing

trunk show

FOR REVIEW

1. Name some specialized market segments served by apparel manufacturers.

2. List the traditional basic categories of women's apparel, giving types of garments in each category.

3. Into what size ranges is women's apparel traditionally divided?

4. List and describe the six major price zones into which women's apparel is divided. What are the major factors contributing to the wholesale price of garments?

5. Why do most fashion producers sell directly to retail stores rather than through wholesalers?

6. Discuss the merchandising activities of women's fashion producers today.

7. How does a manufacturer or designer benefit from attending a trunk show in a retail store?

8. Discuss the major problems facing a manufacturer who is also a retailer.

9. Discuss the development of sportswear and casual wear in the men's market and the influence they have had on the menswear industry as a whole.

10. Name the different segments into which the menswear industry is subdivided, on the basis of the type of product lines each produces. What specific products are produced by each segment?

11. How has the sizing of men's suits and dress shirts been simplified in recent years?

12. What is the role of trade shows in promoting men's fashions? Name and describe five trade shows that command national attention.

13. How have menswear producers tried to compensate for the rising cost of labor and the shortage of skilled workers in the United States?

14. Describe two menswear style trends that are likely to continue.

15. Name and briefly describe the seven size categories of childrenswear. What distinguishes girls' from preteen sizes and boys' from young men's sizes?

16. Explain the statement "Childrenswear . . . must still be viewed as a business that is *fashionable* rather than a *fashion* business." Do you agree with this statement? Explain your reasons.

17. How is consumer advertising handled by different types of firms in the childrenswear business?

18. What accounts for the popularity of character licensing in childrenswear?

19. What is the appeal of designer-label children's clothing?

20. What has been the attitude of U.S. retailers and manufacturers toward the growth of imports in the childrenswear industry?

21. Describe the current trend toward specialty retail outlets for childrenswear.

22. Explain the popularity of resale shops for childrenswear.

FOR DISCUSSION

1. Discuss the advantages and disadvantages of standardization of women's apparel sizes.

2. What are the repercussions of a name-brand or designer manufacturer selling current-season apparel to off-price outlets as well as to department and specialty shops?

3. Is the conservative men's suit dying out, or is it taking on a new life in the wake of more casual business dress codes? In what situations are tailored suits commonly worn in your community? What local trends do you see?

4. What is the role of designer names in menswear? Which men's designer fashions are currently popular?

5. Discuss the influence of modern production techniques on the manufacturing of menswear. What are the effects on costs and pricing?

6. Discuss the importance of licensing in today's childrenswear market. How does the licensing system work? Why is it particularly popular with children?

7. Discuss the pros and cons of school uniforms. What impact does this issue have on the childrenswear industry?

8. What trends do you see in the young adult market today that have filtered into the design of children's clothing?

ACCESSORIES

KEY CONCEPTS

- Categories of accessories
- Merchandising and marketing of accessories
- Market segments in accessories
- Advertising and promotion of accessories
- Trends in the accessories industry

The manufacturers of accessories must constantly forecast the changes in cycles of fashion, so that their accessories are perfect for new fashions. This includes not only the changes in silhouette but also fabrications and color. The marketing of accessories gained an enormous boost with the entrance of well-known designers' names into the business. Today, the fame of the accessories designer is as important as the fame of the clothing designer; in many cases, it is the same famous name.

It is only through constant alertness to trends and degrees of customer acceptance that fashion accessory designers succeed. They must be prepared to design and produce styles that blend, follow or lead, and innovate. The fashion accessories category includes footwear, handbags, gloves, hats, neckwear, eyewear, and jewelry.

FOOTWEAR

Footwear has always conjured up exciting, glamorous, and amusing times in history and literature. We read about gallant heroes in seven-league boots, princesses in glass slippers, Mercury with winged sandals, and, of course, the magic red shoes that took Dorothy from the Land of Oz back home to Kansas.

Feet, the base upon which our bodies stand, have been wrapped, covered, or left uncovered since the beginning of time. Primitive people wrapped their feet in fur, and later people strapped them into sandals. Chinese women bound their feet. Footwear often was—and still is—dictated by profession: Arctic trappers wear snowshoes, while ballet dancers wear *pointes,* or toe shoes; cowboys wear leather boots, and firefighters wear rubber boots.

Organization and Operation

Footwear production was once a major industry in New England, but many of that region's factories have downsized or closed. The largest shoe producer in the United States today is Nike in Beaverton, Oregon. Nike actually does not own any of the manufacturing facilities that produce the shoes and apparel it sells. Rather, it acts more like a wholesaler, and focuses on marketing its products. It designs, develops, and markets footwear and athletic apparel worldwide, and in 2010 had $19 billion in sales and $1.9 billion in profit.[1]

Imports are also a factor in dress shoes that are sold at higher price points. A long-standing reputation for quality craftsmanship and styling has contributed to the success of Italian manufacturers, such as Ferragamo, Prada, Gucci, and Diego Della Valle. Italy is the number one producer of high-end designer shoes, with world-famous designs and quality craftsmanship. The bulk of less expensive imported shoes comes from Asia, mainly China. Other countries that export low-price shoes are Brazil, Portugal, and Spain.

Inventories, production problems, and capital investments in the shoe business are tremendous compared with those of other fashion-related industries. Thus, it is not surprising that giant companies dominate the industry. Among the fashion industries, only cosmetics has a higher percentage of production by giant companies.

Women's Shoes

Styles have run the fashion gamut from pointed to square toes, from high to flat heels, and from naked sandals to thigh-high boots. Typically—but not always—broad-toe shoes have low, chunky heels and narrow,

These brightly colored stilettos from Versace's cruise 2011 collection will not make getting your sea-legs any easier.

pointed-toe shoes are more likely to have stiletto heels. The slim, elegant designs have been popular when apparel fashions have emphasized formality, and the heavier, more down-to-earth styles have been the rage in seasons when more casual clothing styles prevailed.

Men's Shoes

Well-known U.S. brand names for men's dress and casual shoes include Florsheim, Johnston & Murphy, Allen-Edmonds, and Alden. L. B. Evans has been making slippers and sandals in New England since 1804. At the high end of the market are Gokey boots and shoes, which are handmade in the United States to customer's exact specifications; they are sold by Orvis through its catalog and stores.

U.S. designer dress and dress/casual shoes are also predominately produced abroad. High-end imports from Europe include Clark's of England; Bally of Switzerland; and Ferragamo, Gucci, and Bruno Magli of Italy.

Children's Shoes

From an early age, both boys and girls take a serious interest in their shoe wardrobes. Perhaps they are influenced by stories about shoes with magical powers, as in *Cinderella, Puss in Boots,* and *The 12 Dancing Princesses.*

Shoes, especially everyday shoes, are subject to wear and tear, so even though they are outgrown as quickly as apparel, they are not as suitable for handing down or buying secondhand. Furthermore, a professionally fitted new pair of shoes is more likely to ensure health and comfort than used shoes. Children thus must be active participants in the purchasing decision. Having a deciding vote on the comfort of their shoes, children can easily make the next step to expressing opinions on appearances. Dressing in conformity with their peers and older children is an obvious way of showing that they fit into their social group.

As athletic shoes evolved from canvas sneakers, they became the preferred shoe for school wear. Practical features, such as Velcro fastenings; purely decorative features, such as L.A. Gear's briefly popular light-up shoe; and brand and style identification, such as that provided by Nike's Air Jordans, all influence children's preferences.

Athletic Shoes

Sneakers, the original athletic shoe, were made possible by Charles Goodyear, who invented the vulcanizing process for rubber in the late 1800s. Keds were the first shoes to use this process, bonding rubber soles to canvas tops. In 1917, Converse, Inc., of North Framington, Massachusetts, introduced the All Star, which has sold more than 500 million pairs. From these humble beginnings a huge industry has grown—and shod the world.

Perhaps the most significant development in shoes since the 1980s—affecting men's, women's, and children's shoes—has been the proliferation of athletic footwear. Spurred by the trend toward more casual dressing, this separate category is now considered a mature market.

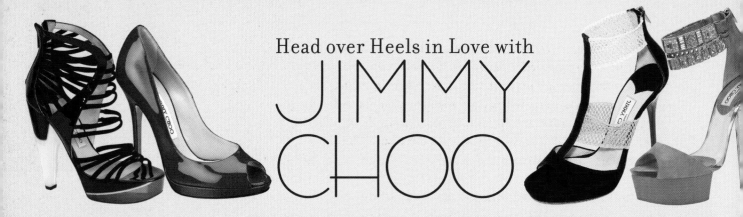

Head over Heels in Love with
JIMMY CHOO

IN THE EARLY NINETIES, TAMARA MELLON, THE ACCESSORIES EDITOR AT BRITISH *VOGUE*, WAS A STEADY CUSTOMER AT THE ATELIER OF JIMMY CHOO, A MALAYSIAN-BORN COBBLER KNOWN FOR CUSTOM-MADE SHOES. Mellon had spotted Choo's talent and often relied on him to make special pieces for the pages of British *Vogue*. With financial backing from her father, she persuaded Choo to start a ready-to-wear business. Here is the story of Jimmy Choo through the years:

1996
- The duo opens the first Jimmy Choo boutique on London's Motcomb Street.

1999
- Jimmy Choo has its first big red-carpet moment when Cate Blanchett wears a pair to the Academy Awards the year she is nominated for *Elizabeth*.
- The brand gets a major television plug when Sarah Jessica Parker's character on *Sex and the City* says, "I lost my Choo."

2001
- Equinox Luxury Holdings Ltd. acquires Jimmy Choo, and Choo exits from the company that bears his name.

2002
- Jimmy Choo kicks off its retail rollout at Harvey Nichols, with a new store and in-store shop concept designed by Milan architect Tiziano Vudafieri.

2003
- The company opens flagships in New York and London.
- Jimmy Choo launches a collection of handbags.

2004
- Lion Capital, then known as Hicks Muse, acquires Jimmy Choo, valuing the company at 101 million pounds (or $187 million).

2005
- Jimmy Choo opens its first boutique in Paris on Avenue Montaigne.

2006
- The London brand inks a distribution agreement with Murjani Group for India: it also forms Jimmy Choo Tokyo K.K., which it owns jointly with Bluebell Japan Ltd.

2007
- TowerBrook Capital Partners LLP snaps up Jimmy Choo in a deal that values the company at 185 million pounds (approximately $364.5 million).
- Jimmy Choo opens a 3,000-square-foot flagship on Rodeo Drive in Beverly Hills.

2008
- Jimmy Choo opens its biggest store in Japan, Tokyo's Ginza neighborhood.
- The brand receives the British Fashion Council's Brand of the Year Award, the ACE Accessory Council Excellence Awards Designer Brand of the Year, and *Footwear News'* Brand of the Year Award.

2009
- Jimmy Choo is honored with the Nordstrom Partner in Excellence Award.
- The accessories firm launches Project PEP, a limited edition collection of handbags, shoes, and small leather goods, in participation with the Elton John AIDS Foundation.
- The brand collaborates with Hunter for boots.
- The house collaborates with H&M on a collection at budget prices.

2010
- Jimmy Choo launches Choo 24:7 Perfect Shoe Closet at retail, putting a fresh spin on some old favorites, including platforms, pointy-toe pumps, and strappy evening stilettos at prices from $395 for a basic flat to $1,200 for the Glenys gladiator stiletto.
- The brand launches a collaboration with Ugg Australia, featuring sheepskin boots with studs, grommets, and fringe details.
- Jimmy Choo opens its largest flagship in Europe at the intersection of Milan's Via Sant'Andrea and Via Montenapoleone.

2011
- The Jimmy Choo fragrance launched at Jimmy Choo stores, followed by worldwide distribution.
- The company adds men's shoes to its offerings.
- Labelux, a privately held luxury group, acquired the high-end shoe and accessories company Jimmy Choo from TowerBrook Capital Partners.

Athletic shoes have become even more specialized. Manufacturers make special shoes for virtually any sports activity—walking, running, climbing, aerobics, racquetball, biking, hiking, and golf. Most of the "super-specialty" shoes are carried in specialty sporting goods stores, while department stores and other general retailers stock a less specialized and more fashion-oriented range of athletic shoes.

Merchandising and Marketing

As with most fashion industries, New York City is the major U.S. market center for shoes. It is there that most producers maintain permanent showrooms, and it is also home to the industry's trade shows. The Fashion Footwear Association of New York (FFANY), with a membership of 300 corporations and 800 brand names, stages the international footwear trade show New York Shoe Expo four times a year.

Some shoe manufacturers operate in the retail field through leased departments in retail stores. Because of the tremendous amount of capital required to stock a shoe department and the expertise needed to fit and sell shoes, many department and specialty stores lease their shoe departments to shoe manufacturers. Surveys by the National Federation of Retailers have repeatedly shown that women's shoe departments are among those most commonly leased by its member stores. Examples of manufacturers of shoes who operate leased shoe departments in stores are the Jones Group, which features Jones New York, Anne Klein, Kasper, and Nine West, and the Brown Shoe Company, which features Buster Brown shoes for children, Naturalizer shoes for women, and Regal shoes for men.

One of many towering sneaker displays at the Nike store in Tokyo.

Industry Trends

U.S. consumption of footwear reached 2.393 billion pairs in 2007, and the percentage of imports to the United States was at 98.7 percent. U.S. imports from China currently supply 83.8 percent of the total U.S. footwear market, with China remaining the largest supplier to the United States. Vietnam is the second-largest supplier and increases from Taiwan have also been seen, according to the American Apparel and Footwear Association.[2]

Whether in athletic or other footwear, there is a strong relationship between shoes and the clothes with which they are worn. Increased emphasis on fashion continues to be the major trend in the footwear industry. Shoe designers and manufacturers regularly attend the Shoe Fair in Bologna, Italy, or the GDS exhibition in Germany. They also attend European apparel openings, as do shoe buyers from retail stores, gathering information on international trends in styling. More and more, apparel fashions influence both the styling and color of footwear. Skirt lengths, silhouette, pants, and sporty or dressy clothes are the fashion keys to women's shoe designs. It is therefore essential for retailers to coordinate shoes and apparel wherever and whenever they can.

HANDBAGS

As fashion statements, handbags are used to dramatize, harmonize, or contrast with whatever else one is wearing. Styles vary from the most casual, used for sportswear, to the more formal, used for formal occasions. A handbag may be small or large, and its shape may be a pouch or a tote, or draped or boxy. So important are handbags as fashion accessories that most women own a wardrobe of them. Perhaps the most-copied handbag of this century was Chanel's "2.55" diamond-quilted bag, with the shoulder strap that slides through golden chains.

Organization and Operation

Compared with other fashion industries, the U.S. handbag industry is small. The number of domestic firms producing handbags diminishes each year, as imports made in Europe, South America, and the Far East increase. Although U.S. manufacturers' brand names are relatively unimportant in the handbag industry (except for certain classics such as Coach, Le Sportsac, and Dooney & Bourke), designer handbags have become popular. Famous names like Anne Klein, Ralph Lauren, Donna Karan, and Marc Jacobs have entered licensing agreements with handbag manufacturers.

Several foreign manufacturers such as Louis Vuitton, Hermès, Ferragamo, Bottega Veneta, and Gucci have always enjoyed enormous status at the high end of the market, and the names of Chanel and, more recently, Prada are associated with distinctive styles of handbags.

Backpacks

Some of the larger manufacturers have recently diversified their lines, reaching out to men, who have flirted with the idea of carrying handbags since the 1960s. The backpack has gained favor with men who are on the go and do not have enough room in their pockets for everything they want to carry. Perhaps the backpack's acceptance is a carryover from its use as a school bookbag. For that purpose, it remains popular with boys and girls from kindergarten through college. Canvas is the most popular material, and names such as L.L. Bean, Lands' End, and JanSport carry status as well as school supplies. Meanwhile, smaller leather backpacks or Prada's nylon backpack have become a trendy handbag style among women.

Merchandising and Marketing

Few handbag manufacturers are large enough to advertise on a national basis in newspapers and television. The customer's impression of what is new and fashionable in handbags is mostly gleaned through store displays and advertising in magazines. Catalogs, home shopping networks, and Internet shopping sites are also increasingly popular ways of reaching customers.

Industry Trends

Faced with severe competition from foreign imports, many domestic handbag manufacturers have themselves become importers of foreign-made handbags. These importers employ U.S. designers to create styles and then have the handbags made in countries with low wage scales.

The industry's trade organization the Fashion Accessories Shipper's Association, Inc., was created by the former National Handbag Association. The organization supports the interests of importers as well as manufacturers of handbags and related accessories, including belts, small leather goods, gloves, and luggage.

The leather goods trade fair, Mipel, held in spring and autumn in Milan, attracts handbag buyers from all over the world.

Elbow-length blue suede gloves by Carolina Herrera complete this opulent look.

GLOVES

Crude animal-skin coverings were the forerunners of mittens, which, in turn, evolved into gloves with individual fingers. Gloves are not new, though; leather gloves were discovered in the tombs of ancient Egyptians.

Gloves have enjoyed a long and varied history, at times even taking on symbolic value. To bring them luck, knights once wore their ladies' gloves on their armor as they went into battle. So long as women wore modest dress, men often cherished the gloves of their beloved as erotic objects. Gloves were once exchanged when property was being sold as a gesture of good faith. And in dueling days, one man would slap another across the face with his glove as an invitation to a duel. Gloves have also been used to denote rank or authority. Until the 16th century, only men of the clergy or of noble rank were allowed to wear them.

For centuries, gloves were coordinated in styling, detail, and color with current apparel styles. To be specific, glove styles correlated to the currently popular sleeve length, especially in coats and suits.

Organization and Operation

The production of gloves varies, depending upon whether they are made of leather or fabric. Leather gloves are among the most difficult accessories to manufacture. Most leather gloves are made, at minimum, with hand-guided operations, and some are still made entirely by hand.

Leather gloves are typically made in small factories, since few machines and workers are required to run such a factory. Glove producers tend to specialize on one part, performing only one manufacturing operation, such as cutting or stitching. Other operations are farmed out to nearby plants, each of which, in turn, has its own specialty.

New York City was once the center of the glove-manufacturing industry. Today, glove manufacturers have turned to offshore production, and most gloves are made in China, the Caribbean, and the Philippines. Some specialist glove manufacturers in the United States are Totes ISOTONER Corporation, which produces a line of leather gloves and the Isotoner line of fabric gloves. Other fashion glove makers in the United States are Fownes Brothers & Co., Inc.; Grandoe; Nolan Glove Company; and LaCrasia.

Merchandising and Marketing

Compared with the dollars spent on consumer advertising for other accessories, the industry outlay for glove advertising is quite modest. Only a few large producers with nationally distributed brand names actively promote their products or offer even limited merchandising support services to retail stores.

Industry Trends

Sales of domestically produced leather gloves have suffered considerably from the competition of less expensive imports. To meet this challenge, the industry is trying to improve manufacturing procedures to reduce costs. Manufacturers have reduced the number of glove sizes, preferring to sell gloves in only small, medium, and large. Stretch fabric gloves, in which one size fits all, are made as well. In addition, improved materials are resulting from product research and development in the leather industry. These are expected to increase the market potential of domestically produced leather gloves. For example, many leather gloves today are hand washable and come in a wide range of fashion colors.

The fabric glove industry is exploring innovative packaging techniques, such as packaging matching hats and gloves (or mittens) together, or matching scarfs and gloves, or matching headbands and gloves for winter wear.

MILLINERY

According to an old saying, whatever is worn on the head is a sign of the mind beneath it. Because the head is one of the more vulnerable parts of the body, hats do have a protective function. But they are also a fashion accessory.

The man's hat of the 19th and 20th centuries in Europe, which was derived from the medieval helmet, protected its wearer both physically and psychologically. The heavy crown kept the head safe from blows, and the brim shaded the face from strong sunlight and close scrutiny. In 19th-century America, the cowboy hat became an enduring national icon. Late in the century, the top hat was a status symbol of a special kind. This was the time of European immigration, and those who wanted to distinguish themselves from the immigrant peasants took care to wear hats.

After decades of prosperity and popularity, the men's **millinery**, or hat, industry began to collapse in the years following World War II. This was soon true for the women's millinery industry as well. Because of the more casual approach to dressing and the popularity of women's beehive and bouffant hairstyles, men's and women's hat sales hit bottom in 1960. During the freewheeling 1960s and 1970s, a hat was worn only on the coldest days—strictly for warmth, not for fashion.

During that time, the millinery industry and its active trade association, the National Millinery Institute, researched, publicized, and campaigned in an extensive effort to reverse the trend, with little success. This was not surprising, since, as we have already learned, no amount of sales promotion can change the direction in which fashion is moving.

With the rise of hip-hop fashion and "ghetto fabulous" clothing styles, a new range of headwear, from streetwise Kangol hats, berets, and caps to elegant fedoras, has become must-haves among young fashion addicts. Many leading luxury houses like Gucci, Louis Vuitton, and Burberry are enjoying tremendous success with their logo-embellished newsboy caps, bucket hats, and fedoras.

Another factor was the featuring of flamboyant hats in designer shows, especially on the runways of Paris and Milan. Although these extreme styles are presented more as a display of the designer's imagination than as an attempt to introduce a trend, they remind fashion arbiters and consumers that hats can be a fun accessory and can make or break an outfit. Philip Treacy, a well-known British hat designer, has designed hats for the runway shows of Chanel, Valentino, and Versace. Treacy has also expanded into handbags. Well-known U.S. millinery designers include Patricia Underwood, Eric Javits, and, at a lower price point, Betmar.

A Marc Jacobs hat in dark, lustrous purple.

The third factor contributing to the increased popularity of hats is the awareness of the dangers of overexposure to the sun. Dermatologists recommend the wearing of hats for protection in all seasons. Straw and canvas hats with large bills or brims offer shade without undesired warmth. Hats are also available that are made of fabrics with SPF (sun protection factor). Baby hats that tie under the chin, or bonnets, have long been popular for infants; they are now widely used for toddlers as well. Along with the popular safari hat for men, hats with neck guards—once only seen in French Foreign Legion movies—have become popular in retirement communities across the country.

As with many fashion trends, the growing popularity of baseball caps as a fashion accessory started with young consumers. In this instance, boys and young men have worn them as a mark of support for their favorite teams. Soon the caps became promotional items for businesses, clubs, and other organizations. Designers took up the trend, putting their names and logos on this activewear accessory, often adding sequins, beading, or braid trims. Caps have proliferated, worn backward or forward, by men, women, and children.

The center of the women's millinery industry is in New York City in the West 30s, between Fifth and Sixth Avenues, with some smaller firms in Los Angeles and St. Louis. One-person millinery shops can be found in many cities, since millinery involves a great deal of handwork and is ideal for custom work.

EYEWEAR

Consumers have become increasingly aware of the need to protect their eyes from the sun's harmful ultraviolet (UV) rays. Even for children, sunglasses are now considered more than a cute, wearable toy.

At the same time, manufacturers of sunglasses have made a concerted effort to produce styles that are high fashion. Wraparound frames, clear frames, and lenses that are reflective or tinted different colors are some of the distinctive design features. Combine these factors with the high visibility of sunglasses on prominent celebrities and on MTV, and it is no wonder that sales of this category exploded.

Dozens of styles are popular at the same time: from aviators to "Jackie O" types, to John Lennon grannies, to "cat eyes," to "alien eyes." Riding the current wave of popularity are many designer names, among them DKNY, Christian Dior, Gucci, Chanel, Kenneth Cole, and Calvin Klein.

In 2004, sunglasses maker Oakley released Thump, sunglasses embedded with a digital music player with $395 and $495 price tags. Too expensive and too goofy, said some, but Thump generated $20 million at Christmas alone. Then, in 2005, Oakley released Razrwire, a line of sunglasses that could be used as a hands-free phone. (Luxottica, a leader of luxury and sports eyewear with license brands including Burberry, Polo, and Ralph Lauren, bought Oakley in 2007.) A more recent trend seen in 2010 was the 24-karat-gold sunglasses. This seems to have stemmed largely from paparazzi shots of Brad Pitt, Angelina Jolie, and Halle Berry, who were seen sporting these glamorous shades. Gold-coated lenses could range in prices from $290 to $1,500; this trend has triggered designers to add them to their collections.[3]

Michael Kors aviators, cast in 22-karat gold, make the world look a little bit brighter.

Designer frames for prescription eyeglasses are another important segment of the fashion eyewear category. Despite the popularity of contact lenses, optometrists now fit their customers to improve their looks as well as their vision. Aging baby boomers have spurred growth in the market for nonprescription reading glasses, or readers. The industry has responded with fashionable styles available at different price points. Designer eyeglasses are available from such famous names as Donna Karan, Hugo Boss, Perry Ellis, Diane von Furstenburg, Tory Burch, Jimmy Choo, and Calvin Klein. Marchon Eyewear is one of the largest manufacturers and distributors for many of these designer brands around the world. Lower-priced readers are available at drugstores.

JEWELRY

A symbol of wealth and importance, jewelry was at certain times worn only by nobility. Laden with gold chains, their clothing adorned with gems, their fingers covered with rings, they carried on their persons the fortunes of their ruling houses. Medieval noblemen displayed elaborate heraldic emblems symbolizing their knighthood, and military men, another privileged class, used to make a great display of their decorations, which were once jewel-encrusted. Jeweled tiaras were in vogue among the upper classes in the Napoleonic era because they simulated the laurel wreaths of antiquity.

Organization and Operation

Methods of making jewelry have changed little over time. Modern jewelers melt and shape metal, cut and carve stones, and string beads and shells much as jewelers have been doing for centuries. Jewelry designers have always used enamel, glass, ceramic, and natural mineral formations as their raw materials.

PIERRE CARTIER
Good Things Come in Red Packages

Coral-and-diam[...]
Cartier bracele[...]

THE BEGINNING OF THE 20TH CENTURY MARKED THE DAWN OF A TRADITION OF INNOVATION AND CREATIVITY THAT CATAPULTED THE HOUSE OF CARTIER TO FAME AND FORTUNE. Founded in 1817 by Louis François Cartier, the house in the 19th century earned a reputation as one of Paris's preeminent jewelers. As the firm achieved greater success at home, it became only a matter of time before it began to look beyond its borders.

In 1909, the company opened a small shop in New York City. It took a while for Americans to become aware of Cartier jewelers. But in 1917, Cartier moved into a famous mansion on Fifth Avenue and 52nd Street. The mansion, a designated New York City landmark, was one of the last private homes constructed in what was then a neighborhood of millionaires' mansions, and for visionary Cartier, it was the most apropos setting. The United States is now the home of 36 Cartier boutiques steeped in old-world elegance.

Cartier sells one important thing: passion! From the house's iconic Love Bracelet, which is meant to signify a lasting bond between two people, to its Trinity rings, which represent the emotional threesome of love (gold), friendship (platinum), and fidelity (yellow gold) all tied into one, both the watches and jewelry remain a haven for romantics. Here are a few of the notable collections:

Panthère de Cartier
In 1914 Cartier made a watch with a panther on it. And in 1949 the Duchess of Windsor commissioned the house to create a one-of-a-kind Panther broach that captured the imagination and excitement of women everywhere.

Trinity
To celebrate its American Centennial, Cartier has designed a new Trinity group that comprises three-ringed bracelets, earrings, and a limited-edition ring accented with 100 diamonds.

Cart[...]
flag[...]
stor[...]

Trinity ring

Love
This collection was created in the 1960s during the Vietnam War protests when catchphrases like "Make love, not war" were commonly heard. The gold bracelet was designed so the wearer could not put it on alone. It is also meant to be locked with a key by his or her significant other, who then holds the key.

"Love" bracelet

And remember, good things come in red packages! The famous red leather Cartier jewelry boxes have become so recognizable that it alone is enough to quicken a woman's heart with joy and anticipation.

Based on the quality of their products, the jewelry industry in the United States can be divided into two primary groups: fine jewelry and costume or fashion jewelry. A third group, bridge jewelry, has gained popularity, as has a fourth group, ethnic jewelry.

Fine Jewelry

Only precious metals such as gold and platinum are used to make fine jewelry. Sterling silver is also considered a precious metal, although its intrinsic value is far less than that of gold or platinum. Too soft to be used alone, these precious metals are alloyed, or combined, with one or more other metals to make them hard enough to be fashioned into jewelry.

Platinum (which includes palladium, rhodium, and iridium) is the most expensive metal. It was first used for jewelry by Cartier, and became a hallmark of the Art Deco movement of the 1920s and 1930s.

The gold content of jewelry is measured by weight in **karats**, which are abbreviated as "K." An item called solid gold actually has only 24 karats of gold—or 1/24 gold to 23/24 alloy. Less costly, 14K gold is popular in the United States, while 18K gold is popular in Europe, and 22K gold is popular in India. Gold-filled jewelry is made of an inexpensive base metal with a heavy layer of gold on top. *White gold* is a substitute for platinum; it is an alloy of gold and another metal, usually nickel. **Vermeil** (pronounced ver-MAY) is a composite of gold over sterling silver. The term **sterling silver** is used for jewelry (and flatware) with at least 92.5 parts of silver; the remaining 7.5 parts are usually copper. Not all sterling silver is equal; thicker items are generally more valuable than thin ones.

The stones used in fine jewelry are called gemstones to distinguish them from lower-quality stones that are used for industrial purposes. Gemstones, which always come from natural mineral formations, have traditionally been classified as either precious or semiprecious. Precious stones include diamonds, emeralds, rubies, and sapphires. Stones are measured by weight in a unit of measure called a **carat**, which equals 200 milligrams, or 1/142 of an ounce. Carats are subdivided into points; there are 100 points to a carat. Thus a half-carat stone is a 50-point stone.

Diamonds are the hardest substance known and are in limited supply. From 250 tons of ore, only one carat of rough diamonds can be recovered, and only 20 percent of them are suitable for gemstones. Diamonds are found in South Africa, Siberia, Australia, and Arkansas. The world supply is dominated by the De Beers cartel of South Africa. It has spent millions to promote the romance of diamonds with its ad slogan, "A diamond is forever."

Diamonds are usually cut into 58 *facets,* which are small, polished planes that are precisely placed to reflect the maximum amount of light. Traditional cuts or shapes of diamonds are round, emerald, marquise, pear, oval, and heart. There is also a cut called the radiant cut, which was developed in 1976. It has about 70 facets and was originally developed to hide flaws.

Advanced technology in the new millennium has unleashed a crop of innovative cuts. Among them is the square-shaped Context Cut, which is not cleaved, but based on the natural twelve-sided rough diamond crystal. Others include the circular Spirit

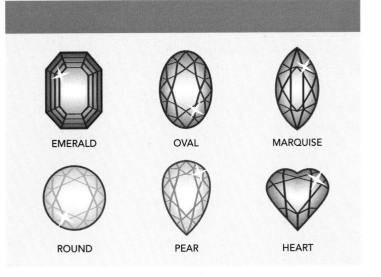

Some classic shapes
for diamond cuts.

EMERALD   OVAL   MARQUISE

ROUND   PEAR   HEART

Sun cut and the triple-brilliant Gabrielle cut, which has 105 facets (compared with the traditional amount of 58). They are available in a wide range of classic shapes.[4]

A *solitaire* is the mounting of a single gemstone; a diamond solitaire is the traditional engagement ring. A *Tiffany setting* refers to a four- or six-prong setting that flares out from the base to the top, with long slender prongs that hold the stone. A *baguette* is a rectangular-shaped small stone used with a larger stone. A *pave setting* is one in which a number of small stones are set as closely together as possible, so that no metal shows between them, and they appear as an all-stone surface.

Real, or *oriental, pearls* are of animal origin but are still considered precious stones. *Tahitian* and *South Sea pearls* are the most expensive real pearls. *Cultured pearls* are pearls formed by an oyster around an irritant placed in the oyster's body by man. They are not considered precious stones, although they can only be raised in limited parts of the world's oceans. *Freshwater pearls* are nugget-shaped pearls that grow in lakes or rivers; they are more abundant and less expensive than real or cultured pearls.

Pearls are measured in millimeters around and in length. Size contributes to the value of pearls; large pearls are hard for oysters to grow, and so are more expensive. Pearls cannot be cut or shaped like other gems. The more symmetrical the pearl, the more expensive it is. Pearls with irregular and asymmetrical shapes are called *baroque pearls.* The rarest—and most expensive—pearls are black; other natural tints are cream, a pinkish hue, or a bluish one.

The so-called semiprecious stones include a host of other natural stones that were once more costly and less rare than precious stones, but are still quite beautiful. The Jewelers of America Association holds that the division of gems into precious and semiprecious is invalid because discoveries have added new varieties that are higher priced because of their rarity than the more well-known gems. For example, fine jade is more valuable than a lesser-quality emerald. Tanzanite, first discovered near Mount Kilimanjaro in 1967, is a deep purple gemstone that Tiffany & Co. has popularized. Although it is considered a semiprecious stone, it is being used by fine-jewelry designers in very expensive pieces.

Chemists have succeeded in creating synthetic stones that are chemically identical to real stones. Synthetic stones are now used in combination with 14-karat gold and sterling silver. The most popular of the synthetics is zirconia, which offers the dazzle of diamonds at a fraction of the cost. Other synthetic stones include synthetic spinel, which looks like emeralds or aquamarines, and synthetic corundum, which looks like amethysts.

212   THE SECONDARY LEVEL—THE PRODUCERS OF FASHION

Fine-jewelry production is still a handcraft industry. A lapidary, or stonecutter, transforms dull-looking stones in their natural states into gems by cutting, carving, and polishing them. Then the jeweler creates a setting for the stones to bring out their brilliance.

In the established fine-jewelry houses, as in haute couture houses, design, production, and retail sales typically take place under one roof—and one management team. Many fine-jewelry firms sell only the jewelry they create, much of which is custom designed for them. Names such as Cartier and Tiffany have always been used to sell jewelry, but in the past, the designers who were in the employ of these companies were not well known. In the past few decades, however, individual designers have taken on new importance, and customers now look for jewelry designed by their favorite designers.

Paloma Picasso and Elsa Peretti designs are sold at Tiffany & Co. Other leading independent designers with large followings include Barry Kieselstein-Cord, Robert Lee Morris, David Yurman, and Steven Lagos. As another example, Bergdorf Goodman's fine-jewelry department carries the work of 50 designers, including Alexander McQueen, Diamond in the Rough, Stephen Dweck, and Stephen Webster.

Blinding pink sapphire-and-diamond clusters in this ring from "The Court of Jewels," a traveling collection of historical jewelry curated by Harry Winston.

Costume Jewelry

Costume or **fashion jewelry** is like mass-produced apparel. A wide range of materials—wood, glass, and base metals such as brass, aluminum, copper, tin, and lead—are used to make it. Base metals are sometimes coated with costlier precious metals such as gold, rhodium, or silver. The stones and simulated (fake) pearls used in costume jewelry are made from clay, glass, or plastic. While they are attractive and interesting in their surface appearance, they are less costly and lack the more desirable properties (durability, for one) of natural stones.

The age of costume jewelry began with designer Coco Chanel. In the 1920s, she introduced long, large, and obviously fake strands of pearls to be worn with her clothes. This new accessory was called costume jewelry because it was meant to coordinate with one's costume. The pearls were called *simulated* in English and *faux,* which means "false" in French.

Chanel, it might be noted, not only helped to create an industry but also continued to wear her trademark pearls for the rest of her life. Today, simulated pearls—indeed Chanel-style pearls—are a staple of the costume jewelry industry. Two first ladies also contributed to the popularity of pearls: Jackie Kennedy Onassis and Barbara Bush.

Mass-production methods are employed in contrast to the handwork that exemplifies the making of fine jewelry. While a fine jeweler pounds and hand shapes metal, manufacturers of costume jewelry cast metal by melting it and then pouring it into molds to harden. Designs are applied to the hardened metal surface by painting it with colored enamel or embossing it by machine. Electroplating is the name of a process that coats inexpensive base materials with a thin coat of silver or gold.

Costume jewelry from Prada provides glamour at an affordable price.

Large firms dominate the industry. Examples are the Monet Group and Carolee. Victoria & Co. Ltd., a division of Jones Apparel Group, is a leading designer and marketer of branded and private label costume jewelry. Victoria manufactures and markets the licensed jewelry collection for Givenchy and also oversees brands such as Nine West, Judith Jack, and Rachel Rachel Roy.[5] While most large firms work with multiple price lines and many different materials, some companies do specialize. An example is Swarovski Jewelry U.S., which specializes in crystal jewelry, made under the company name and the Savvy label.

Still, more than 90 percent of U.S. jewelry producers are small, family-owned companies. Individuals with creative talent often open successful small retail or wholesale operations that cater to customers who are interested in individualized styling and trend-setting fashions. Such operations are an outgrowth of the handcraft movement of the 1960s and 1970s. Handmade jewelry had a major comeback at the beginning of the new millennium, which launched a rise of small, independent jewelry designers across the country. Today, online sites like Etsy also help promote individual jewelry designers.

Bridge Jewelry

Dramatic increases in the price of gold and silver in the early 1980s left jewelers seeking new ways to meet the public's demand for reasonably priced authentic jewelry. The solution was **bridge jewelry**, that is, jewelry that forms a bridge—in price, materials, and style—between fine and costume jewelry. Prices at retail range from about $100 to $2,500 for bridge jewelry. (Also see the discussion of bridge apparel in Chapter 8.)

The development of bridge jewelry led to increased use of sterling silver and its subsequent elevation to a precious metal. The boom in Native American jewelry in the early 1970s also helped to create interest in bridge jewelry. Many department stores and specialty stores created bridge departments to handle sterling silver and Native American jewelry, and when interest in it faded, they were open to other kinds of bridge jewelry that would help them keep the customer base they had developed.

Bridge jewelry departments at stores such as Bloomingdales, Neiman Marcus, and Macy's now carry gold-filled, vermeil, sterling silver, and some 14-carat fashion jewelry set with semiprecious stones. Sterling silver jewelry continues to grow rapidly in popularity. Bridge designers include Zina and M J Savitt. Judith Jack specializes in *marcasite* (crystallized mineral) jewelry, which attracts both costume and fine jewelry customers.

Ethnic Jewelry

The category of ethnic jewelry includes pieces from all over the world at all price points, although some of these items are not made of intrinsically valuable materials, but rather of shells, stones, wood, or fabric. The artistry is so remarkable that these items can command a higher price than costume jewelry. As previously mentioned, Native American jewelry in silver and turquoise has been popular for decades. Two famous styles of silver necklaces, the *squash blossom* necklace and the *liquid silver* necklace, continue to be reinterpreted by modern Native American designers.

Ralph Lauren popularized African jewelry with his 1997 collection that was inspired by the Masai of Kenya; it included arm cuffs, bead chokers, and hoop earrings. Similarly, traditional ethnic jewelry from India, made from 22K gold and decorated with ornate patterns and precious gemstones, became popular in the late 1990s after Nicole Kidman and Goldie Hawn began wearing these styles. Most people, however, bought far less expensive designs in glass, brass, and silver. Chinese-inspired jewelry made of jade, coral, and mother-of-pearl is perennially popular, as is the yin-yang symbol. Moroccan beads, the Egyptian ankh, Guatemalan string figures, Greek worry beads, Caribbean shell necklaces, and Peruvian hammered copper earrings have fans worldwide.

Another category of ethnic jewelry involves wearing religious or spiritual symbols in necklaces, earrings, rings, or pins, such as the Jewish Star of David, the Christian cross, the Buddhist lotus blossom, the Native American eagle feather, and the New Age crystal. The famous Indian "Navratan Haar" ring is made of nine gems with astrological significance: a diamond in the center, circled by eight rainbow-colored stones: ruby, emerald, cinnamon, coral, cat's eye, blue and yellow sapphires, and pearl.

Designers must show sensitivity when adapting these powerful symbols into jewelry. A storm of protest arose when Madonna wore a cross as part of her on-stage costume during the early part of her career; it was interpreted by many as irreverent, even blasphemous.

Many people wear their so-called *birthstone,* to which folklore attributes good luck, according to their sign of the zodiac. In fact, the concept of the birthstone was introduced in the United States in 1912 by the predecessor of the Jewelers of America Association and is matched to calendar months rather than the zodiac.

Another interesting development in ethnic jewelry is the growing number of firms making licensed copies or reproductions of museum pieces of jewelry. Museums around the world, from the State Historical Museum of Moscow to the Vatican Library, to the Metropolitan Museum of Art in New York, are selling vast amounts of inexpensive reproductions of museum pieces in their stores and through catalogs. These pieces come from many different eras and many different cultures; what they have in common is that they have been preserved because of their beauty and power.

Turquoise and silver typify the early Zuni Indian style in this necklace from the 1940s.

THE ACCESSORIES COUNCIL

Adding the Finishing Touches to Any Outfit

Best-selling accessories

LAUDED BY BOTH RETAILERS AND FASHION TRENDERS, THE ACCESSORIES INDUSTRY NOW IS A MAJOR FORCE IN ALL THINGS FASHIONABLE—AND IT HAS THE ACCESSORIES COUNCIL TO THANK FOR ITS GROWTH. The Accessories Council, which began as a small trade organization to help the needs of an overlooked retail and fashion sector, has matured into a vital supporter and player in the fashion industry.

The annual Accessories Council Excellence Awards have become a high-profile celebration of the fashion accessories industry linking brands, retailers, and consumers. From handbags to shoes to watches, accessories are generating the power that is driving the surge in the accessories business. It is a global trend—from the United States to emerging markets such as India, Vietnam, and the Middle East.

Customers are increasingly sophisticated, choosing across categories, brands, and channels for quality style and value in their purchases. Pete Nordstrom, president of merchandising at Nordstrom Inc., said, "Shoes and accessories have been the strongest category for us in the last several years. There is a lot of value in accessories and shoes.... If someone buys a designer handbag, they can use it several times a week. If you bought a designer apparel outfit, you may wear it a few times a year. You get more use of accessories and that is part of the success." David Wolfe, creative director of trend forecasting at the Doneger Group, agrees. He said, "It is natural for accessories to lead the change in the retail recovery."

The Accessories Council's work is hardly done, however, and has significantly increased the scope of the once "teeny trade groups." The council now regularly features educational seminars, lectures, and networking events in the last five years. It has gone from four events a year to one event a month. The council has also initiated a host of new programs, beginning with a few social media ventures. The organization's blog (www.accessoriescouncil.org/blog) posts the council's latest developments and news, as does its Twitter account (www.twitter.com/accessorynews). A new program that stresses socializing has been initiated as a mentorship program named FACE (Future Accessories Council Executive). FACE was created to pair seasoned executives with new talent, to get them networking and active in the industry. There are also a host of educational programs and competitions with the Fashion Institute of Technology and LIM College as well as a job site called "Talent Source."

The real diamond pendant among the Council's string of offerings is the Accessories Council Excellence Awards. The FACE Awards recognize individuals for their contributions to consumer awareness and use of accessories. The event has grown from a trade function to a must-attend celebrity function for anyone and everyone in the fashion, music, and film businesses.

Diane von Furstenberg · Mary-Kate and Ashley Olsen · Kim Cattrall · Eartha Kitt · Lady Gaga and Marc Jacobs

Watches

The useful, dependable wristwatch is a relative newcomer to the 500-year history of mechanical timepieces. Nineteenth-century craftsmen made the pocket watch efficient—and a thing of beauty. In 1904, Louis-Joseph Cartier introduced the first modern wristwatch, the Santos-Dumont, named for a Brazilian aviator.

There are three basic types of watches made today: the mechanical, the self-winding, and the quartz movement. *Mechanical watches* are driven by a balance wheel and powered by a spring, which must be hand wound. *Automatic* or *self-winding* watches wind themselves as the wearer moves a wrist. The *quartz movement* invented in the 1970s offers very accurate timekeeping at a low cost. Most quartz watches have removable batteries that last about one year.

Analog watches have faces with hands that sweep around the numbers "clockwise." *Digital watches* display the time in numbers, generally using a liquid crystal display (LCD). Extra features available in some watches include night-light buttons, calendars, moon-phase indicators, stopwatch (or chronograph) features, alarms, and chimes. Some watches also give the time in other countries or time zones. But watches have always been a fashion statement as well as a useful device.

The inexpensive Timex watch of the 1960s, which "took a licking, but kept on ticking," broadened the market to include a huge number of people who could not afford even the mass market watches of previous decades.

During the 1980s, Swatch made a splash in the market with its casual watches and has now spread its name and contemporary look into a number of other product categories such as sportswear, sunglasses, and other accessories. The Swatch lines have become so popular that some retailers have created Swatch boutiques. As of 2010, they were the number one manufacturer of finished watches in the world.[6] Other well-known companies include Movado, Fossil, and Armitron.

Many companies later jumped onto the sports-watch bandwagon by adding resistance to water, wind, dust, shock, and magnetic fields. Chronograph watches that measure small fractions of a second were best-sellers; some are used to measure speeds, distances, and altitudes.

At the high end of the watch market are leading brands like Rolex, Omega, Patek Philippe, Audemars Piaget, and Cartier, all of which consistently introduce new models. Their watches can cost from $2,000 to $2.7 million.

Tennis star Maria Sharapova exemplifies beauty and toughness in an ad for TAG Heuer.

At the other end of the market are children's watches. The Mickey Mouse watch for children was introduced in the 1930s. Timex makes watches for Disney, Joe Boxer, Nautica, and others. In 2001, Timex introduced TMXessories, a line aimed at tween and teen girls that included colorful, decorative watches disguised as bangle bracelets, rings, and pendant necklaces. Armitron is another maker of cartoon-character watches, such as Tweety, Bugs Bunny, Garfield, and Scooby-Doo. Mattel, the giant toy maker, has a line of Barbie watches.

But have cell phones and iPods made watches obsolete? With the advances in technology, the younger generation may have reduced interest in watches. Many retailers and manufacturers, however, believe the watch business is still thriving. They cite three reasons: fashion, status, and convenience.[7]

Merchandising and Marketing

Jewelry manufacturers present their new styles and, in the case of costume jewelry manufacturers, their new lines at semiannual shows sponsored by the Jewelers of America and the Jewelry Information Center. One of the largest trade shows is the AccessoriesTheShow held in New York in January, February, May, July, August, and September. It also holds shows in Las Vegas in February and August. Other major trade associations include the American Gem Society, the Diamond Council of America, and the Fashion Jewelry and Accessories Trade Association.

Fine-jewelry manufacturers traditionally have concentrated on providing a wide range of basic pieces, most notably, diamond rings and watches. They support their lines with a variety of services offered to stores. Some advertising assistance is offered, but this has not been common in a business where brand names have been relatively unknown. However, with the emergence of designer jewelry names, this is changing.

For all types of jewelry, but especially diamond rings, the Christmas holidays and Valentine's Day are especially busy. Birthdays and anniversaries provide a steady year-round business, while watches show a sales spurt around graduation time. The popularity of vintage clothing has led to a renewed interest in "estate pieces," or fine jewelry of earlier eras, still in the original settings.

Industry Trends

Today, all branches of the jewelry industry emphasize the production of designs that complement currently fashionable styles. For example, when turtlenecks are popular, jewelry companies make long chains and pendants that look graceful on high necklines. When sleeveless dresses are in fashion, bracelets become an important piece of jewelry. When French cuffs are in fashion, both men and women wear cufflinks. When prints are popular, jewelry styles become tailored; but when solid or somber colors are popular, jewelry often moves to center stage with more complex designs and bright colors.

Masculine and unisex designs in gold chains, earrings, rings, shirt studs, nose studs, and fashion/sports watches are popular. More men are also wearing colored gemstones.

New accessories lines debut at Moda Las Vegas and AccessoriesTheShow.

To compete with costume jewelry, which has gained broad acceptance over the past few decades, fine-jewelry companies have begun to diversify. Some have broadened their lines by moving into bridge jewelry. Others have also diversified into complementary non-jewelry areas. Swank, for example, which for years has manufactured men's small jewelry items, now produces colognes, sunglasses, travel accessories, and a variety of men's gifts.

OTHER ACCESSORIES

There are many categories of accessories—and much variation within categories—from dress shoes to jellies, from briefcases to lunch boxes, from hard hats to snoods. Other ornaments, like ribbons, bows, feathers, and fabric flowers, come and go in popularity. The accessory maker needs to move quickly in and out of these trends. Three other categories of accessories deserve mention; they are handkerchiefs, umbrellas, and hair ornaments.

TRENDS IN THE FASHION ACCESSORIES INDUSTRIES

For accessory manufacturers, being supporters of apparel fashions does not necessarily mean being followers. In fact, accessory manufacturers must often be fashion leaders. In the fashion business, which always moves in the fast lane, accessory manufacturers must move in a faster lane than anyone else. They have to be able to adapt or change a style in mid-season if that is what is required to stay on top of current trends.

Market Weeks and Trade Shows

New accessory lines are shown during the five major fashion market weeks in New York so that merchants can buy a coordinated look. These include the following:

- Summer and January
- Transitional and March
- Fall and May
- Holiday and August
- Spring and November

In the United States, the MAGIC and WWDMAGIC shows held in Las Vegas in February and August are the largest trade shows for accessories. The International Fashion Jewelry and Accessory Show (IFJAG) takes place in New York and Rhode Island. Paris Première Classe, the Fashion Accessories Trade Show, is held in Paris in March and October. These shows are a reflection of the growing importance of accessories to retailers and consumers.

SUMMARY AND REVIEW

Specific accessories wax and wane in popularity, but some accessories are always popular as most people do not consider themselves fully dressed until they have accessorized an outfit. In recent years, the business overall has boomed. Many people feel the accessory business, like many other fashion categories, has been given a boost by its association with designer names.

And the benefits are mutual. At the haute couture shows of Paris and Milan, the clothing has become the designer's fashion statement, and accessories have generated the financial support—as well as supporting the look of the season—to allow designers to experiment. Made-to-order gowns and ensembles are individually produced by hand, whereas accessories can be machine-made in larger numbers and sold at higher margins. Similarly, American ready-to-wear designers literally display their names or logos on licensed accessories such as belts, scarfs, caps, handbags, and sunglasses. For the purveyors of fashion as much as for the consumer, accessories support a complete, coordinated image. In addition, they are the source of a more attractive bottom line.

FOR REVIEW

1. Why have U.S. shoe producers moved their factories offshore? How has this trend affected the footwear industry?

2. How do changes in lifestyles and activities affect the shoe industry? Give examples.

3. Describe the merchandising and marketing of handbags in the United States today.

4. What are the current trends in the millinery industry?

5. What are the major types of neckties sold today?

6. Why are shoe and fine jewelry departments often leased?

7. What three metals are considered precious? What is the difference between solid gold and 14-karat gold?

8. What are the major gemstones used in the production of jewelry?

9. Give several examples of how women's apparel fashions influence jewelry fashions.

10. What categories of merchandise are to be found in fashion accessory departments today? In outposts?

FOR DISCUSSION

1. How has the increasing informality of dress affected the accessories industries?

2. List each of the current important fashion accessory items and discuss why they are important to the total fashion look. At which stage of the fashion cycle is each item positioned? Give reasons for your answers.

TRADE TALK

Define or briefly explain the following terms:

bridge jewelry

carat

costume or fashion jewelry

karat

millinery

sterling silver

vermeil

PART 4

THE RETAIL LEVEL— THE MARKETS FOR FASHION

In this part, you will examine the elements of fashion marketing and learn how markets operate to help manufacturers sell their products. You will begin to develop a basic vocabulary and a working knowledge of the following:

- Global sourcing, including its advantages and disadvantages for the U.S. fashion industries—in Chapter 10.

- The history and development of fashion retailing in the United States—in Chapter 11.

- The many fashion services that work with all levels of the fashion industry, including magazines, newspapers, broadcast and TV, the Internet, and fashion reporting services, as well as trade associations— in Chapter 12.

10

GLOBAL SOURCING
AND MERCHANDISING

KEY CONCEPTS

- Meaning of the terms *market, market center, mart*, and *trade show* and the function of each in bringing fashion from producers to consumers in the United States and internationally
- Locations and activities of markets, marts, and trade shows
- Role of offshore production in product development
- International trading laws and agreements between the United States and its trading partners
- Domestic importing and exporting

As the popular children's poem states, "To market, to market, to buy a fat pig; home again, home again, jiggety jig." **Going to market can be an exciting and different experience, whether it is going to buy food, candy, sporting goods, or clothes.** Most of us go to market with great expectations and plans, and once home, sometimes the purchase is perfect and other times it is just not right.

Regardless of the outcome of the trip, it is your money and you can spend it however you wish. However, this is not the case when you spend someone else's money, as is the case for store buyers. When buying for a store, you are using its money, which requires an exhausting amount of planning, organization, and hard work before you can even go to market.

MARKET TERMINOLOGY

Markets . . . market centers . . . marts—what are they? You will hear these terms used frequently and even interchangeably, which makes them that much harder to sort out.

Market

The word *market* has several meanings. We have already spoken of the market, or demand, for a specific product. In this chapter, the word takes on yet another meaning. A **market** is the place where goods are produced and sold at wholesale prices to store buyers. It is an important step in the pipeline that takes clothes and other fashion items from manufacturer to customer. Buyers attend markets, in effect, to choose the styles we will all be wearing within a few months.

Market Center

Actually, there is no one giant shopping mall that serves as a market for the entire U.S. fashion industry. Instead, several market centers, or geographic locations, exist throughout the country and across the globe. A **market center** is a city where fashion is produced and sold at wholesale prices.

The first market center in the United States was New York City. For many people in and out of the fashion industry, New York City epitomizes the allure and excitement of the fashion world. But fashion has become regionalized, and while New York still markets much of the fashion in the United States, it no longer produces all of it. Los Angeles, Dallas, and Miami are all flourishing market centers.

Mart

A **mart** is a building or complex of buildings that houses a wholesale market, that is, an exhibition of fashions that are ready to be sold to retail stores. Most marts are owned and operated by independent investors. Some marts are operated by the cities themselves, and at least one, the Carolina Mart in Charlotte, North Carolina, is operated by a trade association. A permanent, professional staff operates the mart, although a large number of temporary employees are hired for market weeks.

Like convention centers, marts consist almost entirely of exhibition space. Some space is rented out as full-time corporate showrooms, but in many marts, the space is rented only during market weeks. These marts often balance their income by sponsoring other shows and conventions.

New York City, despite the rise of regional marts, in many ways still reigns as the country's premiere market center. Ironically it is the only market center without a mart. Part of the aura of a New York market week is the trek through the garment district from showroom to showroom.

The oldest of marts is the Merchandise Mart in Chicago, which opened its doors in the early 1930s, making Chicago New York's only rival for years. Because the Merchandise Mart was centrally located, buyers from across the country found it convenient to meet in this huge building on the Chicago River several times a year to do their wholesale buying. The Mart is still very much in use today for other goods, such as home furnishings, contract (office/institutional) furnishings, kitchen and bath, and gifts and decorative accessories.

Market Weeks

Buyers can and do travel to market centers and some marts at any time during the year to visit individual producers, but several times a year, they also gather for market week. Few buyers are willing to forego the glamour and excitement of **market week**. During market week, market centers and marts are filled with producers and designers, all of whom exhibit their new lines with as much style and panache as possible. The atmosphere is electrifying, heady with new, innovative ideas and the latest trends.

Trade Shows

In this chapter, you will also learn about **trade shows**, periodic exhibits that are scheduled throughout the year in regional market centers and some marts. Smaller than market weeks, trade shows are typically attended by buyers from one region of the country. Exceptions are a few huge trade shows, such as Magic, which attract buyers from all over the world.

THE DEVELOPMENT OF MARKET CENTERS IN THE UNITED STATES

As discussed, New York City was the first market center in the United States. When design and production clustered in New York, it followed that it would become a center for buying, too. The fact that New York was the most cosmopolitan and fashion conscious of U.S. cities also helped. Even when travel was a strenuous undertaking, buyers at major stores tried to travel to New York twice a year. To service them, manufacturers set up showrooms near their factories in the garment district.

But for many, twice-a-year buying trips were not enough to service a store properly. And many owners and buyers for small stores across the country could not afford to travel to New York. To handle accounts between New York buying trips and to help those who did not come to New York at all, manufacturers hired **sales representatives** who traveled to the stores and the buyers to show the lines.

SERVICES OF MARKET CENTERS AND MARTS

A market week is organized by manufacturers' associations, in cooperation with the market center or mart staff. It is the prime selling opportunity for market centers or mart staffs, fashion producers, and sales reps, all of whom devote themselves to making the visit as easy and convenient as possible for the buyers. Keeping buyers interested, comfortable, and happy encourages them to write orders.

Phillip Lim

Phillip Lim, Fall 2011

Prabal Gurung

Prabal Gurung, Spring 2011

Brian Reyes

Brian Reyes, Fall 2010

GLOBAL SALES
America's Not Enough, So Say New Designers Spanning the Globe

"IF I CAN MAKE IT THERE, I'LL MAKE IT ANYWHERE!"... Once upon a time designers used to live by this famous lyric sung by Liza Minnelli. They would come to Seventh Avenue to build and grow their businesses in New York and the United States before even thinking about opportunities worldwide. Today, young designers are now thinking globally almost from the moment they launch their labels.

To build their overseas presences, designers have either partnered with sales showrooms in other fashion capitols or go to Paris during the city's fashion weeks to show and sell their collections to European and Asian stores.

The young, new designers—such as Jason Wu, Alexa Adams and Flora Gill, Phillip Lim, Peter Som, Prabal Gurung, and Brian Reyes—who have decided to be in as many countries as soon as possible in order to have a successful business feel that constant development on the Web is another factor for global growth. It not only allows potential overseas customers to familiarize themselves with emerging U.S. talent through the click of the mouse but it also makes it easier for designers to communicate with their international stores through e-mail, Skype, social media, BBM, and other tools of online communication.

"Five years ago, if you were a young designer, wherever you were based, it was very much about growing there slowly and eventually international people caught up," designer Prabal Gurung said. "But because of things such as Facebook and Twitter, the way the fashion shows are going viral, information is instant. It's a huge playing field, with countries like India and China and a lot of other Asian countries and the Middle East. It's not just domestic. You can't just focus on domestic and think you can be successful."

Market weeks are scheduled several months before the clothes will be needed in the stores. Four or five market weeks are held each year for womenswear and childrenswear, three to five for menswear and boyswear, and two to five for shoes. Separate market weeks are held in many market centers or marts for accessories, infants' and childrenswear, lingerie, Western wear, sportswear, and bridal apparel.

Publicity

A market week is only as successful as the exhibitors it manages to attract, so most regional markets and marts mount an ongoing publicity program to draw interesting and exciting exhibitors. So the chemistry will be mutual, market centers and marts also do what they can to attract buyers. Flyers and brochures touting market weeks go out to stores and individual buyers several times a year. Buyers are also treated to buyers' breakfasts, luncheons, and cocktail parties throughout market week—all courtesy of the market center, mart, or a supporting organization.

The most popular form of publicity is the fashion shows that highlight every market week. The shows are hectic since they are so huge and so much is going on. They are also among the more extravagant and interesting fashion shows ever staged. Mostly this is because they are the work of many different designers, all of whom enter their most beautiful or interesting designs. To give some coherence to a market week fashion show, it is often organized around a theme, such as a particular color or, more often, an exciting new trend.

An information table welcomes visitors to the L.A. Fashion Market.

Information Services

Once the buyers arrive, they are given a **buyer's directory** and a calendar to help them find their way around and schedule events they want to see. A steady flow of daily publications—trade newspapers, flyers, brochures, and newsletters—continues throughout the week and keeps buyers abreast of breaking market week news.

Educational Services

An orientation program is typically scheduled for the first day, and consultants are on call throughout the week to discuss and deal with specific problems. Seminars and conferences are held to supply buyers with the latest information on fashion. Typical topics are new advances in fiber and fabrics, trends in fashion colors, the latest merchandising techniques, advertising and promotion ideas, and sales training hints.

THE NEW YORK MARKET

As a market, New York belongs in a category by itself, not only because it is the city with the most resources to offer the fashion world but also, as mentioned earlier, because it has no central mart building.

Trading Area and Economic Impact

The New York market is made up of literally thousands of showrooms that line the streets of the garment district, or Fashion Center. The garment district is located between Fifth and Ninth Avenues from 34th to 42nd Streets. Generally, similar-quality apparel is grouped together. In the women's wholesale market, for example, the couture or higher-priced lines are situated primarily along Seventh Avenue in elegant showrooms. Moderate-priced lines and sportswear firms are housed around the corner on Broadway. Obviously, time and coordination are required to shop the New York market—as is a comfortable pair of shoes.

The lack of a central mart is a minor drawback compared with what many buyers consider the glory of shopping this *crème de la crème* of markets. Whatever is new will be seen here first. New York, most industry people agree, is the most dynamic and creative market center. Any buyers servicing stores of any size must come to New York to do so, regardless of the other markets they add to their schedule.

New York offers a wide range of shopping. Every kind of fashion can be found here in every price range. Men's, women's, and children's clothing, accessories, intimate apparel, and cosmetics are located within the garment district. Textile and fiber companies and home furnishings producers maintain showrooms in or near the garment district. Most local manufacturers feel that they must maintain a New York showroom, and many regional manufacturers sponsor one as well, if only during market weeks.

In 1993, Seventh on Sixth was created to organize, centralize, and modernize the American collections, as well as to provide a platform for American designers to become important players in the global fashion business. Originally, New York Fashion Week was under the auspices of the Council of Fashion Designers of America (CFDA), and organized by the CFDA's offshoot known as Seventh on Sixth. In 2001, the former

Seventh on Sixth was acquired by International Management Group (IMG), a sports management and marketing agency. Today, as the producers of Mercedes-Benz Fashion Week in New York and Mercedes-Benz Fashion Week Swim in Miami, IMG has an incredible outreach to thousands of buyers, retailers, and members of the national and international press. They also produce a variety of international fashion shows, including Mercedes-Benz Fashion Week in Berlin and Moscow, Lakmé Fashion Week in Mumbai, and Fashion Fringe in London, among others.

Advantages of the New York Market

Buyers who come to New York can shop not only the market but also the department stores and boutiques for which the city is known. New York is home to the flagship stores of Macy's, Bloomingdale's, Barneys, Bergdorf Goodman, and Saks Fifth Avenue. There is also a high concentration of national and international flagship designer stores. Areas like the Upper East Side, Soho, and the meatpacking district are brimming with elegant flagship boutiques like Marc Jacobs, Donna Karan, and Ralph Lauren. As New York is one of the fashion capitals of the world, practically every important international fashion house has a flagship store there.

New York City is also the hub of the fashion network. Many national organizations have headquarters there, and stand ready to provide assistance and support services to buyers. Even on a personal level, the networking possibilities are good. Local New York buyers attend market weeks as do buyers from all over the country. Buyers who can attend only a few market weeks each year generally head for New York.

THE REGIONAL MARKET CENTERS

Each market center has its own unique flavor, as does each city, and buyers look forward to the varied experiences they will have at different markets. Many small retailers attend New York market weeks less often than they once did, relying instead on regional market centers closer to home. Travel costs are lower, less time is spent away from the stores, and for many, the atmosphere feels more personal. As regional markets become more sophisticated, thus drawing more exhibitors, New York loses even more of its allure. If regional markets can meet their needs, buyers ask, then why struggle through what many consider to be a grueling week in New York? Some retailers have cut out New York entirely, while others have reduced the number of trips they make and fill in with trips to regional markets in Los Angeles, Dallas, or Miami. They can visit them year-round or during special market weeks.

The Los Angeles Market

Much of the look and style of California's markets revolve around its casual lifestyle, which it seems to sell almost as much as it sells its clothing. California leads the nation in retail apparel sales, and Los Angeles is the nation's largest apparel manufacturing center, employing 56,700 workers.[1]

Since the 1930s, when California introduced pants for women, the West Coast has been the source of many important trends in sportswear. Los Angeles is home to some of the country's largest sportswear manufacturers, Guess, L.A. Gear, and Speedo.

Other recent Los Angeles successes are Bisou Bisou, Moschino, Laundry by Shelli Segal, Richard Tyler, St. John's Knits, and Rampage. Bob Mackie, who designs for Hollywood stars, and is frequently seen on television home shopping shows, is also based in Los Angeles. Surf-fashion firms include companies such as Hurley, Billabong, and Blake Kuwahara's Kata Eyewear.

Apparel design, production, and distribution are spread out along the entire West Coast, but the heaviest concentrations remain in Los Angeles.[2] The CaliforniaMart, the nation's largest apparel mart, located in downtown Los Angeles, has permanent and temporary exhibition space not merely for California's lines, but for New York and Dallas lines as well, along with a growing number of foreign producers. The CaliforniaMart is open year-round and offers five market weeks and 20 specialty trade shows, such as ISAM (the International Swimwear & Activewear show), the Los Angeles International Textile Show, and the Los Angeles Shoe Show.

The Dallas Market

The mood at Dallas market weeks is strongly southwestern, as people will find hand-crafted clothes, or clothes that look handcrafted, with bright, vibrant colors. Once a center for budget garments, Dallas has become an important production and market center. It advertises itself as the "marketplace for the Southwest, the nation, and the world." Dallas-produced fashions are shown alongside fashions from New York, California, and around the world. Designers Anthony Marc Hankins and Victor Costa, the firms Jerrell and Poleci, and jewelry designers Elizabeth Showeres, Dian Malouf, and Joan & Co. are based in Dallas.

The Dallas Apparel Mart and the separate Menswear Mart are part of a multi-building complex that offers more than two million square feet of exhibition space and is the nation's leading menswear marketplace. The International Apparel Mart, also part of the multi-marketplace complex, has expanded to become one of the world's largest market-places for apparel and accessories.[3]

The Miami Market

The Miami market weeks have a highly international—mostly Latino and Caribbean—flavor. Colors and styles are lively. The Miami market is also known for an outstanding selection of childrenswear.

Greater Miami has become one of the most dynamic, cosmopolitan, and international fashion-producing centers in the country. Drawn by the temperate climate and quality labor force, many apparel designers and manufacturers now call South Florida home. Retailers find that Miami-produced clothing is well made, reasonably priced, and perfect for the semitropical weather that prevails in the Sun Belt. In Miami, three strong selling seasons—cruise wear, spring, and summer—are available year-round. In addition to cruise and resort wear, Miami design and production center around budget and moderate-priced sportswear, swimwear, and children's clothing. Miami-based designers of better-priced daytime and evening wear are also becoming known for their work.

The Miami International Merchandise Mart, opened in 1968, serves this area. Some exhibitors maintain permanent showrooms but most show only during market week. Buyers from Latin America and the Caribbean account for much of the mart's business.

TRADE SHOWS IN THE UNITED STATES

Trade shows, which are held in market centers throughout the year, are sponsored by **trade associations**—professional organizations of manufacturers and sales representatives. A few of these events are major extravaganzas that attract buyers from across the country and even from abroad. Magic International, held twice a year at the Las Vegas Convention Center, has the atmosphere of an apparel mart market week minus the permanent facilities.

The typical U.S. trade show, however, is much smaller than a mart show and lasts two to four days. Regional trade shows are held in hotels and motels, civic centers, and small exhibition halls. Specialized trade shows cover areas of fashion that may otherwise get lost at major market weeks. The Big and Tall Associates (BATA) is part of the Chicago Collective showing suits and outerwear for big and tall men, for example, and the Surf Expo Florida Show features surf equipment and surf-inspired sportswear.

These small trade shows show every sign of being able to hold their own against the proliferation of marts and market weeks. Trade shows are especially popular with small retailers and exhibitors because they are typically less expensive than market weeks for both groups of participants to attend. Small retailers like to deal with sales reps who are personally familiar with their needs and can cater to them at these smaller exhibits. Buyers from boutiques find that trade shows are their best outlet for the kind of unique and unusual merchandise they seek. Trade shows are known for displaying the work of unusual or small designers who do not ordinarily exhibit at the major marts.

The disadvantage of trade shows is that the exhibitors are limited in number. Buyers have difficulty doing across-the-board buying that is easily accomplished during market weeks at major marts. Trade shows also cannot feature the ongoing service that marts do as they are increasingly open year-round.

A flyer for the Spring 2011 Designers & Agents schedule advertises trade events in three major cities.

FOREIGN FASHION MARKETS

For several centuries, the foreign fashion market consisted entirely of French designers' high fashions. In the 1960s, the ready-to-wear market emerged first in Italy and then in France. Today, cultural and economic changes and a renewed interest in nationalism and ethnicity have combined to encourage the development of fashion markets worldwide. U.S. buyers no longer travel exclusively to France and Italy; they journey to fashion markets all over the globe.

Foreign fashion markets are designed to show off the fashion industries around the world. In the leading foreign markets, clothing is typically designed and presented on two different levels. First in prestige and cost are the **haute couture** (pronounced "oat-koo-TUR") clothes. A French expression originally meaning "fine sewing," haute couture is today synonymous with high fashion. These original designs, which use luxury fabrics and are known for their exquisite detailing, are of necessity expensive and thus are made in very limited numbers. With prices that start in the thousands of dollars for a single garment, haute couture design is affordable to only a small group of wealthy women.

The next layer of fashion design is called **prêt-à-porter**. A French term meaning *ready-to-wear*, prêt-à-porter is produced in far larger numbers than haute couture. Like haute couture, it is introduced in foreign fashion markets at semiannual shows where design collections are revealed to the fashion world. Haute couture and designer prêt-à-porter provide the inspiration for the inexpensive mass-market designs that dominate the fashion market.

France

France first emerged as a fashion showcase during the reign of Louis XIV (1643–1715), often called the Sun King, partly because of his lavish lifestyle. The elaborate clothing worn by his court was widely copied by royalty and the wealthy throughout Europe. The splendor of his court at Versailles created a market for beautiful fabrics, tapestries, and lace. Textile production in Lyons and lace works in Alençon were established to meet these needs. Paris, already an important city and located only a few miles from Versailles, became the fashion capital. Paris is still considered the cradle of the fashion world. New fashion is born there. After it is seen there, it is adopted and adapted by others around the world.

Paris Couture

France has been the center of haute couture since 1858, when the house of Charles Frederick Worth, generally regarded as the father of Parisian couture, opened its doors. Beginning about 1907, Paul Poiret became the second great fashion legend of Paris. Poiret was the first to stage fashion shows and to branch out into the related fields of perfume, accessories, fabric design, and interior decoration.

A **couture house** is an apparel firm for which a designer creates original designs and styles. The proprietor or designer of a couture house is known as a **couturier** if

male, or **couturière** if female. Most Paris couture houses are known by the names of their founders—Yves Saint Laurent, Givenchy, and Chanel, for example. The name may survive even after the original designer's retirement or death, but the signature style changes with his or her successor. In recent years, rapid changes of personnel and licensing of designer names has blurred the identity of the fashion houses and focused attention on individual designers. For example, Karl Lagerfeld designs for Chanel and Fendi, as well as for himself.

In 1868, an elite couture trade association, called the Chambre Syndicale de la Couture Parisienne, came into being. Membership in the Chambre Syndicale (pronounced "shahmbrah seen-dee-KAHL") was by invitation only and was restricted to couture houses that agreed to abide by its strict rules. In 1973, Fédération Francaise de la Couture, du Prêt-à-Porter des Couturiers et des Createurs de Mode was established. La Fédération is the executive organ of all the trade associations (or Chambre Syndicales) of each fashion division. Haute couture, ready-to-wear, and menswear each have their own Chambre Syndicale. You can look up fashion show schedules and general information on the federation's website at www.modeaparis.com.[4]

Intensely dramatic gowns (and hairdos) on the runway for Jean Paul Gaultier's Spring 2011 couture show.

Couture Shows. The Parisian couture house trade shows are held twice yearly: The spring/summer collections are shown in late January, and the fall/winter ones in late July. These shows have evolved into a promotional outlet for the couturiers. The sales of haute couture clothing have steadily declined in recent years as prices have risen and customers have turned to the designer ready-to-wear lines. To survive, couture houses have expanded into other, more lucrative activities, such as the development of ready-to-wear collections and the establishment of boutiques, and the ever-present (and profitable) licensing arrangements.

Couturiers' Ready-to-Wear. Most couturiers' ready-to-wear clothes are sold to department and specialty stores, which often set aside special areas or departments to display these prestigious items.

The exclusivity and cost of producing haute couture lines, in combination with declining craftsmanship skills among designers and atelier staff, have changed the Parisian fashion climate. The ready-to-wear business has completely eclipsed haute couture on the French prestige designer market. Today, many famous fashion houses, like Balenciaga, Chloé, Louis Vuitton, and Yves Saint Laurent, only produce ready-to-wear lines.

Couture Boutiques. The French word for "shop," or **boutique**, has come to mean, more specifically, a shop that carries exclusive merchandise. In the past, many couturiers installed boutiques on the first floor or a lower floor of their design houses. Most famous fashion labels also have their own flagship ready-to-wear stores in key cities around the world. Goods sold in these shops are usually designed by the couture house staff and are sometimes even made in the couture workrooms. All bear the famous label.

Licensing Agreements. The most lucrative business activities for couturiers are the numerous licensing arrangements they establish to sell their accessories and ready-to-wear lines and also a variety of goods produced by others on their behalf. The most popular prestige licenses include perfume, shoes, handbags, sunglasses, and watches.

French Ready-to-Wear

To meet the needs of ready-to-wear designers, the Chambre Syndicale created an autonomous section for designers who work exclusively in ready-to-wear, designating them **créateurs** to distinguish them from couturiers. Among the créateurs are such important names as Karl Lagerfeld, Sonia Rykiel, Christian Lacroix, and Jean-Paul Gaultier.

Although their prestige is great, the couturiers and créateurs represent only a small part of the French fashion industry in terms of numbers and revenue. The remaining 1,200 companies are mass producers of ready-to-wear.

Prêt-à-Porter Trade Shows. The French ready-to-wear producers present their collections at two market shows a year. The first, for the fall/winter collections, is held in March, and the second in October, for the spring/summer collections. Actually, two large trade shows take place simultaneously. The runway shows, sponsored by the Chambre Syndicale for the prêt-à-porter designers, take place at Carousel du Louvre. At the other, sponsored by the Fédération, the mass-market prêt-à-porter collections are exhibited at the Porte de Versailles Exhibition Center. This trade show, known as the *Prêt-à-Porter Paris,* brings together more than 1,000 exhibitors from all around the world. With each succeeding show, the press pays more attention and provides more coverage of this end of the French fashion business. There are approximately 57 percent of French buyers and 43 percent of international buyers that visit the show from areas such as Brazil, the United States, the European Union, or Russia.[5]

Italy

Italy is France's most serious rival in the international fashion industry. In certain areas, such as knitwear and accessories, Italian design is considered superior to the French. Italy has long been recognized as a leader in men's apparel, knitwear, leather accessories, and textiles.

A centuries-old tradition of quality craftsmanship and a close relationship between designers and manufacturers are common features of Italy's otherwise disparate fashion houses.

Italian Couture

Italy has long had couture houses named for the famous designers who head them— Valentino and Giorgio Armani. Its designers are members of Italy's couture trade group (a counterpart to the Chambre Syndicale) known as the Camera Nazionale della Moda Italiana. The Camera Moda organizes the biannual ready-to-wear fashion week runway shows that take place in Milan each year in March and September. You can look up schedule and general information at the association's website at www.cameramoda.com.

Unlike French couture houses, however, Italian couture designers are not all located in a single city. Although Milan is the largest fashion center, couture designers may be found in Rome, Florence, and other Italian cities.

Like their Parisian counterparts, many Italian couture houses have set up boutiques for the sale of exclusive accessories and limited lines of apparel. The designs are usually those of the couture house staff, and the apparel and accessories are sometimes made in the couture workrooms. All items offered in boutiques bear the couture house label.

Italian couture designers also have established licensing agreements with foreign producers. Some design and produce uniforms for employees of business firms, most notably airlines and car rental agencies. Some accept commissions to create fashion products ranging from perfume to menswear to home furnishings.

Italian Ready-to-Wear

Italy began to develop both its women's and men's ready-to-wear industries along with its couture fashions. As a result, it started exporting earlier than France, and today its economy relies heavily on its exporting program. The textile, apparel, footwear, and leather goods industries account for approximately one-fifth of Italy's exports. Much

Ralph Lauren store
on Madison Avenue

Fall/Winter
2011

Ralph Lauren
women's
flagship

Fall/Winter
2011

Ralph Lauren
in his flagship
store

RALPH LAUREN
New in an Old World

AMERICA IS THE NEW WORLD AND EUROPE IS THE OLD WORLD. But on April 19, 2010 Ralph Lauren, designer from the New World, was honored with one of the most prestigious Old World awards.

Ralph Lauren was fêted by the French in a manner not seen since President Charles de Gaulle hosted President John F. Kennedy over 50 years ago.

It was a three-day celebration, starting with a cocktail party at his new store on the first night, moving on to a black-tie dinner at Ralph's—the store's restaurant—on the second night, and culminating in the Légion d'honneur presentation at the American Embassy on the third night.

In his acceptance speech, Lauren said, "This is one of the moments that I will remember for my whole life. My wife, Ricky, has been with me for forty-five years. My children have made me a very happy man. And my career has been a dream because I never went to fashion school. But I was always surrounded by wonderful people and had the luck of having the right eye on the right sense."

Not to be outdone by his new French medal, the City of New York and Mayor Michael Bloomberg presented Lauren with "the Key to the City," lauding him for his "great American success story," and celebrating the opening of a new 22,000-square-foot store on Madison Avenue.

Not bad for a boy from the Bronx, who started his career selling men's ties!

of this exported merchandise is in the medium- to high-price range, especially in knit-wear and accessories.

Designers. Innovative Italian ready-to-wear designers make their shows as exciting as the Paris ready-to-wear shows have become. Giorgio Armani and Versace are considered the standard-bearers for two very different definitions of Italian design. Versace is noted for brightly colored prints, and Armani for classic elegance combined with comfortable styling. Other well-known Italian ready-to-wear designers are equally protective of their reputations for distinctive, recognizable signature styles. Among the leading designers are Dolce & Gabbana, Gianfranco Ferré, Krizia, Missoni, and Miuccia Prada. Ferragamo and Gucci are major names in shoes and accessories, and Fendi is a major name in fur.

Trade Shows and Market Centers. Until the late 1960s, the most important Italian ready-to-wear shows were staged at the elegant Pitti and Strossi palaces in Florence. Milan grew as a fashion center in the 1970s, and many designers began to show there, in addition to or instead of Florence.

In addition to the ready-to-wear shows, Italy hosts a number of shows featuring the categories of apparel, accessories, and textiles for which Italian designers and manufacturers are internationally renowned. Trade shows are held in the regions where the respective industries are centralized. One of Italy's largest textile trade fairs is the Pitti Immagine Filati, held in Florence. This trade show features the latest in yarns and knit fabrics. Leather shoes, handbags, gloves, and small leather goods are one major segment of Italy's fashion industry. Other accessories that are world famous are knitted hats, scarfs, and gloves and silk scarfs and ties. Italy's fashion industry employs approximately 800 thousand people and is home to 30 thousand distribution companies in the textiles, apparel, and footwear industries.[6]

Great Britain

For many years, London's Savile Row was for menswear what Paris has been for women's apparel—the fountainhead of fashion inspiration. Savile Row is a wonderful place where each suit is handcrafted for its new owner.

British Couture

Although Britain has never supported a couture industry the way that France and Italy have, it does offer famous design schools, such as the Royal College of Art, the London College of Fashion, and Central St. Martins. St. Martins alumni include internationally famous names like John Galliano, Alexander McQueen, Hussein Chalayan, Julien MacDonald, Stella McCartney, and Clements-Ribeiro. In addition to their own lines, these designers have or have had designer posts at leading French fashion houses. Other recent graduates of these schools, both British and foreign, are bringing design back to London. Philip Treacy is a five-time winner of the British Fashion Council's Accessory Designer of the Year award for his striking hats.

British Ready-to-Wear

Ready-to-wear was a minor industry in Britain until after World War II. The fact that it entered a period of expansion after the war is largely due to the efforts of the government. According to one English fashion authority, the government became "the fairy godmother" responsible for "the survival of [British] couture and the rapid development of [Britain's] large and excellent ready-to-wear trade."[7]

Vivienne Westwood is a talent who has sparked and shocked the London fashion scene with her unorthodox clothes and lifestyle since the mid-1970s. She continues to be an innovator and leader of the avant-garde pack.

Trade Shows

There was a period in the late 1980s and early 1990s in which the British runway shows and trade shows were dormant. However, today, they are a required stop on the European fashion circuit. British and foreign designers are showing, and British and foreign audiences are looking.

Other European Countries

For leadership in Europe, the fashion industry definitely focuses on France, Italy, and Britain. Other countries do attract international interest, however. In the 1990s and the 2000s, the Belgian town Antwerp became somewhat of a high-fashion mecca. Antwerp natives, like Dries Van Noten, Ann Demeulemeester, Martin Margiela, Veronique Branquinho, AF Vandevorst, and Raf Simons, have achieved great success with their innovative and creative clothes. Although all these designers show and have their business headquarters in Paris, some of them still live in Antwerp. Other European countries that have a presence on the global fashion market are Ireland, with its traditional garments and fine linen, and Spain, with its swimwear, lingerie, and bridal fashion trade shows. As the European Economic Community and other factors globalize the economy, however, national boundaries assume less significance than they once had.

Germany and Scandinavia

Until the mid-1980s, most U.S. fashion buyers skipped Germany on their European buying trips. The country was still divided into East and West, and few West German designers were well known outside Europe. But a new wave of high-fashion women's designers is changing this. Two apparel firms, Escada and Mondi, are noteworthy successes with their high-fashion lines. Designers Hugo Boss and Wolfgang Joop have also developed international followings.

Although Germany's fashion industry is relatively small, its international trade fairs have become a major source of fashion inspiration for new fabric and designs. The Igedo produces the CPD womenswear and menswear fashion shows twice a year in Düsseldorf. Interestingly, this company has exported the fashion trade show through joint ventures with exhibition producers in Hong Kong, London, and Beijing. For textiles, the major international show is Interstoff in Frankfurt, and Cologne hosts shows of menswear, sportswear, childrenswear, and apparel production machinery.

Each of the four Scandinavian countries—Norway, Sweden, Denmark, and Finland—has its own fashion industries and specialties. However, even though each country has its roster of designers, the styles tend to be alike, with emphasis on simple silhouettes and sturdy materials like wool, leather, and linen.

Leather apparel, primarily in menswear, is a popular Swedish product. Both Sweden and Norway are among the important suppliers of mink and other furs to countries around the world. Birger Christiansen and Saga are leading furriers.

Scandinavia also offers some interesting textile designs. The best known, internationally, are the work of Finland's Marimekko.

Excellent jewelry in all price ranges is available in Scandinavia. The area has long been known for its clean-cut designs in gold and silver. Some well-known Swedish-born, contemporary designers include expatriates Lars Nilsson and Richard Bengtsson.

Canada

The development of a group of new and innovative designers has given the Canadian fashion industry a growing sense of confidence that has paid off in real growth. The fashion industry is the fifth-largest employer in Canada and gets larger every year. It has two important centers: the largest is Montreal in Quebec, and the second is Toronto in Ontario. Especially the Montreal fashion scene is gaining more international notoriety for its creativity and independence.

Most Canadian apparel manufacturing is located in Montreal but every province has a stake in the industry, and shows in each province bring local goods to the attention of other Canadians and buyers from the United States and around the world. Montreal and Toronto each have their own fashion week twice a year, where local men's and womenswear designers showcase their new collections in runway shows. Other women's apparel and accessories shows include Western Apparel Market in Vancouver, Trends the Apparel Show in Edmonton, the Prairie Apparel Markets in Winnipeg, the Saskatoon Apparel Market, and Toronto's Mode Accessories show. Childrenswear markets take place in Vancouver and Alberta, and the North American Fur and Fashion Exposition is featured at the Place Bonaventure in Montreal. Alberta, Montreal, Vancouver, and Toronto all host gift shows.

The Americas and the Caribbean Basin

By the mid-1970s, the Central and South American market could be added to the growing list of international fashion markets. The fashion world began visiting market centers in Bogotá (Colombia), Buenos Aires (Argentina), Rio de Janeiro (Brazil), and São Paulo (Brazil).

For buyers and producers from the United States and Canada, the signing of the North American Free Trade Agreement (NAFTA) in 1994 brought new possibilities in the Mexican market. Central and South America and the Caribbean countries began to press for inclusion in this trading pact.

From the perspective of Mexico and the Central and South American governments, the fashion industry has come to be seen as a means of increasing their gross national product and their status in the world marketplace. However, due to the state of the economy in recent years, Mexico has dropped to sixth in rank of importers into the United States.[8]

The combination of Central America and the West Indies have also suffered from the economic downturn, but the Dominican Republic and Honduras remain as major suppliers in the apparel and textile industries.[9]

Fashion Products

The fashion industry in the Americas and the Caribbean Basin offers fashion on three levels. First, several countries have developed their own high-fashion, or couture, industries, many of which are ripe for import to the United States and Europe. The second level revolves around the development of fashion products that reflect each country's national heritage of crafts. With a renewed interest in ethnicity throughout the world, such products are welcome. Lastly, Central America, South America, Mexico, and the West Indies are important "offshore" sources of products made to North American manufacturers' specifications.

Trade Shows in the Americas and the Caribbean Basin

The single most important market center in South America is São Paulo, Brazil. At the turn of the millennium, the emergence of designer talents like Alexandre Herchovitch, Rosa Cha, and Icarius coincided with a major Brazilian boom in fashion in general. When superstar models like Gisele Bündchen appeared in these designers' shows, it attracted enough attention to put São Paulo fashion week on the map. Since then, São Paulo fashion week has been steadily growing in importance, and it may become one of the most attended and publicized fashion events in the world. Other important international fairs featuring textiles and textile products as well as fashion accessories are held in Bogotá, Colombia; Lima, Peru; San Salvador, El Salvador; and Santiago, Chile.

These shows offer not only an opportunity for buyers from North America and elsewhere but also a place for U.S. textile producers to be seen by potential customers in the region.

Asia and Oceania

The United States imports more apparel from Asia than from any other area in the world. The major portion of these imports has been low-priced, high-volume merchandise, but hardly any of the apparel had qualified as "designer merchandise" in the past. However, this is changing with innovative styles offered by design-oriented Asian stylists. Buyers have used certain countries in Asia as a market in which to have fashions they saw in the European fashion centers copied and adapted. A fashion buyer needs to know which areas in Asia are best equipped to handle specific types of manufacturing. Japan and Hong Kong were once the two major contract or copyist countries. But Japan has upgraded its fashion image so that today it is a producer of outstanding high-styled, high-priced fashion apparel. Hong Kong is working to develop the apparel industry of China and promoting Chinese goods in its international trade fairs. In addition, recent patterns show that Vietnam and India may take over as leaders if costs get higher in China.

Oceania, which is made up of Australia and New Zealand, is connected to Asia economically. These markets are small in the industry and produce only a few apparel lines for export. However, Australia remains the world's top producer of wool fiber and fabric.[10]

Japan

Japan, long known for its export of silks and pearls, has moved most apparel production out of Japan, to lower-cost countries like Thailand, China, and the Philippines. Many Japanese designer boutiques in Tokyo—Japan's fashion center—have their own design staffs who create exciting new looks. Because of their ability to produce fashion goods quickly, the Tokyo fashion scene is often six months to one year ahead of other fashion centers.

Japanese Ready-to-Wear. In the 1970s, as Western dress had finally won acceptance in Japan, a group of highly original Japanese designers—Hanae Mori, Kenzo Takada, Issey Miyake, and Kansai Yamamoto—emerged. They first worked in Paris, where their lines were design sensations that rivaled the French prêt-à-porter designers. For over a decade, in fact, these daring designers were thought of as French rather than Japanese. Some of them still show in Paris.

Japanese Designers. In the early 1980s, a mostly new wave of avant-garde designers—Rei Kawakubo of Comme des Garçons, Yohji Yamamoto, and Matsuhiro Matsuda—stormed the U.S. fashion scene.

In the 1990s, the latest generation of Japanese designers, catering to a domestic market, have, like their British contemporaries, focused on retro pop-cultural influences such as hippie beads and T-shirts and 1970s punk.

More recently, Japanese designers like Hiroyuki Horihata and Makiko Sekiguchi, Ayako Kon and Hiromi Sato, Takeshi Osumi, and Yoshio Kubo have come on to the scene with ingenious designs that incorporate themes, gimmicks, and an eclectic mix of styles.[11]

China

In 2000, the United States entered a trade agreement with China that gave China normal trader status. This paved the way for the country's entry into the WTO (World Trade Organization). Since then, China's growth in the apparel industry has been clear—today the United States imports more goods from China than from any other country in the world.

Among the products that China exports, one of the most sought after is silk. Although it is the world's largest silk producer, it is just beginning to acquire the modern technology needed for quality weaving, printing, and dyeing. As the Chinese have been more proficient in these finishing processes, they have exported more finished

Intertextile Beijing showcases apparel fabrics and accessories from China and around the world.

silk fabrics and apparel products. Cotton and polyester production, once big exports, now barely meet China's domestic needs. Inexpensive plastic shoes are another major export. Leather and fur are also important exports. Several trade shows in Beijing and Shanghai have been instituted by Western-owned exhibition producers to promote Chinese leather to the international market.

Hong Kong. In July 1997, Hong Kong rejoined mainland China after 156 years as a British Crown Colony. The world held its collective breath, waiting to see what would become of this quintessentially market-driven world trading center when it came under Communist rule. The agreement between Britain and China calls for the governing of Hong Kong as a Special Administrative Region for 50 years, and local businesses are reassuring their international customers that Hong Kong will continue to offer all the advantages they have enjoyed plus more. In addition to the political change, Hong Kong has experienced a move in its economy from manufacturing to trade and service industries.

The Hong Kong Trade Development Council sponsors an international fashion week semiannually as well as several smaller shows. UBM Asia, a trade show producer based in Hong Kong, produces the All China Leather Exhibition in Shanghai and the

APLF-Materials Manufacturing and Technology Fair in Hong Kong—the premier events of their kind—and the Cosmoprof Asia beauty fair.

India

India's centuries-old textile industry continues to make it a major force in the Asian textile market, and recently the industry has seen its potential to surpass China as a leader in the industry. India also has its own rapidly expanding fashion industry, with a variety of homegrown designers. Most set up their businesses at the end of the 1990s in response to India's growing upper class and its appetite for global styles. Mumbai has had its own Lakmé India Fashion Week since 1999, which draws tremendous attention and is produced by IMG—the same event marketing conglomerate that runs the Mercedes-Benz Fashion Week. Manish Arora, Rohit Bal, Ritu Beri, and Raghavendra Rathore are among the more well-known designers from India.

India is also the home of the largest handloom industry in the world, and cotton and silk are the strongest growth areas of the Indian textile industry. In 2010, India was the world's largest organic cotton exporter, ranking top three in overall cotton production, along with China and the United States.[12] It is the only country in the world that produces all four silk varieties: mulberry, tussah, eriand, and muga. Its textile industry alone employs more than 35 million people, and it is expected to grow and generate more jobs.[13]

The India Trade Promotion Organization (ITPO) conducts promotions and fashion events with major retailers and assists U.S. and European designers in developing sourcing contacts in India.

Other Asian Countries

Indonesia, Thailand, Malaysia, Sri Lanka, Vietnam, and the Philippines are regarded by many Americans in the apparel industry as sites of offshore production, but that is only part of the story. As these developing countries become more industrialized and the standard of living improves, their own industries and markets are taking their place in the global economy. Thailand, for example, has for many years been a producer of fine printed silk and cotton. As discussed earlier, Vietnam has also increased its production capabilities, and as of 2008 ranked number seven in apparel exports globally.[14]

Singapore has many of the advantages of Hong Kong—an easily accessible location, a multinational population, and expertise in international trade. It is Hong Kong's chief rival as a center for trade shows.

Korea, with a design history similar to Japan's, has some exciting young designers creating for the Korean fashion-conscious market. Much of the production of ready-to-wear in Korea is still contract work. But because of the fashion design movement among young Koreans, this is beginning to change.

Oceania

Australia is not a large producer in the textile and apparel industries, but it is known for wool. Australia produced more than 1.05 billion pounds of wool, accounting for almost 50 percent of the global total. There has been a slow decline of wool output for several years, but as of late 2009 it was steadying.[15] Australia is also credited with the origin of UGG boots, which became a major trend in the United States in the 2000s.

New Zealand is similar to Australia in that it imports more than it exports. Their retail market operates approximately a season behind Europe and the United States. Due to this, local importers are able to purchase end-of-season surplus goods and sell them at the start of the season in New Zealand.[16]

IMPORTING BY RETAILERS

The fashion industry is very much a part of the global economy, so much so that those who work in the business invented a term to describe the process of shopping for and purchasing imported goods: **global sourcing**. When a firm in a country, such as the United States, buys foreign goods, it **imports** them. The country that furnishes the goods, such as Italy, **exports** them. Most countries are both importers and exporters, although, as we shall see, they do not necessarily do each activity in equal amounts.

Retailers are the primary importers of foreign goods in the fashion industry, although manufacturers also seek global sourcing. Retailers like imports for several reasons: their uniqueness, quality, cost, and the variety they add to their stock. They constantly seek merchandise that will make their stores stand out in special and unique ways that will set them apart from the competition. Foreign merchandise often fits that bill.

Anyone who intends to buy goods from a foreign country needs to have a thorough knowledge of its local laws and regulations, particularly the laws that regulate exporting and importing, the efficiency of the transportation system, and the availability and skill of the labor force. The buyer must be well versed on the tax system and exchange rates. He or she must understand local and national customs and must be well informed about the current political and economic climate. Finally, the buyer must be up-to-date on U.S. import-export regulations, including any pending legislation and must know all this for any country in which he or she intends to do business. This is why importing is best done by someone with access to good suppliers and extensive experience in dealing with foreign manufacturers and import regulations.

To gain entry to foreign fashion markets, as well as to cover them extensively, U.S. buyers rely on the help and experience of intermediaries. These specialists help U.S. buyers shop in the international markets successfully. Foreign-made goods can be purchased at and by the following:

- Foreign fashion markets
- Store-owned foreign buying offices
- Commissionaires or independent agents
- Import fairs held in the United States
- Importers

American Buyers' Visits to International Fashion Markets

Buyers like and need to travel to foreign fashion markets so they can observe new trends firsthand and buy goods suited to their customers. By personally shopping in international markets, often during market weeks, U.S. buyers can be sure they are obtaining goods that will sell at home. They are also able to soak up the cultural and social climates of the countries to which they travel, which, in turn, helps them translate what is new and exciting to their customers.

Store-Owned Foreign Buying Offices

Some stores—those that are large enough to do so or whose image is very special— maintain company-owned foreign buying offices. Buyers who work in these offices support and advise store buyers by surveying the market for new trends, supervising purchases, and following up on deliveries. Because they are an extension of the store, buyers in foreign buying offices are often authorized to make purchases just as store buyers are when they shop in foreign and domestic markets.

If the purchase is part of a new trend, stores need the goods when they are still new and customers are still eager to buy them. If it is part of a foreign theme promotion, goods must be delivered while the promotion is in progress. Delivery—especially timely delivery—has been a major problem with imported goods.

Stores generally locate their buying offices in major fashion capitals such as Paris, Milan, London, Hong Kong, Beijing, and Tokyo, from which their buyers can travel to smaller markets around the world. Saks Fifth Avenue, Neiman Marcus, and Macy's, Inc., all maintain store-owned foreign buying offices, as do the large general-merchandise chains such as Sears, JCPenney, and Wal-mart.

Foreign Commissionaires or Agents

In contrast to store-owned foreign buying offices are **commissionaires**, or foreign-owned independent agents. Commissionaires, whose offices are also located in key buying cities, tend to be smaller than store-owned offices. Commissionaires also represent both retailers and manufacturers.

Apart from these differences, however, they provide many of the same services as store-owned foreign buying offices. They often have specialized buyers, or market representatives, who work closely with clients, keeping them abreast of what is generally available and helping them locate specific goods. As is the case with store-owned buying offices, a substantial part of the staff's time is spent following up on purchases to make sure they are delivered when they are needed.

Unlike store buyers, who are authorized to purchase on the store's behalf, commissionaires do not purchase unless they have been authorized to do so. Commissionaires are paid on a fee basis. Usually, they take a percentage of the **first cost**, or wholesale price, in the country of origin.

Foreign Import Fairs in the United States

Another way to buy foreign goods is to attend one or more of the foreign import fairs that are now regularly held in the United States. Many foreign countries participate in such shows or stage their own fashion fairs in the United States. The New York Prêt, a semiannual event in New York City, is one of the largest and most prestigious of these U.S.-based shows.

COUNTERFEITING
The Fight Against the FAKES

CHILD LABOR, TERRORISM, AND HUMAN TRAFFICKING. Buying counterfeit goods is hardly harmless.

It is estimated that up to 7 percent of our annual world trade—$600 billion worth—is counterfeit or pirated, and that includes more than handbags. Everything from baby formula to medicine is counterfeited. Fakes are believed to be directly responsible for the loss of more than 750,000 American jobs, and counterfeiters and the crime syndicates they work with have been linked to sinister deeds such as terrorism.

OK, counterfeiting is a dastardly business but what has that got to do with buying fashion goods such as shoes, handbags, apparel, and harmless purchases that keep us looking good—and buying them at lower prices!

The thought that fake designer goods are harmless fun is shared by many people, but that view is changing as the fashion industry is battling against the counterfeit industry with new laws and criminal penalties. However,

it is now easier and more comfortable to buy these so-called bargains. No more chasing around vendors in the streets or basement stores for the goods. You may think you're getting a bargain when you buy online, but the truth is the Internet is becoming a "Worldwide Web of Counterfeits." Online counterfeit sales cost businesses $135 billion in revenue. The problem is growing because the amount of fake goods produced is rapidly increasing. For years, almost all counterfeit fashion has been produced in China, Korea, and Taiwan, but today we now have American companies making counterfeit goods.

How can consumers become more aware of counterfeit goods? Check Bazaar's "Fakes Are Never In Fashion" website (www.fakesareneverinfashion.com) the next time you shop for a "bargain" in retail stores or on the Internet.

Counterfeit Louis Vuitton bag

Police crackd on Chinatowr counterfeiting

I am **original**, I don't buy **fake**
www.unifab.com

These foreign import fairs increase the size and depth of the import market by giving buyers of small- and intermediate-size stores who would not ordinarily tap into the foreign market a chance to do so. To provide their customers with imported merchandise, these buyers need not maintain foreign representatives or shop in the foreign markets, neither of which would be cost-effective for their operations.

Importing by U.S. Businesses

Last but hardly least in a market that relies increasingly on foreign goods is U.S. buyers' purchase from U.S.-owned importing firms. Import firms shop in the international markets to purchase their own "lines," which they put together and display to retailers. U.S. manufacturers, initially upset about the growth of direct importing done by retailers, have increasingly turned to offshore sources for the same reasons that retailers do: price advantage, exclusivity, and workmanship. Like retailers, they often cite high domestic labor costs as a primary reason for resorting to imports. But labor costs must be viewed in light of the other considerations if a manufacturer is to maintain control of its brands' images. For example, a sportswear manufacturer may combine fine-quality knitwear produced overseas with domestically produced skirts or pants to create a line of separates.

PRODUCT DEVELOPMENT: SPECIFICATION AND PRIVATE LABEL BUYING

In addition to importing unique or distinctive goods, many retail operations use product development to set their assortment apart from those of their competitors. They may rely on domestic manufacturers or foreign sources for specification and private label buying.

These two terms may be used to describe the same items of merchandise, but the meanings are slightly different. If the retailer agrees, the manufacturer may design private label merchandise for the retailer. On the other hand, **specification buying** is a type of purchasing that is done to the store's rather than the manufacturer's standards. Retailers provide the standards and guidelines for the manufacture of clothes they order.

INTERNATIONAL TRADING LAWS

In the global economy, trade is truly international, not merely a set of bilateral agreements between pairs of nations. (A "bilateral agreement" is one in which two countries reach a separate agreement.) The trade relationship between any two nations affects the relationship of each party with its other trading partners as well. International trade laws have therefore developed out of need.

Counterfeit, Black Market, and Gray Market Goods

Three illegal practices that plague both importers and exporters are the importing of counterfeit, black market, and gray market goods. Counterfeit goods, like counterfeit currency, are inferior imitations passed off as the genuine article. Luxury goods and designer brands are the chief objects of counterfeiters. The sale of counterfeit goods at "bargain" prices devalues the real brand and deprives legitimate businesses of their fairly earned profits. U.S. Customs officials are authorized to seize imported counterfeit goods.

Another problem for manufacturers is **bootleg goods**. Many of these goods are not cheap rip-offs, rather they cannot be distinguished from the real ones. They are being made by the same manufacturers that make the real ones, but who are selling some goods to the black market.

Gray market goods are those that were not intended for sale in the country in which they are being sold; for example, an expensive Swiss watch is sold at a remarkably low price in the United States, but it does not have a warranty valid in the United States. The unfortunate customer usually does not realize this until repairs are needed.

North American Free Trade Agreement (NAFTA) and Central American Free Trade Agreement (CAFTA)

The **North American Free Trade Agreement (NAFTA)**, which went into effect in January 1994, eliminated quotas and tariffs for goods shipped among the United States and Canada and Mexico. Free trade agreements with China have complicated the issue further. The **Central American Free Trade Agreement (CAFTA)**, which was passed in July 2005, eliminated most trade barriers between the United States and Costa Rica, the Dominican Republic, El Salvador, Guatemala, Honduras, and Nicaragua. In 2005, quotas were lifted on all apparel and textile imports for the 144 countries in the World Trade Organization. The full implementation of free trade with Mexico began on January 1, 2008.[17]

PENETRATION OF THE U.S. MARKET BY FOREIGN INVESTORS

Direct investment in U.S. properties and businesses is extremely attractive to foreigners. Since so many textile and apparel items are imported into the United States, foreign investors have long been interested in buying into U.S. textile and apparel manufacturing companies. Only recently have they succeeded in doing so. Foreign investors, mostly from Europe and Asia, have taken three routes to ownership: joint ventures, total ownership, and licensing.

For example, L'Oréal of France purchased three important U.S. cosmetic labels: Maybelline, Redken, and Helena Rubenstein. While the purchasing of manufacturers is a relatively new form of foreign investment, many retail operations have been foreign-owned for some time, and there is even more activity in this sector than in manufacturing. Other foreign retailing successes are Laura Ashley, which is British owned; United Colors of Benetton, which is Italian owned; Zara, which is Spanish owned; and H&M, which is Swedish.

New York's Madison Avenue, Chicago's Michigan Avenue, and Los Angeles' Rodeo Drive are lined with the boutiques of Italian designers such as Valentino, Armani, Ungaro, Dolce & Gabbana, Missoni, and Prada. Their presence in the United States is just a part of their global retailing strategy.

Licensing

Actually, investment by foreign manufacturers in the fashion industry is not entirely new. Licensing arrangements, which often involve ownership of domestic companies, were initiated more than 25 years ago by companies such as Christian Dior, Pierre Cardin, and Hubert Givenchy. Today, the European presence is widespread. For example, Donna Karan's and Marc Jacobs's collections are financed by the French LVMH Moët Hennessy-Louis Vuitton family.

PENETRATION OF FOREIGN MARKETS BY U.S. COMPANIES

To counterbalance foreign investment, U.S. businesses have been interested in investing in foreign countries, where U.S. management is often welcomed because U.S. know-how and standards for high quality are much-respected commodities. U.S. investment in foreign countries also helps the balance of trade.

Licensing

Just as foreign manufacturers first penetrated the U.S. retail market with licensed products, so too have U.S. companies been able to license products abroad. Character licenses such as Mickey Mouse, Superman, and Dora the Explorer have been great successes abroad, as have sports licenses and brand names, such as Nike, and designer names, such as Calvin Klein, Donna Karan, and Ralph Lauren.

Many companies are now switching from licensing to importing strategies to establish and strengthen brand identity. As international distribution continues to develop, U.S. manufacturers are finding that a mix of locally licensed products and U.S.-manufactured apparel is the most effective way to sell locally.

Joint Ownership

While the United States permits total ownership by foreign investors, most other countries only allow foreign investors to be partners or joint owners. Among the U.S. companies that are joint owners in foreign manufacturing firms is Blue Bell, producer of Wrangler jeans in Asia, Italy, and Spain.

U.S. EXPORTING

Because the "Made in the U.S.A." label is desirable all over the world, the United States can export its fashion products around the globe. Increased U.S. exports, in fact, are seen by many industry experts as the solution to the U.S. trade deficit. The United States does not need to keep out foreign competitors as much as it needs to sell and promote its products abroad.

By the mid-1990s, U.S. fashion producers had begun to see exporting as a solution to another challenge as well. With the domestic market saturated with their goods, they turned to other countries as a source of growth. The U.S. industry's reputation for quality and trendsetting styles continues to grow. U.S. exports of textiles and apparel in 2010 increased to record levels of more than $15.8 billion.[18]

Although U.S. designer fashions are available in upscale department stores around the globe, a common strategy is to establish a presence in a new foreign market with a freestanding "signature store," or boutique. The ability to monitor consumer reaction to the designer's merchandise allows for rapid adjustment to local tastes and preferences, just as is true at home. Bud Kohnheim, chief executive officer of Nicole Miller, predicted in 1998 that "by the end of the century, the term 'going global' will have lost its meaning. Foreign sales will just be another part of every firm's account list."[19] He was right!

TRENDS IN GLOBAL FASHION SOURCING AND MERCHANDISING

The fashion industry survives through change. International fashion markets are working furiously to remain viable in a highly competitive global market. Fashion is increasingly becoming a global business. At the present moment, there are international fashion weeks in Australia, Brazil, New Zealand, Canada, India, Colombia, Mexico, Iceland, Hong Kong, Thailand, Japan, China, and South Africa.

The expense of attending markets and trade shows has had an impact on buyers and exhibitors at home and abroad. Economic globalization has made fashion capitals like Paris, Milan, and New York showplaces for designers from all over the world, not just from the home country. Retail buying trips to the national and international market centers have become the province of senior staff, who must make decisions for more departments or store units. Designers and other vendors carefully weigh the costs and benefits of several less elaborate exhibitions against fewer more lavish ones.

Another aspect of globalization is that developing countries are now becoming major players in the fashion industries, primarily as sources of materials and production, but also as importers and exporters of finished goods.

The increased worldwide use of computers and the Internet for buying, especially the basics, has had a great impact. The Internet also provides buyers, press, and consumers with instant information. For example, Fairchild Fashion Group's site Style.com (www.style.com) publishes runway reviews and pictures of a collection only hours after it has been shown on the catwalks in Paris, New York, London, or Milan. Some people argue that all this product information has made the consumer's attention span for trends shorter. Photos of collections are now available so quickly that the clothes look old by the time they hit the stores.

SUMMARY AND REVIEW

A market is a meeting place of buyers and sellers. Retail buyers of fashion goods go to market several times a year during market weeks, at the market centers of New York, Los Angeles, and Miami, and regional marts in other cities, including Atlanta, Chicago, Dallas, and Denver. With the exception of New York, where an entire district serves as a marketplace, markets are located in large convention centers with exhibition halls called marts. In addition to visiting the manufacturers' sales representatives in their showrooms or multiline sales representatives in temporary exhibition spaces, the buyers may attend trade shows and seminars sponsored by trade organizations.

In Europe, market weeks are semiannual. Designers' haute couture (custom designs) and ready-to-wear collections are shown in the market centers of Paris, Milan, and London. Numerous trade shows for apparel, accessories, and textiles are presented in other cities.

In Canada, market weeks and trade shows take place more frequently. Quebec is the province with the largest fashion industry, but all the provinces have apparel manufacturers, and market weeks and trade shows are held in major cities across the country.

The Americas and the Caribbean Basin are developing as centers for the production of wool and wool products, leather goods, and costume jewelry. Australia is also a big supplier of wool.

Japan's fashion designers and producers operate on an international scale with showings, boutiques, and manufacturing facilities at home and abroad. The largest international market for fashion goods is in Asia, with increasing production development in India and Vietnam. Apparel businesses in these areas are using their manufacturing and marketing expertise to develop the silk, leather, and fur industries on the Chinese mainland. Singapore is also emerging as an important market center. The fashion industry is truly operating in a global economy.

Through imports, offshore production, and exports, the U.S. textile and apparel industry is a major player in the global economy. Importing is a major source of merchandise for retailers, who rely on visits to foreign markets, store-owned foreign buying offices, commissionaires, import fairs, and U.S. import firms. Apparel manufacturers are also purchasers of foreign products, especially fabrics and other materials and trimmings. Retailers may develop products bearing their private label by having their designs produced by foreign manufacturers.

U.S. apparel manufacturers have turned to offshore sources for all or part of the production of their goods. To improve the unfavorable balance of trade that has resulted from this extensive import activity, the government has imposed quotas and tariffs on selected goods from countries whose products have a competitive advantage. The United States participates in multinational agreements such as those of the World Trade Organization and in separate trade agreements with individual countries or groups of countries.

U.S. and foreign businesses mutually penetrate one another's markets through licensing arrangements, investments in manufacturing, and establishment of retail outlets. Export of U.S.-made fashion goods is a growing aspect of the country's role in the global economy.

FOR REVIEW

1. What criteria must be met for an area to be considered a market center?

2. What support services for buyers are offered by the marts during and between market weeks?

3. What distinguishes New York City as the major fashion market center in the United States?

4. Describe the distinctive characteristics of the three regional market centers.

5. What business activities have the Paris couture houses undertaken to offset the decline in sales of haute couture clothing?

6. Name the fashion products for which Italy and Britain, respectively, are considered leaders.

7. What advantages do imports give retailers?

8. Name the five ways foreign-made fashion merchandise can be purchased.

9. What are the two important functions of foreign import shows in the United States?

10. What are the concerns that arise when retailers do specification buying of private label merchandise?

11. What forms do American investing in foreign countries' fashion industries take?

FOR DISCUSSION

1. Discuss the importance of Asia to producers and retailers of fashion goods. What are some current emerging global markets?

2. The reputation of Paris as a prime source of fashion inspiration began to develop several centuries ago as the result of many interrelating factors. Identify those factors and discuss their importance in the development of any major fashion design center.

3. As a fashion consumer, do you advocate protectionism or free trade? What major items of your current wardrobe would you have been unable to purchase if broad protective legislation prohibiting imports had been in place?

4. What are the advantages of using a store-owned foreign buying office? A commissionaire?

TRADE TALK

Define or briefly explain the following terms:

bootleg goods

boutique

buyer's directory

Central American Free Trade Agreement (CAFTA)

commissionaire

couture house

couturier/couturière

créateur

export

first cost

global sourcing

gray market goods

haute couture

import

market

market center

market week

mart

North American Free Trade Agreement (NAFTA)

prêt-à-porter

sales representative

specification buying

trade association

trade show

FASHION
RETAILING

KEY CONCEPTS

- History and development of fashion retailing in the United States
- Organization for buying and merchandising in department, specialty, and discount stores
- Discussion of sole proprietors, chains, leased departments, and franchises
- Operation of off-price retailers, factory outlets, category killers, and boutiques/showcase stores
- Operation of nonstore retailers, including direct sellers, catalog retailers, TV home shopping, and Internet sites
- Trends in retail patterns

The business of everybody in the fashion business is store business, whether one designs, manufactures, buys, sells, promotes, displays, reports, or photographs clothes, shoes, accessories, or beauty products. Eventually, the goods must be where the people are, and the people must come to where the goods are, and what is in the stores must be desired and bought by people—people continuously shopping, seeing, desiring, paying, and possessing.

—Estelle Hamburger, *Fashion Business—It's All Yours*[1]

Retailing is the business of buying and selling goods to those who will use them: the ultimate consumers. Retailing is a vital industry in the United States today. With more than two million retailers, the nation generates more than $3 million in sales annually.[2] Fashion retailing involves the business of buying and selling—or merchandising—apparel, accessories, and home fashions. It is the way fashion products are moved from the designer or manufacturer to the customer.

Retailing is in many ways the heart of the fashion industry. It is the most challenging end of the fashion business, existing as it does in a constant state of change. Retailers must, for example, be among the first to spot and act on new trends. They must be attuned to their customers' needs and desires to a degree that is required in few other businesses. Retailers must react to a constantly changing and often unsettled economic climate.

An extraordinary amount of planning and effort goes into the merchandising of fashion products. For people who are not in the fashion business, the process of merchandising fashion products can look very easy. Fashion moves from concept to customer, that is, from designer to manufacturer to retailer to you—the customer! The most intricate part lies in the merchandising and retailing of the goods. As mentioned previously, an old adage among fashion retailers is called the five Rs, and stands for choosing the following:

- The right merchandise
- At the right price
- In the right place
- At the right time
- In the right quantities

If any one of these Rs is incorrect, it will collapse the remaining Rs. Think of it as smoothly juggling five balls at once. You must keep them all in the air at the same time: constantly moving, never touching. Your timing must be flawless. If you let one ball slip, they will all fall. And you must keep smiling and make it look effortless, just like in fashion merchandising—it looks easy but is difficult to do!

HISTORY AND DEVELOPMENT OF FASHION RETAILING

People have been swapping, trading, or selling one another various goods for thousands of years. In the Orient and eastern Mediterranean, bazaars and marketplaces still operate on the sites they have occupied for centuries. Not until the mid-1800s and the opening of the first department store—Bon Marché in Paris—did modern merchandising as we know it begin to develop. Even then, it developed differently in the United States from the way it did in Europe. In this chapter, we shall explore the development of retailing in the United States.

TRADITIONAL TYPES OF FASHION RETAILERS

As the frontier turned into towns and cities, peddlers became sales representatives and general stores and mail-order businesses evolved into something entirely different from their ancestors.

Retailers today usually can be classified into one of two broad categories—general and specialized—depending on the kinds of merchandise they carry. In each of these categories are many different kinds of retail operations: department stores, specialty stores, chain operations, discount stores, and leased departments, to name a few. Almost all retail stores offer some form of mail-order, telephone, or e-commerce. More recently, there are retailers who are exclusively online, like Zappos.com and Blue Fly. We will discuss Internet shopping sites later in this chapter. Some stores have grown into giant operations, but many others are still small independently owned and operated businesses.

The retail scene is dominated by **general merchandise retailers**, such as JCPenney, Sears, and Target. These retailers typically sell many kinds of merchandise in addition to clothing. They try to appeal to a broad range of customers. Most general merchandisers very broadly target their merchandise to several price ranges, and only a few limit themselves to narrow price ranges.

Specialty retailers, in contrast, offer limited lines of related merchandise targeted to a more specific customer. They define their customers by age, size, or shared tastes. Their customers are more homogeneous than those of general merchandisers. Examples are Crate & Barrel, Tiffany's, and Talbots.

The differences between types of retailers are not as clearly defined as they used to be. It has, for example, become increasingly difficult to distinguish a department store from a chain operation, a discounter from an off-pricer, a franchiser from a chain. In this section, we will look at three traditional types of fashion retailers: department stores, specialty stores, and discount stores.

Department Stores

The **department store** is the type of general retailer most familiar to the buying public. Many are even tourist landmarks. Few people, for example, visit New York without seeing Macy's or Bloomingdale's. In London, Harrods is a big tourist attraction, as is Printemps in Paris.

Department stores reigned as kings of retailers well into the 1960s, when there was only about 4 square feet of retail space per person in the United States. They had long dominated downtowns with main stores called *flagships*. In the 1960s and 1970s, department stores anchored malls. But in the turbulent 1980s, department stores failed all across the country, victims of overexpansion, mergers and acquisitions, and increased competition. By 2005, the retail space was occupied by many different types of stores.

Before getting into the ways in which stores are changing, let us look at how various kinds of traditional retailers operate and merchandise themselves. As general merchandisers, department stores typically serve a larger portion of the community than other stores and often offer a variety of quality and price ranges. A department store usually offers a category of apparel at several price points, each in a different part of the store.

Department stores have also traditionally enjoyed a certain prestige that often extends even beyond the communities they serve. They are usually actively involved in their communities. A department store, for example, will eagerly stage a fashion show for a local charity, knowing that such activities create goodwill and enhance the store's overall reputation.

TERRY J. LUNDGREN

Macy's Chairman, President, and CEO

THE TITLE SAYS IT ALL! He is the only chairman, president, and CEO in the world of major retail organizations.

Born and raised in Southern California, he aspired to be a veterinarian but abandoned that dream for a lifelong career in retailing. After graduating from the University of Arizona in 1974, he started as a trainee at Bullock's, in California, a division of the then Federated Department Stores. He held positions of increasing responsibility over the next decade in buying, store management, human resources, and senior-level management.

His career in retailing had been very successful from 1975 to 1988 as he moved from Federated Department Stores, the Bullock's division, to Neiman Marcus. He went back to Federated in 1994 and Macy's, Inc. (formerly Federated Department Stores, Inc.).

Throughout his career, Lundgren is credited with being an innovator in merchandising, branding, and localization. Lundgren lead the 2005 merger of Federated Department Stores, Inc., and Macy's Department Stores, Inc., creating one of the largest retailers in the world with more than 800 U.S. stores.

In an interview with Tracy Mullin, former president and CEO of the National Retail Federation (NRF), he was asked if department stores are dead. He said, "When I graduated from college at the University of Arizona, I decided to take the job at Bullock's and my professor said, 'Aren't department stores dead?' That was 1975."

When asked of what he is most proud, he said, "After being with Bullock's for a year and a half, I was handwriting transfers from one store to another and I was really bored. And so I went to the head of HR, and I said to Gene Ross, 'Listen, I'm bored to death.' He has this sign in his office that said, 'Bloom where you are planted,' which I took to mean basically shut up and get back to work. I can honestly say that ever since that moment, my perception changed. I focused on the job I was in instead of focusing on my next job, and things just kind of worked for me."

Macy's, NYC

Terry Lundgren

Organization for Buying and Merchandising

Department stores are organized into special areas, or departments, such as sportswear, dresses, men's clothing, and furniture. Generally, buyers purchase for their departments, although in very large department stores, even the departments may be departmentalized, with individual buyers purchasing only part of the stock for a department. In some sportswear departments, for example, one buyer may purchase tops, while another buys bottoms.

Entertainment Values

The weaving of entertainment into modern retailing is reshaping the shopping experience. Entertainment values in retailing are defined in a number of ways. The most traditional way is by "simply having a compelling, often changing, merchandise assortment." Many retailers think of their stores as theaters that provide entertainment. The walls are the stage, the fixtures are the sets, and the merchandise is the star. Other popular entertainment strategies include providing video walls, interactive Internet sites, store visits by celebrities, designer trunk shows, sponsoring charity fund-raisers, and so on.

Contrary to the rumors that the department store is a dinosaur, many department stores are fighting back by adding entertainment value. One way that department stores have built relationships with their customers is through award and loyalty programs. These programs reward high-spending customers with bonuses, and make members feel as if they are part of a VIP club. The stores will arrange events that range from meet-the-designer product launches to luncheons and cocktail parties. Neiman Marcus, for example, hosts lunches for its InCircle program that has featured guests, many from the world of entertainment, such as singers, TV personalities, and famous designers.

The traditional department store "look" features separate, departmentalized classifications.

Specialty Stores

A specialty store carries a limited line of merchandise, whether it is clothing, accessories, or furniture. Examples of specialty stores include shoe stores, jewelry stores, maternity-wear stores, and boutiques. As noted, specialty merchandisers tend to target a more specific customer than do general merchandisers. They may offer a single line—just shoes, for example. Or they may offer related limited lines, for example, children's apparel, shoes, and other accessories. Or they may offer a subspecialty, like just athletic shoes or even socks.

Another variation of the specialty store is the private label retailer, which sells only what it manufactures itself. Gap, Ann Taylor, and Brooks Brothers are leading examples.

Organization for Buying and Merchandising

In small specialty stores, the buying and merchandising are done by the owner or a store manager, sometimes with the assistance of a small staff. Large multidepartment specialty stores are organized along the lines of department stores, with buyers purchasing merchandise for their own departments. Multiunit specialty stores belonging to chain organizations are set up in a unique way that is described under chain organizations, discussed later in this chapter.

Entertainment Values

Entertainment is a natural activity for specialty stores. In addition to exciting visual merchandising, many specialty stores now offer related entertainment. Niketown began the trend with its video wall, and then expanded to a Town Square with a staffed counter, banks of video monitors, and information about local and national sports teams. Gaylan's Trading Company, now owned by Dick's Sporting Goods, Inc., offers indoor and outdoor climbing walls, and an in-line skating area.

The Seven For All Mankind store offers jeans in a wide variety of sizes and fits.

Discount Stores

The discount business got its start after World War II, when servicemen and servicewomen came home with a well-thought-out agenda for their lives: get married, establish a home, and start a family. Within a few years, with the help of the G.I. Bill, which funded both education and mortgages, they had managed to achieve at least one of their wishes. Millions of new houses were built in "new" suburban towns. The next step was to furnish them.

A **discount store** today is any retail operation that sells goods at less than full retail prices. Discounters are called *discount stores, mass merchandisers, promotional department stores*, and *off-pricers*. Discounters may be either general or specialty merchandisers, selling everything from cosmetics, accessories, and apparel to health and beauty aids, to major appliances.

Organization for Buying and Merchandising

Early discounters searched the marketplace for closeout and special-price promotions. Their inventories consisted almost entirely of this type of goods. Today, discounters specialize in low-end open-market goods or special lines made exclusively for them. Most conventional retail operations do not want their buyers to purchase goods that will be sold to discounters, but this has not stopped manufacturers from making special lines for discounters. Some designers and manufacturers use discount outlets to sell their overstocks or slow-moving items.

FORMS OF OWNERSHIP

There are four types of ownership commonly found in U.S. retailing today: sole proprietors, chain organizations, leased departments, and franchises. Partnerships, once a very popular form of retail ownership (Sears and Roebuck, Abraham and Straus, and so on), are seldom found today because of liability issues and tax considerations. Owners use many different formats, including the traditional department store, specialty store, or discount store, or the newer off-price, factory outlet, or category killer formats.

Sole Proprietors

Sole proprietors, or owners, are the entrepreneurs who shaped U.S. retailing. Many of the retailing greats—JCPenney, John Wanamaker, Adam Gimbel, and Isaac and Mary Ann Magnin—began as sole proprietors with a great idea and went on to found great retailing empires.

More than 90 percent of all U.S. retailers own and operate a single store. Sole proprietors usually have small stores because of the huge amount of capital required to support an adequate inventory for a large business. These so-called **mom-and-pop stores** are usually single stores, managed by the owner with a few assistants. They are most frequently specialty stores because department stores require more space and inventory. If the owner prospers and expands to more than four stores, he or she is said to have a *chain*.

POP-UP STORES

Here Today, Gone Tomorrow, or Are They?

WELCOME TO THE ERA OF THE POP-UP STORE, the once temporary and rare fixture during holidays like Christmas and Halloween that have suddenly become much more permanent.

Pop-up stores are not entirely new. Target is one of the first national retailers to use the idea when it moved into a 1,500-square-foot store in Rockefeller Center in New York City for six weeks in 2003, to launch Isaac Mizrahi's new women's clothing line. In 2004, a Target pop-up opened in the Hamptons, selling barbeque and summer accessories, and for the Christmas season, set up a floating pop-up store on the Hudson River. JCPenney also tested out the New York City retail market six years ago that featured new home decor lines that were not available in their brick-and-mortar stores. Even eBay, the online auction site, has used the pop-up concept to create a physical space.

The boom in pop-up stores has brought some relief to the unemployed through the recent revival in temporary hiring in the retail sector. Many retailers see pop-ups as a reflection of the changing times and are taking their best-selling merchandise and putting it into smaller stores. The new stores can also serve as a valuable marketing tool for companies. The existing retail brand is "bricks, clicks, and quicks"—with "quicks" representing temporary retail like pop-ups as the newest trend to emerge.

Baron Hanson, owner and founder of Red-Baron Consulting and OpenPop-UpShops.com, estimates that nearly 99 percent of pop-up shops are independent from big-box brands and want to maintain a sense of exclusivity.

According to Hanson, cheap rent in high-traffic areas of metropolitan cities like New York and Los Angeles has given emerging retail entrepreneurs the ability to open up a store, however temporary, and really interact with their customers. "The pop-ups [are] a very youthful and very energetic type of expression," said Hanson. "It is a great way for younger entrepreneurs to test whatever they want."

eBay
pop-up
store

Chain Organizations

A **chain organization** is a group of centrally owned stores, four or more according to the Bureau of the Census definition, each of which handles similar goods and merchandise. A chain organization may be local, regional, or national, although it is the national chains that have had the largest impact on retailing. They also may be general or specialty merchandisers, and depending upon the kinds of stores they are, they will target their customer broadly or narrowly. A chain organization can be a mass merchandiser known for its low prices, a department store known for high-quality mid-priced goods, or a specialty merchandiser selling exclusive designs at high prices. Apparel chains may focus on a special size, age, or income group.

The oldest and best-known chain organizations are JCPenney and Sears, which *Stores* magazine categorizes as department stores. Other chains include Kmart and Walmart, which are categorized as discount stores. Prestigious specialty chains are Talbots and Eddie Bauer. Wet Seal is a juniors' specialty chain. The Limited is an example of a women's apparel specialty chain.

Organization for Buying and Merchandising

Most chain stores are departmentalized but not in the same way as department stores. Chain-store buyers are typically assigned to buy a specific category or classification of apparel within a department instead of buying all categories for a department the way a department store buyer does. This practice is referred to as **category buying** or **classification buying**. Buyers in department stores, in contrast, are said to be responsible for **departmental buying**.

A departmental buyer in a sportswear department, for example, would buy swimwear, tops, jeans, sweaters, and slacks. A chain-store buyer who bought in the sportswear department might buy only swimsuits or only swimwear accessories. Category buying is necessary because huge quantities of goods are needed to stock the individual stores of a chain operation. Some chain operations have merchandise units numbering in the hundreds of thousands.

In addition to centralized buying and merchandising, most chains also have a system of central distribution. Merchandise is distributed to the units from a central warehouse or from regional distribution centers. Computer systems keep track of stock so that it can be reordered as needed; they also keep buyers informed of what is selling.

Leased Departments

Leased departments, which were first discussed in Chapter 4, are sections of a retail store that are owned and operated by outside organizations. The outside organization usually owns the department's stock, merchandises and staffs the department, and pays for its own advertising. It is, in turn, required to abide by the host store's policies and regulations. In return for the leasing arrangement, the outside organization pays the store a percentage of its sales as rent.

Leased departments work best where some specialized knowledge is required. Jewelry, fur, and shoe departments are often leased, as are beauty salons. Glemby Company and

Seligman and Latz, for example, lease many of the beauty salons in stores. Another example is Macy's, Inc., which has a leased agreement with Sunglass Hut.[3]

Department stores, chains, and discount organizations will lease both service and merchandise departments, while specialty stores usually restrict leased operations to services, such as jewelry or shoe repair or leather and suede cleaning.

Franchises

Franchises established themselves as a viable form of retailing when shops featuring fast food, bath linens, cookware, fabrics, unfinished furniture, electronics, and computers were successfully franchised. In a **franchise** agreement, the franchisee (owner-operator) pays a fee plus a royalty on all sales for the right to operate a store with an established name in an exclusive trading area. The franchiser (parent company) provides merchandise and assistance in organizing and merchandising, plus training. Firms as diverse as United Colors of Benetton and Gymboree have adopted this form of ownership. Athletic footwear, tennis apparel, and men's sportswear have all produced lucrative and popular franchises. The Athlete's Foot, for example, which sells athletic footwear and activewear, has 530 locations in 36 countries.[4]

The latest trend is for designers to get in the act. Examples of successful worldwide franchises by designers are Ralph Lauren's Polo Shops, Calvin Klein shops, and Yves Saint Laurent's Rive Gauche shops.

Industry experts see no signs that franchising will slow its pace and many feel that this form of retailing will continue to grow.

OTHER TYPES OF FASHION RETAILERS

In addition to the traditional retail formats discussed above, a new group of businesses have evolved throughout the past 30 years that adapt some of the attributes of the traditional retailers with some new ideas.

Types of retail formats popular today include off-price retailers, factory outlet stores, convenience stores, category killers, catalog showrooms, boutique/showcase stores, and nonstore retailers. Many overlap with existing traditional formats. Many are chains. We will focus on those that are most important to apparel, accessories, and home furnishings.

Off-Price Retailers

One area that is experiencing strong growth is **off-price retailing**, the selling of brand-name and designer merchandise at lower-than-normal retail prices when they are at the late rise or early peak in the fashion cycle. In contrast, regular discounters sell merchandise in the late peak and decline stages of the fashion cycle.

Off-price retailers attribute part of their success to the fact that they provide an invaluable service to manufacturers and price-conscious customers. Because manufacturers must commit to fabric houses so far in advance (up to 18 months before garments will be in the stores), they risk not having enough orders to use the fabric they have ordered. Off-pricers have in effect helped to smooth out the cyclical and often financially disastrous course of apparel manufacturing. Customers, in turn, benefit from being able to buy garments very similar to those that are being sold in exclusive stores for less than they would pay in those stores.

Off-pricers managed to capture an important share of the brand-name market. The success of brand names such as Donna Karan, Bill Blass, and Calvin Klein meant that designers no longer had to give department stores exclusives, and they were soon selling their products to off-pricers. More recently, however, many designers have begun to sell their overstocks in their own stores. This has put severe pressure on off-pricers like Loehmann's and Syms to get enough inventory.

One other disadvantage seems to be built into off-price retailing: Off-price retailers get the goods later than regular-priced retailers. While a department store puts designer spring and summer clothing on the selling floor during the winter, the off-pricer does not get the same merchandise until several months later. As a result, the off-pricer has a shorter selling season than the regular-price retailer.

Factory Outlet Stores

Factory outlet stores, a discount operation run by a manufacturer—or increasingly these days by a designer—are another booming area of discount retailing. Factory outlets have grown at a furious pace over the past few decades. There are entire communities, such as Freeport, Maine; Manchester, Vermont; and Secaucus, New Jersey, that devote almost exclusively to the selling of factory outlet goods. The draw in Freeport was the presence of L.L.Bean, an established force in mail-order retailing that expanded its factory store outlet throughout the 1980s from a small outpost to a huge multibuilding operation.

Like off-price discounters, factory outlets offer certain advantages to manufacturers and customers. Most important is the fact that they provide manufacturers and designers with a backup channel of distribution, which improves inventory control. Canceled orders and overstocks can be funneled into discount stores, which, if run correctly, also can be enormous image enhancers. Not to be underestimated is the possibility of strong profits. An outlet buys merchandise from the parent company for 30 percent off the regular wholesale prices and sells it for the same markup percentage as regular-priced retailers.

One of Neiman Marcus's Last Call discount stores [left] and inside, overstocks and canceled orders are unloaded to shoppers looking for a bargain [right].

Fall 2011

Spring 2011

Jessica Simpson

Spring 2011

Spring 2011

JESSICA SIMPSON

Billion-Dollar Baby

HERE TODAY—GONE TOMORROW, THE USUAL PATH OF "CELEBRITY" FASHION IDOLS. But there is a surprise survivor that is on her way to becoming a fashion powerhouse—Jessica Simpson.

Yes, Jessica Simpson, famous for marriage and divorce from Nick Lachey, liaisons with singer John Mayer and Dallas Cowboys' quarterback Tony Romo, and her infamous wondering whether "Chicken of the Sea" tuna was actually chicken!

The singer-actress, tabloid favorite has proven to have staying power. In the fashion world, she has outlasted the likes of Jennifer Lopez and, at least for now, is even outperforming Madonna. Only a few years ago, it would have been hard to believe that Jessica Simpson would be the celebrity fashion brand that would break the one-billion-dollar retail barrier.

Jessica was born in Texas on July 10, 1980, and her first success was as a singer whose rise to fame began in 1999. Since that time, she has achieved many recording milestones and starred in several television shows, movies, and commercials.

"She is the girl next door and has great product that surrounds her," said Vince Camuto, founder and Chief Executive officer of Camuto Group. "People like her. People look at her as a style icon."

Since 2005, the Camuto Group, which makes her footwear, has linked licensing partnerships for twenty-two categories ranging from fashion accessories, swimwear, dresses, outerwear, watches, and fragrance. In 2010, Jessica Simpson's brand rang up $750 million in retail sales across all product categories.

In 2011, the Jones Group Inc. was chosen to design, develop, produce, and distribute Jessica Simpson sportswear. Designed to sell to better junior areas, the sportswear complemented the Jessica Simpson Jeanswear also done by the Jones Group Inc.

Jack Gross, CEO of Jeanswear for the Jones Group said, "She's very communicative to the fans. Fifteen- and sixteen-year-olds through forty-year-olds like her. Sometimes she has missteps, and they identify with her."

Over 650 department stores carry Simpson's collection, including Macy's, Dillard's, Belk, and Bon-Ton. Gross noted that Simpson has approved rights, as well as input into the line.

All of this is happening at the same time as the launch of Jennifer Lopez and Marc Anthony's apparel and accessories collection with Kohl's, and on the heels of Madonna's Material Girl collection exclusively at Macy's. Other "celebrity" designers that have already gained success are Gwen Stefani, Mary-Kate and Ashley Olsen, and Victoria Beckham.

Time will tell whether Jessica Simpson will be the Billion-Dollar Baby of celebrity fashion icons.

While designers and brand-name manufacturers use their outlets for overstocks and canceled orders, large manufacturers, such as Kayser-Roth and Carter, are careful to use their outlets only for closeouts and seconds. The latter are unwilling to risk offending department stores and other major customers with more direct competition. But now even the department stores have opened outlet stores: Saks Fifth Avenue has Saks Off Fifth, while Nordstrom has Nordstrom Rack.

Category Killers

Superstores or category specialists carry one type of goods that they are able to offer in great amounts at low prices because of volume buying. They so dominate a market that they drive out or "kill" smaller specialty stores, and so are known as **category killers**. They offer a narrow but deep assortment of goods in stores more than 8,000 square feet. Because of their buying power they can get not only rock-bottom prices but also excellent terms and an assured supply of scarce goods.

Examples of category killers include Bed Bath & Beyond, Home Depot, Barnes & Noble, and Babies 'R' Us. Typically these are huge freestanding stores, often called *big boxes*. They are rarely located in malls. They carry thousands of related products at low prices, which they think offset no-frills service and decor.

Boutiques/Showcase Stores

Although boutiques originated as small shops with French couture houses, they really came to life as small, individually owned shops in the anti-establishment 1960s. The first freestanding boutiques opened in London and quickly spread to the United States. Their appeal lies in their potential for individuality. These stores are often owned and operated by highly creative people who are eager to promote their own fashion enthusiasms. Their target customers are like-minded souls who share their unique attitudes about dressing.

Some boutique owners design their own merchandise; others buy and sell other people's designs. Boutiques are one of the few outlets for avant-garde merchandise that is too risky for department and specialty stores to carry.

A trend in boutiques has been for designers to open their own shops. The French designers were the first to experiment with freestanding boutiques in the United States, but U.S. designers soon followed suit. Among the French who have opened successful boutiques in the United States are Pierre Cardin, Valentino, Yves Saint Laurent, and Givenchy. Italian designers and manufacturers such as Armani, Gucci, and Ferragamo

Foreign designers open boutiques in the United States, such as Ferragamo on Fifth Avenue in New York City.

were quick to follow. Successful British firms that pioneered boutique selling on both sides of the Atlantic were Laura Ashley and Liberty of London.

Many U.S. designers are expanding by opening showcase stores. A **showcase store** is a manufacturer's or designer's store that sells merchandise at the introductory and early rise stages of the fashion cycle. In addition to generating income, showcase stores are testing grounds for new products. Ralph Lauren, Donna Karan, Calvin Klein, Tommy Hilfiger, Anna Sui, and Esprit operate showcase stores in addition to factory outlets. As less well-known designers rush to open showcase stores, there is little doubt that this form of retailing will continue to grow.

Nonstore Retailers

Nonstore retailing today is composed of four major formats: direct selling, catalog retailers, TV home shopping, and Internet shopping sites. The lines between these types are already starting to blur, as are those between nonstore retailers and traditional retailers. Store-based retailers are looking to expand their customer base through catalogs and electronic options. For example, leading catalogers such as Lillian Vernon and Spiegel have established a major presence on the Internet, as have retailers such as JCPenney and Gap, which have giant online virtual storefronts.

Direct Selling

Direct selling, which used to be known as direct-to-the-home selling, is still a major force in the United States. According to the Direct Selling Association, in 2009 direct selling sales was estimated to be more than a $30 billion dollar industry.[5] Almost all people who work in direct sales in the United States are independent part-time salespeople, who buy merchandise from a large firm and distribute it by selling it to customers in their territories. The Connault Group is a leader in direct sales fashion for women and is the creator of the Carlisle Collection, Per Se Collection, and Casuals Etcetera, Inc.[6]

Catalog Retailers

Catalog retailing, or mail-order retailing, as it was traditionally called, has been popular in the United States since the 1880s. But by 1982, the explosive growth of mail-order retailers had reached such proportions that *Time* magazine ran a cover story on it. The evolution of air delivery and computerized distribution played a vital role in increasing direct-mail and catalog sales. Companies had become able to target their customers in very specific ways: by age, income, geographic region, lifestyle, and interests. As a result, almost 90 percent of all catalog sales is now from specialized catalogs. Other boosts to mail-order selling include providing customers with toll-free 800 numbers, fax, and website information for placing orders; the ability to use credit cards to pay for merchandise; and the discount key codes. Retailers have established their own direct-selling programs, and store bills arrive stuffed with offers to purchase products. Some companies also send **magalogs**, which are catalogs that have editorial content, not just advertising.

However, there are a few big problems that are plaguing catalog retailers: the steadily increasing cost of paper, growth in Internet shopping, and the movement to be more "green." Another is that the average U.S. household receives about 140 catalogs a year—a deluge that is prompting negative customer response.

Still, many customers respond enthusiastically to catalogs as providing great entertainment value, as well as shopping venues. Think of the romantic travelogue copy, the informative product information, or the provocative photos featured in your favorite catalog.

TV Home Shopping

One of the most talked about developments in retailing has been the growth of home TV shopping, a form of retailing that takes the catalog sales techniques one step further. The potential of television as a direct-mail sales tool has long been recognized; witness the late-night gadget demonstrations and the ubiquitous storm window advertisements.

Not until the advent of cable television, however, with its lower production standards and costs, was it feasible to produce infomercials and to set up home shopping services that sell an array of goods. The cable TV infomercial with its enthusiastic host and wildly appreciative audience has been used to sell a large variety of goods, from Justin Bieber and Katy Perry for ProActiv to Susan Lucci's Malibu Pilates.

In 1977 Home Shopping Network, Inc. was the pioneer in the TV home shopping business. On the air 24 hours a day, 7 days a week, HSN is the world's most widely distributed TV shopping network and is the only service that offers shopping by remote. It also has an e-commerce site and apps for the iPad and mobile phones. HSN reaches at least 90 million homes and ships 50 million products annually. Its fashion and accessories area includes collections from designers, models, and athletes like Badgley Mischka, DKNYC, Iman, Twiggy, and Serena Williams.[7]

The second-largest television shopping service is QVC and has grown significantly since it was founded in 1986. QVC was the first multimedia retailer to offer native high-definition service to customers in May 2009. It offers on-screen demonstrations of merchandise that ranges from simple cookware to enormous amounts of apparel and accessories, especially jewelry. It also offers a wide array of home furnishings, table-top goods, and gift items. QVC has separate weekly shows for gold jewelry, silver jewelry, simulated-diamond jewelry, men's jewelry, and watches. Los Angeles designer Bob Mackie has made many appearances on QVC, selling out their stock of his scarves and tops. Isaac Mizrahi, Joan Rivers, and Rachel Zoe are other examples of effectively combining selling and entertainment. QVC also operates sales through its website; mobile phone applications; and retail operations, including a store at the Mall of America in Bloomington called QVC @ The Mall.[8]

ShopNBC, which is owned and operated by Value Vision, is a multichannel electronic retailer. This shopping network reaches 73 million homes in the United States through cable and satellite television. It too offers an extensive array of products, including apparel and accessories from Anne Klein, Suzanne Somers, Ed Hardy, and Harley-Davidson.[9]

With flat-screen TVs and new advances in technology, customers get a better view of the products, enticing them to place even more orders.

Internet Shopping Sites

Apparel sales moved into the top spot online in 2006 and have continued its phenomonal growth at a rate of 19.4 percent per year. Worldwide e-commerce totaled $572.5 billion in 2010, according to Goldman Sachs.[10] And in December 2010, Cyber Monday (Monday after Thankgiving) raked in more than $1 billion to become the biggest online spending day in history.[11]

Key reasons for growth of apparel, accessories, and footwear online are the variety of sites available, liberal shipping policies, a larger customer base, and easy search options for customers. High-speed broadband allows users to navigate quickly, and some sites give customers the opportunity to zoom in and see multiple views of products.

The e-tail players that have been the most successful are the online channels of apparel retail and catalog giants like JCPenney.com, Landsend.com, JCrew.com, and LLBean.com. NeimanMarcus.com offers interactivity with live chats and assistance. And let's not forget about the exclusively online retailers like Amazon, Zappos, and Bluefly.

Gucci's platform for the iPad lets customers easily shop for high-end timepieces wherever they might be.

A more recent trend in e-tailing that has emerged is member-only and flash-sale websites. Four major players in the flash-sales arena are Gilt Groupe, HauteLook, Ideeli, and Rue La La. Gilt Groupe, which is considered more "luxe," has about three million members. These sites give customers exclusive discounts with sales that last for only a certain number of hours, creating a sense of urgency to buy.[12]

MERGERS AND ACQUISITIONS

Until the 1930s, most department stores in the United States were independently owned. Most, in fact, were owned by the families whose names they bore, such as Marshall Field, John Wanamaker, Gimbel Bros., and J. L. Hudson. By the 1980s, most of these long-established stores had changed hands, and with these changes in ownership came new images and sometimes even new names.

So much change has occurred in the retail business recently that you need a scorecard to track the remaining players. Consolidations, changes in distribution channels, bankruptcies, altered buying organizations, and foreign investments have all caused the retail scene as we knew it to change.

Although mergers have taken their toll on department stores, causing some old, established stores to close their doors, some good has been served. Without mergers, many of the established department stores would not have survived the onslaught of competition from chains and discounters. In fact, mergers generally occur for one of two reasons: a need to reorganize for greater efficiency and a need to expand.

Merging for Efficiency

In the early 1980s, chain organizations, with their centralized buying, had developed a competitive edge over department stores even though department stores had tried to keep up by expanding the number of branch stores. The department stores soon realized that the real way to meet the competition was to develop more streamlined, efficient internal organizations. This was often achieved by merging one or more internal divisions to create a parent organization large enough to sponsor centralized buying, shipping, and merchandising.

Bal Harbour Shops—a luxury upscale mall featuring designer goods.

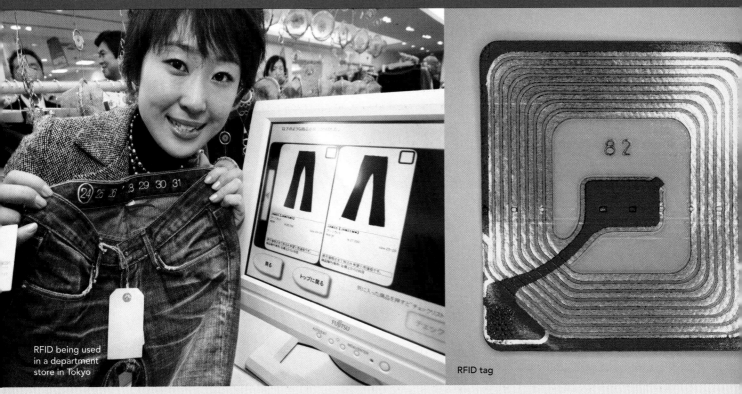

RFID being used in a department store in Tokyo

RFID tag

RFID
Radio Frequency Identification

WHEN WAS THE LAST TIME YOU COULD NOT BUY AN ITEM YOU WANTED BECAUSE THE STORE WAS OUT OF YOUR SIZE AND COLOR? Today? Yesterday? We all have had this experience and many times we never shopped in that store again!

Retailers' biggest problem for decades has been the difficulty in keeping track of their inventory. Radio Frequency Identification (RFID) is reported to be the answer for this problem, giving greater inventory accuracy, high responsibility, and vastly improved consistency. Keeping customers happy and buying in their stores, Wal-mart; JCPenney; Macy's, Inc.; and Bloomingdale's have all begun to use RFID tags on many of their apparel classifications. The tags empower retailers to identify each garment by size, style, color, and inventory. This dramatically enhances their ability to be fully stocked with the "right goods" at the "right store" at the "right time" more often.

The great upside for customers are lower prices and fewer missing sizes thanks to technology-driven efficiencies. The downside for customers: fewer markdown sales to unload unsold inventory.

"The power of accurate on-hand inventory is the driving factor from which all anticipated improvement will flow. Inventory accuracy is powerful and imperative for making right decisions," said Peter Longo, president of Macy's, Inc. logistics and operations. "Everything flows from it—from decisions about replenishment to the appropriate time to take a markdown—and the ability of shoppers to find the item they're looking for in the size and color they desire. Bottom line: RFID is a powerful tool to drive the selling environment, customer experience, and everything that goes with it."

TRENDS: CHANGING RETAIL PATTERNS

Retail operations must not only constantly respond to change in their environments but also must change themselves if they are to survive. One theory, suggested by Malcolm P. McNair, retailing authority and professor emeritus at the Harvard Business School, describes the way in which retail organizations naturally change or evolve.

According to McNair's theory, called the *Wheel of Retailing*, most retail organizations begin life as lower-priced distributors. They offer strictly functional facilities, limited assortments, and minimal customer services. As time elapses, the successful businesses need to grow to survive, so they begin to trade up in an effort to broaden their customer profile. Facilities are modernized. Store decor becomes more attractive. Assortments become more varied and of higher quality. Promotional efforts are initiated or increased, and some customer services are introduced.

The process of trading up, however, involves considerable capital investment in the physical plant, equipment, and stock. Operating expenses spiral. As a result, retailers are forced to charge higher prices to cover the increased cost of doing business. To justify the higher prices, they also begin to stock more expensive merchandise.

According to McNair's theory, as retailers move out of the low-priced end of the market into the moderate-to-high-priced field, they create a vacuum at the bottom of the retailing structure. The vacuum does not exist for long, however. Enterprising new retailers move quickly to fill the vacated and temporarily uncompetitive low-priced area to meet the demands of customers who either need or prefer to patronize low-priced retailers. This pattern keeps repeating itself as successful retailers trade up and new ones move into the vacuum. This theory also applies to catalog companies—Spiegel is one example of a firm that moved upscale.

Even those who move up must still constantly cope with the ever-changing nature of the fashion business.

The environment of this Ralph Lauren store is designed to reach out to the customer.

SUMMARY AND REVIEW

The history of fashion retailing in the United States is an interesting one. From general stores and peddlers to the earliest mail-order sellers, all early retailers sought customer satisfaction. Today's retailers seek the same goals through a variety of formats.

Three traditional retailing formats were the department store, the specialty store, and the discount store. Other formats include off-price retailers, factory outlet stores, category killers, and boutiques and showcase stores. All of these formats can be owned in one of four ways: sole proprietors, chain organizations, leased departments, or franchises.

Four types of nonstore retailing are popular today: direct selling, catalog or mail-order selling, TV home shopping, and Internet sites.

Mergers and acquisitions have changed the face of retailing as we knew it, and will probably continue to do so. Malcolm McNair's theory of how retailers evolve and change proposes that most retailers begin as lower-priced distributors and then move upscale. This creates an opportunity for new retailers to fill the lower-priced niche. McNair calls this the *Wheel of Retailing*.

FOR REVIEW

1. Name and briefly explain the characteristics and importance of three early forms of retail distribution in the United States.

2. How is the buying function handled by a department store?

3. What is a specialty store? How are buying and merchandising handled in a specialty store?

4. What is a chain organization? How are buying and merchandising handled in chain operations?

5. How do successful discounters make a profit?

6. What is a leased department, and how does it operate? Name the departments in a retail store that are frequently leased.

7. What is a category killer?

8. What stage or stages of the fashion cycle would most likely be emphasized by a specialty store, a department store, and a discount store?

9. What is the difference between home TV shopping and shopping on the Internet?

10. According to Malcolm P. McNair, how do retail organizations typically evolve?

FOR DISCUSSION

1. Compare and contrast the organization for buying and merchandising among prestigious chain organizations, department stores, and large specialty stores; discounters and off-price mass merchandisers; and franchises and leased departments. Give examples of different types of retailers in your community.

2. What examples in your community can you cite that support McNair's theory of trading up by retailers?

TRADE TALK

Define or briefly explain the following terms:

category buying or classification buying

category killer

chain organization

departmental buying

department store

discount store

factory outlet store

franchise

general merchandise retailer

leased departments

mom-and-pop stores

magalogs

off-price retailing

showcase stores

SO YOU WANT TO BE IN FASHION?
FASHION AUXILIARY SERVICES

KEY CONCEPTS

- Information provided to fashion producers and retailers by fashion consultants and research agencies; trade associations and trade shows; and buying, merchandising, and product development offices
- Differences among advertising, publicity, and public relations
- Services provided to fashion merchandisers by media such as trade and consumer publications, broadcast media, and the Internet and social media
- Overview of store design and visual merchandising services

As consumers we expect to find what we want, when we want it, and where we want it every day of the year. In the fall, back-to-school merchandise better be in stores, and the colors must be new and up-to-date. During the holiday months, gift merchandise and new items for holiday parties are expected. During spring and summer months we expect new colors, silhouettes, and fabrics to brighten up our wardrobes and take us through spring days to the hot, muggy days of summer.

How do the stores see into the future and anticipate our needs and wants? How do they keep stocks peaked when we want them and marked down when we are tired of them? They do not have crystal balls, or fortune tellers leading the way; what they do have are the fashion auxiliary services.

Bringing you and your fellow consumers the styles you want to wear is so huge and all-encompassing a task that the fashion industry requires many support, or auxiliary, services. These services have either been created specifically to serve it, as in the case of buying, merchandising, and product development organizations, or their function has been tailored to the fashion industry's specific needs, as in the case of advertising and public relations agencies, fashion magazines, and the variety of consultants and marketing groups.

FASHION AUXILIARY SERVICES OFFERED BY THE MEDIA

The media offer three broad categories of fashion auxiliary services: advertising, publicity, and public relations. **Advertising**, which appears in everything from magazines and newspapers to radio, television, and on the Internet is space and time for which an advertiser pays. **Publicity** is the free and voluntary mention of a firm, product, or person in the media. Its purpose is to inform or enhance public interest about something specific. **Public relations**, a broader term than publicity, is also free and voluntary mention, but it is designed to enhance a long-term goal, such as the shaping of a company's public image. All three efforts are important elements of the remaining auxiliary services.

One difference between advertising and publicity/public relations is the amount of control a manufacturer or retailer can exercise over each. Since advertising is purchased, a great deal of control can be exercised over its execution. Public relations and publicity can be carefully developed and well presented to the media, but there is no guarantee that the material and information supplied will be used well—or at all.

Some media—like newspapers and magazines—are moving away from print and transitioning to digital formats. Regardless of the form it may be in the future, it will continue to be a vital part of communications for the fashion industry.

Fashion Magazines

Fashion magazines, which combine advertising, publicity, and public relations, came into existence about 150 years ago in the form of a single publication called *Godey's Lady's Book*. Prior to that, women discussed the newest fashions with one another but had no authoritative source from which they could learn what was new and exciting. The magazine's first editor, Sara Joseph Hale, is now best remembered for her early feminism, especially her struggle to help women win acceptance in professions, but her influence on fashion was equally important. *Godey's Lady's Book* reported on the latest styles and was the forerunner of today's fashion magazines, such as *Vogue, Harper's Bazaar, Glamour,* and *Seventeen* (for young women). Several other magazines have also established themselves as fashion arbiters, most notably *Elle,* which competes with

Glamour, Marie Claire, and Nylon, which specializes in avant-garde fashion. In the mid- to late 1990s, two new important lifestyle magazines appeared on the scene. The first was InStyle, a monthly glossy that married celebrity and style editorial by covering fashion trends among celebrities and rigorously reporting on red-carpet ceremony dressing. InStyle was launched in 1994, and quickly became hugely successful. In 2009 their circulation was up to 1.7 million copies. Another important newcomer was Lucky, a publication that called itself "the magazine about shopping." The concept behind Lucky was very close to that of a catalog. It is almost exclusively based on still-life pictures of clothing and brief descriptions on what a garment is and where it is retailed. It has had much success over the years, with a circulation today of more than one million.[1] Magazines that appeal to specific ethnic markets include Essence, Ebony, and Today's Black Woman for African Americans, and the bilingual Latina for Hispanics. Even more specialized are magazines such as Bride's, which reports on wedding fashions, and Mode, which caters to full-figured women.

Well over a century after its first publication, Vogue continues to exert tremendous influence over the fashion world.

Gentlemen's Quarterly (GQ) is the largest circulating men's fashion magazine. Esquire, which covers topics beyond fashion, is still widely regarded as an authority on the latest trends in menswear. Other men's magazines that cover fashion in addition to other topics like health and sports include Details, Playboy, Men's Journal, Outside, FHM, and Maxim. Some men's magazines, like Maxim and FHM, also have their own biannual men's fashion magazine editions, which tend to be considerably more upscale than their parent magazines.

The "shelter magazines" are devoted to home fashions. Among the better known are Elle Decor, Architectural Digest, House Beautiful, Martha Stewart Living, Wallpaper, and Surface.

Fashions that appear in magazine articles are accompanied by an **editorial credit**, a unique form of publicity that names the manufacturer and lists retail stores where the clothes may be purchased. Editorial credit benefits even stores that are not listed because, if they have seen a magazine in advance, they can often stock the fashions. For advertisers whose merchandise is featured and credited in the editorial pages of a magazine, this publicity reinforces the paid advertising message.

FASHION WALK of FAME

BONNIE CASHIN

Following a career in costume design, Cashin launched her fashion business in the 1950s. Calling her clothing "kinetic art forms for living," she adapted simple cuts from the history of world clothing to meet the needs of modern women. She advocated playful but subtle exoticism and introduced layered, interlocking garments that could be rearranged to suit the wearer's taste and activity. Fusing practicality and whimsy, Cashin's distinctive style and philosophy celebrated independence.

2001

Bonnie Cashin's Fashion Walk of Fame plaque

FASHION WALK of FAME

MARC JACOBS

A fashion prodigy, Marc Jacobs has attracted attention from the very beginning of his career. Known first for his clever, witty designs, as in his "Freudian slip" dress, he became controversial with his "grunge" collection for Perry Ellis in 1992. His current success, both for Louis Vuitton in Paris and for his own New York-based collections, rests on his ability to meld the past with the present.

2002

Marc Jacobs Fashion Walk of Fame plaque

FASHION SHOWTIME GOES GLOBAL

FROM SIDEWALK CATWALK TO FASHION'S WALK OF FAME, from Mercedes-Benz Fashion Shows at Lincoln Center to Fashion's Night Out, fashion's showtime has gone global.

The Sidewalk Catwalk, strutting down Broadway from Times Square to Herald Square in New York City, was a one-of-a-kind public art exhibition of New York City's top fashion designers. It was a project of the Fashion Center Business Improvement District (FCBID), a nonprofit corporation, to promote development of New York's Fashion District. The FCBID works on specialized and ongoing programs to improve the image and importance of the Fashion Center. The Sidewalk Catwalk provided excitement and fashion awareness for NYC residents and the world.

The FCBID also sponsors the Fashion Walk of Fame in which individuals who have had an extraordinary impact on fashion have decorative plaques honoring them. Embedded in the plaques are an original sketch by the designer, a brief description of the designer's contribution to fashion, and the designer's signature.

The Fashion Walk of Fame is the only permanent landmark that celebrates achievements in American fashion design and is a destination point for tourists and fashionistas.

The biannual NY Mercedes-Benz Fashion Week has moved from Bryant Park at 6th Avenue and 42nd Street to Damrosch Park at Lincoln Center located at Broadway and 65th Street—not a global move—but important because of the larger space at Lincoln Center so that 250

designers can "strut their stuff" for the professional members of the fashion industry, as well as the general public who can buy tickets for the shows at $25 to $400.

In 2009 the newest and most exciting fashion event in the U.S. was Fashion's Night Out—geared to celebrate fashion, spur the economy, and so attendees could "shop till they drop." It was such a success that it became bigger and better in 2010, going global with Fashion's Night Out being celebrated from London to Paris to Milan to Tokyo to Sydney and across America from Los Angeles to Boston.

Retailers all joined the party by having designers, celebrities, and movie stars appear in their stores, having special items and events for customers, and generally inviting the public to enjoy a fashionable and happening experience.

Nanette Lepore's sidewalk catwalk design

PLEASE DO

General Consumer Publications

General interest consumer publications also play a role in disseminating fashion news to the public. Practically every newspaper reports on fashion, and some, such as the *New York Times*, the *Los Angeles Times*, the *Chicago Tribune*, and the *Washington Post*, devote regular weekly sections to apparel and home fashion design. Their fashion editors cover fashion openings, press weeks, and trade shows around the world. Twice a year, the *New York Times Magazine* has a second section for each of three fashion markets, *Fashions of the Times* for women's fashions, *Men's Fashions of the Times*, and *Home Design*. In *Paper, Time Out, City*, and other magazines that deal with pop culture, fashion gets extensive coverage. *Time, Newsweek*, and *People* provide occasional but important fashion coverage, as do the traditional women's magazines such as *Good Housekeeping* and *Ladies' Home Journal. Cosmopolitan*, whose primary market is young singles, has a circulation of 2.6 million. Other women's magazines that are geared to women who are not full-time homemakers also carry fashion news for their market segments. Among the most influential are *O, The Oprah Magazine; Ms.*; and *Working Mother*, which covers career fashions. *Seventeen* and *Teen Vogue* are designed for young teenagers. Women's sports magazines, such as *Self, Shape, Fitness*, and *Sports Illustrated Women/Sport*, include articles that cater to the fashion interests of female athletes and sports fans.

The New Yorker, Vanity Fair, Harper's, and the *Atlantic Monthly* occasionally bring fashion news to their urbane, sophisticated audiences.

Spanish-language versions of *People, Playboy, Cosmopolitan, Harper's Bazaar, Elle*, and *Marie Claire* are also in the market. The Spanish version of *Reader's Digest*, called *Selecciones*, is widely circulated. The publicity departments of most stores across the United States usually have no difficulty getting their messages across in local newspapers, since apparel stores are a major source of advertising revenue for newspapers.

Trade Publications

One of the most important aids to the merchandising of fashion is the **trade publication**. Unlike the fashion magazines, trade newspapers and magazines are published just for the industry. Many discourage subscriptions from people outside their field; few are available at newsstands, except in fashion markets and marts.

These publications announce new technical developments, analyze fashion trends, report on current business conditions, and generally help all who work in the fashion industry keep up-to-date on a staggering number of new products, techniques, and markets. Even government regulations are covered, as are personnel changes and classified ads for jobs.

The best-known fashion trade publication is *Women's Wear Daily*, often referred to as the bible of the industry. It is one of the oldest publications of its kind, having first been published in 1910. *Women's Wear Daily*, called *WWD* by those who read it, covers every aspect of the fashion industry from fiber and fabric to apparel, from day-to-day developments to new directions and trends. Each daily issue highlights a different segment of the fashion industry. In 2008 *WWD* started including coverage of

Women's Wear Daily
is constantly reporting
from fashion's
front lines.

men's fashion, retail, and related industries in its pages. Special *WWD/Global* issues are published, providing an overview of the major international markets that prepare readers for the upcoming spring and fall fashion weeks.

Footwear News and *Accessories* cover their specialties as intensely as *WWD* covers the women's market. The youth market is covered in *Earnshaw's Infants', Girls' and Boys' Wear Review*. Department store and specialty store management and merchandising executives read *Stores* and *Chain Store Age*. The fiber and fabric professionals read *Bobbins* magazine and *Textile World*.

The Broadcast Media

Fashion merchandisers have a choice of standard broadcast mediums: television, cable television, and radio. Or they may choose the newest medium—the Internet. Unlike the print media, the broadcast media are time- rather than space-oriented. Radio and television stations sell three levels of commercials in descending order of cost: network, spot, and local.

Broadcast media focused on children have received a good deal of critical attention over the years. Many new children's channels were launched and the kids' market seemed like a place of golden opportunity for advertisers. However, the climate slowed down at the turn of the millennium and the children's channels that turned a profit were the already established and relatively inexpensive giants like Cartoon Network and Nickelodeon. Other channels that have shows geared to children include Fox Kids, Kids' CW 11, and ABC/Disney.

Television

One cannot turn on the television today without learning something about current apparel fashions. The fashion industry obtains invaluable publicity from the simple fact that everyone who acts in a show or hosts or appears on a newscast or talk show wants to—and usually does—wear the latest fashions.

Because of the technical expertise and high level of quality required for network television, outside advertising agencies are usually hired to produce television advertising. Agencies develop an idea, present it in storyboard form to their client, photograph the advertisement, obtain or create the music, and provide tapes to individual stations for on-air viewing. Daytime talk shows and television commercials are another avenue of promotion for national brands of apparel. There is also a members-only website SeenOn.com that offers customers exclusive deals on products from celebrity looks "seen on" TV. For example, a customer could find an outfit that was worn on *Gossip Girl*, original designs straight from *Project Runway*, or collections from top stylists.[2]

Websites like private shopping hub SeenOn.com bring customers much closer to the brands and styles they see on TV.

Cable Television

Cable television has become an increasingly attractive option for fashion advertisers, largely because it costs so much less than network television. Many more outlets also exist for cable television, which reduces the competition to buy space. Cable television is also the home of the infomercial, the extended commercial in which a sponsor presents information about its product in a program format. Several celebrity-owned or franchised cosmetics lines have relied on this advertising medium. The 1982 debut of the Home Shopping Network (HSN) marked the beginning of a new outlet for sales as well as advertising. (See Chapter 11 for more information on HSN and QVC.) Fashion-inspired shows on cable television include *The Rachel Zoe Project* on Bravo and *Project Runway* on Lifetime.

Radio

While television is unsurpassed as a fashion advertising medium because of its visual qualities, radio is popular because it is inexpensive and can reach large but targeted audiences. Stations exist that serve only the youth market; others, such as classical radio stations, are geared to an older market. Others broadcast news and can deliver a virtual captive audience during the morning and evening commutes, the so-called *drive time.*

Commercials announcing sales and other storewide events can use radio effectively because they do not depend on visual appeals. To attract advertisers, stations provide assistance with the preparation of copy, which may be delivered by disk jockeys and other announcers. Radio is also a source of publicity as products and fashion news are discussed on regular shows.

eBay fashion iPhone app

EBAY
Looming Even Larger in Fashion

THE EBAY WEBSITE, WHICH REVOLUTIONIZED E-COMMERCE IN 1995 BY CONNECTING BUYERS AND SELLERS IN AN AUCTION FORMAT WHERE PRICE WAS SET BY THE MEETING OF SUPPLY AND DEMAND, unveiled its first fashion app for the iPhone in July 2010. The company also introduced fashion apps for the iPad and Blackberry.

Narciso Rodriguez for eBay

eBay president & CEO John Donahoe

Users will have access to 20 million fashion items offered through eBay's marketplace. The app allows users to browse, virtually try on, and buy products at any time of the day. One of the features of the mobile phone app includes a virtual style gallery of the latest trends and a "browse similar items" option that brings up more choices. A tap on the closet icon opens a user's personal closet, where favorite fashions can be stored. With the outfit builder, looks can be assembled by mixing and matching pieces from the closet and virtually trying on clothing. Users could either download their own photos and "dress" themselves, or drag and drop items onto a simple dress form to find the perfect look. There are also the requisite social-media functions so that friends and family can either veto or support any potential purchases.

With $5.45 billion in worldwide gross merchandise volume in apparel in 2009, eBay sells more apparel online than any other company. EBay wants to offer even more exclusive fashion to its client base of more than 90 million active users. For example, in 2010 it introduced exclusive capsule collections by Narcisco Rodriguez and Norma Kamali. Products are listed under the headings women's, men's, kids, baby, and vintage (with vintage organized by decade).

EBay is eager to build its stable of brands and outlet stores. For the first time, the company is hiring people with fashion merchandising backgrounds to help sellers position their products. A dedicated fashion buyer monitors what's selling through eBay, and then approaches the brands directly and asks them to consider selling their products. With its own fashion portal, www.fashion.ebay.com, eBay has improved its visuals, included pages of editorial features, and started hosting videos on the site.

Fashion is on the move in a big way on eBay!

The Internet and Social Media

Smart marketers acknowledge they need to be where the customer is—whether that's on a website, mobile device, Twitter, Facebook, or YouTube.

A web page is a reflection of a firm's identity, and in the fashion industry especially it is necessary to have a website that is well-designed and user-friendly. Web pages also allow the company to reach selected market segments and respond to their specific needs at any given moment. For example, retail customers can locate the nearest outlet of a favorite chain store, job applicants can find out about available positions and submit their résumés, and employees can communicate with one another, as well as with customers and vendors. Customers also have the ability to view and purchase products online within minutes.

Besides creating a whole new vocabulary, social media has managed to make the global fashion industry seem small. **Social media** are forms of electronic communication in which users create online communities and share information, including photos, videos, and messages. What the fashionable are wearing all over the world can be discovered with a push of a button or click of the mouse. Companies have responded to the social media explosion by jumping onto social networking sites and accumulating fans on Facebook, while promoting new products and delivering instant information via Twitter. And many design houses, including Ralph Lauren, Chanel, DKNY, and Gucci, "tweet" about their fashion shows right from the runway.[3] The bloggers, who have become just as famous as the designers themselves, send their reviews from the front row of fashion shows straight to the rest of the world. YouTube is another medium used to show off collections and related fashion videos.

According to Forrester Research Inc., there is certainly a shift from traditional media marketing to more interactive marketing. It is expected that this category will grow to $55 billion and represent 21 percent of all marketing spending by 2014.[4]

Everyone with a networked computer is able to find like-minded others, to share and publish, to create an audience or a market, and to collaborate with others to create things. The phenomenon is changing the world from a one-to-many broadcast format to a many-to-many interactive conversation.

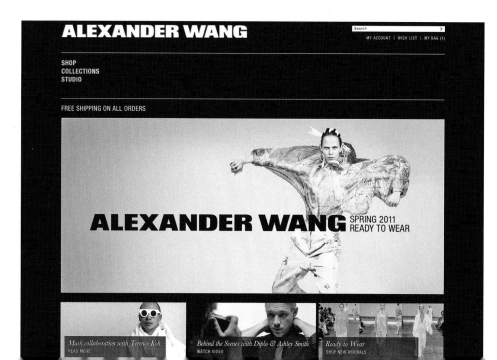

Alexander Wang, like most modern designers, has a strong Internet presence.

Donna Karan's Twitter page provides insider scoops—140 characters at a time.

ADVERTISING, PUBLICITY, AND PUBLIC RELATIONS AGENCIES

Advertising, publicity, and public relations agencies do far more for the fashion industry than prepare and sell advertising. An agency in any of these three areas may be deeply involved in creating a multimedia campaign designed to shape the public's image of a client company. These campaigns are used for ongoing maintenance of a company's image as well as for an image change.

Advertising Agencies

Advertising agencies provide many services, all of which are tied to the selling of commercial advertising space and/or time. Some agencies are specialized and deal only with one medium or one type of client, while others are general, offering a full range of services for many different types of clients. Agencies vary from one-person shops to giant agencies that employ hundreds of people around the world. Small agencies claim to offer personal attention, but even large agencies divide their staff into creative teams so they, too, promise and often deliver a specialized service.

Public Relations Agencies

Public relations firms are involved in the creation of publicity as well as in public relations. Publicity and public relations require that the agency work closely with its client, keeping abreast of what is new and newsworthy and announcing it to the world, either through press releases, often accompanied by photographs, or with story ideas presented to trade and consumer magazines and newspapers. As noted, public relations also involves, on a much deeper level, the shaping of a company's image. To this end, a public relations agency may suggest or help to plan and coordinate an event or activity, such as the rendering of a public service or gift to a charity or community or the presentation of a scholarship or endowment to an institution or foundation.

Other Advertising and Public Relations Services

Maintaining the corporate image of a fashion producer or retailer requires the services of a number of "creative" specialists, who may be company employees, agency employees, or freelancers. For example, fashion stylists may select and coordinate the apparel and accessories for store catalogs and print ads, for magazine articles, or for commercials. The job of the stylist involves juggling many tasks in one day and often includes charming celebrities into posing in outfits they dislike. Many stylists work in either Los Angeles or New York, but more job opportunities are growing across the country. Hollywood's top stylists include Phillip Bloch, Jeannine Braden, Deborah Waknin, Lisa Michelle, Stacy Young, Patricia Field, and Rachel Zoe. Stylists must work cooperatively with the rest of the team: the photographers, the makeup artist, the hairdresser, the magazine editor, and the celebrity's agent or publicist.

Fashion illustrators' and photographers' work appears in advertising and in the editorial pages of consumer and trade publications. Skilled fashion photographers command creative control of a shoot as well as high pay. Independent fashion show production companies offer their services to producers, retailers, and trade organizations.

STORE DESIGN AND VISUAL MERCHANDISING

Two important on-site promotional activities that support the selling of fashion merchandise are store design and visual merchandising. The term **visual merchandising** includes the arrangement and presentation of merchandise in store windows and on the selling floor. It covers the arrangement of items that are on sale as well as the display and sample items on mannequins and other props. The layout and design of any retail business have an impact on sales. For the traditional retailer operating in a store, the selling floor serves the critical purpose of presenting the merchandise to the customer, a function that is essential in selling fashion goods, for which appearance is a primary feature. Manufacturers' and designers' showrooms are their selling floors and, thus, require the same attention to interior design and visual merchandising.

Signs and Graphics

Signs and graphics enhance merchandise presentations both in windows and on the selling floor. Temporary signs to announce a sale or special event or inform shoppers of a price could be produced easily with computer software. More permanent signage, such as directional signs for elevators, escalators, departments, and restrooms, are more typically prepared by professionals. Like other aspects of visual merchandising, signs should be in keeping with the store's image.

Celebrity stylists, like *Sex and the City*'s Patricia Field, have increasingly found the spotlight through behind-the-scenes work.

Diane von Furstenberg,
inducted to the Fashion Hall of Fame

Fall
2011

Diane von
Furstenberg

Spring
2011

DIANE VON FURSTENBERG

Just Can't Get Enough!

THERE ARE MANY DESCRIPTIONS OF DIANE VON FURSTENBERG. Among them are: candid, coquettish, feline, strong, outspoken, powerful. She is the Belgium-born daughter of Auschwitz survivor Lily Nahmias. At 22 she married Prince Egon von Furstenberg, and her nights at Studio 54 were splashed across headlines; Andy Warhol immortalized her in pop-art portraits. But beyond a lofty title and the role of wife and mother, she created the famous wrap dress in 1974 and became an overnight fashion sensation.

However, her fashion business took a bad hit in the 80s, and she left the United States and went to Paris where she stayed for over five years. She made a triumphant comeback in 1997, rebuilding her company and becoming one of the most popular and well-known American designers. She is currently the president of the CFDA, American fashion's governing body, and has achieved numerous awards and a place on the Fashion Walk of Fame.

From the pace of Diane von Furstenberg's social calendar, one might presume that the CFDA's commander in chief is hot on the reelection trail. Not only is she a favorite of the "fashion crowd" but also is very much involved in empowering women worldwide. When asked by a reporter, "What do you feel is the greatest lesson that you've learned?" von Furstenberg replied, "In life? It's funny, but I think that I have learned that to be kind, to give, is the best gift. I think that's the big

lesson. You have to be your best friend in life because the relationship that matters most is the one you have with yourself."

Under her leadership and part of the CFDA's commitment to design education, the Geoffrey Beene Design Scholarship, the Liz Claiborne Fashion Scholarship, and the CFDA/TEEN Scholarship all support fashion design students across the country. CFDA has also cultivated emerging talent like no other single fashion capitol by supporting the CFDA Fashion Incubator. The initiative consists of a full floor with studios at the building in the Fashion Center of the Garment District and includes mentorship from top industry professionals for the young designers.

Diane von Furstenberg told the last, sold-out CFDA Fashion Awards show, "Tonight is the night we designers and members of our industry salute our peers and celebrate their talents. We are a family."

INFORMATION RESOURCES

The fashion business is so huge and complex that no one individual or company can keep abreast of everything that is happening in it. It is a business made up in large part of trends and news in addition to its products. As a result, the auxiliary service provided by fashion consultants and research agencies, whose role is to supply information, is vital to the industry.

Fashion Consultants and Information Services

Fashion consultants are individuals and groups who provide information and services to producers and retailers. The most famous pioneer in fashion consulting was Tobé Coller Davis, who founded her agency, Tobé Associates, in 1927. It has continued to be an important source of information for the industry for decades. Other well-known consultants today are Kurt Barnard and Walter F. Loeb. Additionally, firms working in the fashion and retailing consulting area include Kurt Salmon Associates in Atlanta; Greenhouse Inc. in Chicago; State Street Research in Boston; Retail Management Consultants in San Marcos, California; and WSL Strategic Retail in New York.

The Fashion Group International, Inc.

Another vital source of industry information is the Fashion Group International, Inc., a nonprofit global association of professional women who work in the industry and the associated beauty and home fashions industries. It was founded in 1930 to create executive jobs for women. Over the ensuing decades, however, it has become an important consulting and research agency. Its services are offered to members and, in some instances, nonmembers. Originally a group of 17 fashion leaders in New York, it now has more than 6,000 members in chapters in fashion centers across the world.

The Fashion Group is known for its exciting and prophetic fashion presentations. Through lavish fashion shows and fiber displays, it offers the fashion industry its expert and insightful analysis of upcoming trends. It covers the U.S., European, and Far Eastern fashion scene. The Fashion Group also publishes monthly news bulletins and maintains a valuable website (www.fgi.org), an online information service featuring directories of industry executives and professional services, calendars of events, trend reports and forecasts, classified job listings, public announcements, and conferences.

Specialized Information Services

A number of services disseminate reports on various segments of the fashion industry. For example, Nigel French, a British company, issues reports on fabrics, knitwear, and color. The *International Colour Authority,* a British publication, and the Color Association of the United States (CAUS) specialize in reporting on color trends in womenswear and menswear.

Market Research Agencies

Because knowing what is new and what is now is at the very heart of fashion, businesses in all segments of the industry avidly consume the raw data and trend analyses published by market research agencies. The services of these professional prophets are expensive, but many of their findings are made public in time to be useful to a larger following. Among the better-known agencies is Kurt Salmon Associates (KSA), known for its extensive work with textile and apparel manufacturers and softgoods retailers.

The major accounting firms also have special divisions devoted to the fashion industries. Ernst & Young, Deloitte & Touche USA, and Management Horizons (a division of PricewaterhouseCoopers) all offer respected management consulting services on a global basis.

A new breed of researchers and forecasters who rely on a variety of resources—including their own anecdotal observations and gut instincts as well as polls and surveys—is epitomized by Faith Popcorn. BrainReserve, the company she founded in 1974, has a staff of 28, but it also retains its "TalentBank" of 5,000 authorities in a variety of businesses whom it consults regularly. Brain Reserve's public opinion surveying technique involves hour-long face-to-face interviews. Popcorn boasts a 95 percent accuracy rate in her predictions.

Exemplifying a trend themselves, a number of trend-forecasting agencies specialize, and the youth culture is a well-studied specialty. Cheskin in Southern California is a typical fashion forecaster who follows their subjects to their natural habitats: night-clubs, rock concerts, health-food stores, and so on. Much of their information is collected by insiders, under-30 interviewers and observers, some armed with video cameras to document the trends they see. As consumers become more aware of trends, they become more aware that they are trendsetters, and the fashion industry, instead of attempting to dictate what will be worn next season, is actively seeking out the influential consumers and taking a cue from them. Other trend forecasting firms include the Doneger Group, Stylesight, and Mudpie.

Trade Associations and Trade Shows

Associations of manufacturers and retailers assist fashion buyers in many ways. The nature and frequency of assistance available, however, are not uniform throughout the industry, and buyers soon learn how much assistance will be forthcoming from their particular trade.

Retailers Group

The National Retail Federation (NRF) is the largest retail trade association in the United States, counting among its members all the major department and specialty stores. It disseminates information and advice through its monthly magazine, *Stores*, and other periodicals and through regional and national meetings. An annual general convention is sponsored by the National Retail Federation in New York City in January. Vendors of products and services as diverse as market research, management software, and shopping bags exhibit at this meeting. Members gather at seminars and workshops to learn from retailing authorities and from one another. A special feature at this convention is a session devoted to outstanding fashion promotions during the previous year.

Buyers Groups

Specialized associations or buying clubs provide an opportunity for an exchange of opinions and ideas among members. Retail buyers' groups also transmit the preferences of their members on matters as varied as the dates when lines should be opened and the appropriate sizes of stock boxes for specific products. Trade associations are often subsidized by outside sources—either the industry itself or a trade publication.

Trade Shows

Retail and manufacturing groups, as well as independent organizations, sometimes sponsor trade shows at which many exhibitors gather to show their products and lines in one place, usually a hotel or convention center. Trade shows save time that would otherwise be spent trudging from showroom to showroom and provide buyers with a chance to meet and exchange ideas with one another. They are especially helpful in fashion areas made up of many small firms. Exhibitors also find them a place to meet their counterparts from other regions or countries.

BUYING, MERCHANDISING, AND PRODUCT DEVELOPMENT ORGANIZATIONS

Another type of auxiliary service—one developed especially for the fashion industry—is the **buying, merchandising, and product development organization**. This type of organization evolved from a service called a *resident buying office (RBO)*, and to understand the function of a buying, merchandising, and product development organization, one must first know something about RBOs. The buying offices came into being to serve the ongoing needs of a store or group of stores for a steady supply of new merchandise. Because a store's buyers worked out of the store and made only occasional market trips, they came to rely on a service located at the market centers for ongoing, daily attention to the store's needs. Originally, RBOs existed only for out-of-town retailers to place orders. Today, their functions and their clients have become so diverse that the term "resident buying office" is no longer complete or accurate.

Although their main job remains buying and coordinating orders, buying offices provide many support services—not just to retailer buyers but also, in some instances, to wholesalers and apparel manufacturers. They watch and report on fashion trends, help with strategic planning, make vendor recommendations, coordinate imports, and assist in product development. They help to organize fashion weeks and ensure that they go smoothly for their client stores' buyers. A good buying office continually adds to its list of services, and many have even expanded into areas such as sales promotion and advertising, personnel operations, and computer processing.

HOPE REIGNS HIGH ON THE JOB FRONT

THE PROSPECTS FOR COLLEGE GRADUATES LOOKING FOR FASHION AND RETAIL JOBS ARE IMPROVING BUT ARE STILL DIFFICULT. During the past few years, many firms pulled back from recruiting on college campuses, reduced payrolls, and have depended on unpaid interns to fill in the gaps. But it is not all doom and gloom! A rise in expected hiring provides hope for college graduates seeking jobs in retail. Hiring retailers range from large department stores such as Macy's, Inc., and big-box retailers such as Lowe's, Home Depot, and Bed Bath & Beyond, to small boutiques.

WWD contacted retailers, fashion companies, universities, and headhunters about the job market, especially for those looking to enter the retail-fashion sector. Among the retailers who have training programs for college graduates is Macy's, Inc., which has a ten-week program. JCPenney also offers a ten-week internship program. Gap offers a competitive nine-month training program for grads that focuses on three core areas of the business: merchandising, production, and inventory management. The TJX Companies, Inc., have a corporate merchandise-planning program to develop the quantitative and fashion-planning skills needed by off-price retail professionals.

The fashion companies that do the most on-campus recruitment are Macy's, Inc.; JCPenney Co. Inc.; Target Corp.; Kohl's Corp.; Liz Claiborne Inc.; Li & Fung USA; TJX Companies, Inc.; and Polo Ralph Lauren Corp. Many of the colleges and universities report that seniors are using social networking tools to find jobs. They post their own career pages and are encouraged to create their own brands.

Hiring experts believe it is imperative that retailers and fashion firms recruit young people. "They've got to bring in young talent," said Hal Reiter, CEO of Herbert Mines Associates. "We're suffering a material dearth of talent, and unless we recruit retailers and retain these young people, then there'll be nobody to run these businesses in 15 years."

University of Michigan commencement

This computer rendering previews the look of *TeenVogue*'s booth at the upcoming *WWD* Magic convention.

Functions of the Buying, Merchandising, and Product Development Organization

Even with instant communication by e-mail and the Internet, the buying function benefits from the services of a representative and adviser who is actually at the market. Some of the functions that buying offices perform on behalf of their clients are purchasing, preparing for market weeks, importing, and developing products.

Purchasing

Buying offices offer store buyers advice and support in various buying situations. For example, an office can place an order large enough to qualify for a manufacturer's quantity discount and then divide the goods among several small clients. The organization's staff can visit manufacturers' showrooms and make recommendations to their clients about specials, trends, and hot items. Size and location give the buying office clout with vendors when it comes to reordering in midseason or making sure the right goods are delivered on schedule.

Preparing for Market Weeks

Market weeks are hectic times for fashion buyers, filled with many showroom visits and other information-gathering events. A buying office can provide services similar to those of a tour guide to make the buying trip smooth and efficient. Staff members visit the showrooms in advance and assess each manufacturer's lines on behalf of their various clients. When the store buyers arrive, the buying office may give presentations to let them know what to expect. Sometimes personnel from a buying office accompany visiting buyers to vendors' showrooms and offer on-the-spot advice about orders.

Importing

In response to the increasingly global nature of the fashion business, many buying offices maintain divisions in key foreign cities or affiliate with a *commissionaires* overseas. (A commissionaire is an agent that represents stores in foreign markets. See Chapter 10 for further discussion.) Overseas divisions and commissionaires work closely with the merchandising division and with client stores. In addition to performing the buying functions of a domestic buying office, these services deal with the unique challenges of importing, such as quotas, tariffs, long lead times for delivery, and interpretation of the buyers' orders for vendors who speak a different language. Having an adviser and consultant overseas is especially beneficial for buyers who are attending a market week or trade show or having private label goods produced in a foreign country.

Developing Products

Buying offices have played an important role in the development of private labels. Most corporate-owned buying offices have a private label program for their member stores.

Corporate offices have also aggressively pursued private label business and product development. Macy's, Inc., has a well-established product development and private label program. They employ more than 500 people in more than 18 countries to design, develop, and identify manufacturers for its product development private label business.

SUMMARY AND REVIEW

Fashion producers and retailers depend on a variety of auxiliary services to support the merchandising function. Depending on the size and resources of a company, it may rely on its own staff for these services or hire outside firms to perform them.

The media regard fashion businesses as clients and offer assistance in preparing and placing advertising in newspapers, consumer and trade magazines, and on the Internet. They also air commercials on television and radio. Today, the use of social media is a fast-growing marketing tool for the industry. To attract advertisers, the media offer fashion businesses color and style forecasts and other trend information. Advertising and public relations agencies also provide auxiliary services in placing paid advertisements and free publicity in the media. Store design and visual merchandising are other promotional services that may be performed by staff members or independent suppliers.

For information about industry trends and fashion forecasts, retailers and producers can take advantage of the services offered by fashion consulting firms, market research agencies, trade associations, and trade shows.

A source of information unique to the fashion industry is the buying, merchandising, and product development organization. This type of business began as resident buying offices, representing out-of-town retailers in the major markets. Some firms were independent, selling their services to noncompeting retailers. Others were corporate-owned, either as cooperatives owned by several retailers or as divisions of large retail chains. Resident buying offices have evolved into businesses that include wholesalers and producers among their clients and that provide a full range of services, including liaisons with vendors, advice and assistance in buying and merchandising, and forecasting and other information services.

FOR REVIEW

1. What is the difference between advertising and publicity/public relations?

2. Describe the contents of *Women's Wear Daily.*

3. What are the advantages of television, radio, the Internet, and social media for fashion exposure? Do you prefer one instead of another? Why?

4. What tasks do public relations firms undertake for their clients?

5. What advantages does a website offer as a promotional medium?

6. How does a store design contribute to the store's image?

7. Describe the research methods that trend forecasters use.

8. What is the major function of buying, merchandising, and product development organizations? What additional services do they perform?

9. What are the similarities and differences between independent and corporate buying, merchandising, and product development offices?

FOR DISCUSSION

1. As a consumer, where do you get your information about fashion? How does each medium influence your buying decisions?

2. You own a small boutique that caters to upscale young women. What services of a buying, merchandising, and product development organization would be most useful to you? Why?

TRADE TALK

Define or briefly explain the following terms:

advertising

buying, merchandising, and product development organization

editorial credit

publicity

public relations

social media

trade publication

visual merchandising

GLOSSARY

activewear The sector of sportswear that includes casual attire worn for sports such as running, jogging, tennis, and racquetball. Sometimes called *active sportswear*.

adaptations Designs that have all the dominant features of the styles that inspired them but do not claim to be exact copies.

advertising The paid use of space or time in any medium. This includes newspapers, magazines, direct-mail pieces, shopping news bulletins, theater programs, catalogs, business cards, billboards, radio, TV, and the Internet.

anchor A design from a previous season reworked in a different color of fabric.

apparel contractor A producer whose sole function is to supply sewing services to the industry, here it is sometimes called an outside shop.

apparel jobber (manufacturing) A firm that handles the designing, planning, and purchasing of materials and usually the cutting, selling, and shipping of apparel, but not the actual garment sewing.

apparel manufacturer Performs all the operations required to produce apparel, from buying the fabric to selling and shipping the finished garments.

auxiliary level Composed of all the support services that work with primary producers, secondary manufacturers, and retailers to keep consumers aware of the fashion merchandise produced for ultimate consumption.

bootleg goods Quality products made by the same manufacturer that produces the genuine branded products; these are sold to the black market.

boutique A shop associated with few-of-a-kind merchandise, generally of very new and extreme styles, with an imaginative presentation of goods. French word for *shop.*

brand names A word, name, symbol, etc., especially one legally registered as a trademark, used by a manufacturer or merchant to identify its products distinctively from others of the same type and usually prominently displayed on its goods, in advertising, etc.

bridge (apparel—women's and men's) A price zone that bridges the gap between designer prices and better prices.

bridge jewelry Merchandise ranging from costume to fine jewelry in price, materials, and newness of styling.

bundling Assembling the cut pieces of each pattern—sleeves, collars, fronts, and backs—into bundles according to their sizes. Usually done by hand.

buyer's directory A list (and often a map) of the manufacturer's showrooms in a particular market or mart; it is furnished to retail buyers to assist them in "working the market."

buying, merchandising, and product development office *Associated/cooperative:* One that is jointly owned and operated by a group of independently owned stores. *Private:* One that is owned and operated by a single, out-of-town store organization, and which performs market work exclusively for that store organization. *Salaried, Fee,* or *Paid:* One that is independently owned and operated and which charges the stores it represents for the work it does. *Syndicate/Corporate:* One that is maintained by a parent organization that owns a group of stores and which performs market work exclusively for those stores.

carat A measure of weight of precious stones equal to 200 milligrams or 1/142 of an ounce. See also *karat.*

category or classification buying A practice whereby a chain store buyer located in a central buying office is usually assigned to purchase only a specific category or classification of merchandise instead of buying all categories carried in a single department. See also *departmental buying.*

category killer Superstores or category specialists who so dominate a market that they drive out or *kill* smaller specialty stores.

chain organization A group of 12 or more centrally owned stores, each handling somewhat similar goods that are merchandised and controlled from a central headquarters office (as defined by the Bureau of the Census).

chargebacks Financial penalties imposed on manufacturers by retailers.

classic A style or design that satisfies a basic need and remains in general fashion acceptance for an extended period of time.

collection A term used in the United States and Europe for an expensive line.

commissionaire (pronounced *ko-mee-see-oh-NAIR*) An independent retailer's service organization usually located in the major city of a foreign market area. It is roughly the foreign equivalent of an American resident buying office.

Computer-Aided Design (CAD) A computer program that allows designers to manipulate their designs easily.

Computer-Aided Manufacturing (CAM) Stand-alone computerized manufacturing equipment, including computerized sewing, pattern-making, and cutting machines.

Computer-Integrated Manufacturing (CIM) Many computers within a manufacturing company are linked from the design through the production stages.

consignment selling A manufacturer places merchandise in a retail store for resale but permits any unsold portion to be returned to the wholesale source by a specific date.

contract buying See *specification buying.*

contract tanneries Business firms that process hides and skins to the specifications of converters but are not involved in the sale of the finished product.

corporate licensing The use of a company's name on (sometimes) related merchandise.

costume jewelry Mass-produced jewelry made of brass or other base metals, plastic, wood, or glass, and set with simulated or nonprecious stones. Also called *fashion jewelry.*

couture house (pronounced *koo-TOUR*) An apparel firm for which the designer creates original styles.

couturier (male) or **couturière** (female) (pronounced *koo-tour-ee-AY* and *koo-tour-ee-AIR*) The proprietor or designer of a French couture house.

créateurs (pronounced *kray-ah-TOURS*) French ready-to-wear designers.

culmination (stage) See *fashion cycle.*

custom-made Clothing fitted specifically to the wearer.

decline (stage) See *fashion cycle.*

demographics Studies that divide broad groups of consumers into smaller, more homogeneous target segments; the variables include population distribution, age, sex, family life cycle, race, religion, nationality, education, occupation, and income.

departmental buying A practice whereby a department buyer is responsible for buying all the various categories of merchandise carried in that department. See also *category buying.*

department store As defined by the Bureau of the Census, a store that employs 25 or more people and sells general lines of merchandise in each of three categories: home furnishings, household linens and dry goods (an old trade term meaning *piece goods* and *sewing notions*), and apparel and accessories for the entire family.

design A specific version of a variation of a style. In everyday usage, however, fashion producers and retailers refer to a design as a *style,* a *style number,* or simply a *number.*

details The individual elements that give a silhouette its form or shape. These include trimmings; skirt and pant length and width; and shoulder, waist, and sleeve treatment.

discount store A departmentalized retail store using many self-service techniques to sell its goods. It operates usually at low profit margins, has a minimum annual volume of $500,000, and is at least 10,000 square feet in size.

discretionary income The money that an individual or family has to spend or save after buying necessities such as food, clothing, shelter, and basic transportation.

disposable personal income The amount of money a person has left to spend or save after paying taxes. It is roughly equivalent to what an employee calls *take-home pay* and provides an approximation of the purchasing power of each consumer during any given year.

diversification The addition of various lines, products, or services to serve different markets.

downward-flow theory The theory of fashion adoption, which maintains that to be identified as a true fashion, a style must first be adopted by people at the top of the social pyramid. The style then gradually wins acceptance at progressively lower social levels. Also called the *trickle-down* theory.

editorial credit The mention in a magazine or newspaper of a store name as a retail source for merchandise that is being editorially featured by the publication.

electronic data interchange (EDI) The electronic exchange of machine-readable data in standard formats between one company's computers and another company's computers.

environment The conditions under which we live that affect our lives and influence our actions.

erogenous Sexually stimulating.

export When a country provides goods to another country.

fabrics Materials formed from knitted, woven, or bonded yarns.

factor Financial institution that specializes in buying accounts receivable at a discount.

factory outlet store Manufacturer-owned store that sells company products at reduced prices in austere surroundings with minimum services.

fad A short-lived fashion.

fashion A style that is accepted and used by the majority of groups at any one time.

fashion business Any business concerned with goods or services in which fashion is an element—including fiber, fabric, and apparel manufacturing, distribution, advertising, publishing, and consulting.

fashion cycle The rise, widespread popularity, and then decline in acceptance of a style. *Rise:* The acceptance of either a newly introduced design or its adaptions by an increasing number of consumers. *Culmination:* The period when a fashion is at the height of its popularity and use. The fashion then is in such demand that it can be mass-produced, mass-distributed, and sold at prices within the reach of most consumers. *Decline:* The decrease in consumer demand because of boredom resulting from widespread use of a fashion. *Obsolescence:* When disinterest occurs and a style can no longer be sold at any price.

fashion industries Those engaged in producing the materials used in the production of apparel and accessories for men, women, and children.

fashion influential A person whose advice is sought by

associates. A fashion influential's adoption of a new style gives it prestige among a group.

fashion innovator A person first to try out a new style.

fashion jewelry See *costume jewelry.*

fast fashion A strategy of constantly changing fashion to keep it fresh by basing the collections on the most recent fashion trends presented at Fashion Week and manufacturing it quickly in an affordable way to the mainstream consumer, allowing retailers to develop ways to create and offically manage a variety.

fiber A threadlike unit of raw material from which yarn and, eventually, textile fabric is made.

first cost The wholesale price of merchandise in the country of origin.

floor ready Merchandise that has been ticketed with bar-coded price and packed in labeled cartons with all shipping documents attached. If the merchandise is a garment, it has been pressed and folded or hung on a hanger with a plastic bag over it.

franchise A contracted agreement in which a firm or individual buys the exclusive right to conduct retail business within a specified trading area under a franchiser's registered or trademark name.

free trade The unrestricted exchange of goods among nations.

fur farming The breeding and raising of fur-bearing animals under controlled conditions.

general merchandise retailer Retail stores that sell a number of lines of merchandise—for example, apparel and accessories; furniture and home furnishings; household linens and dry goods; and hardware, appliances, and smallwares—under one roof. Stores included in this group are commonly known as mass-merchandisers, department stores, variety stores, general merchandise stores, or general stores.

generic name Non-trademarked names assigned by the Federal Trade Commission to 23 manufactured fibers.

geographics Population studies that focus on where people live.

geotextiles Manufactured, permeable textiles currently used in reinforcing or stabilizing civil engineering projects.

global sourcing Term used to describe the process of shopping for and purchasing imported goods.

graded Adjustment of a style's sample pattern to meet the dimensional requirements of each size in which the style is to be made. Also referred to as sloping.

gray market goods Goods not intended for sale in the country in which they are being sold, often with an invalid warranty.

greige goods (pronounced *grayzh goods*) Fabric that has received no preparation, dyeing, or finishing treatment after having been produced by any textile process.

group A subdivision of a line, linked by a common theme such as color, fabric, or style.

haute couture (pronounced *oat-koo-TOUR*) The French term literally meaning *fine sewing* but actually having much the same sense as our own term *high fashion.*

hides Animal skins that weigh over 25 pounds when shipped to a tannery.

high fashion Styles or designs accepted by a limited group of fashion leaders—the elite among consumers—who are first to accept fashion change.

high-tech fabrics A fabric that has been constructed, finished, or processed in a way that gives it certain innovative, unusual, or hard-to-achieve qualities not normally available.

horizontal growth A company expands on the level on which it has been performing. See also *vertical growth.*

horizontal-flow theory The theory of fashion adoption that holds that fashions move horizontally between groups on similar social levels rather than vertically from one level to another. Also called the *mass-market theory.*

import When a country buys goods from a foreign country.

inflation A substantial and continuing rise in the general price level.

item house Contractors that specialize in the production of one product.

karat A measure of the weight of the gold content of jewelry; abbreviated as *K*.

kips Animal skins weighing from 15 to 25 pounds when shipped to a tannery.

knockoffs A trade term referring to the copying, at a lower price, of an item that has had good acceptance at higher prices.

leased department A department ostensibly operated by the store in which it is found but actually run by an outsider who pays a percentage of sales to the store as rent.

let-out (furs) A cutting and re-sewing operation to make short skins into longer-length skins adequate for garment purposes.

licensing An arrangement whereby firms are given permission to produce and market merchandise in the name of the licensor, who is paid a percentage of sales for permitting his or her name to be used.

line An assortment of new designs offered by manufacturers to their customers, usually on a seasonal basis.

line-for-line These are exactly like the original designs except that they have been mass-produced in less expensive fabrics in standard size measurements.

magalogs Catalogs that have editorial content, not just advertising.

manufactured fiber A fiber invented in a laboratory; also called "man-made" or "synthetic."

marker (apparel manufacturing) A long piece of paper upon which the pieces of the pattern of a garment in all its sizes are outlined and that is placed on top of many layers of material for cutting purposes.

market A group of potential customers. Also the place or area in which buyers and sellers meet for the purpose of trading ownership of goods at wholesale prices.

market center A geographic center for the creation and production of fashion merchandise, as well as for exchanging ownership.

market segmentation The separating of the total consumer market into smaller groups known as *market segments.*

market weeks Scheduled periods throughout the year during which producers and their sales representatives introduce new lines for the upcoming season to retail buyers.

marketing A total system of business activities designed to plan, price, promote, and place (distribute) products and services to existing and potential customers.

mart A building or building complex housing both permanent and transient showrooms of producers and their sales representatives.

mass customization The idea to tailor the product to fit one particular customer—not one size fits all—and to supply thousands of individuals, at mass prices, not custom-made prices.

mass or volume fashion Styles or designs that are widely accepted.

masstige When luxury designers apply their creativity to create apparel intended for mass market.

merchandising Sales promotion as a comprehensive function including market research, development of new products, coordination of manufacture and marketing, and effective advertising and selling.

merger A sale of one company to another with the result that only one company exists.

microfiber A fiber two or three times thinner than a human hair and thinner than wool, cotton, flax, or silk fibers. It has a texture similar to silk or cashmere but is wrinkle-resistant.

millinery The women's hat industry.

mom-and-pop store A small store run by the proprietor with few or no hired assistants.

North American Free Trade Agreement (NAFTA) An agreement that eliminated quotas and tariffs for goods shipped among Canada, the United States, and Mexico.

obsolescence (stage) See *fashion cycle.*

off-price retailing The selling of brand name and designer merchandise at lower-than-normal retail prices when they are at the late rise or early peak in the fashion cycle.

offshore production The importation of goods by domestic apparel producers, either from their own plants operating in cheap, labor-rich foreign areas, or through their long-term supply arrangements with foreign producers.

outside shop See *apparel contractor.*

pelt The skin of a fur-bearing animal.

per capita personal income The wages, salaries, interest, dividends, and all other income received by the population as a whole, divided by the number of people in the population.

personal income The total or gross amount of income received from all sources by the population as a whole. It consist of wages, salaries, interest, dividends, and all other income for everyone in the country. See also *disposable personal income* and *discretionary income.*

PETA People for the Ethical Treatment of Animals, a nonprofit organization devoted to animal rights.

piecework A production method in which each operator sews only a section of the garment to speed the production process. See section work.

prêt-à-porter (pronounced *preht-ah-por-TAY*) A French term meaning "ready-to-wear."

price zone A series of somewhat contiguous price lines that appeal to specific target groups of customers.

primary level Composed of the growers and producers of the raw materials of fashion—the fiber, fabric, leather, and fur producers who function in the raw materials market.

primary suppliers Producers of fibers, textile fabrics, finished leathers, and furs.

private label or store brand Merchandise that meets standards specified by a retail firm and belongs to it exclusively. Primarily used to ensure consistent quality of products as well as to meet price competition.

product development The teaming of market and trend research, with the merchandising, design, and technical processes that develop a final product used by both wholesale manufacturers, who develop products for signature brands, and retailers, who use it for private label development at their own stores.

product manager See *specification manager.*

profit The amount of money a business earns in addition to its expenses; net income.

prophetic styles Particularly interesting new styles that are still in the introductory phases of their fashion cycles.

psychographics Studies that develop fuller, more personal portraits of potential customers, including personality, attitude, interest, personal opinions, and actual product benefits desired.

public relations Works to improve a client's public image and may develop long-range plans and directions for this purpose.

publicity The mention of a firm, brand, product, or person in some form of media.

purchasing power The value of the dollar as it relates to the amount of goods or services it will buy. A decline in purchasing power is caused by inflation.

quality assurance (QA) Inspection of each component of a garment to ensure that it meets the standards established for it.

quick response (QR) A strategy used by manufacturers to shorten the ordering cycle to compete with foreign imports.

radio frequency identification (RFID) Uses electronic tags for storing data; using a unique serial number that allows the tracking of products, cartons, containers, and individual items as they move through the supply chain. They hold more data than bar codes and can be read many times faster.

ramie A minor natural fiber from a woody-leafed plant grown mostly in China.

ready-to-wear (RTW) Apparel made in factories to standard size measurements.

recession A low point in a business cycle when money and credit become scarce and unemployment is high.

retail level The ultimate distribution-level outlets for fashion goods directly to the consumer.

rise (stage) See *fashion cycle*.

royalty fee Percentage of licensee sales paid to the licensor. See also *licensing*.

sales representatives Company representatives who exhibit merchandise to potential customers.

sample hand The designer's assistant who sews the sample garment.

secondary level Composed of industries—manufacturers and contractors—that produce the semifinished or finished fashion goods from the materials supplied by the primary level.

section work The division of labor in apparel manufacturing whereby each sewing-machine operator sews only a certain section of the garment, such as a sleeve or hem.

short-run fashion A fashion that takes fewer seasons to complete its cycle than what might be considered its average life expectancy.

silhouette The overall outline or contour of a costume. Also frequently referred to as *shape* or *form*.

skins Animal skins that weigh 15 or fewer pounds when shipped to a tannery.

sloping See *graded*.

social media Forms of electronic communication in which users create online communities and share information, including photos, videos, and messages.

social mobility When an individual or group moves within a social hierarchy. There is also an effort to associate with a higher class by imitation.

specification buying A type of purchasing that is done to the store's rather than to the manufacturer's standards. See also *private label*.

specification manager Manager who oversees the purchasing and manufacturing process for a private label. Also called *product manager*.

spinnerette A mechanical device through which a thick liquid base is forced to produced fibers of varying lengths.

spreader A laying-up machine that carries material along a guide on either side of a cutting table, spreading the material evenly, layer upon layer.

sterling silver A term used for jewelry and flatware with at least 92.5 parts of silver; the remaining 7.5 parts are usually copper.

style A characteristic or distinctive mode of presentation or conceptualization in a particular field. In apparel, style is the characteristic or distinctive appearance of a garment, the combination of features that makes it different from other garments.

style number The number manufacturers and retailers assigned. The number identifies the product for manufacturing, ordering, and selling.

suit separates (menswear) Sports jacket and trousers worn much as the tailored suit used to be.

sumptuary laws Laws regulating consumer purchases (for example, dress) on religious or moral grounds.

supply chain management (SCM) Allows companies to share forecasting, point-of-sale data, inventory information, and the supply and demand for materials or products.

sustainable use An environmental program that encourages land owners to preserve animal young and habitats in return for the right to use a percentage of the grown animals.

sweatshop A garment manufacturing plant employing workers under unfair, unsanitary, and sometimes dangerous conditions.

tailored suit A structured suit that is designed to fit close to the body, rather than being loose.

tanning The process of transforming animal skins into leather.

target market A specific group of potential customers that manufacturers and retailers are attempting to turn into regular customers.

taste The recognition of what is and is not attractive and appropriate. Good taste in fashion means sensitivity not only to what is artistic but also to these considerations.

textile fabric Cloth or material made from fibers by weaving, knitting, braiding, felting, crocheting, knotting, laminating, or bonding.

texture The look and feel of material, woven or nonwoven.

trade association Professional organizations for manufacturers or sales representatives.

trade publications Newspapers or magazines published specifically for professionals in a special field, such as fashion.

trade shows Periodic merchandising exhibits staged in various regional trading areas around the country by groups of producers and their sales representatives for the specific purpose of making sales of their products to retailers in that area.

trend A general direction or movement.

trimmings All the materials—excluding the fabric—used in the construction of a garment, including braid, bows, buckles, buttons, elastic, interfacing, padding, self-belts, thread, zippers, etc.

trunk show A form of pre-testing that involves a designer or manufacturer sending a representative to a store with samples of the current line and exhibiting those samples to customers at scheduled, announced showings.

universal product code (UPC) One of a number of bar codes used for automatic identification of items scanned at retail cash registers. UPC is the symbol that has been most widely accepted by retailers and manufacturers.

upward-flow theory The theory of fashion adoption that holds that the young—particularly those of low-income families as well as those of higher income who adopt low-income lifestyles—are quicker than any other social group to create or adopt new and different fashions.

vendor One who sells goods to others; a source of supply.

vermeil (pronounced *vur-MAY*) A composite of gold over sterling silver.

vertical growth When a company expands on a level different from its original one.

visual merchandising Everything visual that is done to, with, or for a product and its surroundings to encourage its sales. This includes display, store layout, and store decor.

wicking Fabrics that are capable of transporting moisture, have resistance to radiation, corrosive chemicals, and other stresses, and adjust to extreme weather changes.

yarn A continuous thread formed by spinning or twisting fibers together.

TOP 100 APPAREL DESIGNERS

What makes top 100 lists so much fun? The intense debate, evaluation, and reevaluation they inspire; it's also what makes them such a valuable learning experience.

Some of the people included are famous figures in the history of design; others are more recent designers whom I have known personally or through their clothes. Others are included because their work strikes a chord with the times they designed in—and others captivated the young!

So, enjoy the list. Then add your own favorites and subtract those names you don't agree with. And, of course, state the reasons for your choices.

	NAME	DECADES OF INFLUENCE	DEFINING CHARACTERISTICS
1	Adolfo	1960s–1980s	Chanel-inspired knit suits … has a devoted following of "status" dressers
2	Alaïa, Azzedine	1980s–2000s	Famous for seductive clothes … "King of Cling"
3	Armani, Giorgio	1980s–2000s	Impacted both men's and women's fashions … fluid tailoring, luxurious light fabrics, self-assured style
4	Balenciaga, Cristobal	1940s–1960s	One of the 20th century's greatest … his influence inspired the later work of Hubert de Givenchy, Emanuel Ungaro, and André Courrèges
5	Balmain, Pierre	1940s–1950s	Classic daytime looks and extravagant evening gowns … opened Paris house in 1945
6	Beene, Geoffrey	1960s–1980s	Relaxed, elegant look, superb cut, and beautiful fabrics
7	Blass, Bill	1970s–1990s	Mr. Sophistication … great taste, refined cut, and innovative use of fabrics
8	Bohan, Marc	1960s–1980s	Started in early 1960s with Dior and was the lead designer there until 1989
9	Callot Soeurs	1900s–1950s	Four sisters' design house … credited for training famous French designers
10	Boss, Hugo	1980s–2000s	First name in menswear
11	Cardin, Pierre	1950s–1960s	King of the licensing game … first designer to show his line in China
12	Carnegie, Hattie	1930s–1940s	Influential in the 1930s and 1940s … her designs influenced Norell, Trigère, and McCardell
13	Cashin, Bonnie	1940s–1950s	Mother of the American Sportswear Look … championed separates and the "layered look" … stretch ski pants, pedal pushers, capri pants
14	Cassini, Oleg	1960s–1980s	Official designer for Jacqueline Kennedy in her White House years … now king of the licensed suit
15	Cavalli, Roberto	1970s–2000	Big success with blasted jeans … designs for men, women, and youth
16	Chalayan, Hussein	2000s…	Internationally regarded designer famous for his innovative use of materials
17	Chanel, "Coco"	1920s–1940s	Her innovations have become timeless classics: sweaters, sailor looks, tweed suits
18	Claiborne, Liz	1980s–2000s	The "Executive Lady" … innovator of career apparel
19	Costa, Francisco	2000s…	Creative director of the Calvin Klein Collection for women, one of fashion's highest posts
20	Courrèges, André	1960s–1970s	First couturier to raise hemlines to mid-thigh … white boots, tough chic
21	de la Renta, Oscar	1960s–2000s	Luxury designer … opulent eveningwear, sophisticated daywear
22	Dior, Christian	1940s–1950s	The "New Look" in 1947 … cinched waist, pushed-up bosom, short jacket emphasized hips, full long skirts

	NAME	DECADES OF INFLUENCE	DEFINING CHARACTERISTICS
23	Dolce, Domenico, and Gabbana, Stefano	1990s–2000s	Inspired the young to dress up … sexy lingerie looks are their signature … glorification of female physique is the message of their designs
24	Elbaz, Alber	2000s …	Known for his simple, feminine clothing … lauded by the fashion press
25	Ellis, Perry	1970s–1980s	Added high-fashion pizzazz to classic looks … young in spirit … natural fibers, hand-knitted sweaters
26	Fath, Jacques	1940s–1950s	Sexy clothes … hourglass shapes … plunging necklines
27	Ferré, Gianfranco	1980s–1990s	Architectural look to his designs … was educated as an architect and he shows well-defined construction in his clothes
28	Ford, Tom	1990s–2000s	Design voice of Gucci … now speaks for himself
29	Galanos, James	1940s–1950s	First American couturier … elegant haute couture designs
30	Gaultier, Jean-Paul	1980s–2000s	Trendy and controversial … advocate of the "punk look" … daring and avant-garde
31	Ghesquière, Nicolas	2000s …	Designer of Balenciaga … one of a handful of young visionaries looking to the believable future of fashion
32	Giannini, Frida	2000s …	Creative director of Gucci … holds the reigns of one of Italy's most powerful fashion houses … followed Tom Ford
33	Givenchy, Hubert	1950s–1980s	His fashion muse was Audrey Hepburn … introduced chemise or sack dress
34	Grès, Alix	1930s–1950s	The duchess of draping … her Grecian column dresses are draped to perfection
35	Gurung, Prabal	2000s …	After showing for the first time in 2009, he has skyrocketed into the fashion world as one of its premiere darlings
36	Halston	1970s–1980s	Unconstructed separates, lush cashmeres … Studio 54
37	Herrera, Carolina	1980s–2000s	Caters to high-society clientele … dressy eveningwear … luxurious fabrics
38	Hilfiger, Tommy	1980s–2000s	"Brand image" designer
39	Jacobs, Marc	1990s–2000s	Designed for the Perry Ellis label … exceptional in leather and fur design
40	James, Charles	1940s–1950s	The Dalí of Design
41	Johnson, Betsey	1960s–1970s	The Betsey of "Betsey, Bunky, and Nini" … designed for "Paraphernalia" stores
42	Kamali, Norma	1980s–1990s	Sweatshirt clothes made high-fashion news … appeals to the young
43	Karan, Donna	1980s–2000s	High-fashion elegant sportswear … simple silhouettes, sarong skirts, easy-fitting dresses
44	Kawabuko, Rei	1980s–1990s	Avant-garde clothes challenged classic idea of femininity
45	Klein, Anne	1950s–1960s	Classic American sportswear designer … "Junior Sophisticates" was her company

NAME	DECADES OF INFLUENCE	DEFINING CHARACTERISTICS
46 Klein, Calvin	1970s–2000s	King of the minimalism look … designer jeans … sexually charged advertising
47 Kors, Michael	1990s–2000s	Strong on shape and line, devoid of ornamentation
48 Lagerfeld, Karl	1980s–2000s	Produces 16 collections a year! … perfect technique and witty design resurrected the Chanel name
49 Lanvin, Jeanne	1920s–1930s	One of the earliest Paris couturiers
50 Lauren, Ralph	1980s–2000s	Western look for men and women … creates upper-crust lifestyle looks … classic silhouettes
51 McCardell, Claire	1940s–1950s	Introduced dirndl skirt as a high-fashion icon … leading proponent of American sportswear look
52 McCartney, Stella	2000s…	Loved worldwide for her sharp tailoring and sexy femininity
53 McQueen, Alexander	1990s–2000s	Started as a Saville Row tailor in London … now designs couture for Givenchy
54 Mainbocher	1930s–1940s	An American in Paris … introduced strapless evening gowns … designed the wedding dress of Wallis Simpson, the Duchess of Windsor
55 Missoni, Rosita and Ottavio	1950s–1990s	Bold, multiple-color combinations in knitwear … simple but sophisticated knitwear designs
56 Mizrahi, Isaac	1980s–2000s	Flashed on fashion scene under Chanel backing … moved on to theatrical and movie works
57 Molyneux, Captain Edward	1920s–1960s	British … "a designer to whom a fashionable woman would turn if she wanted to be absolutely 'right'"
58 Montana, Claude	1980s–1990s	Wedge-shaped silhouette … architectural shapes in original designs
59 Mori, Hanae	1980s…	Mines the gap between East and West … Chanel inspired her designs
60 Mugler, Thierry	1970s–1990s	Extravagant and innovative … spans from lots of ornamentation to rigorous minimalism
61 Norell, Norman	1940s–1960s	Winner of first Coty award in 1943 … his shimmering sequined dresses are worn and treasured forever
62 Natori, Josie	1980s–2000s	Banished the borders between inner and outerwear … success based on mix of comfort, practicality, and style
63 Norell, Norman	1940s–1960s	Winner of first Coty award in 1943 … his shimmering sequined dresses are worn and treasured forever
64 Panichgul, Thakoon	2000s…	His designs are described as "timeless feminine," "romantic and sensual," "modern and innovative" … dresses First Lady Michelle Obama
65 Patou, Jean	1920s–1930s	Elegant, ladylike couture clothes … successful businessman and showman
66 Philo, Phoebe	2000s…	British designer … creative director for Céline and Chloé

	NAME	DECADES OF INFLUENCE	DEFINING CHARACTERISTICS
67	Pilati, Stefano	1990s–2000s…	Design director at Yves Saint Laurent … often way ahead of his time, his designs are questioned—then widely accepted
68	Poiret, Paul	1920s–1930s	First Paris couturier of the 20th century to become a trendsetter… liberated women from corsets
69	Prada, Miuccia	1990s–2000s	Clothing and accessories global trendsetters … secondary line Miu Miu a rage with the young
70	Pucci, Emilio	1950s–1960s	His colorful graphic prints on jersey revolutionized Italian fashion at that time
71	Quant, Mary	1960s–1970s	Swinging sixties London scene … popularized miniskirts, colored tights, and football sweaters
72	Rabanne, Paco	1970s–1980s	Produced clothes of plastic, chain metal, fiber-optic wire, and doorknobs … fashion's heavy metal guru … a revolution in fashion
73	Reid, Billy	2000s…	Selected by *GQ* as the 2010 best new menswear designer in America … Southern-bred luxury in menswear
74	Rodarte	2000s…	Sisters Kate and Laura Mulleavy … California designers who impressed critics and clients with their use of old-world techniques that look like couture … Tenacity and Talent
75	Rodriguez, Narciso	1990s–2000s	Designs for Loewe, a Spanish design company
76	Rykiel, Sonia	1970s–1980s	Knitwear her forte … sense of fashion humor, mixing the outrageous with the feminine
77	Saint Laurent, Yves	1960s–1990s	Exploded on scene in 1960s … "Infant Terrible" … famous for pantsuits, pea jackets, "le smoking," safari suits … Rive Gauche
78	Sander, Jil	1990s–2000s	Highest quality in materials and craftsmanship … expert tailoring in suits and coats
79	Sant'Angelo, Giorgio	1960s–1990s	Diana Vreeland, *Vogue* editor, set his career in motion. He cited native and ethnic cultures as his inspiration and introduced stretch fabrics
80	Scaasi, Arnold	1950s–2000	Acclaimed designer who created gowns for the "ladies who lunch" and White House First Ladies
81	Schiaparelli, Elsa	1930s–1940s	Avant-garde designer in Paris … famous for introducing "shocking pink"
82	Simons, Raf	2000s…	Belgium men's fashion designer … He takes his inspiration from the rebellion of post and present youth cultures
83	Sprouse, Steven	1980s–1990s	Was a fashion designer and artist credited with pioneering the 1980s mix of "uptown sophistication in clothing with a downtown punk and pop sensibility"
84	Sui, Anna	1990s–2000s	Free-spirited approach to design … mix of hip and haute couture
85	Theyskens, Olivier	2000s…	Creating couture lines for both Nina Ricci and Rochas, all received with great acclaim … Now is artistic director for Theory
86	Tisci, Riccardo	2000s…	Officially appointed creative director of the haute couture, ready-to-wear, and accessories lines for Givenchy in 2005 … He was a huge success

	NAME	DECODES OF INFLUENCE	DEFINING CHARACTERISTICS
87	Trigère, Pauline	1940s–1980s	Pioneer American designer … her coat silhouettes are famous … attention to detail
88	Ungaro, Emanuel	1970s–1980s	Space-age inspired … bold colors … sharp edged
89	Valentino	1960s–1990s	His famous V-shaped emblems crown his collection … simple, subtle design
90	Van Noten, Dries	1990s–2000	Belgium designer … the New York Times described him as "one of fashion's most cerebral designers"
91	Versace, Donatella	2000s…	One year and three days after Gianni's death, she mounted her first couture show … Today she oversees the production of a dozen collections a year
92	Versace, Gianni	1980s–1990s	Kinetic, kaleidoscope prints … metallic mesh garments … king of fashion for the rock-and-roll set
93	Vionnet, Madeleine	1920s–1930s	Called the "Queen of the bias cut" and "the architect among dressmakers" … considered one of the most influential designers of the twentieth century … Influence many past and present-day designers
94	von Furstenberg, Diane	1970s–2000	Best known for her "wrap dress" and signature prints, DVF has grown into a global luxury lifestyle brand
95	Wang, Alexander	2000s	Known for his edgy, somewhat masculine womenswear design … In 2007, he launched his first collection and received $200,000 as CFDA's 2008 Fashion Fund Prize winner
96	Wang, Vera	1990s–2000s	Was senior editor of Vogue for 16 years … Started her wedding gown design business in 1990 … She made wedding gowns for famous women and expanded her brand today to include ready-to-wear, accessories, home fashion, and perfume
97	Westwood, Vivienne	1980s–1990s	Punk rock fashion … T-shirts with outrageous messages … named her boutique "Sex"
98	Worth, Charles Frederick	The originator of fashion—1860s	He created the "designer name" as we know it … established the pattern of regular seasoned fashion shows
99	Wu, Jason	2000s…	He started designing clothes for dolls … in 2006, his first designer collection won the Fashion Group International Rising Star Award … First Lady Michelle Obama put him on the fashion map by buying and wearing four of his dresses
100	Yamamoto, Yohji	1980s–1990s	Sparse, understated fashions … dark, strong designs … asymmetrical cuts

Adapted from a variety of sources, including *WWD: 75 Years in Fashion 1910–1985; WWD Century,* September 1998; and *WWD 100 Years | 100 Designers,* November 1, 2011.

NOTES

CHAPTER 1

1. *Merriam-Webster's Collegiate® Dictionary*, Eleventh Edition (Springfield, MA: Merriam Webster, Inc., 2004), p. 455.
2. IBID, p. 776.
3. Agnes Brooke Young, *Recurring Cycles of Fashion: 1760–1937* (New York: Harper & Brothers, 1937; reprint, New York: Cooper Square Publishers, Inc., 1966), p. 30.
4. "Fast Fashion," *IESE Insight, Iss. 3, Fourth Quarter 2009*, p. 8.
5. Maryam Banikarim, "Seeing Shades in Green Consumers," *Adweek,* April 19, 2010, p. 18. Full text copyright © 2010 Nielsen Business Media, Inc.

Features

In the Fashion Spotlight: Michael Kors: Michael's Magic Moment

"Message to Michael." *WWD*, August 8, 2010, pp. 1, 6, and 7.

Rosemary Feitelberg, "Michael Kors to Open Store in Paris," *WWD*, June 5, 2010, p. 2.

Bridget Foley, "Michael Kors: A Lifetime in Fashion and Still Under 30." *WWD*, June 4, 2010, p. 12.

Amanda Kaiser, "Michael Kors' Big Plans for the East," *WWD*, September 13, 2010.

Amy Larocca, "Park Avenue Jesus," *New York Magazine*, August 23, 2010.

George Wayne, "Man in Black," *Vanity Fair,* September 2009.

Timeless Treasures: Betsey: Fashion's Magic Johnson

Rosemary Feitelberg, "Chantal Bacon Exits Betsey Johnson," *WWD*, October 5, 2010, p. 2.

Jessica Iredale, "Magic Johnson" *WWD Milestones*, July 22, 2008.

Arnold J. Karr, "Not Doing Cartwheels: Betsey Johnson Defaults, Steve Madden Steps In," *WWD*, September 3, 2010, pp. 1 and 10.

Ray A. Smith, "Betsey Johnson Faces a Makeover," the *Wall Street Journal*, November 18, 2008, pp. 1–4.

Everything Old Is New Again: Pierre Cardin: He's Everywhere and Into Everything

Joelle Diderich, "Cardin Talks About 60 Years in Business" *WWD*, March 9, 2010, p. 11.

____. "Q&A-Pierre Cardin," *WWD*, 2010.

Jamie Huckbody, "Pierre Cardin, He's Everywhere" *theage.com.au.* August 1, 2003.

Sandy Mitchell, "All About Pierre Cardin," http://www.essortment.com/lifestyle/pierrecardininfa_solw.htm, acccessed April 2011.

CHAPTER 2

1. "Lifestyle and behavior segmentation: Nielsen PRIZM," Nielsen Corporation, 2010, http://www.nielsen.com.

2. U.S. Department of Commerce, Economics and Statistics Administration, "Middle Class in America," January 2010, http://www.commerce.gov/s/groups/public/@doc/@os/documents/content/prod01008833.pdf, accessed March 2011.

3. *Merriam-Webster's Collegiate Dictionary,* Eleventh Edition (Springfield, MA: Merriam-Webster, Inc., 2004), p. 641.

4. National Bureau of Economic Research, Business Cycle Dating Committee, Memo, January 7, 2008, p. 3, http://www.nber.org/cycles/jan08bcdc_meo.html.

5. U.S. Census Bureau, "Monthly Population Estimates for the United States," http://www.census.gov/popest/national/tables/NA-EST2008-01.xls, (released December 22, 2008).

6. U.S. Census Bureau, "2008 National Population Projections" (released August 2008), http://www.census.gov/population/www/projections/2008projections.html, accessed March 2011.

7. Doug Anderson, "Below the Topline: U.S. Hispanics and Acculturation," *Nielsen Wire,* November 2, 2009, http://blog.nielsen.com/nielsenwire/consumer/u-s-hispanics-and-acculturation.

8. U.S. Census Bureau, "2004 American Community Survey, Selected Population Profiles, SO201" (released Febuary 2007).

9. U.S. Census Bureau, "2008 National Population Estimates," http://www.census.gov/population/www/socdemo/race/Asian-slide-presentation.html, accessed March 2011.

10. U.S. Census Bureau, "The American Community—Asians: 2004" (released February 2007).

11. U.S. Census Bureau, "2009 American Community Survey," http://www.census.gov/newsroom/releases/archives/facts_for_features_special_editions/cb11-ff06.html, accessed March 2011.

12. Institute for Women's Policy Research, "Fact Sheet: The Gender Wage Gap: 2009," September 2010.

13. U.S. Department of Labor, U.S. Bureau of Labor Statistics. "Highlights of Women's Earnings in 2009," Report 1025, June 2010.

14. U.S. Department of Labor, U.S. Bureau of Labor Statistics, "Educational Attainment: 2005–2009, American Community 5-Year Estimates," http://factfinder.census.gov/servlet/STTable?_bm=y&-geo_id=01000US&-qr_name=ACS_2009_5YR_G00_S1501&-ds_name=ACS_2009_5YR_G00_&-redoLog=false&-CONTEXT=st, accessed March 2011.

15. Cate T. Corcoran, "Fashion's New Fever: Bloggers in Spotlight As They Aim for Fame," *WWD,* February 19, 2010, http://www.wwd.com/media-news/fashions-new-fever-bloggers-inspotlight-as-they-aim-for-Fame, accessed January 7, 2011.

16. Paul H. Nystrom, *Economics of Fashion* (New York: The Ronald Press, 1928), pp. 66–81.

Features

In the Fashion Spotlight: Donna Karan

Leslie Bennetts, "Donna's NEW Direction," *Town & Country,* July 2010, pp. 74–79, and 106.

Marc Karimzadeh, "Karan Brings Her Touch to the Table," *WWD,* October 4, 2010, p. 15.

Nancy Jo Sales, "Donna Karan's Journey," *Harper's Bazaar,* September 21, 2010, pp. 342–354.

Timeless Treasures: Tobé Reports: The Original Trend Spotter Just Got Trendier

Rachel Dodes, "The 80-Year Hunt for 'It' Fashions," the *Wall Street Journal,* July 14, 2010.

Everything Old Is New Again: Lilly Pulitzer: Life in Lilly Land

Julee Kaplan, "In the Land of Pink and Green," *WWD Special Report,* December 2, 2008, pp. 2, 4, 6, 13, and 15.

CHAPTER 3

1. "Burberry Winter 2010 Catwalk streamed in 3D from the New York Fashion Week," *Instablogs.com,* September 9, 2010.
2. Pearl Binder, *Muffs and Morals* (London: George G. Harrop & Co., Ltd., 1953), pp. 162–164.
3. James Laver, *Taste and Fashion,* rev. ed. (London: George G. Harrop & Co., Ltd., 1946), p. 201.
4. "That 70's Show." *WWD,* September 15, 2010, p. 10.
5. Madge Garland, *The Changing Form of Fashion* (New York: Praeger Publishers, 1971), p. 11.
6. J. C. Flügel, *The Psychology of Clothes* (New York: International Universities Press, 1966), p. 163.
7. Laver, *Taste and Fashion,* p. 200.
8. IBID, p. 201.
9. "Power to the People." *WWD,* July 26, 2010, p. 20.
10. Charles King, "Fashion Adoption," p. 124.
11. Edward Sapir, "Fashion," *Encyclopedia of the Social Sciences,* vol. V1 (London: Macmillan & Co., 1931), p. 140.
12. "Rules of Style: Kenneth Cole." *Details,* http://www.details.com/style-advice/rules-of-style/200907/rules-of-style-from-designer-kenneth-cole, accessed March 2011.

Features

In the Fashion Spotlight: Jason Wu

"All About Jason Wu," *W Magazine,* January 21, 2009.

Venessa Lau, "Wu From the Top," *WWD,* February 3, 2010, pp. 6 and 7.

Melissa Magsaysay, "Jason Wu Wows Hollywood," *L.A. Times,* November 19, 2008.

Shane Mitchell, "Jason Wu: Designer," *Travel and Leisure,* October 2009, p. 66.

Cheryl Tan, "The Michelle Obama 'Career-Launcher' for Emerging Designer Jason Wu," the *Wall Street Journal,* December 1, 2008.

Timeless Treasures: Roots: What Inspires Designers?
Marjorie Rosen, "Roots," the *New York Times Style,* August 19, 2001, pp. 1 and 2.

Everything Old Is New Again: Esprit: Looking Back and Forward
"Time Line," *WWD Special Report,* Section II, September 18, 2008, p. 3.
Melissa Drier, "Youth Movement," *WWD Special Report,* Section II, September 18, 2008, pp. 4 and 5.
Sharon Edelson, "Esprit Aims High with 34th Street Flagship," *WWD,* March 23, 2010, p. 17.
Sarah Haight, "High Concept," *WWD Special Report,* Section II, September 18, 2008, pp. 10 and 11.

CHAPTER 4

1. U.S. Bureau of Labor Statistics, Career Guide to Industries, 2010–11 Edition, http://data.bls.gov/cgi-bin/print.pl/oco/cg/cgs015.htm, accessed March 2011.
2. Douglas MacMillan, "Psst! Private-Sale Shopping Sites Are Hot," *BusinessWeek* Online, November 15, 2009, http://www.businessweek.com/technology/content/nov2009/tc2009114_771888.htm, accessed March 2011.
3. PricewaterhouseCoopers LLP, "2010 Franchise Business Economic Outlook" (prepared for The International Franchise Association Educational Foundation), December 21, 2009.
4. EPM Communications, Inc., "Licensed Merchandise Sales Worldwide Down 10.8% In '09; Properties From Chanel To Coca-Cola, Bakugan To Nate Berkus Span The Globe In Search Of New Profit Opportunities," *The Licensing Letter,* June 1, 2010, http://www.epmcom.com/public/Licensed_Merchandise_Sales_Worldwide_Down_108_In_09_Properties_From_Chanel_To_CocaCola_Bakugan_To_Nate_Berkus_Span_The_Globe_In_Search_Of_New_Profit_Opportunities.cfm, accessed June 2011.
5. "Disney Takes the High-End Road," *License! Global,* August 2010, vol. 13 (6), p. 39.
6. Dwight E. Robinson, "Fashion Theory and Product Design," *Harvard Business Review,* November–December 1958, vol. 36, p. 129.

Features
Timeless Treasures: Tom Ford: "You Ought to Be in Pictures": From Fashion to Film
"Tom Ford Ready for Return to Women's" *WWD,* October 21, 2009, pp. 1 and 7.
Bridget Foley, "Venice Gives Tom's Movie Thumbs Up," *WWD,* September 14, 2009, pp. 1 and 12.
Dave Karger, "From Fashion to Film," *Entertainment Weekly,* November 13, 2009, pp. 62–65.

In the Fashion Spotlight: Vera Wang: Skating Her Way to Fashion Success
Bridget Foley, "Vera Wang," *WWD Milestones,* May 12, 2010, pp. 7 and 8.

Everything Old Is New Again: Roberto Cavalli: Four Decades in Fashion's Jungle

Alessandra Ilari, "Cavalli on Cavalli," *WWD Milestones,* September 23, 2010, pp. 2, 4.

Eric Wilson, "Cavalli, 69, Still Prowling," the *New York Times,* October 3, 2010.

CHAPTER 5

1. Jane Dorner, *Fashion in the Forties and Fifties* (New Rochelle, NY: Arlington House, 1975), p. 38.

2. Supima, http://www.supimacotton.org, accessed April 2011.

3. Stan Gellers, "CMA Seminar Addresses Global Issues for Millenium," *DNR,* September 1999, p. 1B.

4. American Fiber Manufacturers Association, Inc., http://www.fibersource.com/afma/afma.htm.

5. Robert S. Reichard, "A Changing Industry," *Textile World,* http://www.textileworld.com/articles/2010/March/Issue/Departments/Business_x_Financial.html, accessed March 2011.

6. National Council of Textile Organizations, http://ncto.org/ustextiles/index.asp, accessed April 2011.

7. ___, http://ncto.org/ustextiles/closings.asp, accessed October 2010.

8. Unifi, Inc. "Haggar Chooses Unifi's Repreve Recycled Fiber for 'Green' Line of Pants," http://unifi.com/un_news_pr.aspx?id=32, accessed April 2011.

9. Patagonia. *Patagonia Environmental Initiatives* (booklet), http://www.patagonia.com/pdf/en_US/2010_enviro_grants.pdf, accessed April 2011.

10. Kristi Ellis and Ivan Castano, "Sourcing Horizons: Warming Up to CAFTA," *WWD Style Issue,* March 29, 2011, http://www.wwwd.com/business-news/cafta-starting-to-come-alive-3566914/print, accessed April 2011.

11. Mayu Saini, "India Textile Industry Seen Tripling," *WWD,* September 21, 2010.

12. Kristi Ellis and Ivan Castano, "Sourcing Horizons: Warming Up to CAFTA," *WWD Style Issue,* March 29, 2011, http://www.wwd.com/business-news/cafta-starting-to-come-alive-3566914/print, accessed April 2011.

13. Mayu Saini, "India Textile Industry Seen Tripling," *WWD,* September 21, 2010.

14. National Council of Textile Organizations, "NCTO Hails House Passage of China Currency Bill," September 29, 2010.

15. Bureau of Consumer Protection, "Threading Your Way Through the Labeling Requirements Under the Textile and Wool Acts," http://business.ftc.gov/documents/bus21-threading-your-way-through-labeling-requirements-under-textile-and-wool-acts, accessed April 2011.

16. "Technology Report: Texile Printing—Fabrics a la mode," *Print Week,* March 12, 2010, p. 25. Original text from Business and Company ASAP.

Features

Timeless Treasures: Cotton Incorporated: Keeping Cotton Growing and Going

"FTC Green Guides To Deter Bamboo-zling," *WWD,* September 2, 2010.

Liza Casabona, "Forty Years Cultivating the Industry," *WWD Special Report,* October 26, 2010, pp. 10 and 11.

Kristi Ellis, "Keeping Cotton Growing," *WWD Special Report,* October 26, 2010, pp. 7–9.

In the Fashion Spotlight: Home Textiles: "You Can't Live Without Them!"

"Drapery & Theatrical Soft Goods," *SGASi Production Services,* 2010, pp. 1–3.

"Home Furnishings–A Review," *Textile Exchange,* pp. 1–3.

Anjali Athavaley, "Make Room for Junior Decorators," the *Wall Street Journal,* December 1, 2010, pp. 1 and 2.

Tracy Bulla, "Light, Colorful Fabrics Top the Soft Goods Trend," *Home Accents Today,* August 1, 2004, p. 1.

Allessandra Iiari, "Custom House," *WWD Section II,* April 12, p. 2.

Marc Karimzadeh, "Designing a Fashionable Home," *WWD,* June 1, 2010, p. 10.

J.J. Martin, "Home Bodies," the *New York Times Style Magazine,* August 26, 2007, p. 117.

Everything Old Is New Again: Recycled Fashion: From Discarded to Divine

Elsa Blaine, "22 Dresses From Unusual Materials," *Trend Hunter,* November 2, 2008, pp. 1–3.

Marissa Brassfield, "Sci-Fi Origami Dresses," *Trend Hunter,* January 7, 2010, p. 1.

Gloria Dawson, "The Trench Coat Is Dead. Long Live the Trench Coat (Dress)!" *The Daily Green,* 2010, pp. 1–15.

Joelle Diderich, "Miyake Designs Origami-Inspired Fashion Line," *WWD,* September 7, 2010.

Joanna Ramey, "What's Old Is New Again," *WWD,* April 8, 2008, p. 9.

David Lipke, "Greg Lauren Launches Fashion Collection," *WWD Style,* February 7, 2011, p. 16.

Matthew Stoker, "Top Ten Unusual Pieces of Clothing Worn by Celebrities," *Associated Content,* September 14, 2010, p. 1.

CHAPTER 6

1. Robin Givhan, "Equine Finery for Fall, Designers Gallop Toward the Tony Pony," *Washington Post,* October 23, 1996, p. D1.

2. "AAC Annual Report," Alligator Advisory Council, December 2009, http://www.alligatorfur.com/alligator/alligatorannual09.pdf, accessed October 2010.

3. "Guandong Market for leather weathers storm, spells demand for American hides and finished leather," USDA Global Agricultural Information Network, Guangzhou, China, November 16, 2009.

4. Leather Industries of America, http://leatherusa.com/LIA-Membership.htm, accessed October 2010.

5. "About Us," APLF Website, http://www.aplf.com/AboutUs/tabid/1664/language/en-US/Default.aspx, accessed August 2010.

6. APLF Ltd, http://www.aplf.com/AboutUs/tabid/16641language/en-US/Default.aspx, accessed April 2011.

7. International Fur Trade Federation, "The Socio-Economic Impact of International Fur Farming," http://www.iftf.com.

8. "Mink," National Agricultural Statistics Service, USDA, July 2010.

9. The American Legend, http://www.americanlegend.com/alcompany.html, accessed March 2011.

10. Fur Information Council of America, http://www.fur.org/fica-facts, accessed April 2011.

11. The American Legend, www.americanlegend.com/alcompany.html, accessed March 2011.

12. Fur Commission USA, "U.S. Fur Sales Hurt By Economic Concerns in 2007," November 20, 2008, http://www.furcommission.com/news/newsF11h.htm, accessed April 2011.

13. Fur Information Council of America, "Retail Sales of Fur Up For 2010," March 24, 2011, http://www.fur.org/retail-sales-of-fur-up-for-2010/, accessed April 2011.

14. Saga Furs of Scandinavia, "Who Where," http://www.sagafurs.com.

15. Fur Information Council of America, http://www.fur.org/fica-facts, accessed April 2011.

16. International Fur Trade Federation, http://www.iftf.com/#/press-releases/174, accessed April 2011.

Features

In the Fashion Spotlight: Luxurious Leather

Maria C. Thiry, "Luxurious Leather," *American Association of Textile Chemists & Colorists*, January/February 2010, pp. 39–43.

Everything Old Is New Again: Fur: Makes a Comeback

Samantha Critchell, "Fur Makes Comeback with More Humane Claims," *The Leaf Chronicle*, November 21, 2010.

Samantha Musumeci, "Fur–The Real Thing–in Disguise," *L.A. Times*, October 4, 1991.

Timeless Treasures: Rachel Zoe: Stylist, Designer, and Mother of Invention

"Married to Fashion," *Harper's Bazaar*, January 10, 2011, p. 74.

Jessica Iredale, "Mother of Invention," *WWD*, January 11, 2011, pp. 12–13.

"Bravo's "The Rachel Zoe Project" Premiere Shuts It Down Becoming Most Watched Episode in Series History," the *Futon Critic*, http://www.thefutoncritic.com/ratings/2010/08/04/bravos-the-rachel-zoe-project-premiere-shuts-it-down-becoming-most-watched-episode-in-series-history-36853/20100804bravo02/, accessed March 2011.

CHAPTER 7

1. Susan S. Nichols, "Product Development, Innovation in Demand from Top-Tier Retailers: (Exclusive Report From SPESA)," *Apparel*, July 2010, p. 28.

2. Muditha M. Senanayake and Trevor J. Little, ""Measures for New Product Development," *Journal of Textile and Apparel Technology and Management*, Volume 1, Issue 3, Spring 2001, p. 9.

3. Valerie Seckler, "NPD: National Brand Shoppers Outspend Private Label Fans," *WWD Infotracs* (Fashion Trends), February 28, 2006, p. 23.

4. The NPD Group, Inc. "NPD Reports on the Men's Apparel Market," *PR Web*, April 5, 2011. Copyright © Vocus PRW Holdings, LLC, http://www.prweb.com/printer/8271585.htm, accessed April 2011.

5. American Apparel and Footwear Association, "AAFA Continues Call for Elimination of Trade Barriers Worldwide," March 30, 2011, https://www.apparelandfootwear.org/UserFiles/File/PressReleases/2011/033011AAFAContinuesCallforEliminationofTradeBarriersWorldwide.pdf, accessed April 2011.

6. Evan Clark, "Fashion Refinancing Back in Vogue," *WWD*, August 4, 2009, http://www.wwd.com/business-news/fashion-refinancing-back-in-vogue-222931/print/, accessed April 2011.

7. Janet Suleski and Lucie Draper, "PLM for Apparel 2010: Decision Support Meets Value Chain Orchestration, *Apparel*, June 2010.

8. *PC Magazine*, http://www.pcmag.com/encyclopedia_term/0,2542,t=RFID&i=50512,00.asp, accessed April 2011.

9. Amanda Dematto, "5 Ways Body Scanners Could Make Fitting Rooms Obsolete," *Popular Mechanics*, June 29, 2010.

Features

Timeless Treasures: Phillips-Van Heusen: Big-Bigger-Biggest in the World

Vicki M. Young and Marc Karimzadeh, "Grow, Grow, Grow: Phillips-Van Heusen Aims to Be Biggest in World," *WWD*, June 25, 2010, pp. 1 and 11.

In the Fashion Spotlight: Birth of a Notion

Venessa Lau and Alec Badia, "Fierce About Fashion," *WWD*, February 13, 2010, p. 15.

Venessa Lau and Luis Campuzano, "Spring Things," *WWD*, September 9, 2010, pp. 10 and 12.

Venessa Lau, "What Were They Thinking?" *WWD*, February 12, 2011, pp. 7 and 9.

Tools of the Trade: Digital Fitting Experiences

"Macy's Herald Square Unveils 'Magic Fitting Room'" *DDi*, October 05, 2010, p. 1.

"Macy's Magic Fitting Room Features Mirror with Multi-Touch Technology," *Screen Media Daily*, October 6, 2010, p. 1.

Bonnie McCarthy, "No Need to Take Clothes off in Macy's Magic Fitting Room," *Wallet Pop*, October 15, 2010, pp. 1–2.

CHAPTER 8

1. Destination Maternity Corporation, May 31, 2011.

2. Miles Socha, "Masstige Gains Power," *WWD*, October 5, 2010, http://www.wwd.com/markets-news/masstige-gains-pwer-3326578/print, accessed April 2011.

3. "Mayor Bloomberg Announces New Home for Fashion Week at Lincoln Center," February 3, 2009, http://www.nyc.gov/portal/site/nycgov/menuitem.c0935b9a57bb4ef3daf2f1c701c789a0/index.jsp?pageID=mayor_press_release&catID=1194&doc_name=http%3A%2F%2Fwww.nyc.gov%2Fhtml%2Fom%2Fhtml%2F2009a%2Fpr058-09.html&cc=unused1978&rc=1194&ndi=1, accessed April 2011.

4. The NPD Group, Inc. "NPD Reports on the U.S. Apparel Market for 2010," http://www.npd.com/press/releases/press_110210.html, accessed April 2011.

5. Allison Golub, "Size Matters," *Earnshaw's*, February 2007.

6. Cynthia Ogden, Ph.D., and Margaret Carroll, M.S.P.H., "Prevalence of Obesity Among Children and Adolescents: United States, Trends 1963–1965 Through 2007–2008," Centers for Disease Control and Prevention, http://www.cdc.gov/nchs/data/hestat/obesity_child_07_08/obesity_child_07_08.pdf, accessed April 2011.

7. Zak Stambor, "Children's Clothing Manufacturer Carter's Launches Two E-Commerce Sites," *Internet Retailer*, April 2, 2010, http://www.internetretailer.com/2010/04/02/children-s-clothing-manufacturer-carter-s-launches-two-e-com, accessed April 2011.

Features

Timeless Treasures: The American Woman: Fashioning a National Identity
"American Idols," *WWD*, May 4, 2010, pp. 4–7.
Marc Karimzadeh, "American Style in All Its Glory," *WWD*, April 28, 2010, pp. 12–13.
___. "The Style of the American Woman," *WWD*, April 30, 2010, p. 13.

Everything Old Is New Again: It's a Mad, Mad World!
Bill Keveney, "Distinctive 'Mad Men' Reaches Out to Today's Style, Culture," *USA Today*, August 13, 2009.
Irene Lacher, "Costume Designer Jenny Beavan Has a Royal Time on 'The King's Speech,'" the *Los Angeles Times*, January 5, 2011, http://articles.latimes.com/print/2011/jan/05/news/la-en-costume-kings-20101216, accessed April 2011.
Lauren A.E. Schuker, "'Mad Men': Threads of the Story," the *Wall Street Journal*, June 10, 2010.
Brenner Thomas, "'Mad Men' Designers Find Opportunity Outside the Show," *WWD*, October 15, 2009, p. 9.
___. "Men on Film," *WWD*, October 15, 2009, p. 10.

In the Fashion Spotlight: Teens, Tweens, and Justin Bieber: Talking Technology
Bruce Horovitz, "J.C. Penney, Others Turn to YouTube 'Haul' Videos for Help," *USA Today*, July 13, 2010, p. 1.
Margaret Case Little, "Retail Relationship: Tweens Influencing More Than Just Products," *National Retail Federation*, April 26, 2010.
Lisa Robinson, "Justin Bieber! Is This the Adorable, Inescapable Face of 2011?" *Vanity Fair*, February 2011, pp. 98, 100, 104, 105, and 150.
Alexandra Steigrad, "Searching for a New Look: Teen Retailers Hit by Fashion Shift," *WWD*, June 14, 2010, p. 14.
Khanh T.L. Tran, "Internet Generation: To Keep Up With Teens Brands Go High Tech," *WWD*, May 24, 2010, p. 12.

CHAPTER 9

1. "Nike, Inc., Ten Year Financial History," http://invest.nike.com.
2. American Apparel and Footwear Association, "ShoeStats 2008," August 2008, http://www.apparelandfootwear.org/statistics.asp, accessed April 2011.

3. Lauren Benet Stephenson, "A Golden Era for Eyewear," *WWD*, July 19, 2010, p. 12b.
4. "Revolutionary New Cuts Add Spice to Engagement Rings," Jewelry Information Center, http://www.jic.org, March 2008.
5. Caroline Tell, "Lukas Named President at Victoria & Co.," *WWD*, April 28, 2009, p. 5.
6. The Swatch Group, Ltd., "The Swatch Group History (today)," http://www.swatchgroup.com/en/group_profile/history/today, accessed April 2011.
7. William George Shuster, "Retailers Still High on Watches," *Jewelers Circular Keystone*, June 1, 2007.

Features

In the Fashion Spotlight: Head over Heels in Love with Jimmy Choo

"Jimmy Choo at 15," *WWD Special Report*, Section II, December 17, 2010, p. 1.
"Jimmy Choo Through the Years," *WWD Special Report*, Section II, December 17, 2010, p. 2.
Marc Karimzadeh and Lauren Benet Stephenson, "Head Over Heels," *WWD Special Report*, Section II, December 17, 2010, p. 4.
Roxanne Robinson-Escriout, "Choos Wisely," *WWD Special Report*, Section II, December 17, 2010, pp. 10–11.

Timeless Treasures: Pierre Cartier: Good Things Come in Red Packages

Sharon Edelson, "The Network" *WWD Milestones*, May 18, 2009, p. 22.
Katya Foreman, "House Specials" *WWD Milestones*, May 18, 2009, p. 35.
David Moin, "The Mansion," *WWD Milestones*, May 18, 2009, pp. 15–20.
Robert Murphy, "History, Buffed," *WWD Milestones*, May 18, 2009, pp. 9–13.

Everything Old Is New Again: The Accessories Council: Adding the Finishing Touches to Any Outfit

Lauren Benet Stephenson, "Putting the Accent on Accessories," *WWD Special Report*, July 26, 2010, pp. 12 and 13.
Marc Karimzadeh and Katyz Foreman, "Accessories Propel Ascent of Luxury," *WWD*, December 20, 2010, pp. 1, 8, and 9.

CHAPTER 10

1. Los Angeles Economic Development Corporation, "Los Angeles County Profile," http://www.laedc.org/reports/LA%20County%20Profile.pdf, accessed April 2011.
2. Kristi Ellis and Liza Casabona with contributors from Arthur Friedman and Khanh T.L. Tran, "U.S. Apparel Manufacturing Showing Signs of Life," *WWD*, January 10, 2011.
3. Dallas Market Center, "Trammell Crow, Dallas Market Center Found, 1914–2009," http://dallasmarketcenter.com/press/trammell-crow-dallas-market-center-founder-1914-2009, accessed April 2011.
4. Mode à Paris, http://www.modeaparis.com/spip.php?rubrique8#toppage8, accessed April 2011.

5. Prêt à Porter, "Report of Prêt à Porter Paris," September 2010 Edition, http://www.pretparis.com/images/stories/images_articles/presse/communique/septembre2010/bilan_papp_sept10_gb.pdf, accessed April 2011.

6. L. Zargani, "Italian Government to Boost Fashion," *WWD*, March 6, 2009, http://www.wwd.com/business-news/italian-government-to-boost-fashion-2042397, accessed April 2011.

7. Madge Garland, *The Changing Form of Fashion* (New York: Praeger Publishers, 1971), p. 73.

8. Maquila Solidarity Network, "The Crisis and Its Effect on Mexico's Textile and Apparel Industry," http://en.maquilasolidarity.org/sites/maquilasolidarity.org/files/MSN-Crisis_and-Garment_Sector_in_Mexico-2009-10.pdf, accessed March 2011.

9. Grace I. Kunz and Myrna B. Garner, *Going Global: The Textile and Apparel Industry*, Second ed. (New York: Fairchild Books, 2011), pp. 325–329.

10. IBID, pp. 284–385.

11. Amanda Keiser and Kelly Wetherille, "Diversity in Japan Fashion," *WWD*, October 21, 2010, p. 9.

12. Grace I. Kunz and Myrna B. Garner, *Going Global: The Textile and Apparel Industry*, Second ed. (New York: Fairchild Books, 2011), p. 379.

13. Business Maps of India.com. "India Textile Industry," http://business.mapsofindia.com/india-industry/textile.html, accessed April 2011.

14. World Trade Organization, "International Trade Statistics, 2009," http://www.wto.org/english/res_e/statis_e/its2009_e/its09_toc_e.htm, accessed April 2011.

15. R. Tucker, "Australian Wool Industry in Two-Sided Tangle" *WWD*, July 27, 2005, p. 8.

16. Grace I. Kunz and Myrna B. Garner, *Going Global: The Textile and Apparel Industry*, *Second ed.* (New York: Fairchild Books, 2011), pp. 384–385.

17. United States Department of Agriculture, "North American Free Trade Agreement (NAFTA)," http://www.fas.usda.gov/itp/Policy/NAFTA/nafta.asp, accessed April 2011.

18. Office of Textiles and Apparel (OTEXA), "U.S. Export Markets by Group, December 2010 Data," http://otexa.ita.doc.gov/exports.grp0.htm, accessed December 18, 2010.

19. "Exports Hit Their Stride," *WWD*, August 7, 1996, p. 28.

Features

Everything Old Is New Again: Global Sales: America's Not Enough, So Say New Designers Spanning the Globe

Marc Karimzadeh, "Light Up the Night," *WWD*, May 4, 2010, pp. 1, 10–11.

Timeless Treasures: Ralph Lauren: New in an Old World

Stephanis Clifford, "At Polo Store, the Feel of a Mansion to Bolster a Brand," the *New York Times*, October 12, 2010, http://www.nytimes.com/2010/10/14/business/14polo.html, accessed April 2011.

Pamela Fiori, "Monsieur Ralph," *Town & Country*, August 2010, pp. 72–77 and 115.

Marc Karimzadeh, "Mad About Madison," *WWD*, October 14, 2010, pp. 1, 4, and 5.

___. "Ralph Lauren Gets Key to the City," *WWD*, October 15, 2010, p. 2.

___. "Ralph Lauren Lights Up Crowd," *WWD*, November 12, 2010, p. 8.

___. "Ralph Lauren Telling the Story of 'The RL Gang,'" *WWD*, August 5, 2010, p. 3.

Suzy Menkes, "Ralph Lauren: New in an Old World," the *New York Times*, April 19, 2010.

Adrianne Pasquarelli, "Ralph Lauren wears it well," *Crain's New York*, November 21, 2010, http://crainsnewyork.com/article/20101121/FREE/311219969, accessed April 2011.

Anamaria Wilson, "Ralph's Reign," *Bazaar*, August 12, 2010, pp. 491–496.

Vicki M. Young, "Polo First-Quarter Profit Rises 57.3 Percent," *WWD*, August 5, 2010, p. 3.

In the Fashion Spotlight: Counterfeiting: The Fight Against FAKES

Liza Casabona, "Feds Shut Down Counterfeit Sites," *WWD*, November 30, 2010, p. 2.

___. "Counterfeit Crackdown: Successes but new Worries." *WWD*, December 21, 2010, p. 9.

Katie Deatsch, "Online counterfeit sales will cost businesses $135 billion this year," http://www.internetretailer.com/2011/01/05/online-counterfeit-sales-will-cost-businesses-135-billion, accessed April 2011.

Matthew Lynch, "NYC Counterfeit Raid Yields Big Haul." *WWD*, December 9, 2009, p. 2.

Alexandra Steigrad, "Luxury Counterfeiters Found Guilty," *WWD*, June 14, 2010, p. 2.

Dana Thomas, "If you buy one of these fake bags, you are supporting child labor, organized crime, even terrorism . . . Bazaar investigates," *Bazaar*, January 2005, p. 18.

CHAPTER 11

1. Estelle Hamburger, *Fashion Business—It's All Yours* (New York: Harper & Row), 1976.

2. National Retail Federation, "Retail Sales Growth, 2008–2009," http://www.nrf.com/modules.php?name=Pages&sp_id=1237&op=printerfriendly&txt=National+Retail+Federation++-+Retail+Sales, accessed April 2011.

3. David Moin, "Macy's Names Langenstein Fashion Director," *WWD*, July 12, 2010, p. 2.

4. Hoovers, Inc., "The Athlete's Foot Brands, LLC: Overview," http://theathletesfoot.com, accessed December 20, 2010.

5. Direct Selling Association, "DSA Releases 2009 Sales and Salesforce Figures," http://dsa.org/files/DSA_2009_GO_Survey_Release_-_FINAL_7-20.pdf, July 22,2010.

6. The Connaught Group," http://www.theconnaughtgroup.com, accessed December 20, 2010.

7. Home Shopping Network, Inc. "About HSNi," http://www.hsni.com/about.cfm, accessed April 2011.

8. QVC, "QVC at a Glance," http://www.qvc.com/qic/qvcapp.aspx/app.html/params.file.%7Ccp%7Cmainhqbusovr,html/left.html.file.%7Cnav%7Cnavhqabout,html/walk.html.%7Cnav%7Cnavhqabout.html, accessed April 2011.

9. ShopNBC, "About ShopNBC," http://www.shopnbc.com/CustomerService/default.aspx?cm_re=BN-_-AboutUs-_-N&WhereAmIGoing=http://shopnbc.custhelp.com/app/answers/detail/a_id/57, accessed April 2011.

10. Internet Retailer, "Global E-commerce Sales By Region 2010 (source: Goldman Sachs)," http://www.internetretailer.com/trends/sales/, accessed April 2011.

11. Adrianne Pasquarelli, "Retailers Expect Full Stockings This Holiday Season; Now the Coal: Pain Could Return In 2001 as Higher Supplier Costs Push Up Apparel Prices," *Crain's New York Business,* December 6, 2010, p. 2.

12. Jenny B. Fine, "Instant Gratification, Beauty Inc. Issue," *WWD,* April 22, 2011, http://www.wwd.com/beauty-industry-news/instant-gratification-3587336/print, accessed April 2011.

Features

Timeless Treasures: Terry J. Lundgren: Macy's Chairman, President, and CEO

"Executive Management Team Bios/Photos," *Macy's, Inc.,* p.1.

Ellen Davis, "Tracy Mullin's burning questions for Terry Lundgren," *NRF,* September 27, 2009, pp. 1–3.

"Terry Lundgren," *WWD,* 2010, p. 1.

Everything Old Is New Again: Pop-up Stores: Here Today, Gone Tomorrow, or Are They?

Pop Up Retail Concept, Pop up Retail Group, 2008.

Sarag Duxbury, "Gap Opens Piperlime Pop-Up Store in NYC," *San Francisco Business Times,* August 10, 2010.

Sharon Edelson, "Plethora of Pop-ups: When Is There Too Much of a Good Thing?" *WWD,* December 21, 2009, pp. 1 and 10.

Christina Fierro, "Pop-up Stores: No Longer Temporary," *The Recovery Times,* November 18, 2010, pp. 1–3.

Joyce King, "Pop-up Stores Offer Bridge to Better Times," *USA Today,* October 14, 2010, p. 1.

Sarah E. Needleman, "Stores That Can't Stay," the *Wall Street Journal,* August 5, 2010.

In the Fashion Spotlight: Jessica Simpson: Billion-Dollar Baby

Lisa Lockwood, "Jessica Simpson's Growing Empire," *WWD,* December 6, 2010, pp. 1 and 3.

Tools of the Trade: RFID: Radio Frequency Identification

Mark Albright, "Retailers Test New ID Tech to Try and 'Wow' Individual Consumers," *St. Petersburg Times,* January 18, 2011.

Miguel Bustillo, "Wal-Mart Radio Tags to Track Clothing," the *Wall Street Journal,* July 23, 2010, http://www.online.wsj.com, accessed April 2011.

Susan Reda, "Ready (Finally) for Item-Level Deployment, *Stores,* November 17, 2010, http://www.stores.org/print/book/export/html/5701, accessed April 2011.

CHAPTER 12

1. *Lucky* Media Kit, http://www.condenastmediakit.com/luc/circulation.cfm, accessed April 2011.

2. SeenOn, http://www.seenon.com/info.php#about-us, accessed April 2011.

3. Marc Karimzadeh and Nina Jones with contributions from Samantha Conti, "Got Tweet?," *WWD*, WWD Collections Issue, April 12, 2010, http://wwd.com/media-news/got-tweet-3030762/print, accessed April 2011.

4. Shar VanBoskirk, "U.S. Interactive Marketing Forecast, 2009 to 2014: Spend Will Reach Nearly $55 Billion as Interactive Cannibalizes Traditional Media," January 11, 2010 (updated), http://www.forrester.com/rb/Research/us_interactive_marketing_forecast,2009_to_2014, accessed April 2011.

Features

In the Fashion Spotlight: Fashion Showtimes Goes Global

Rosemary Feitelberg and Marc Karimzadeh, "Showtime for Designers at Lincoln Center," *WWD*, May 25, 2010, p. 12.

Jessica Iredale, Marc Karimzadeh, and Amanda FitzSimons, "The Fashion Circle," *WWD*, September 8, 2010, p. 4.

Marc Karimzadeh, "New Look For Fashion Week" *WWD*, April 30, 2010, p. 11.

Ruby Charles, "New York Fashion Week Relocates to Damrosch Park, Lincoln Center," *Examiner*, February 4, 2010, pp. 1–5.

David Moin, "Fashion's Night Out Gains Steam," *WWD*, August 17, 2009, p. 3.

"Spanning the Globe," *WWD*, August 24, 2010, p. 4.

Tools of the Trade: EBay: Looming Even Larger in Fashion

Sharon Edelson, "Looming Ever Larger: EBay Ups Fashion Game With New iPhone App," July 16, 2010, pp. 1 and 3.

Timeless Treasures: Diane von Furstenberg: Just Can't Get Enough!

"Block Party" *WWD*, May 10, 2010, p. 16.

"Just Can't Get Enough" *WWD*, May 7, 2010, p. 10.

DVF.com, http://inside.dvf.com/about/dianes_bio/, accessed April 2011.

Elizabeth Thurman, "Diane von Furstenberg Receives Talley Lifetime Achievement Award," *WWD*, May 18, 2010, p. 3.

Anamaria Wilson, "DVF Unwrapped," *Harper's Bazaar*, September 14, 2009, pp. 215–222.

Everything Old Is New Again: Hope Reigns High On the Job Front

Armold J. Karr, "Future Leaders Need Different Skillset," *WWD*, November 1, 2010, p. 1.

Lisa Lockwood, "Class of 2010: Glimmer of Hope on the Job Front," *WWD*, May 18, 2010, pp. 12–13.

CREDITS

Page 36 (left to right) Courtesy of Bryan Derballa; Courtesy of Bryan Derballa

Page 42 (left, top to bottom) Courtesy of WWD; Courtesy of WWD; Courtesy of WWD/Stefan Sveensson; Courtesy of WWD; Courtesy of WWD/Talaya Centeno

Page 42 (right, bottom) Courtesy of WWD

CHAPTER 3

Page 50 Courtesy of WWD/Giovanni Giannoni: Christian Dior Spring 2011 HC

Page 55 Courtesy of WWD

Page 57 Courtesy of WWD/Stephane Feugere

Page 58 (left to right) Courtesy of WWD/Giovanni Giannoni; Courtesy of WWD/Giovanni Giannoni

Page 67 New Line Cinema/The Kobal Collection

Page 68 Courtesy of WWD/Jason Laveris

Page 69 Courtesy of WWD/Stefanie Keenan

Page 71 Image Courtesy of The Advertising Archives

Features

Page 54 (top, left to right) Courtesy of WWD/Talaya Centeno; © SHAWN THEW/epa/Corbis; Courtesy of WWD/John Aquino; Courtesy of WWD/Thomas Iannaccone

Page 54 (bottom, right) Courtesy of WWD/Robert Mitra

Page 60 (left, top to bottom) Courtesy of WWD/Steve Eichner; Courtesy of WWD/Kyle Ericksen; Courtesy of WWD/Steve Eichner; Courtesy of WWD/Dave Yoder

Page 60 (right, top to bottom) Courtesy of WWD/Thomas Iannaccone; Courtesy of WWD/Talaya Centeno; Courtesy of WWD/Dominique Maitre; Courtesy of WWD/John Aquino

Page 64 (left to right) Courtesy of WWD; Courtesy of Esprit; Courtesy of Esprit

CHAPTER 4

Page 76 Courtesy of WWD/ John Aquino: J. Crew store on Fifth Avenue in New York

Page 84 Courtesy of WWD/Robert Rooks

Page 85 Courtesy of WWD

Page 91 Courtesy of WWD

Features

Page 80 (right, top) Courtesy of WWD

Page 80 (left, top to bottom) Courtesy of WWD/Eli Schmidt; Courtesy of WWD/Steve Eichner; Courtesy of WWD; Courtesy of WWD/Amy Graves

Page 88 (top, right) Courtesy of WWD

Page 88 (bottom, left to right) Courtesy of WWD/George Chinsee; Courtesy of Condé Nast; Courtesy of WWD/George Chinsee; Courtesy of WWD/Thomas Iannaccone; Courtesy of WWD/Robert Mitra

Page 92 (top, left to right) Courtesy of WWD/Mauricio Miranda; Courtesy of WWD/Sakis Lalas; Courtesy of WWD

Page 92 (bottom, right) Courtesy of WWD

PART 2

Pages 96–97 Courtesy of WWD/Stephane Feugere: D&G Fall 2011

CHAPTER 5

Page 98 Courtesy of WWD/Talaya Centeno: Libertine Fall 2011 RTW

Page 100 Courtesy of WWD/Giovanni Giannoni

Page 101 Courtesy of WWD/Cotton

Page 110 Courtesy of DuPont

Page 112 © Anuruddha Lokuhapuarachchi/Reuters/Corbis

Page 114 Courtesy of WWD/Davide Maestri

Page 115 Courtesy of WWD

Page 175 (left to right) Courtesy of WWD/Giovanni Giannoni; Courtesy of WWD/Thomas Iannaccone

Page 177 Courtesy of WWD

Page 178 © Brooks Kraft/Corbis

Page 179 (left to right) Courtesy of Destination Maternity Corporation; Courtesy of Destination Maternity Corporation

Page 180 Courtesy of WWD/Kyle Ericksen

Page 181 Courtesy of WWD/Giovanni Giannoni

Page 182 Courtesy of Fairchild Publication, Inc.

Page 185 Photo by John Sciulli/Getty Images for Kenneth Cole

Page 186 Courtesy of WWD/Luca Bellumore

Page 187 (top to bottom) Courtesy of WWD/Davide Maestri; Courtesy of WWD/Steve Eichner

Page 188 Courtesy of WWD/Ralph Lauren

Page 192 Courtesy of WWD/Marc Jacobs

Page 194 Courtesy of WWD/J. Crew

Features

Page 176 (right, top) Courtesy of WWD/Kyle Ericksen

Page 176 (left, top to bottom) Courtesy of WWD/Kyle Ericksen; Courtesy of WWD/Kyle Ericksen; Courtesy of WWD/Kyle Ericksen; Courtesy of WWD/Kyle Ericksen

Page 184 (top, right) Courtesy of WWD

Page 184 (bottom number order) 1. Courtesy of the Everett Collection; 2. Courtesy of the Everett Collection; 3. Universal Tv/The Kobal Collection; 4. See-Saw Films/The Kobal Collection

Page 190 (top, left to right) © PhotoEdit/Alamy; © PhotoEdit /Alamy; © PhotoEdit / Alamy; © Rune Hellestad/Corbis

Page 190 (bottom, left to right) Courtesy of WWD/ George Pimentel; Courtesy of Getty Images; © Jeff Daly/Retna Ltd./Corbis

CHAPTER 9
Page 198 Courtesy of WWD/Mauricio Miranda: Fendi Spring 2011 RTW

Page 200 Courtesy of WWD/Giovanna Pavesi

Page 203 Courtesy of WWD/Yukie Kasuga

Page 204 (left to right) Courtesy of WWD; Courtesy of WWD/Giovanna Pavesi; Courtesy of WWD

Page 205 Courtesy of WWD/Kyle Ericksen

Page 207 Courtesy of WWD/Thomas Iannaccone

Page 209 Courtesy of WWD

Page 213 Courtesy of WWD

Page 214 Courtesy of WWD

Page 215 © George H.H. Huey/Alamy

Page 217 Image Courtesy of The Advertising Archives

Page 219 Courtesy of WWD/Ronda Churchill

Features

Page 202 (left to right) Courtesy of WWD; Courtesy of WWD; Courtesy of WWD; Courtesy of WWD/ Thomas Iannaccone

Page 210 (top, right) © Christie's Images/Corbis

Page 210 (bottom, left to right) Courtesy of WWD; Courtesy of WWD; Courtesy of WWD/Thomas Iannaccone

Page 216 (top, right) Courtesy of WWD/George Chinsee

Page 216 (bottom, left to right) Courtesy of WWD/ Steve Eichner; Courtesy of WWD/Dimitrios Kambouris; Courtesy of WWD/Billy Farrell; Courtesy of WWD; Courtesy of WWD/Steve Eichner

PART 4
Pages 222–223 (left to right) Courtesy of WWD/ Philip Stone; Courtesy of WWD: Nordstrom at Perimeter Mall in Atlanta, Georgia; Victoria's Secret in Dallas, Texas (bottom) Courtesy of WWD: Target Store

CHAPTER 10

Page 224 Courtesy of WWD/Giovanni Giannoni and Dominique Maitre: Kenzo Spring 2011

Page 229 Courtesy of WWD

Page 233 Courtesy of Designers&Agents

Page 235(left to right) Courtesy of WWD/Giovanni Giannoni and Stephane Feugere; Courtesy of WWD/ Giovanni Giannoni

Page 244 Courtesy of Fairchild Publications, Inc.

Page 249 Courtesy of WWD

Features

Page 228 (left to right) Courtesy of WWD/Lexie Moreland; Courtesy of WWD/Talaya Centeno; Courtesy of WWD/Talaya Centeno; Courtesy of WWD/George Chinsee; Courtesy of WWD/Steve Eichner; Courtesy of WWD/George Chinsee

Page 238 (right, top) Courtesy of WWD/Robert Mitra

Page 238 (left, top to bottom) Courtesy of WWD/ Robert Mitra; Courtesy of WWD/John Aquino; Courtesy of WWD/Robert Mitra; Courtesy of WWD/John Aquino

Page 248 (left to right) Courtesy of Eric Gaillard/ Reuters/Landov; Courtesy of WWD/John Aquino

CHAPTER 11

Page 256 Courtesy of WWD: Holt Renfrew contemporary space

Page 261 Courtesy of WWD/Kyle Ericksen

Page 262 Courtesy of WWD

Page 267 (left to right) Courtesy of WWD; Courtesy of WWD/Nan Coulter

Page 269 © Maurice Savage/Alamy

Page 272 Courtesy of WWD

Page 273 Courtesy of Bal Harbour Shops

Page 275 Courtesy of WWD/Dominique Maitre

Features

Page 260 (left to right) Courtesy of WWD/John Aquino; Courtesy of WWD/Jimi Celeste

Page 264 (left to right) Courtesy of WWD/George Chinsee; Courtesy of WWD/Brad Forth; Courtesy of WWD/Jonathan Netek

Page 268 (left to right) Courtesy of WWD/Thomas Iannaccone; Courtesy of WWD/Thomas Iannaccone; Courtesy of WWD/Kyle Erickson; Courtesy of WWD/Thomas Iannaccone; Courtesy of WWD/ Thomas Iannaccone

Page 274 (left to right) Courtesy of AFP/Getty Images; Courtesy of Veer

CHAPTER 12

Page 278 Courtesy of WWD/Giovanni Giannoni: Manish Arora Fall 2011 RTW

Page 281 Courtesy of Condé Nast

Page 284 Courtesy of WWD

Page 285 Courtesy of SeenOn

Page 287 Courtesy of WWD/Alexander Wang

Page 288 Courtesy of WWD/Twitter

Page 289 Courtesy of WireImage

Page 295 Courtesy of WWD

Features

Page 282 (top, left to right) © Richard Levine/Alamy; © Richard Levine/Alamy

Page 282 (bottom, right) Courtesy of WWD/John Aquino

Page 286 (top to bottom) Courtesy of WWD; Courtesy of WWD/George Chinsee; Courtesy of WWD

Page 290 (left to right) Courtesy of WWD/John Aquino; Courtesy of WWD/George Chinsee; Courtesy of WWD/Scott Rudd; Courtesy of WWD/ George Chinsee

Page 294 © Jeff Kowalsky/epa/Corbis

INDEX

Page numbers in italics refer to figures.

haute couture, 234
hemp, 104
hides, 129
high fashion, 9
Hilfiger, Tommy, 60, 91
Hispanics, 40
Home Shopping Network, 271, 285
home textiles, 106
horizontal-flow theory, 63, 65–66

I

imports, 246–47, 249–50, 295–96
    see also global sourcing
income, personal, 33–34, 52, 56
India, 245
individuality, and fashion, 72–73
inflation, 34
Italy, 237, 239
item houses, 151

J

Jacobs, Marc, 46, 57, 192, 207
Japan, 243
Jersey Shore, 23
jewelry, 209–19
jobbers, 151, 153
Johnson, Betsey. See Betsey Johnson

K

Karan, Donna. See Donna Karan
karats, 211
King, Charles, 65, 68
kips, 129
knockoffs, 17
Kors, Michael, 12, 60

L

Lady Gaga, 10, 216
Lagerfeld, Karl, 60, 180
Lauren, Ralph. See Ralph Lauren
Laver, James, 56, 58
leased departments, 265–66
leather, 126–33
    categories, 126–27, 129

merchandising and marketing,
    130–31
processing, 129–30
research and developments, 131
trade associations and shows, 131
trends, 131–33
leisure time, 38, 52–53
let out, 140
licensing, 86–87, 163–64, 192–93,
    236, 251, 252
line-for-line, 150
lines, 90, 150, 153–54, 160
Los Angeles market, 231–32
Lundgren, Terry J., 260

M

Macy's, Inc., 91, 93, 259–60, 266
Mad Men, 184
magalogs, 270
magazines, 280–81
MAGIC trade show, 220
manufacturers, 89–90, 151
    CAM (computer-aided
        manufacturing), 157
    as retailers, 163
    see also product development
marker, 159
market centers, 226, 227, 229–30,
    239
marketing, 7
    see also merchandising
market penetration, 251–52
market research
    economic environment, 33–35,
        37
    market segmentation, 30–31, 33
    population, 35, 37
    psychological factors, 47
    sociological environment, 38–41,
        43–46
markets, 226
    Americas and the Caribbean
        Basin, 241–42
    Asia and Oceania, 242–46

Canada, 241
Dallas market, 232
France, 234–37
Germany and Scandinavia,
    240–41
Great Britain, 239–40
Italy, 237, 239
Los Angeles market, 231–32
Miami market, 232–33
New York market, 230–31
penetration, 251–52
market segmentation, 30–31, 33
market weeks, 227, 229–30
marts, 226, 227
mass customization, 169
mass fashion, 9
mass-market theory, 63, 65–66
mass merchandisers, 263
masstige, 180
maternity clothing, 178, 179
McCartney, Stella, 60, 181
McNair, Malcolm P., 275, 276
McQueen, Alexander, 40, 178
men's apparel, 183–87
    designer names, 185
    merchandising and marketing,
        187
    organization and operation, 183,
        185–86
    tailored clothing, 185
    trends, 187
merchandising, 7
    and adoption theories, 63, 65, 67
    children's, tween's, and teen's
        apparel, 191–93
    fabrics, 113–16
    fibers, 109–11
    footwear, 203
    gloves, 206
    handbags, 205
    jewelry, 218
    leather, 130–31
    men's apparel, 187
    and product lines, 150–51